Tears on the Sand

an American doctor's mission of mercy becomes the successful search for the world's most wanted man

Joseph Agris, M.D.

Tears on the Sand

an American doctor's mission of mercy
becomes the successful search for
the world's most wanted man

A to Z Publishing
(In cooperation with The Children's Foundation)
Scurlock Tower
6560 Fannin, Suite 1730
Houston, Texas 77030

ISBN: 978-0-9712348-9-5 (cloth)
ISBN: 978-0-9712348-5-7 (paper)

Literary collaboration & graphic design services provided by

Professional Literary Services
Ron Kaye & Connie L. Schmidt
www.schmidtkaye.com

Dedication

To Terry

Our life together has been and will always be
an exciting journey.
There is no predicting the outcome,
but of one thing I am certain:
I will always love you.

You are the one I want to spend the rest of my life with,
and I will hold on to you forever,
not to control, but to cherish,
to encourage,
and to protect.

My sweet soul mate,
this book is for you.

Love,
Joe

Acknowledgements

My journeys, the work that I love to do, and this book would not have been possible without the gracious and tireless assistance I've gotten from many people, far more than I can list here. I want to especially thank the following:

The Children's Foundation – U.S.
The House Of Charity – Houston
for so faithfully supporting the efforts to improve the lives of people who are too frequently overlooked
Dow University – Karachi and all their faculty
Shalmar Hospital – Lahore and all their personnel
Jacobabad Civil Hospital – all the doctors and personnel
Civil Burns Center Karachi – all the doctors and personnel
for your tireless and highly professional efforts under incredibly difficult conditions
The many government officials in Pakistan *who worked closely with our medical staff*
The U.S. Embassy and its staff in Pakistan
The Frontier Medical College in Abbottabad – *with whose faculty and staff I have truly enjoyed working*
and finally,
Schmidt Kaye and Company Literary Services – *the literary world's equivalent of a seasoned O.R. Nurse: demanding, yet gentle*

Before Beginning....

A Note from the Author

*T*his book is both a journal of my travels and experiences that I hope you will find enlightening, and a novel that I hope you will find entertaining. That's why I present it as an autobiographical novel... or a novelized memoir, if you prefer. Some of the passages have been dramatized somewhat in an effort to emphasize truths learned, or to protect the innocent (and not so innocent) from unfair reprisals. However, the accounts of the women whose bodies have been so disfigured and whose lives have been destroyed have been, if anything, downplayed somewhat. I felt that had I offered their accounts in complete detail, the narrative would end up being too painful to read, forcing readers to turn away from the pain and allow the horror to continue.

I invite you to take away from this narrative what you will, to look within your minds for the truth, even as you look to your hearts for compassion. For without both truth and compassion, the worst of what we are will ultimately prevail, and the horrors that I have seen and so many have suffered first-hand will be little more than a footnote in the ongoing victory march of hate and suffering. We must do better than that if we are to survive at all, and to be able to call ourselves human beings.

"Doc Joe" Agris, M.D., D.D.S., F.A.C.S.
Texas, December, 2012

Tears on the Sand

Prologue

Sitting in the makeshift conference room in the Civil Burn Center in Karachi, alongside the Pakistani physicians with whom I had spent so many hours over the past several years, I am struck by the image of the young woman seated across from me. She is the only female in the room. She had obviously been quite attractive once, but what I find most remarkable is the intelligence and intensity that she exudes, so unlike the demeanor of most of the women I have encountered during my journeys in this region.

Smoothing the material of her sari, she holds the gaze of each of us for a moment before speaking. And once she speaks, it becomes obvious that she has a gift for languages, as well as a passion for the well-being of her homeland and all who live there. I wonder whether the passion has always been there, or is simply an outgrowth of the horrific ordeal to which she has been subjected. Whatever its source, it has the power to still the tongues of a room full of physicians. Not just the outspoken surgeon from Houston, Texas, but even the men who have been born to her world: a world that expects – demands – silent acquiescence of its women. This woman will not be silent. Neither will she bow to the traditions that have not only allowed but have also encouraged the disfigurement that she has endured. She speaks with the strength of justice denied, and it is a strength born not of anger, but of the steely determination to see that justice realized, so that no other young girls or women will ever find themselves subjected to the horror that she and thousands of other women throughout the Middle East have suffered.

Tears on the Sand

She is twenty-two years old, but the scars have left her looking much older. Her face has literally been burned away, and the burns extend over her neck and on to her chest and upper arms. The acid completely dissolved her left eye, and left her with only partial vision in her right. She tells us that she had attended school and taught herself English, and had hoped to use her education and skills to improve her life and that of her family. As she describes her life, it becomes apparent that she has a gift for writing, as well, for her imagination seems to bring forth something different from what I expected, and likely very different from anything to which her countrymen seated around the table with me are accustomed. I can easily imagine this young woman being successful, influential, and someday, well-married, if that were her choice. I can only assume that she once held such dreams for herself, as well. Then came the acid attack that almost took her life and burned away the beauty of her youth.

The stated cause of the attack was her failure to abide by some aspect of Sharia law, which forbids a woman from venturing out alone, even in the middle of the day; from being accompanied by a man other than the woman's husband or family; and from exposing – even accidentally – the merest hint of her beauty. The real cause, however, was and is far more serious. It is the ignorance and fear that allows, even promotes, such complete subjugation of women, and looks unfeelingly upon the torture of any woman who somehow fails to follow the archaic law to the letter. I can't help but wonder what sort of creep could resort to such cruelty.

But this young woman is not unique. Over the past five years, I have seen many young women with acid burns. I have spoken out against this practice, have appeared on television and in newspaper articles, and have addressed the various press clubs in major cities around the world – all in hopes of making the world aware of this culturally-supported but grossly unacceptable treatment of women that has not only shattered thousands of their lives, but also serves to coarsen and dehumanize an entire region's culture.

Under normal circumstances, I have tried not to bring my own cultural morals into my work in a foreign country, because I know that doing so has a tendency to create unwelcome turmoil. Such turmoil could actually result in my being denied access to those who need help so desperately. But this is different, and demands that I not keep silent. The cultural dictates of the Middle East are admittedly quite different than my own, but the practice of throwing acid in women's faces should be unacceptable in any culture. And the fact that the men who commit such crimes – with the full support and blessings of Sharia law – often walk away without any form of punishment makes my blood boil. There is no choice for me in this matter; I feel I have to do something to change the attitudes, and barring that, at least to put a stop to the practice. This is truly a cultural cancer that must be cured, and I am willing to do whatever it takes to see that a cure becomes real.

Early on in one of my medical missions to Pakistan, someone told me: "*When you go looking for Osama bin Laden, you don't find him. He finds you.*" I didn't know quite what to make of that statement then. But in time I would be struck by the truth of that simple but ominous-sounding declaration.

Over the years during which my travels had taken me deep into the remote areas of Pakistan and Afghanistan, I have found myself falling in love with the people. Most of them live their lives in much the same way as had their ancestors for millennia. Their needs are simple, their possessions few, and their lives unimaginably hard, yet they remain charming and humble. But I quickly learned something very important about them. Whereas they tend to welcome trusted friends with the same warmth one would expect to be limited to close family, they are also quick to violence when faced with a threat.

It has taken me years to convince them that I am no threat to them, but rather, a friend. I did not win their trust with words; they have heard too many words from the Americans, and have seen that Americans' actions rarely mirrored the kindness that the words had promised. I knew that telling these people that I was their friend would be a useless effort. But, notwithstanding that propensity for outspokenness I mentioned earlier, words aren't my stock in trade. I am a surgeon, and have made my statements by traveling to the poorest villages and treating people who have probably never seen a physician before. Over the years, I have performed surgery on thousands of children who had been born with terrible birth defects, or who had been maimed by the violence that has long defined life in the region.

In time, these people began referring to me as Dr. Angel, and I have to admit that I take more pride in that title than in any of the other accolades I have ever received. For that title was borne not of politics or social standing or respect for wealth, but rather of a genuine appreciation and caring for one who does his small part to make their lives a bit less difficult.

As I treated and was befriended by these people, I couldn't help but wonder at the seeming paradox that Osama bin Laden represented. To most Westerners, he was viewed as the human incarnation of evil, a killer of thousands, and a fanatic who took great joy in the spilling of innocent blood, including that of his own people. And yet, to the people of these villages, he was a saint and a savior, sent to protect them from the very kind of evil he represented to the West. The more familiar I became with the villagers and physicians with whom I worked, the more intent I became on meeting with bin Laden, face to face, to learn for myself what drove this monster/saint, and to discover the source of the power he wielded, not only in this remote region, but throughout the world.

Maybe it was crazy for me to go off in search of bin Laden, but then again, another nickname my Pakistani friends have given me was "Crazy Texan." I will not argue with their assessment.

My initial efforts to find and meet with bin Laden had been marked by my passing out large amounts of money in hopes of purchasing information as to his whereabouts. I eventually learned the folly of those attempts, as the same methods had been employed for years, by people with far more money than I could ever imagine. Those people, including my country's own military and intelligence services, had but one objective: to kill the man and parade his death before the world as testament to their cunning and strength. And despite their monumental efforts, they had failed. Over and over again, I was reminded of the truth of that earlier admonition: *"When you go looking for Osama bin Laden, you don't find him. He finds you."* I would have to find a better way if I were to learn the truth, and to sit with and get to know the man who personified both evil and salvation to so many people.

This book is my story. Of how I came to a devastated region, hoping to demonstrate in some small way my gratitude for the many blessings that had been bestowed upon my life. Of how I managed to befriend a people whom so many of my countrymen would call their enemies. Of how I have been able to change lives by using and sharing the skills I have acquired in my many years as a surgeon. And somewhere in there is the tale of how one *"Crazy Texan"* was ultimately able to do what thousands of soldiers, spies, and diplomats were unable to do: to find and get to know a figure who would mold the history of one region by instilling hope, and shape the attitudes of the rest of the world by instilling fear and hatred. I neither confirm nor deny the veracity of the details.

I originally came to the Middle East to offer my help and to change a few lives for the better. But as I have come to realize, the change that is most desperately needed cannot be accomplished with a surgeon's scalpel, and the most malignant sickness and horrible injury is inflicted not on the bodies of those few for whom I have provided treatment, but on the minds of people from the mountain villages of Pakistan to the "sophisticated" power centers of the greater world. This book is my attempt to excise the ignorance and hatred that so drives us all, and to help demonstrate that we are not, in our essence, enemies, but rather friends who have yet to get to know each other. Whether my efforts will bear any fruit, I cannot say. Others with greater influence and better skills than I possess have tried, only to fail. But like them, I know that I have to try.

Dr. Joseph Agris, M.D, D.D.S., F.A.C.S
Houston, Texas, January 2013

Joseph Agris, M.D.

Tears on the Sand

The Journey Begins

I am often asked what it was that initiated my interest in the Middle East in general, and Pakistan in particular. In truth, there were a number of things that caused my fascination with the region. My first taste of the Arab world was, like many Westerners, found in early movies such as *Arabian Nights* and *The Thief of Baghdad*. The characters in those old movies were, as a rule, strikingly attractive, yet somehow menacing. The region itself was typically portrayed as a hotbed of mysticism and intrigue, an image that seems to still linger somewhere in my mind, as I suspect it does in many people's. When I was a bit older, I read T.E. Lawrence's *Seven Pillars of Wisdom*, which provided an altogether different view of the Arab world than did the paradoxical world of incredible beauty and passion, albeit with ever-present sinister undertones, that came out of Hollywood. When I began learning the history of the ancient and storied Silk Road, and how those who traversed it often strove unsuccessfully to change the culture of the people, particularly along the Karakoram route into Pakistan, I found myself completely entranced.

Then, as I grew into adulthood, I became aware of the more modern history of the region, and how the discovery of its abundant oil deposits had made it the target of a succession of enterprises whose goals lay far beyond those of earlier traders, with each new venture supported by military intervention. Mystique fell before subterfuge, and the fabled flying carpets of the Arabian Nights were supplanted by the all-too-real images of fighter jets, helicopters, and most recently, faceless but deadly drones. Despite all this, my fascination with that part of the world was not diminished.

As I began my career as a dentist and then as a plastic and reconstructive surgeon, I began to hear reports of the horrifying conditions in much of the region, in marked contrast to the opulent luxury with which the sheiks and their courts surrounded themselves.

Then, there's the terrible way that those who lack power are treated – including the entire female half of the population.

Here in the US, when a woman is even just verbally abused in public, there is often a rush of media reports detailing the outrage, followed by a burst of emotionally charged responses from the public. In Pakistan, Afghanistan, and virtually throughout that part of the world, however, the abuse of women is systemic and occurs on a daily basis. It's not merely verbal abuse, either. It is nothing out of the ordinary for a woman in those countries to be beaten to death in front of a crowd of apparently unconcerned onlookers, or to have acid thrown in her face, leaving her blinded and permanently disfigured. And when some unfortunate woman (or young girl, for that matter) suffers such a fate, it is not uncommon for even her parents and siblings to turn against her for allegedly bringing shame to the family. Even the woman or girl who is "fortunate" enough to survive becomes a pariah in her own home and village, frequently being forced to flee for her very life.

In this country, we would demand to know what the authorities are doing to bring the perpetrators to justice. In that world, however, if the authorities react at all, it is generally with nothing more than a shrug of the shoulders and a silent acquiescence to accepted traditions.

What ultimately led me to begin my journeys to Pakistan, however, was the plight of the children there. Thousands of them die every year of diseases and injuries that we in the West don't give a second's thought to. These are diseases against which there are effective vaccines, and wounds that – in the

U.S. - are treated quickly in a doctor's office or emergency room, with the child sent home to recover fully in a matter of days or weeks. In the tribal villages of Pakistan, however, the vaccines that could save so many lives are virtually nonexistent, and the wounds we take so lightly in the U.S. often get infected to the point where gangrene or sepsis takes hold, leaving the child to die a slow and agonizing death. And then there are the thousands of children born with easily correctable birth defects such as a cleft palate - children who might survive, but are doomed to be forever ostracized for their appearance.

What future do these children have? To die miserably for lack of treatment, to live their lives being constantly stared at and avoided because an accident of birth has marked them as different, defective, or damned? As a physician, the more I learned of the plight of so many women and children, the more I realized that I had the wherewithal to make a real difference in at least a few of their lives. And as a human being, I realized that I could not look the other way and pretend that their suffering was not a part of my own life. My journeys to Pakistan were not inspired by some grandiose sense of my own nobility. I have never seen myself as a savior to anyone. But I could not look at myself in the mirror and know that I had turned my back on such desperate need. I decided I would go to Pakistan, and I would do what I could to make a few lives less miserable. What I did not expect was for all my earlier images of a people to be so thoroughly dashed before the harsh reality of their lives. Or for my perception of my own culture to be so deeply challenged by witnessing the repercussions of even our most high-minded actions, to say nothing of our more cynical endeavors.

I have to admit that somewhere underneath my desire to ease the suffering of the people of Pakistan, I still felt that burning curiosity about a culture so removed from my own, and a desire to unravel the paradox that lies at the core of most Westerners' image of the people in that section of the world. How could a culture that is known for bringing such beauty into the world – and for being the birthplace of a religion that is at its core so remarkably compassionate – also be the birthplace of acts of random brutality the likes of which the world has never before seen? I knew that I would never find the answers to these questions in the comfort and security of my own little world. I would have to go to their world, not as a tourist, but as a participant in their daily lives. I knew there would be a degree of danger far beyond that of sleepless nights in beds not as soft as my own. I also suspected that I would feel a sense of satisfaction at being able to change lives for the better by using my skills as a physician.

What I did not expect was that I would ultimately find myself at times fighting for my very survival, or humbled to tears by the sweetness and joy that managed to survive amid the bloodshed and turmoil. Where I had originally thought to ease some suffering and dry the tears of children, I was to learn the true meaning of strength, to encounter people who could and should serve as role models to all of us, and who strive daily to move beyond their many challenges and live joyful lives. I was and am humbled by what I have learned along the way, and hope that one day, the suffering of these people will be eased and their future made much brighter. And most of all, I feel honored. Blessed by the opportunities I've been given, and proud to acknowledge that some of the tears on the sand have been my own.

A Day at the Office, Pakistani Style

I learned many years ago that the daily routine of a physician in Pakistan – particularly that of a visiting American physician – bears little resemblance to the routine followed by most American physicians. Here in Texas, I awaken early every morning, shower, and enjoy what is, by American standards, a simple breakfast like a toasted bagel and juice, or something similar. Sometimes, I'll read over the day's headlines for a few minutes, and when I'm done, set the dishes in the sink. Then, it's into my air-conditioned car for the quick drive to the hospital to perform whatever surgeries I've scheduled. Then on to hospital rounds to check on my patients, add my notes to their charts, and issue any treatment and medication orders that might be required. The time spent documenting everything I do or order to be done can get to be a pain sometimes. However, it's an essential fact of life for physicians, especially nowadays, what with government agencies' inserting themselves more and more into the relationships between doctors and patients.

After making my rounds and jotting down my notes, I walk through air-conditioned corridors to my comfortable office to begin seeing the day's schedule of patients. Some of my patients come to me, desperate to have some mistake of nature or a souvenir from one of life's less enjoyable experiences modified, hidden, or removed. Others come because they want to be, as author Richard Brautigan once wrote, "fifteen percent prettier." And yes, this includes men as well as women. I certainly don't fault anyone for wanting to look his or her very best, and I really enjoy the work I do with all my patients. It is my greatest passion in life, after all. Besides, the comfortable living I make performing surgeries – both reconstructive and purely aesthetic – is what gives me the freedom to help others who would otherwise have no options but to continue suffering from whatever had befallen them.

Still, no matter how much I enjoy working with my patients here in Houston, at the end of the day, when I'm reasonably assured that all is right with my little corner of the world, my thoughts will frequently return to my wider practice, in places most Americans would have great difficulty even pronouncing, much less imagining. I try to stay in contact with my colleagues in the far corners of the world, fellow physicians who, while every bit as passionate about and devoted to their work as their counterparts in more highly developed countries, are profoundly handicapped by the extreme poverty (and all too often, ignorance) they must strive to overcome to provide even the most rudimentary level of care.

My efforts are sometimes hindered by the fact that I'm not overly inclined to make use of many online communications tools. I am much more inclined to make a telephone call or write a brief letter than to go to an online forum, access to which is either severely limited or downright unavailable to many of those physicians, anyway. My wife Terry has dragged me – kicking and screaming, but thankful, nonetheless – into the new-fangled world of email, but I still use it less than I could, and Terry has all but given up on getting me to use the different social media sites available to me. But who knows? That might change, as well. She can be very persuasive!

No matter how engaging I find my life in Houston, at some point the call of my "desert practice" grows so compelling that I have little choice but to begin planning a trip to the region. That planning usually takes almost as much time as the trip itself, as I always have a list of patients either awaiting surgery or requiring a followup. Add to that the numerous referrals for patients who are in need of my services, and it takes weeks, if not months, to arrange an opening in my practice large enough to allow me to disappear for even a couple of weeks.

One of the first things I do when preparing for a trip (something that elicits no small amount of questions and teasing from colleagues and patients alike) is to begin growing my beard. While for some Westerners, facial hair is little more than a cosmetic decision or a minor affectation, for an American man traveling in the tribal areas of the Middle East, it is virtually a necessity – not as a nod to the fashion dictates of the region, but as a disguise, to conceal the fact that I am an outsider. In too many areas, being an outsider, especially an American outsider, can mean death.

Because the region has a long history of hostile occupation, and particularly because of American involvement in the wars of the last decade, the Pakistani people are very suspicious of Westerners in general, and of Americans in particular. While our country's stated motives have been noble, and I have to tell myself that those noble motives have been real for the most part, the fact remains that in pursuing our objectives in the "war on terror," we have also been responsible for significant levels of death and suffering, even among those people who hold the Taliban and al Qaeda in little regard. And although there have always been inordinately frequent incidents that we in the West so casually call "collateral damage," the frequency and scale of the deaths of innocents has risen quite dramatically with our recent dependence upon unmanned and heavily armed drones. Contrary to what the news reports indicate, the drone attacks are far from being "surgical" in their accuracy and selectivity – so much so that virtually all who dwell in the remote countryside and tribal villages throughout Pakistan live in constant fear, knowing that a drone attack can come at any time, anywhere. And the people know that when the drones do strike, there will be no survivors.

Furthermore, we still represent to these people a desire to change the Arab/Persian culture so that it more closely resembles our own. No matter how much our politicians might claim to be struggling to improve the lives of the Pakistani people, those people have seen far too much evidence to the contrary, and they are not likely to forget it... at least, those who are still alive.

Despite the fact that I am first and foremost a physician, sworn to do no harm, and that I have managed to earn the trust and respect of people throughout the region, the need to be constantly vigilant and prepared to defend myself if necessary remains a harsh and difficult reality. The fact that I must, of necessity, carry a weapon on my journeys frankly angers and depresses me, as it runs contrary to everything I believe and hold dear. But the sad fact remains that there are those who would jump at the opportunity to kill an American, and wouldn't hesitate long enough to discover that I am not an enemy. And there are those who wouldn't hesitate to kill me and all who travel with me, despite being reassured by the fact that I am the one whom tribesmen throughout the region have nicknamed "Doctor Angel," or (affectionately) "Crazy Texan." I realize, and am forced to accept, the fact that if I am not both vigilant and prepared, I could very easily be killed, and as a result, others would be deprived of the care I could give them, and the local doctors would be further handicapped in their efforts to bring comfort and healing to their people.

As I mentioned earlier, I certainly don't see myself as some kind of savior, but I am able to bring supplies and surgical expertise to people whose lives would be diminished or even ended without them. For that reason, I am able to (barely) justify doing whatever I must do to survive in what is at once the most beautiful and most tragic part of the world I have ever encountered. And despite the hardships, dangers, and frustrations that are part and parcel of my time in Pakistan, those times have become as important to me as the very air I breathe.

Despite the searing heat that comes with the rising sun, the nights here are often bitterly cold, especially in the oddly-described "foothills" of the Himalayas, which would, in most other countries, be considered mountains in their own right, since they can rise twelve thousand feet or more. Most nights, I find myself a guest in the home of one of my fellow physicians who lives in the village, or in the home of one of the village elders, or in some cases I am shown remarkable hospitality by the family of one of my little patients. No matter where I stay I am always shown the most congenial level of hospitality possible, but the conditions are inevitably more austere than those to which we who live in more highly developed countries have grown accustomed. My quarters usually consist of a simple room, often with a single open window, and devoid of furnishings beyond a simple mat for sleeping, laid upon a bare floor, and sometimes a single chair or small table, upon which I put the few personal items I carry in with me. But I honestly don't feel that the accommodations I am offered represent any hardship, and I find that I sleep quite well, despite the lack of heat, as the heavy woolen blankets my hosts provide keep me quite warm against the chill of the night.

A typical day in Pakistan begins before the sun shows its face above the mountains. I awaken after a few hours' sleep – typical for me – and attend my morning rituals in a bathroom that is shared by all, thankful that I have awakened before my hosts and fellow guests. There are some mornings, however, when I am awakened by one of those other guests, but these generally occur when the day has been spent traveling from one village to another on what pass for roads, which I find infinitely more tiring and stressful than the days spent actually treating patients and performing or assisting in surgeries. There's just something about being bounced about all day in the sweltering heat, and breathing the omnipresent dust that follows travelers in the region, as you make your way from one police or military checkpoint or tribal roadblock to another, with the constant awareness that you might be fired upon at any moment.

Once I've had a chance to attend to my toilet and clear my head in the morning air for a few moments, our hosts will serve a breakfast that is a veritable feast by their standards, but would probably leave any guest at an American hotel grumbling and swearing never to return. Most mornings, the fare will consist of fried eggs, flatbread, and fresh dates, which are infinitely more delicious than any we can obtain back home. I find myself relishing these simple meals and I wolf them down, much to the delight of my hosts, who are extremely conscious of their duty to please their honored guests.

My colleagues and I depart before the sun has risen completely, and make our way to the hospital or clinic, where we always seem to encounter a crowd of people patiently awaiting our arrival (if only all of my American patients were so... well, patient!). We begin with what must appear to be a chaotic approach to triage, quickly checking each patient to determine whose medical needs are most pressing, and moving those people to the front of the "line." This being a primarily agricultural society, we see many hand and leg injuries, often inflicted as the result of a moment's inattention in the fields tending their crops or their herds of goats and sheep. We also see a number of children with some congenital defect such as a cleft lip or palate, and we assign these children to the day's surgery schedule. No critical cases, these, so we have the luxury of attending to them as we can between the more critical cases.

Among the latter, we see an alarmingly large number of women and girls who have fallen victim to brutally harsh punishments, either in response to having broken some archaic rule, or for doing something that allegedly brings dishonor to their families. It is these unfortunate women and girls who concern me the most. A child who has been born with a cleft lip can be treated quickly, with the result being that she or he has a real chance at living out a normal life. For the women, however, there is no "cure" to which a physician can turn. We can treat the broken bones and bruises left by the most recent beating, and can perform operations to graft skin to cover the bared flesh where the acid, thrown by an outraged husband, father, brother, or neighbor, has dissolved the original skin. But we simply cannot return every one of these women and girls to whatever state of beauty with which they had once been graced. Even if we were able to miraculously restore them to their former, un-butchered state, we know it is beyond our power to heal the emotional damage, and we also know that it is quite possible – even likely – that they will suffer the same kind of agonizing disfigurement again, in response to some new infraction. And there are some – too many – who have been so horribly brutalized that there is no hope of restoring them to anything but hideous reminders of the power that the men in their culture have over them. The worst of these, we cannot even keep alive, and I often find myself wondering whether they might actually be the most fortunate ones, finally realizing an escape from a life where the greatest promise is of future and unending torture.

Of course, there are also the casualties of the conflict that has raged in this part of the world for times beyond living memory. Skirmishes between tribes are common, as they have been for centuries, the main difference being that nowadays, even boys as young as ten carry fully-automatic AK-47 rifles, and are expected to use them against their enemies. While I feel compassion for the adults who come into the hospitals and clinics with injuries from the wars, I am filled with a burning rage when I see young children whose childhood has been stolen from them, their toys set aside in favor of killing machines, and the games that should fill their young lives replaced by having to attack or defend against attacks by others – often themselves only young boys – with whom they probably have no quarrel. They fight, bleed, and die in their grandfathers' or great-great-grandfathers' wars, with no sign of an end to the dying in sight.

* * * * *

The hospitals and clinics in which we work are beyond primitive by Western standards. The waiting areas often are merely unfurnished rooms, always crowded with patients, their families, and even the occasional goat. Unlike American waiting rooms, there is no sense of impatience among the throngs of people awaiting treatment. They sit, quiet for the most part, accepting the fact that they might be waiting for hours before being taken into a room for treatment or surgery. When one is called, that individual's appreciation is palpable, and those around them seem satisfied with being ever closer to being treated themselves.

The treatment and operating rooms bear no resemblance to those to which I'm accustomed back home, more closely resembling an even cruder version of the army field hospitals portrayed in the old MASH television series, but without all the modern conveniences, beyond the few that I am able to bring with me from the States. There are no expensive machines to monitor every aspect of patients' life processes. No vast supply of surgical kits, suture sets, and all the other "necessities" that we physicians take for granted. And while an American operating room will be the scene of only one surgical procedure, on one patient at a time, the OR in a Pakistani hospital will often be the stage for two or more patients' procedures at a time.

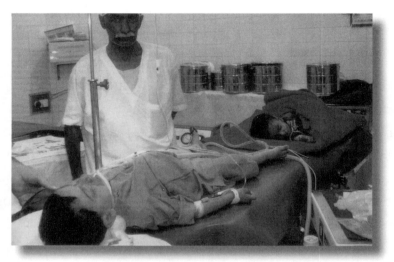

Here is an example of a typical operating room, with two young patients on adjoining tables.

Back in Houston, it takes at least an hour or two after completing a procedure to prepare the room for the next patient. The entire room is sterilized, with fresh materials brought in to be used in the subsequent procedure. In Pakistan, by contrast, the time between surgeries is often fifteen minutes or less. There is no fastidious effort to sterilize the entire environment. The instruments used in the previous operation are cleaned, autoclaved (in an autoclave that would have been obsolete even in the Korean theater where MASH was supposed to have taken place), and returned, to be used in the next procedure. Floors are swept and mopped between procedures, but there is no pretense of maintaining a sterile environment, because it would be a futile effort, at any rate. But despite what one would think, and what I as a physician know to be the general case, the incidents of infections in these primitive facilities are actually less than what we encounter in the most advanced surgical facilities in the world. I wouldn't have believed this when I first began coming to the region, or would have written it off as an aberration – beginner's luck, if you will. But year after year, with thousands upon thousands of procedures having been performed, the post-surgical infection rate has remained remarkably low. If it is beginner's luck, it has lasted a miraculously long time.

Another dramatic difference I see between this region and the surgical system back home is the very notable reduction in the amount of documentation required of the medical staff. Working in an American hospital, I have to devote literally hours to the process of documenting every minute element of every procedure I perform, just to keep the hospitals' administrators, attorneys, and insurance carriers satisfied. Such extensive additional effort is not only not required in the Pakistani clinics, it is forbidden by the laws of practicality. The hours I would spend writing my surgical notes, progress notes, and assorted observations just aren't available, and are better spent treating additional patients, anyway. And there is always an abundant supply of additional patients.

I have to admit that despite the crude and seemingly unsanitary conditions, I find that I actually enjoy operating in the village clinics and hospitals. Stripped of all but the most austere essentials, I feel as if I'm practicing medicine in a purer sense than when I'm back in a state-of-the-art, multi-billion dollar facility. Virtually every ounce of effort, by surgeons, nurses, and staff alike, is devoted directly to caring for patients. There is no "covering your behind," no song and dance to protect yourself and your hospital from liability. The patients in the outlands come to the clinics and hospitals for one reason only: to be treated. And to a person, they genuinely appreciate the treatment they receive. I wonder sometimes if the healthcare profession in more "developed" parts of the world has become so sophisticated that actual patient care has suffered in the process, too often taking a back seat to the efforts to prove and reinforce our level of sophistication.

My day at the hospital or clinic doesn't end until late in the evening, and sometimes stretches into the early morning hours. During the day, meals (or more often, snacks) are taken whenever a few free moments present themselves. Yet no matter what the hour of our return to our hosts' dwellings, we are served a meal that is, by village standards, a veritable feast. Very shortly after our return, our senses are titillated by the aromas of broiling meats and simmering vegetables, bringing to the forefront the awareness of a deep hunger that we had successfully ignored, often for hours. The dishes, alternately sweet and quite savory, have burned themselves into my memory (some, quite literally!), assuming a prominent place in my characterization of my travels. Grilled, curried lamb, with its inevitable heat, is offset by the soothing blandness of yogurt and rice, with all of it balanced by the sweetness of dates and fruits. I have to admit that I look forward to these meals every bit as much a s I do a foray into the finest restaurants the world has to offer, for the meals our hosts set before us speak not only to the tongue, but to all the senses, and even the soul.

Each dish is served by the women of the house, but custom dictates that they do not join us. They simply bring the foods, set the dishes on the floor in the center of our circle, and retreat in silence to the kitchen. And when all have had their fill, interspersed with talk about the day just passed, the health of crops and herds, and whatever rumors have passed through the area, the women return, again in silence, and remove the dishes, replacing them with bowls of sweet fruits and confections, and refilling our cups of tea.

After the meal, I often like to stretch my legs and drink in the first chill on the night air. I never wander far from the dwelling, however, for even in a village, surrounded by friends and co-workers, there always exists the danger of some outsider who is eager to avenge any wrongs or slights he or his people might have suffered. It is usually late in the evening or early morning before I wash and prepare myself for bed. The thin mats are most comfortable after an eighteen-hour day, and once I lay myself down, wrap myself in the thick, coarse wool blankets, and close my eyes, sleep comes quickly, as if it knows it must hurry to prepare me for the day that shall come all too soon.

Joseph Agris, M.D.

Mohammed: More Than a Driver

My driver in Pakistan, Mohammed, is an interesting character – a study in contrasts, as the old saying goes. Actually, he is more than a driver; he's my bodyguard when he needs to be. But he's much more than that. He is also my friend.

Mohammed is a good-looking man with olive skin and black hair that is graying on the sides and at the temples. A small, well-trimmed mustache sets off his features: deep, wide-set eyes, a handsome nose, and a broad, beautiful smile. A muscular guy with large arms and hands, Mohammed is mildly rotund but hardly what you would call overweight. Though he weighs at least 260 pounds, at six-feet-four he has the height to carry it. All told, he cuts quite an impressive figure.

Mohammed believes that jobs involving the sweat of his brow are not his forte. This doesn't mean that he is afraid of work; in fact, he is really not afraid of much at all. That's not surprising when you consider his background. When a young man, he served in the military, and is comfortable with both small and large automatic weapons. At first appearance he presents as a formidable adversary, and he certainly can be – but underneath he has a heart of gold, and for the most part is soft-spoken and mild-tempered.

Mohammed is Kurdish, a refugee from Iraq. He was born in northern Iraq, in the city of Mosul. His family was middle class, and he was able to attend the university, from which he graduated as a mechanical engineer in the mid-1970s. But he was not destined for an easy, comfortable life in Iraq. For in Saddam Hussein's Iraq, Mohammed was considered a potential political activist – and a criminal – simply because he was a Kurd, despite the fact that he had never joined a political group or participated in any criminal activities.

Because he was a Kurd, he faced difficulties getting a good job after graduating from university. However, he was talented, skilled, and smart, and engineers were in great demand in Iraq in the late 1970s and early 1980s. Construction – both military and civilian – was booming. So Mohammed was ultimately able to find work, and was peacefully employed for a number of years. He developed a reputation as a good worker and a team player, and a good friend and companion to his co-workers.

His happiness was not to last. One day in 1990, the Iraqi secret police stormed the engineering company where Mohammed was working, and arrested him and several other Kurdish employees. They were all taken to a prison outside Mosul, where they were tortured for several months in an attempt to make them "confess." Confess to what? That never became clear to Mohammed or his co-workers. They had no idea what they were supposed to be confessing, so the tortures continued.

During this time, Mohammed's elderly father was also arrested and charged with being a suspected Kurdish militant. This was absurd. At the time his father had medical problems, and could barely even walk, yet the secret police marked him as a suspicious militant simply because he was Kurdish. There was no elaboration beyond that, and apparently no trial. Mohammed's father was executed the month after he was arrested.

Yet Mohammed was luckier than most, having a paternal uncle who was a well-respected businessman in Mosul. His uncle owned a large appliance outlet, and with his international connections was able to obtain Western household appliances without any difficulty. He had the usual line of refrigerators, freezers, gas stoves, and electric coffee makers, but his biggest sellers – and by far his most profitable items – were flat-panel, wide-screen televisions with international satellite connections.

Although it was not illegal to own a satellite dish connection, Saddam Hussein's regime and the secret police were beginning to worry about the fact that so many people were acquiring satellite TV. After all, having a satellite dish invited the world into one's home, and of course, dictators such as Saddam Hussein have always preferred their people to be uneducated and ignorant about world affairs. Keeping people insulated from world news is just another means of absolute control.

In April following the year that Mohammed's father was executed, Mohammed's uncle fell into a small fortune of $25,000 in gold. Mohammed was still in prison, of course, and his uncle immediately contacted the Ba'ath Party leader and began the process of buying Mohammed's freedom. His initial offer was $10,000 in gold, and the negotiations went back and forth for several weeks until finally a price of $20,000 in gold was agreed upon, as "compensation" for the "injuries" that Mohammed had caused the Iraqi state.

Keep in mind that as an engineer, Mohammed had worked for years for a company that had completed many state projects. He had done an excellent job for them. Since his imprisonment, he had been repeatedly tortured so he would "confess," though of course he had no idea to what he was expected to confess. Yet his release papers stated that the $20,000 in gold was compensation for injuries *Mohammed* had caused the state. Unthinkable, unbelievable, outrageous, yes – but it happened, and all because Mohammed was a Kurd.

Unfortunately, his story was far from unique.

Though he had weighed 264 pounds at the time of his imprisonment, this 6'4" man only weighed 102 pounds when he was released. He had sores all over his body from the torture, as well as from the insects and vermin that lived in the cells – and on him. He had been burned, cut, and struck with mallets, resulting in broken bones, which of course went untreated during his confinement. He was short of breath and could barely walk when his uncle came to the prison to bring him home.

But he was free.

A cousin owned a small farm away from the city of Mosul, so Mohammed's uncle took him to the farm, where, it was hoped, he would be far from prying eyes and the Iraqi secret police. As you can imagine, when the family saw the shrunken, shriveled, ghost of a man who arrived on their doorstep, they were appalled. There were no doctors in the area, and the family members were afraid to bring a physician in from the city, since that would most likely draw unwelcome attention to his hiding place.

Mohammed literally hovered between life and death for several months, but with clean country air and wholesome, home-cooked meals on the farm, his strength slowly returned. He began a self-imposed exercise program, and walked the perimeter of the farm several times each day. By the fall, he was up to 180 pounds and was all muscle. He began to help out with daily chores at the farm, and this further improved his strength. Even so, he was always in pain as a result of the tortures he had undergone.

Now the big question was what he was going to do in the future. What options were open to him? What kind of work could he find that would pay a decent wage, with a minimal risk of imprisonment due to his ethnic origin? There didn't seem to be too many choices. Mohammed had survived a terrible ordeal, but his future didn't look very bright.

Things began to look even darker when, in late October, he and his uncle learned that some other family members who lived and worked in Mosul had been arrested. These people were not as lucky as Mohammed, and would never be seen by their family again.

Fortunately for Mohammed, however, his uncle seemed to remain immune to the consequences suffered by most people of Kurdish descent in Saddam's Iraq. No doubt this was because the uncle was able to import not only satellite TV equipment, but also the electronic devices for which members of the secret police and the political parties clambered. Through these connections, the uncle was tipped off that Saddam's secret police were once again looking for Mohammed. With the remaining gold coins that he had hidden under the floorboards of his store, he was able to acquire a false passport for his nephew, and arrange for a secret nighttime border crossing. He loved Mohammed and hated to see him go, but felt it was the only option. If Mohammed did not escape, the uncle feared, he would lose him as well.

So Mohammed escaped across the northern border between Iraq and Iran. He made his way to the northern city of Tabriz, where he applied for a job as a lorry driver. Being educated, and being fluent in several languages, he was immediately accepted. This was an ideal situation for him, as he could remain more or less anonymous and could always be on the move.

He quickly made friends with the dispatcher at the trucking company, often bringing him lunch to his office. This afforded Mohammed the opportunity to see the shipping orders. And it was this access that ultimately provided him with an opportunity to truly escape, and to secure his future in Pakistan.

One day a bill of lading appeared on the dispatcher's desk, for a job that entailed taking a truckload of equipment from Tabriz to the city of Zahedan in southeastern Iran. From there the equipment would be unloaded at the railhead, and would then be transported across the Pakistani border. It would then go north through the Indus Valley to Islamabad. Because of his friendship with the dispatcher, Mohammed was able to secure the assignment to drive the truck that would be going to the Zahedan rail station.

He knew that this could be his best chance at a decent life, a life where he would not always have to be looking over his shoulder. He realized that he would never again be able to return home, but then again, there was little to draw him back there. Other than his uncle and elderly mother, all of his family had been killed by Saddam's secret police. So Mohammed took his chance.

It was a slow and dangerous trip in the overloaded lorry. Driving a sixteen-wheeler through the Iranian mountains, on roads that were nothing more than jeep tracks, Mohammed and Amman, the young assistant who had come along with him, made their way south from Tabriz to Tehran without incident. From there they continued south along the western rim of the Great Salt Desert to the city of Yazd. Then they climbed back into the mountains, continuing south by southeast to Kerman.

Though the trip was exceedingly difficult, the truck was running well and the load of equipment remained intact. Fortunately, they were only stopped once, and were not questioned about the bill of lading or their personal papers. After that incident, Mohammed said a silent prayer of thanks to Allah, and told himself, *Tomorrow is Friday. I will stop at the mosque and really thank Allah for looking after me during these arduous ten days.*

When Mohammed and Amman left Kerman, they turned directly east across the lowlands between the two mountain ranges, before again climbing upwards to the city of Zahedan, their destination. The equipment was offloaded in the rail yard as planned, and Mohammed was given the receipt. He calmly handed it to Amman, who was shocked when Mohammed told him he was not taking the truck back to Tabriz.

Amman protested, "If you do not return with the truck, you will not be paid. This has been a difficult and hazardous venture; you'd have to be crazy not to collect your payment!"

Mohammed replied, "I don't care about that. I will write you a short note, which should allow you to collect the fee for both of us. You may keep my share."

"What are you planning? Where will you go?"

"When the train leaves for Pakistan," Mohammed replied, "I am going to be hiding among the crates and barrels. I feel I have to do this. Because I am of Kurdish descent, I will never feel safe until I am in Pakistan. But I'll be all right. I am an engineer, and if I do not find engineering work I can always drive a truck."

"But...but...what am I to do?"

"Take the truck back to Tabriz. There is no reason to rush. Make it a safe journey. Then collect your fee and mine. You may keep all of the money."

Amman was still uncertain. "This is a long and difficult trip to make alone."

"Well, then, hire a young assistant who can help with the driving, and offer him half of my fee to make the trip. You'll still come out ahead."

Seeing that Amman was still not completely convinced, Mohammed added, "I'm sure you can find someone in Zahedan, at a truck depot or the rail station. There's bound to be a man who is looking for work and would appreciate a job. Now, Amman, I expect you to keep my secret and not talk about this to anyone. It could cost me my life." With that, Mohammed gave the keys to the lorry to Amman, and they parted company.

Mohammed left the next morning, hidden among the crates in the baggage compartment of the train. A few days later, he arrived in Islamabad: free at last.

Though he was unable to find employment as an engineer – a fact that didn't really surprise him – Mohammed had no trouble getting a job as a lorry driver to transport supplies through the Swat Valley and into the Northwest Frontier Provinces along the dangerous Karakoram Highway, or KKH, to China. The task was to carry trade goods north to China, and return with Chinese-made products to Islamabad, the capital of Pakistan. The pay for drivers on this route was exceptionally good; all you had to do was survive the trip, which was easier said than done. Many unlucky drivers ended up thousands of feet down in a ravine along the KKH. Many others were attacked by bandits, who would relieve the drivers of their Chinese merchandise, which would then be sold on the black market.

Mohammed was well aware of the potential hazards, but nevertheless was extremely grateful, and once again stopped at the mosque to give thanks, for he felt that Allah had truly looked after him.

* * * * *

During one of his trips through Islamabad, Mohammed met a man who ran an agency that provided cars and drivers for the occasional tourist, as well as for local politicians and other celebrities. Mohammed had a good reputation for safety and caution, and being so well educated, he was very comfortable with these types of clients, and they with him. So it was a natural step for him to sign on as a driver for the agency.

It was definitely a step up for him, and one he welcomed. He had long since realized that being an educated, experienced construction engineer counted for nothing in Pakistan. He was destined to be a driver. But that suited him just fine, for he liked driving, and he enjoyed being with and talking to the people he met.

It took him no time to learn the main streets and back roads, which allowed him to avoid the traffic and congestion of the city. The only drawback was that he could not sit for more than a few hours, because the pain in his back from the beatings he'd received while imprisoned in Mosul would become unbearable. However, most of the trips within the city were short, and this gave him a chance to stand and walk about to relieve the discomfort.

Now Mohammed was earning a good living, and was able to afford his own apartment. He got a second job at a car repair shop, where he could put his engineering skills to good use.

He started putting money aside so he could buy his own van and become an independent driver. With two jobs, he earned enough to purchase his van within a few months.

The van Mohammed bought was ten years old, but it had a good engine, and the owner of the repair shop allowed him to use the facility to upgrade the vehicle. It ran on natural gas and had several cylinders in the rear compartment, but Mohammed modified it so he could piggyback additional cylinders, which would allow him to make longer trips without stopping. The compressed gas was easily available and inexpensive.

One of Mohammed's easier – and more profitable – jobs was transporting prominent people between Islamabad and the city of Lahore, only a few hours south of the capital. The road that connected the two cities was a major six-lane highway that was well paved: a complete contrast to the hazardous jeep trails he had driven in the mountains.

It wasn't long before Mohammed had a list of regular customers, which included the private Shalamar Hospital in Lahore. He felt he was fortunate to obtain a contract with this hospital – and I tend to agree with him. For that is how he and I met.

While many in the region have called me "Doctor Angel," Mohammed is one of those who has referred to me by my other nickname, "The Crazy Texan," from the beginning. I think it is because we both share the same sense of adventure and the same – sometimes crazy – feeling of invincibility. The trips we have made together at my behest have taken Mohammed into areas of Pakistan that he normally would never consider visiting. But he always says that traveling with me diverts him from the monotonous routine of driving within the city. "It gives my life new meaning," he has said, and I don't think he is exaggerating.

Early on in our association, Mohammed introduced me to Sultan, and we immediately took a liking to each other. Sultan became my bodyguard and he, Mohammed, and I became the Three Musketeers. We were inseparable; there wasn't anything that we wouldn't do for each other's safety. Not long afterward, Saleem joined up with us as my interpreter and "backup" bodyguard, and we became the Four Musketeers.

In our quest to locate and meet Osama bin Laden, we came up with a pseudonym for me, and my three new friends did what they could to help me improve my Urdu language skills. They also saw to it that I was always dressed appropriately, so I would blend in. These tactics would serve me well on my dangerous quest.

Learning of Mohammed's experiences was an eye-opener for me, and made me all the more impressed with him. Here is a man who survived utter brutality, but it did not make him brutal. There is much to admire about this man, and I am proud to call him my friend.

As I noted above, Mohammed's suffering under Saddam's regime was hardly unique. Over the past several years I have met many victims of that vile regime who were lucky enough to survive and escape. For instance, there were the "Brothers Seven" – seven unrelated businessmen who had been taken from their homes in different towns, and thrown into the Abu Ghraib Prison as political prisoners. Their "crime?" Speaking out against Saddam Hussein and his regime. Their punishment was to have their right hands cut off. With only a functioning left hand, they became outcasts within the prison walls, and would not have survived had they not banded together. Their story is one of courage, cooperation, and determination to stay alive within the walls of the horrific prison.

But I'll have to save that story for another chapter – or perhaps another book.

Saving Babies

The truck driver asks, "Where are the children I'm supposed to pick up?" He is clearly anxious to collect his young charges and be on his way. The driver, a Pakistani working for the United Nations, has been told to take some severely injured infants to the closest hospital. This is something entirely new for him. He is young and single, continually on the road, living out of his truck. And while he has been through many adventures – and misadventures – during his time on the road, he has absolutely no experience with children, particularly infants. In fact, they scare him. He is afraid that they will die on his watch and he will be held responsible.

Traveling south, Quetta is an essential stopping point for the driver, where he will be able to refuel the truck, make any necessary repairs, and stop at a teahouse where northbound drivers gather. There he can inquire as to the road conditions along his intended path through the mountains and southeast through the Indus Valley to the city of Jacobabad. The driver also knows that there is a hospital in Quetta, and that the sooner he can get help for these infants, and relieve himself of their responsibility, the better he will feel.

Quetta, the capital of the Pakistani province of Balochistan, sits in a dramatic mountaintop setting at an altitude of almost eighteen hundred meters. Being higher in the mountains, it is cooler than most parts of Pakistan, and in the winter the wind cascading down from the glaciers produces a bone-chilling cold. There is only one road, if you can call it that, that allows passage through the mountains in a southeasterly direction through Dadhar and the village of Sibi en route to Jacobabad.

Quetta is strategically positioned in the mountains, only a few miles away from the Afghan border. An ancient fort was constructed there to protect the roads passing from Afghanistan to India, via an important trade route through what is now Pakistan. (In the Pashto language, the word for fort is *kwatta*, from which it is believed the city's name Quetta is derived.) In more recent times, the Taliban members who were based to the north in Kandahar took advantage of this proximity and used Quetta as a logistical springboard for their comings and goings. As such, Quetta exudes an air of a wild frontier town.

Quetta consists of three main tribal groups. The original indigenous inhabitants were the dominant Pashtuns, as well as the Balochi and Brahui. This tribal area was under the control of the Khan of Kalat. The British entering the region from India realized the strategic importance of Quetta to the region, and it became the largest garrison in British India. All of that changed in May 1935 when a devastating earthquake shook the region and reduced Quetta to rubble.

Counts were not accurate, but it was estimated that more than twenty thousand people lost their lives when the unstable seismic fault that transverses the Harboi Mountains gave way. Because of its strategic location, the British contributed to the reconstruction of the city, including a train station on the rail line in the southwest corner of the town.

The British presence did not change the frontier style atmosphere, nor did it hamper the actions of the stalwart tribesmen who spent much of their time in the teahouses and strolling in the bazaar district around Mizan Chowk. It is not uncommon for regional tribal tensions to occasionally flare up in the narrow streets of the bazaar, where automatic weapons are commonly fired into the air to show disapproval or disagreement on the one hand, or extreme pleasure on the other.

* * * * *

The truck driver enters Quetta from the north and continues to travel south along its main street, Jinnah Road. He then turns to a familiar area, the Suraj Ganj Bazaar. There he gets directions to the mission hospital. Maneuvering the truck through the bazaar is slow and difficult because of the parade of vendors and their colorful pushcarts filling the narrow streets as they passionately haggle with their customers. Once clear of the bazaar area, the driver easily locates the train station and continues west to the hospital, which is really not more than a clinic. There is no physician. Supplies and equipment are limited. All that can be provided are some sweet water and juice.

As he enters the hospital, the driver is greeted with anguished screams, coming from a patient whose dressing the poorly trained and ill-prepared technician on duty is attempting – and failing – to change. Much to the patient's relief, the technician soon abandons the attempt. When the driver tells the technician about the infants in his charge, the latter shakes his head, saying, "We are not able to offer any medical care, and we are not equipped to take care of infants and children. We can try to get them to take something to eat and drink. Where are you going from here?"

The driver says, "My usual route takes me south to Jacobabad."

"You are in luck. The American medical team is at the Civil Hospital in Jacobabad. The only hope for these children – if they survive the trip – is to get them to the American doctors there."

After the technician helps feed the babies and makes them as comfortable as possible, the driver begins the 329-kilometer trip southwest to Jacobabad. There will be no stopping. He is painfully aware that these infants are his responsibility, and that their lives depend upon him. They are the only living survivors of the American drone attack on their poor Balochistan village. The driver feels it was a miracle that they are still alive. He believes that Allah had a purpose in sustaining them, and that it is now his duty to see that they are brought to the American doctors as quickly as possible.

The late lunch over and prayers said, the surgical team and I return to the operating room. As I described earlier in this narrative, the conditions under which we have to operate are very different from those in more privileged parts of the world. Unlike most operating rooms in the United States, there are two surgical tables in each room, with two procedures being performed simultaneously. With one child already asleep and surgery started, a portable screen is placed between the two tables, and the second child is intubated. The screen is then removed, and the doctors can discuss the procedures and even assist each other by changing gloves and moving just two feet from table to table. This is very conducive to teaching and instruction.

I am undertaking the more difficult procedures, and explaining their intricacies, while simultaneously instructing one of the Pakistani surgeons who is performing a less complicated procedure on the table only inches away from me. The procedures take a little over an hour, after which there is a complete turnover of linen and instruments, and during which time I visit my next patient. The turnover consists of removing the instruments, which will be washed and re-sterilized, then cleaning of the operating tables and the room, followed by discarding all of the used materials from the last two patients. Once thoroughly cleaned, the operating room is restocked with two sterile instrument packs, intravenous solutions, antibiotics, and whatever other equipment and supplies are needed and available.

Earlier we received a call about the three infants from Balochistan, so we have been expecting them. We are surprised when the truck driver arrives; we had all been expecting an ambulance transfer, but this is Pakistan. The truck driver is amazing, having done everything he possibly could to make this trip as comfortable as possible for these infants, and getting them from Quetta to Jacobabad as fast as he did.

The oldest of the children is perhaps two years old. Nobody knows her name, and we are told that in Quetta they had began calling her *Khufhdakth*, which means "good destiny." We will soon come to give her another nickname, *Shakira*, derived from the Arab word for "Thank you." We will grow to love her as if she were our own child. Surprisingly, despite her terrible injuries she is alert and responsive to all those who are participating in her care. Her face is horribly damaged; most of her nose is gone, as are her eyelids. She also has second and third degree burns on her scalp, neck, forearms, and hand. It appears that she threw her hands up in front of her in a defensive manner when the blast of the rockets from the unmanned drone occurred, but those little hands could not protect her from the horror that rained down upon her.

Within minutes the team has her IV started to administer antibiotic therapy, and pain medication is then administered. She will be stabilized first, rehydrated, and then blood tests will be completed. Perhaps in a few days she will be taken to the operating room for debridement and cleaning of the burn wounds. For now the wounds are gently cleaned, with topical antibiotic ointment and soft burn dressings applied. Her eyes are examined as well.

Unfortunately, and very disheartening, the other two children are probably less than a year of age and have suffered from both dehydration and more extensive burns. They are semi-comatose, and it is very questionable whether they will survive the next several days. There are no intensive care units. There are no respirators or specialized equipment. The medical teams will have to do the best that we can with what we have, and everyone of us is compelled to offer up prayers for them.

The sun has set, and it is already getting dark. Oddly enough, this is the hardest moment of the night, now that the initial work is over, the hospital is quiet, and most of my co-workers have eaten and retired for the evening. My own adrenaline is still pumping, and I have no interest in dinner, despite having ignored a growing hunger for hours. I need to take a walk, to somehow shake off the frustration and heartache that I feel. Regardless of the danger, I cannot resist the temptation.

I feel ashamed that there was nothing else that we could offer our little burn victims. I walk toward the main entrance, where I see a spark of light hovering in the darkness. As I draw closer, I can see that it is the glow of the cigarette in the hand of one of the sentries at the front entrance. A damp mist rises from the hillsides in the distance, and I walk silently onto the path leading from the hospital to the main gate.

Shakira:
The Thankful One

The relationship between the United States and Pakistan has long been a complicated one, and has been made increasingly complex by the Americans' implementation of unmanned drone attacks in the region. Where the Pakistani government has at least been superficially supportive of American efforts to diminish al Qaeda control, it has also come under significant pressure from the public whenever it has been discovered that American military incursions have crossed into Pakistani territory without the government's permission.

The use of unmanned drones has reinforced the distrust that many Pakistanis feel toward the U.S., and has placed the government in the untenable position of trying to calm its people's anger, while at the same time, reassuring them that the government is not under American control. Matters are made even worse when the United States publicly claims that the drone attacks are surgical in their scope, with casualties restricted to high-value al Qaeda and Taliban targets. Unfortunately, as I have mentioned, the people in the tribal areas know that such claims are untrue, and that many of the drone attacks miss their intended targets and strike innocent civilians who are guilty of nothing more than trying to live their own lives.

Even when the drones manage to strike their intended targets, the results can hardly be considered surgical, and the euphemistically named "collateral damage" – the death toll of innocent civilians who happen to be nearby – is much higher than the U.S. claims would indicate. The common wisdom among the tribes, which I have heard expressed and seen the effects of firsthand, is that when a drone strikes, none survive. And the strikes occur all too frequently in small villages, where a target is suspected of hiding. When the village is hit, it is frequently (to use another horrific euphemism) neutralized. And that means that the entire village, along with all its residents – men, women, children, and even livestock – are wiped in a blinding instant from the face of the earth.

One of the rare exceptions to this grim statistic is the young child we nicknamed Shakira, derived from the Arab word for "thankful." Though she had been through more suffering and pain in her short life than many people experience in a lifetime, Shakira was always visibly grateful for the care she received. She was always saying, "Thank you" to us.

Nine months have passed since Shakira and the other two small children were brought to us. I've thought of them now and then and wondered about their fates, but have been busy with hundreds of other patients. My team and I only arrived in Lahore twenty-four hours ago, and have spent the last eighteen hours dealing with almost five hundred patients, preparing operating schedules, setting up pharmacies, sorting equipment, and preparing the operating rooms. Everyone is mentally and physically exhausted.

The day begins at 6:00 AM. The clinic has remained open, and the hospital staff and I first see those who had spent the night waiting to see the doctors. We then continue throughout the day, examining and treating new arrivals. The operating room runs from 7:00 AM to almost midnight, and as my American team integrates with the local Pakistani doctors and nurses, the efficiency level rapidly increases, and a very strong camaraderie develops. We know we are facing another eighteen-hour day.

Everything goes well, and judging by the number of new patients coming to the clinic, it is evident that word of our arrival has spread into the Indus Valley and the tribal areas of the Northwest Territories, and across the borders of Balochistan into Afghanistan.

On the afternoon of the third day, a friendly face appears at the operating room door. It is a young orderly. "An ambulance has arrived and is parked next to the emergency wing. The doctors would like you to come to the outpatient emergency area as soon as you finish this case."

"Is this an emergency?"

"No, it's urgent, but it is not an emergency situation."

"Can you tell me more about the patient?"

"I was not given any other information."

"Tell them approximately ten minutes."

"Thank you."

As suddenly as he had arrived, the young orderly disappears from the operating room doorway. I am finishing a wide, complicated cleft-lip repair, and after placing the sutures that will align the muscle and overlying lip section, I leave it to the most experienced Pakistani surgeon to complete. I remove my gloves and surgical gown and exit the operating room, grabbing my white lab coat from the hook by the door. I slip into a pair of sandals and walk through the doors toward the main entrance, then down the corridor leading to the outpatient clinic wing and emergency room.

The orderly's statement that the request was urgent but not an emergency is a little confusing, and stirs my curiosity. I enter the outpatient clinic area, and am directed by a grinning nurse to one of the examining rooms. There, I discover an ambulance attendant and another nurse sitting on an examining table, with a nearly three-year-old burn patient between them. She is dressed in a typical colorful Balochistan sari. She has a small scarf around her neck and a multi-colored ribbon in her hair. The nurse and attendant have given her one of the small, cuddly stuffed animals that we give to all of the children at the hospital, and she is playing with it. As the door to the examining room closes behind me, she looks up. I will never forget those beautiful big eyes and their life-giving glow. As our eyes meet, I stand there mesmerized...in

shock. I step forward, and her little arms reach out and latch onto my neck. Nine months have passed since I treated her, and she is still alive... and she recognizes me!

**Shakira the Thankful One
and Doc Joe**

She holds me tightly as I softly whisper into her ear, "Shakira... Shakira, the thankful one."

She whispers back, "My doctor. My doctor."

At that instant I make up my mind that this time, there will be no political or administrative decisions to send this child back to Balochistan again. Not only will we be caring for her injuries at the Shalimar Hospital in Lahore, but with my good friend Hashmat's help, we will bring this child to the Texas Medical Center and coordinate her treatment with the Shriner's Burn Hospital.

"So what was the urgency?" I ask the attendant and nurse.

"Ambulances are in short supply and the driver needs to return to Balochistan."

I don't understand why his departure seems to be hinging upon my pronouncement, and tell her, "Give him something to eat and some bottled water for his return trip."

"But doctor, first we have to know if you accept this patient."

I can't believe that there could be any question in the matter, and bark at her, somewhat more tersely than she deserves, "Of course we accept this patient! She is our patient. We treated her nine months ago in Jacobabad. She is a survivor of a drone rocket attack. Tell Hashmat, Arsala, and Riaz to complete her admission forms and get her a bed on the children's ward."

Turning to the ambulance driver, I ask him if he knows what happened to the other two children who had been brought in with Shakira those many months before. When he tells me that they died of their injuries months ago, I am overwhelmed with a sense of sadness and profound loss, and begin weeping uncontrollably. Shakira loosens her grip on my neck and begins wiping away my tears, saying, "It's okay. It's okay." Her tenderness, her desire to comfort me when it is I who should be comforting her, brings my heart to my throat, and I know that I have to step away if I am to be able to function for the patients who await my care. I hug her once more, tightly, then step away to return to the operating room. The nurse takes Shakira to the children's ward, where Hashmat and Arsala are just as surprised to see her as I was.

As I walk down the long corridor back to the operating room, I decide that as soon as our scheduled surgical procedures are completed, the next procedure I perform will be on Shakira. The blast from the drone had destroyed her upper eyelids, and as a result of her burns, she has ectropion of the lower eyelids, and they are contracted and folded down. The lack of protective eyelids has resulted in the conjunctiva and cornea of her eyes being badly irritated and red. Surprisingly, she still has good vision, but I know that if we are to maintain that, she needs eyelids to protect the delicate membranes of her eyes from irritation and ulceration caused by the sun, the dryness of the desert air, and the blowing sand and dirt. If the delicate task of grafting new eyelids is not performed, the child will be permanently blinded.

I am so pleased – and yet so shaken – by my encounter with Shakira that I walk absent-mindedly into the operating room un-scrubbed, still wearing my white coat and sandals rather than the required surgical gown and slippers. Within seconds, one of the nurses scolds me, asking me respectfully but firmly to return outside, hang up my coat, and remove my sandals.

I do so without comment, and wash longer than usual at the scrub sink, in order to regain my composure. As I enter the operating room, two children are being put to sleep in preparation for their surgical procedures. I had begun to feel tired a little earlier, but now the adrenaline is pumping. I am filled with renewed strength and couldn't be happier. The sun has set, but we continue working. The last evening call to prayer echoes through the hallways of the hospital and into the operating rooms, but we all continue to work.

I lose all track of time. Finally at one point, when setting up for the next procedure by cleaning the tables and opening the new instrument pack, I realize the room is almost empty. Where has everyone gone? I look up at the clock and see that it is midnight. That can't be correct, I think. I pull off my gloves, reach into my pocket, and look at my own watch, which also indicates that it is midnight. I walk through the swinging doors adjoining the operating rooms to the area where the handwritten surgery schedule is posted. I see that a line has been drawn through every one of the names. There are no more patients scheduled for today. I count the names on the list and am amazed to see that our team has completed forty-two procedures. It seems that we started our day only minutes ago, and now it is past midnight. There is nothing like a busy day – and an adrenaline rush – to make the time fly.

I leave the operating room for the doctor's lounge, where my associates are sitting with their feet up on the old, well-worn coffee table, their heads back and their eyes closed. I decide to have some fun with them. I shout out, "Who is going to help me with the next case?"

Their heads pop up, their eyes fly open, and their startled expressions almost make me laugh aloud. Nothing is said for a few moments, and then, from the back of the room, I hear a quiet little voice: "What next case?"

I begin to laugh and say, "I'm just having some fun with you. We are not sleeping here tonight. Take off your operating room garments, put on your street clothes, and meet me in the front in a few minutes. We're going to the Gymkhana Club, and for those who are hungry, there will be some food available."

There is an audible sigh of relief throughout the room.

Presently I join Hashmat and Arsala in the lead car, and our little convoy leaves for the Gymkhana Club for some food and a good night's sleep. I am sitting in the front next to the driver, as it is not proper for me to sit with the ladies in the back seat. Adjusting my seat belt, I turn so I can face them, saying, "It's a miracle that Shakira has been returned to us, isn't it?"

Hashmat's face lights up as she says, "Yes it is! We will treat her here, of course?"

"That's right," I say.

"And then," says Hashmat, "we will immediately start making arrangements for her to continue treatment in Houston, Texas."

I smile broadly. "Yes, that's the plan."

I have all the faith in the world that if anyone can make this happen, Hashmat and her husband Tarak will be the ones to do so. My heart as well as my face is smiling as I think of Shakira and realize that at last, there is real hope for her. I can't save every child, but I can help save some.

When Shakira had first been brought to us nine months ago, her features, or rather, what was left of them, were delicate. All that remained of her nose was the cartilage framework, the skin and underlying tissue having been seared away. Despite the damage to her eyelids, her large, staring eyes had remained miraculously uninjured by the blast of the powerful rocket fired upon her village by the American drone. When she spoke, those beautiful, undamaged eyes sparkled. As I examined her wounds, she looked up at me, her innocence remarkably intact, and said matter-of-factly, "I like toys. I like nail polish. I like to play. I do not like bombs." And she pointed at her ravaged face for emphasis.

Her face was horribly scarred by the burn and pigmented by the sun. Those areas somehow not injured by the blast were as white as sugar and unblemished except for her hairline. The hair closest to her forehead had been burned off in the blast, and her skin was mottled with alternately light and dark pigmentation. Her lips had been dried and cracked in some areas, but were for the most part uninjured.

It seems so long and so many thousands of patients ago that she was first brought to us with the other two children, but the memory of our first meeting is as clear as if it had been an hour ago. Now that she has returned, I notice that she is developing an increasing awareness of herself and the medical team, and asks us ever more difficult questions every day. "How did I get hurt? How did I get lost?"

Her questions are difficult for us to hear and consider, and we know that we have no real answers for her. Is she referring to the time nine months ago when they secretly took her away from the Jacobabad hospital and returned her to the orphanage in Quetta, leaving her lost from the medical team, the only people she had left in the world? Or does she mean that she is lost, taken from a village and a family who are all now dead?

When she was secretly returned to Quetta, every member of the medical team missed her. She had changed – and continues to change – our lives as we have taken care of her. We have become her only family. With each day, she smiles more. It is interesting that at times when she is happy and things are progressing well, she speaks more and more English, but when she gets upset, she returns to her mother-language, Urdu, and becomes more withdrawn, almost as if she is an island unto herself. When she looks in the mirror, she does not comment on the scars that are there, but does say that she misses her hair. Enough hair remains in the middle and posterior portion of her scalp that with the use of balloon expanders, it should be possible to recreate a hairline.

Once again, I am reminded of the limitations as to what is possible in this small hospital, and I know that it would be best if the necessary but difficult reconstructive procedures could be done back in the States, perhaps at the Shriner's Burn Center. To pull this off, we will need to obtain passports and a visa for our little patient. Hashmat says she will speak to Muhammad Mian Soomro, the past chairman of the Pakistani Senate, and enlist his help in obtaining a passport. We do not have a birth date for Shakira, so in a gesture of good will, Mr. Soomro suggests that we use the 19th of August, his own birth date, on her passport application, to which we happily agree.

I write the letter of medical necessity, which will be sent to the American Embassy in Pakistan to obtain a United States visa for medical reasons. The people at the embassy know me well. Such maneuverings have become a common practice over the past five years, and all the children for whom I have submitted such requests have been allowed to come to the U.S. for their continued medical care, without political interference from either the Pakistani or the United States governments. This has allowed us to provide care for many children in the United States that is beyond the level of equipment and expertise available in Pakistan.

It has been interesting to watch the progress of these children as they became bilingual and returned to Pakistan, where they have continued their education and gone on to become productive citizens. Without such care, they would have inevitably spent the rest of their lives sitting in their homes, hidden away from the public, uneducated and lost. These children have become powerful goodwill ambassadors and spokespersons, who speak highly of the United States. They have also become advocates for women's rights and the freedoms that should be available to all, but are withheld from the vast majority of the population in their home country.

It will take a few weeks, perhaps a little longer, but the arduous paperwork process for obtaining her passport and visa will be completed, and Shakira and some of the other children will be returning with us to Houston for their medical care. Thanks to the generosity of the medical community and numerous benefactors, there are no fees charged for the children's treatment. When these grateful and hope-filled children return home, they are without a doubt the best ambassadors the United States could ever have. And the total cost of each child's care is far less than the cost of even one of the rockets launched by the unmanned drones.

Contrast this with the profound emotional toll on the Pakistani people of the countless child warriors conscripted by the Taliban and al Qaeda, and it would seem to me that such unofficial diplomatic efforts could be infinitely more success-ful – and less costly – than our strategic efforts in winning a war on hate.

Adventures on the Road to Peshawar

hy am I in Pakistan? I am asked that all the time, and even after reading this far in the narrative you may still be asking the same thing. To really understand it, maybe you just "have to be there." Beyond my desire to help the people of Pakistan, beyond my concern with the cruel violation of women's rights (particularly in the rural areas), even beyond my growing obsession with finding, meeting, and conversing with Osama bin Laden, there is something deeper. As I said, perhaps you just "have to be there."

* * * * *

I am in the van with my driver Mohammed, my bodyguard Sultan, and my interpreter/guide (and "backup" bodyguard), Saleem. We're leaving the breadbasket of the Indus Valley and climbing into the highlands, our destination being Peshawar. I have heard that the headmaster at a famous *madrasa* (school) in the area may be able to give me some insights about Osama bin Laden. And on the way I intend to take every opportunity to photograph the amazing scenery.

The air has become much cooler, and a light breeze caresses my face. I sit in the van's front passenger seat – appropriately termed "riding shotgun" in this case, as I have my weapon close at hand, as well as multiple cameras at my feet, one camera on my lap, and a telephoto lens positioned between the seat and the door.

When we first set out, Sultan was not happy with this arrangement. In a short but very direct conversation I made it clear that I was in charge. After all, I explained, one of my purposes for making this trip is to photograph the Northern Territories. In order to do that properly, I need to sit in the front seat of the van and take the pictures. Sultan protested, feeling that he was not fulfilling his job of looking after me if I sat up front. He told me that riding in the front seat made me a target.

I explained to Sultan that I fully understood the risk, and said I would be happy to alter our seating arrangements if and when he – and the others – thought we were in an area where there was a significantly increased threat. "Now, this will have to be a group decision," I clarified. "But I will abide by whatever the group decides." Sultan reluctantly consented, so here I am.

I look out the window now and ponder the distant snow-capped mountains and rocky ledges that extend upward into the sky. I love this weather. We are leaving the grasslands behind and driving on a gravel road along the steep rocky cliffs that have been shaped since the beginning of time by relentless winds and rain. There are scattered clusters of small mud brick homes with adjacent gardens, and I see mountain goats, sheep, and an occasional yak.

This land is wild, beautiful, visual…and incredibly sensual. I take a deep breath and smile to myself as one does when thinking of an old lover. Stripped of its violent history, this place is very romantic. There is definitely something magical about these mountains – almost mystical. For me they evoke thoughts of a truly nomadic society, where a man can journey to the far corners of the earth for no reason other than that he wants to go there. My imagination is now running wild as I envision a life so completely different from the one I have lived: a life where one can simply go forth into the mountain passes and valleys and seek whatever one wishes. This is a freedom that most contemporary city dwellers will never know or understand.

When you come right down to it, I suppose it is a freedom that very few nomads, past or present, could truly experience either, since the poorest wanderers have always been engaged chiefly in the struggle for survival in a harsh and sometimes brutal environment. No doubt those who live in areas such as these highlands do appreciate the beauty around them, and would miss it sorely if they were suddenly plunked down into "civilization." But I imagine that very few of these poor nomads ever just pick up and go for the sake of going. There is always a goal in mind related to their survival: better grazing, better weather, escape from some adversity. I realize that this is a region where breathtaking beauty is countered by the reality of tribal conflicts and politics, not to mention natural disasters such as earthquakes, floods, and landslides.

Without a doubt I am romanticizing this place, and I know it. Believe me, I am grateful to be in a position to do so. Most of the time I am very aware that I have the best of all worlds. I have the affluence that permits me to travel, as well as the education and perspective that allow me to appreciate every experience, and to see the beauty in even the most troubled parts of the world. I also have skills that people need, both at home and abroad. The fact that so many people need me keeps me grounded most of the time. But sometimes – right now, for example – those wild mountains call to me in a way that is beyond all rational thought.

Mohammed interrupts my reverie by saying, "Our destination is a river crossing. An all-wooden suspension bridge that extends across a tributary of the Indus River."

"Okay," I say. "That sounds interesting."

He continues, "There is a small teahouse built into the side of the cliff where we can stop, stretch our legs and get something to eat and drink. I know the owner. I was there last year and the food and drink were acceptable. Also, from that vantage point a man can see for miles. The visibility couldn't be more perfect."

Sultan knows what he is getting at, and calls out from the backseat, "Bring your cameras! Bring your cameras!" As if I needed to be prompted.

Mohammed says, "When I hiked this area last year I discovered a handmade metal belt and a rusted sword. I imagined that perhaps a soldier had been placed on watch on the peak long ago. Maybe the soldier died here defending this territory." He muses that such individual tragedies leave little evidence behind and are submerged in the rivers of time. Unless there is a historical marker of some sort, most of these stories remain untold and are irreversibly lost. It is up to the finder of the odd artifact, years or decades or perhaps even centuries later, to fill in the pieces of the puzzle.

We are now well above the tree line, and as we approach our destination, the road is very narrow. Fortunately we have not seen another vehicle in the past several hours. When we get to the small teahouse/restaurant, I see that it is really nothing more than a cave in the side of the mountain facing the road. Several wooden posts support a lean-to like structure that extends outward from the entrance of the cave. There are a few very old, hand-built wooden tables. Under the lean-to covering, as well as inside the cave, are some rope platforms.

Sultan says, "At night when the tea shop is closed, truck drivers and travelers can put their blankets on these rope platforms and sleep here for the night. It only costs a few pennies."

We are approached and greeted by a young man. He notices that I am peering curiously at the dark interior of the restaurant, and he hastily says, "You should sit out front and enjoy the mountain view. You will be more comfortable out here."

So we all sit down at one of the outside tables. The young man tells us that rice with chicken is the only thing on the menu, and that tea and flatbread come with the dinner. That sounds fine to us, since we're very hungry by now. He rushes off to get our orders.

Our server's insistence that we sit outside has put us on full alert, but of course has done nothing to abate my curiosity about what is inside the cave. I get up from my seat, saying something about needing to walk around a little after having sat so long in the van. Of course I cannot resist venturing into the area behind the lean-to covering, so I can get a closer look at what – and who – might be in the cave. The area is dimly lit by the little sunlight that trickles in through the entrance, so it takes a few moments for my eyes to grow accustomed to the darkness.

I see that there are similar tables and rope-like platforms within, and small groups of men are smoking and drinking tea. They look up for a moment when I enter, and then return to their conversations. I notice that they are all dressed in black and are wearing dark turbans, and as my eyes adjust to the low light I also see that they all have automatic weapons lying across their laps, or propped up against the table next to them.

I have seen enough to know that I do not need to enter into the cave itself. It has become abundantly clear to me why our host advised us to sit outside. On the other hand, the photographer within me is screaming for me to go to the van and get a camera. Yet the more sensible part of my brain is telling me, *Don't you dare do it. You need to get the hell out and join the others outside!*

In the end I yield to my more sensible self and return to the table, where I say nothing to the others about my rather unsettling discovery.

Sultan looks at me and says, "My legs are stiff from riding in the van too. While our dinner is being prepared, would you like to join me for a walk along the rocky crags?"

I tell him I think that would be a good idea, and I think but don't say aloud that perhaps while we are gone, those within the cave will finish and leave. I think I would feel more at ease without their presence. But I soon forget my trepidation about the men in the cave, and give myself up to enjoyment of the wildflowers blowing along our path as we walk.

I notice, however, that Sultan has slung his heavy double-barreled shotgun over one shoulder. I can see he is scanning possible hiding places behind rocks and trees. Of course he is doing his job and I am very appreciative of it. I realize now that I was being too trusting, and was underestimating the potential dangers in this area. It's an understandable oversight, I think; it is just too beautiful here to think of anything unpleasant, to say nothing of anything really dangerous.

And it *is* beautiful. The view of the glacier-covered mountains is stunning, and this place is more than just a feast for the eyes. The many streams, rushing swiftly down over the rocks and the rope bridge, produce a haunting song that is carried on the wind. I want to stay here forever.

Nearby I notice the young man who greeted and seated us, carrying pots and dishes from the kitchen to the stream to wash them. He is barely more than a teenager. His bare feet are thick with calluses, and the white apron he wears around his waist is discolored and stained. After returning the clean dishes to the kitchen, he comes back with a scratched and dented metal jug, and grasping a branch of a tree in one hand, he leans over the stream and fills the pitcher with water. My photographic instincts get the better of me, and I pull one of the cameras from my belt pack. I gesture to the young man, pointing to the camera and then back to him. He gives me a big smile and a nod.

As he leans over the stream with the big metal jug, I take a series of photos, and then walk back with him to the kitchen. I manage to find out that his name is Mohammed, just like my driver. Of course it is quite a common name in these parts.

The cooking area is outside the cave entrance to our left, and is sheltered by a rocky overhang. The kitchen itself consists of a round brick oven in which they bake the flatbread, and a fifty-five gallon steel drum, which has been cut in half and is supported on short legs. Within this is a charcoal fire for cooking. A metal grill covers the drum, and perched on the grill are several large blackened metal pots and iron skillets in which tea is boiling and the chicken and rice are cooking. I feel comfortable eating here since the food has obviously been boiling for hours, and there is little chance of any bacterial contamination. The doctor in me is still cognizant of food and drink safety.

Sultan and I return to our table. The owner – who is also the cook – stands with one hand leaning on a post that supports the lean-to, watching us. He is a big man, at least six-foot-two, with a full head of charcoal colored curly hair specked with gray. His beard is a similar color and extends to his waist. His eyes are partly covered over by hanging lids and thick curly brows. He is barefoot, and his rotund abdomen is covered with a cook's apron, stained from long years of use. It does not appear to have been washed recently. He glances over at our group and as we make eye contact, he smiles. It is clear that he knows our driver, Mohammed, but equally clear that he is very curious about the rest of us. What are we doing here? Why have we come?

I can see the questions in his eyes as I look at him. I quickly turn my gaze away from him, and look up into the heavens, where I can see several clouds moving swiftly over the mountaintops, driven by the wild winds above us in the Himalayas. I can still feel the cook's steady gaze, and feel that I am the one who has aroused most of his curiosity. But he finally turns away and heads toward the kitchen area.

In short order the younger Mohammed brings two full plates to our table, and then returns with two more. He quickly follows with an old worn wooden tray, stacked with hot flatbreads. Gratefully we began eating.

I am beginning to relax. I feel we are dressed appropriately and that I blend in quite satisfactorily, but my Nikon cameras betray the fact that I'm not from around here. Our server is obviously curious, and he and Sultan strike up a conversation.

Sultan explains what we were doing, telling him I am a doctor who is working in Pakistan to provide medical care, surgery and education to all who need it. He adds that I do not charge for my services.

The owner makes another appearance. He must have felt that his young server has been taking too long with his new guests, and with a quick wave of the hand he signals for him to go into the cave and see to the others. The young man does not walk; he runs. A few minutes later he comes out of the cave, stops at the kitchen area, and picks up the large teapot. He brings the large teapot to our table and dutifully begins refilling our cups.

Apparently we have also stirred the curiosity of one of the black-garbed strangers who had been sitting closest to the cave entrance. The man suddenly gets up and comes over to our table, and before long he and my driver are engrossed in a conversation.

I quickly review the correct pronunciations in my mind, and in my rudimentary Urdu I invite the man to sit and join us for tea. Then I glance around our little table and see that the others have concerned looks on their faces. Once again Sultan comes to the rescue and takes over the conversation. I am relieved because frankly, my very limited Urdu vocabulary does not allow me to say much more.

I gently elbow Saleem and whisper in his ear to order more chicken, rice and flatbread for our guest. Saleem seems puzzled at first, so I nudge him again with my elbow. It is only then that he gets up and walks to the kitchen to place the additional order. Plates and food quickly arrive, and our guest eats with relish and gusto as if he hadn't had a meal for some time. Between mouthfuls he is full of questions, and I am only too glad to let Sultan and Saleem answer.

As Sultan, Saleem, and our guest are engaged in their conversation, a military vehicle with a .50 caliber machine gun mounted on top pulls in behind our van. Four men in full

Pakistani military uniforms, with automatic weapons slung over their shoulders, exit the vehicle and walk directly to the counter. I can hear them ordering tea, after which they select a table outside across from ours. They too seem very interested in who we are and what we are doing at this out-of-the-way spot. Another round of questions begins. I get up from the table, thinking that this might be a good time to share the photos I have in the van, depicting the surgical team's works in Pakistan. Maybe this will change the antagonistic atmosphere that seems to be developing.

As I walk from our table toward the van I pass the table of military men, and one of them stands up, pats me on the shoulder, and softly speaks into my ear. "These are dangerous men – Taliban."

I thank him with a smile but continue on to the van, thinking that there is still a chance I can turn a potentially adversarial situation around. I open the sliding door and search through the blankets and other supplies at the rear of the van until I locate several of the photo albums of the children. I gather them up, shut the van, and quickly return to our table. I feel more comfortable having Sultan and Saleem handle the explanations; they're pretty well versed by now. So I pass the photo albums to them and retreat to the kitchen area under the pretext of wanting more tea. From there I can observe what is taking place. It only takes a minute before the Taliban fighter is heading back into the cave with one of my photo books. I remain discreetly in the kitchen area just outside the cave entrance until the young waiter finishes serving, and then I motion for him to come over and pour me another cup of tea. It gives me a reason to remain away from our table a little while longer.

Within minutes the black-clad men I had seen earlier emerge from the cave with their automatic weapons slung casually over their shoulders, and they walk towards our table. I remain where I am in the kitchen, observing to my relief that a friendly conversation has started. The military men at the adjacent table stand up; they also want to see the photos and join in the conversation.

I watch the goings-on from my vantage point a few feet away, sipping my tea until the cup is empty. Young Mohammed refills my small metal teacup one more time, after which I saunter back to the table. Saleem gets up and offers me his seat, saying, "These men all wanted to meet you and shake your hand."

The atmosphere and attitude have completely changed with the appearance of the photos.

A few minutes later our young server returns to the table bearing a small silver tray with several slips of paper on it; I assume these are the checks. I immediately take the tray from him, explaining that I will pay for the entire group – my small group, the Taliban fighters, and the military men.

Everyone else is still talking and reviewing the photos, so I get up and walk the short distance to the van, where I grab my Nikon camera and some wide-angle lenses, hoping everyone will agree to a photo.

When I return the conversation is relaxed and pleasant, and everyone has a smile on his face. This makes me feel a lot better, as, let's face it, these are a couple of groups of very tough fighters. Encouraged, I hold up my camera and point to the group. They all nod their heads and smile. After I take several photos, one of the Taliban indicates that he wants me to be in a photo with them. This is something I had also secretly wanted since our arrival.

I call out, "Mohammed, Mohammed," and our young server comes running to the table. I focus the camera for him and show him how to use it. He considers this a great honor, and clicks away like an experienced photographer. When he finishes, I find some small coins in my pocket, and slip them into his hand. This puts a big smile on his face.

Things are working out much better than I had expected. After a while Mohammed, my driver, comes over to me and says in a low voice, "The military commander is continuing north to a mountain outpost where they are stationed. They will be happy to escort us through the area, which is considered to be a Taliban controlled road. There are many possible dangers."

I tell Mohammed to thank them and to let them know that we accept their gracious offer. "Tell the military commander that we will be ready to leave when they finish their tea."

The military men finish their tea and begin walking toward their Jeep. I say a proper goodbye to the men in black and request one last photo.

Then at my request, Saleem extends my offer of medical care to any of their children – and adults – in the tribal area. He explains that if they can secure transportation to the Frontier Medical College in Abbottabad, or the Shalamar Hospital in Lahore, I will treat them. They seem appreciative.

We walk to the van, where I see that Sultan is already in the shotgun seat, his facial expression and folded arms making it abundantly clear that this time, our seating arrangements are not negotiable. However, after what has just been said regarding the dangers along this section of the road, I am not going to get in an argument with him. So I take my pride – and my cameras – to the rear seat in the van. I am quickly learning that if I am to maintain Sultan's friendship, which I value deeply beyond his function as my bodyguard, there are times when I will simply have to allow his instincts and experience to prevail. I need to keep focused and pick the fights I can win. So we all settle into our respective spots, and I say, "Let's go." And once again we are on our way.

* * * * *

The military Jeep takes the point position, and we follow at a safe distance behind. We are erring on the side of caution; after all, getting killed is not going to get the job done. I am feeling a little anxious, but don't know whether my anxiety is warranted. But as I glance from face to face, everybody seems tranquil, even pleased. A surge of relief washes over me.

Now we have to decide how much further we're going to drive before stopping somewhere for the night. I ask Mohammed, "What is your recommendation?"

He says, "I do not want to be on these roads at night."

On that we can all agree, and we all nod our heads.

"Perhaps we should go as far as the military escort will take us and then find lodging," I suggest.

"We can probably find lodging in Nowshera," Mohammed says.

I do not feel we will be able to reach Peshawar before dark, but we'll go as far as we can. We drive for several hours, still following our military escort at a reasonable distance, and then suddenly they turn off the main road. Mohammed follows them, and we drive on for about a mile through the mountains. At last we enter a gated compound and stop. This is the local mountain military base.

We get out and our escorts lead us to a small wooden building. Upon entering, we see that there are a half dozen uniformed men inside. A few chairs are set against the wall, and there's a desk at the far end of the room. The commander sitting behind the desk stands and greets us, and we exchange introductions.

The commander asks, "How long will you be in the area, and what is your destination?"

I reply, "We are going on to Peshawar in the morning."

The commander asks to see our papers and requests that we sign his log book. His face hardens when I hand him an American passport.

"Americans don't come here," he says, with more than a hint of accusation in his voice.

Several of the military men who have acted as our escorts begin to speak rapidly, and from what I can understand they are giving him a quick summary of the work I am doing in Pakistan, and describing the photos they have just seen. They explain that they had encountered us at the teashop with the Taliban fighters.

The officer in charge softens immediately, and says, "Good, good. We appreciate this type of help. It is very nice, and much needed in Pakistan."

He then turns the logbook around on his desk and asks that I write my passport number and have Mohammed, Sultan, and Saleem show him their papers as well.

With this completed, the commander says, "Everything seems in order."

Saleem asks, "Is there a place that would be safe and appropriate for us to spend the night? It will be dark soon, and we don't wish to continue onto Peshawar at night."

The commander and the other military men in the room enter into a discussion, and in a few minutes come to a conclusion as to the best place for us to spend the night. They provide directions to Mohammed, and we thank them and leave. Climbing back into the van, we resume our trip along the gravel road.

We have been driving only about thirty minutes when the sun begins to disappear behind the tall mountains. Mohammed, who has already been driving pretty slowly, slows down even more. After all, the road is unlit, and as is so often the case in this area, there are no guardrails. There is no way to summon help should the need occur.

Our discussion turns to Peshawar and our plans. The most famous *madrasa* in the area is Darul Uloom Haqqania. It is located just outside Peshawar, and its headmaster is the senior *Maulana*, or respected religious scholar. The *Maulana* oversees approximately three thousand students at the *madrasa*. The students come from all over, including Afghanistan and the Central Asian Republics, but most are from Pakistan. Our plan is to meet the *Maulana* in the morning.

The school is sometimes called "The University of Jihad" because of the curriculum and some of the activities of its alumni. But I feel that only by visiting this school and speaking with the *Maulana* will I be able to get some of the answers I am seeking.

Saleem is familiar with the school and says he has several friends who were in attendance there only a few years ago. He tells me a little of its history, explaining that the school was established just after the partition of India into India and Pakistan in 1947. Originally, the *madrasa* was a modest institution. Saleem says, "The students originally came only for an education, and the funding was initially quite limited. As the school grew in importance, however, monetary support came from wealthy Muslims. With this funding, the *madrasa* enlarged and improved, and attracted hundreds of Pakistanis who were in search of higher education."

I know that Saleem has presented a somewhat sanitized history of this school, which is, to put it mildly, no stranger to controversy. But I am eager to visit and speak to the *Maulana*.

After we drive a while in silence, Saleem asks, "Can we stop for a few minutes so we can say our evening prayers?"

Mohammed says, "We will be in town in only a few minutes, and there is a mosque surrounded by a beautiful garden. It isn't far from the boarding house where we will stay."

True to his description, we soon enter a little town, and approach a beautiful garden in a small courtyard in which about fifteen men are gathered. Mohammed finds a space off to the side of the road to park the van. We all disembark and Mohammed, Sultan, and Saleem first stop at the fountain and wash, and then enter the lovely little garden adjacent to the mosque. It is clear that the others there are preparing for their evening prayers.

I have found watching a group of Muslim men praying to be a moving experience. This choreographed activity of synchronous worship – something that we have lost in the West – has been well adapted to the daily routine in the Middle East.

I sit in the corner of this gorgeous garden with my back leaning against the wall. Once again my mind is wandering, and I think about ritual prayer as practiced in the West. I recall the poignant nineteenth-century French painting, *The Angelus*, by Jean-François Millet. Originally titled, *Prayer for the Potato Crop*, this painting depicts two humble farmers pausing in their labors to recite The Angelus, a Catholic prayer ritual to commemorate the Incarnation. People so often pray for divine intervention when they are in trouble, but ritual prayer has a different goal in mind: it is an expression of devotion and of gratitude. It is, I think, a beautiful thing to watch.

When the prayer services finish, we all leave together through the garden gate. Mohammed speaks with several of the men, making inquiries as to road conditions and the safety of driving the area at night. He also confirms directions to our destination.

It is almost completely dark now, and there are no street-lights. This is the most dangerous time of the evening to be traveling. There are still many people along the road riding motorbikes, donkey carts, and camel wagons, but they are almost invisible. And this is in addition to the occasional water buffalo, sheep or goat that wanders across the road.

We turn west, crossing the Kabul River, and pass through the small town of Jahangira. About twenty minutes later we arrive at our destination. Mohammed stops at a ramshackle two-story wooden building and announces, "We have arrived."

I remain in the van with Mohammed, and send Sultan and Saleem to negotiate the price for rooms and make any other arrangements they deem necessary.

They return in a few minutes and tell me the accommodations are clean but simple, and that the room fee is $4.00 a night per room. I will be able to have the room that has its own bath, so I won't have to share with anyone else.

"That will be fine. I am in agreement with those arrangements," I say, and Sultan returns to the clerk to close the deal.

Mohammed warns me, "Do not leave anything in the van. We must take everything with us. And be sure to lock your door when you go to bed tonight."

The desk clerk comes out to help us carry our things into our rooms. He seems quite excited to have paying guests. Most Westerners reading this might think that we are getting a bargain at only $4.00 a night per room. But I think we have overpaid, considering that the average salary for a desk clerk in an establishment like this is probably about $4.00 a month. The desk clerk is probably pocketing a few dollars for himself, I think. In comparison, a nurse in Pakistan only earns $75.00 a month, or approximately $2.50 a day. Professionals, such as doctors, earn $1,200 to $1,500 a year, and they consider themselves lucky.

But I am tired, and there is nowhere else to stay, and I am certainly not going to squabble over a four-dollar room fee.

The desk clerk makes multiple trips up and down the stairs with our luggage, running each time. I have just remembered that it is the holiday of Ramadan. I am feeling generous, and I give him the equivalent of $5.00. He embraces me with such force that it takes my breath away.

I say to him, "This is for your family for Ramadan. Eat well!"

He thanks me again and again and whispers, "Don't tell anyone here about this gift."

I smile, patting him on the shoulder as he passes through my doorway with the last piece of luggage. Then, heeding Mohammed's warning, I slide the heavy steel bolt into place behind the door and go to wash up.

A few minutes later, Sultan is knocking at my door saying, "We must hurry if we hope to find some place that is still open in order to get something to eat. Remember, this is Ramadan."

During the month of Ramadan, from sunrise to sunset, the Muslim is expected to fast. Now that the sun has set, the Muslim families will be gathering for their evening meal. It is our hope that somewhere a teahouse is still open, so we can get something to eat. I am aware that the Taliban have imposed an ultra-orthodox version of Islam in this territory, and Ramadan will be strictly observed.

In keeping with this strict observation of Islam, men are not allowed to shave or trim their beards. Even though there is no legal compulsion to wear a *burqa*, women in this area nonetheless don the garment. Women are also required to stay at home unless accompanied by their husband or another male relative when going out. "*Women belong in the house or in the grave*" sounds pretty grim, but it pretty much sums up the status of women under Taliban rule.

You need to understand the thinking behind the confinement of women in this part of the world. You must look at this, not with a Westerner's mindset, but from within the culture to which these women were born. This culture does not allow women their full rights as set forth in International Law, or even in Sharia Law. The Taliban's attitude is that women's rights are set by Allah and his Messenger Mohammed, who (according to their interpretation) instructed, "Women are to stay in their home and tend to their family."

I don't like it but have learned to accept it as the local norm.

The Taliban could actually have been a force for good, had their priorities been different. For instance, there have been many unsustainable Pakistani governmental projects.

There has been a shortage of food, and there is wide-scale unemployment; the recent floods in the Indus Valley have exacerbated the problem. But these are not the concerns of the Taliban. They have been preoccupied with religious matters and enforcing Sharia laws. The Taliban has gone further than anyone before them, requiring the Hindu population of the area to wear distinguishing clothing, setting them apart from the Muslims. This is reminiscent of Hitler requiring the Jews to wear the Star of David on their clothing.

In Western countries, the Taliban is often depicted as a unified front. But in fact the Taliban is split between hardliners and those who want to engage more with the outside world. What many Westerners do not realize is that in the major cities of Pakistan such as Karachi, Lahore, and Islamabad, it has been very difficult for the Taliban to enforce more radical policies such as the banning of education for girls, or the prohibition of women working outside the home.

The Taliban really control only the rural and tribal areas. The major cities have become much more cosmopolitan. In the major cities, women wear fitted suits, high heels and make-up. Rarely is a women seen in a *burqa* or other garb that is so typical of Muslim women in the rural and tribal areas. At posh city restaurants, women can even be seen wearing mini-skirts – a fashion that could cause them to be stoned to death in the tribal region.

The Taliban are reluctant to acknowledge these changes. They do not want to admit openly to this weakening of fundamentalist Islamic ideals and Sharia laws. However, they are gradually coming to the realization that they are losing their control, and have recently acquiesced to the education of girls – but only to the age of twelve. Small girls' schools have been established discreetly, located off of main streets or in private homes. These schools are supported by donations from the girls' families and other concerned citizens. The makeshift classrooms lack teaching materials, and the courses given simply consist of basic reading, writing, and arithmetic, and occasionally a foreign language.

There have been other cultural shifts as well. These include allowing women to be treated by male doctors, and women are also now permitted to enter the practice of medicine. There have been increased opportunities for women to work outside the home in other professions, too. As with the modernization of fashion, these changes have occurred only in the major cities, but are quickly spreading to the suburbs. However, the tribal areas of the west and north are under the control of the Taliban, and still impose restrictions on women's rights. The Religious Police that exist for *"the promotion of virtue and prevention of vice"* still remain very active. And overall, as you can imagine, the Taliban human rights record remains very poor – a ludicrous oxymoron, you might say.

* * * * *

With our personal items and equipment stored safely in our rooms, the four of us meet in the hotel lobby and leave as a group. We make our way down the unlit streets, where all of the shops are already closed. Several of the teashops have also closed. We are the only ones out on the street tonight – most of the people are now in their homes, breaking their Ramadan fast with their families – and as we walk slowly down the middle of the road I have an unsettling feeling.

With the setting of the sun, the temperature has dropped quickly. The wind begins to cascade down the canyons of the mountains into the vacant streets. A sudden chill comes upon me and I wrap my woolen shawl tightly around my shoulders. I cover the lower portion of my face to prevent the swirling dust and sand from stinging my cheeks. I notice the others doing the same. We continue walking down the center of this gravel road, which passes for the town's main street.

All at once, Sultan springs to life and begins walking quickly towards a shop several meters away and to our right. It has a single light bulb hanging from an electric cord. This is the only illumination. Within the shop I can see the shadow of a man and hear the sound of water running.

We all quickly pick up the pace, following Sultan's lead till we reach the entrance to a small restaurant. Sultan is already conversing with the man inside. The man had been closing and was ready to go home for his evening meal with the family, but he takes pity on us – or more likely sees the opportunity to earn a little extra money tonight.

The shopkeeper says, "I can only offer lamb and rice with mixed vegetables. It will take a few minutes to heat."

Sultan answers, "We have been traveling all day and have not eaten for many hours. We stopped and said our prayers at the mosque before entering your village. Now the sun has set and we are very hungry. We would much appreciate anything you can offer us."

Sultan presents this request in a very quiet, humble manner, and continues, "We appreciate your efforts and we will compensate you well for this food, as well as for your kindness and this special consideration on Ramadan."

The restaurant's proprietor motions us toward a wooden table with four wooden chairs. We are very appreciative of this opportunity to get out of the cold and the blowing sand. In a few minutes the restaurateur returns with hot rice and lamb and some vegetables, served on metal plates. He also brings some flatbreads, which must have been made earlier in the day because they are a little too firm. But when you are hungry and it is very late – and this is the only teahouse that is still open – you are thankful for what you get. We begin eating as our host goes to fetch a pot of hot tea, which he pours into little dented metal cups for each of us.

Suddenly he asks, "May I join you?" I can see the curiosity burning in his eyes. We bid him to pull up a chair and he does.

"Where are you from? What do you do, and where are you going?" he asks. The questions come fast, and I let Sultan and Saleem answer them. They are smart enough to stick with generalities and not to divulge too many details. The only information they disclose is that we were going to Peshawar, where we plan to stop at the *madrasa*.

The proprietor says he knows exactly where it is located and can provide directions. "I wish you a safe trip," he adds.

Since we are all so hungry, we eat quickly, and when we finish our meal we thank him profusely. In a very humble manner he tells us what our meals will cost us: the equivalent of about one U.S. dollar for each of us. "Would that be acceptable?" he asks.

I nod to Sultan and hold up five fingers, indicating he should be paid in Pakistani rupees equivalent to five U.S. dollars.

Our host is a big man with long arms and huge powerful hands. His dark beard extends to the middle of his chest, and he has a full, round face and high cheekbones. His eyes are small, but they sparkle, particularly when he receives the money. He gives us a wide contagious grin, and we thank him again for his kindness and for staying open so late on Ramadan.

We wrap our woolen shawls tightly over our faces, as the wind is now howling off the mountain peaks with a blistering force, and carrying a cold mist along with the sand. We are all exhausted after such a long day.

When I reach my room, Sultan puts his hand on my shoulder and says, "Remember to put the steel bolt across the door." He really didn't have to remind me. I'm very aware that there is danger lurking everywhere in these dark, remote places – even during a holy time such as Ramadan.

My rope bed is quite firm, and the pillow is nothing more than a hard bed roll, but that doesn't seem to matter. As soon as I lie down, I am asleep.

* * * * *

The following morning I am awakened by the call to prayer, which echoes off the mountain peaks and through the town. I look out the window and can see there is a red fireball reflecting off the mountains. Opening the shutters to let some light and air into the room, I notice that the chilling wind that whipped us the night before has dissipated.

I wash in cold water and dress in a clean *shalwar kameez*, and then snap on my handmade sandals, which are covered with dust. When I open the door I see that Sultan is already in the hallway. There will be no breakfast this morning, for the sun has already risen, and the people here are all observing the Ramadan fast.

As I pack the last of my things, I noticed a slip of paper fall from my daily diary. It is a copy of the recent U.S. State Department travel advisory that my secretary had printed from their website for me. It reads, "Americans remain vulnerable to political and criminally motivated attacks and violence, including robbery, kidnapping and hostage taking. There are an estimated five to seven million landmines scattered throughout the countryside and along the Afghanistan-Pakistan border. This poses an imminent danger. The U.S. State Department urges Americans not to venture into these areas."

And yet, in spite of this warning, here we are.

The statement goes on to say that one should take extreme caution, should monitor their security situation closely, and should "make plans to respond to a sudden deterioration in conditions.

I wonder who writes this stuff for the State Department? I am absolutely certain it is written by someone who has never been in the tribal areas of Pakistan and has no appreciation of what "sudden imminent danger" is.

I toss the warning in the circular file in the corner of the room, and quickly shift back to packing my treasured diary, which I place in the inner pocket of my backpack. Then we all get into the van and are on our way to Peshawar.

We enter the old city, pass through the traffic circle, and find a safe place to park the van. Here I notice that Mohammed does not lock the van. The shops are already open and we purchase some clothing items that are typical of this area, including some skullcaps. We are determined to blend in. Mohammed inquires about directions to the famous *madrasa*. This will be our first stop.

I am hoping to be granted an interview with the *Maulana*. It is very important to me because in this region he is more than just a headmaster. He is the law. He has the money. I have been told that he is politically well connected to the Taliban and other Islamic parties in Peshawar. I have also been told that he is an admirer of Osama bin Laden, and this is a particularly important point I wish to discuss with him – including my desire to meet and interview bin Laden.

We arrive unannounced, because I think that will be our best chance of meeting with the *Maulana*. The decision turns out to work very much in our favor.

My research has provided me with enough information to speak in an intelligent yet humble manner with this prominent scholar. I have also prepared a list of questions for the *Maulana* to answer.

When at last we sit down together and he asks for my first question I do not hesitate. "What are your thoughts on Osama bin Laden?"

"I think he is more popular than any political leader in Pakistan."

Bin Laden's ideas resonate deeply with members of the Pakistani clergy. as well as with many political leaders. The

Sheik is a large contributor to this *madrasa*, and others as well.

I push on. "Please, please tell me what you think of Osama bin Laden as a person."

"He is not a saboteur. He is not a terrorist, as some think. I do not think he has an aggressive attitude. Bin Laden feels the Americans want to take everything from the Middle East – most notably, all of our oil and gas. He thinks Americans are like the Russians in Afghanistan, whom bin Laden fought against and won. Now he has taken up the fight against the American Army that has located itself on the Saudi Arabian peninsula, the site of the two Holy Cities."

After taking a deep breath the *Maulana* continues, "Nowhere is Bin Laden more popular than in the Pakistani *madrasas*."

"Am I being naïve, or is it from these *madrasas* that the Taliban drew many of its recruits?" I ask. Before he has a chance to reply I add, "I also understand that your graduates learn much of the Qur'an by rote memory, and literacy is not a priority, to say nothing of interpretation. Also, the *madrasas* I have visited do not teach a wide variety of subjects. Everything seems to center around the Qur'an."

The *Maulana* says, "America is in a war with Muslims, and under Sharia the shedding of American blood is permitted. It is a holy war."

I notice that he has not really answered any of my questions, but, like all good politicians, he has simply expressed his own feelings on the matter.

The *Maulana* continues, "I understand you want to interview Osama bin Laden for a book you are writing. *You may seek Osama bin Laden, but it is he that will find you. He knows!*"

That will not be the last time I hear this.

The *Maulana* says, "I understand from your driver, Mohammed, that you plan to travel east toward the city of Abbottabad. I strongly suggest that you keep to these plans. That is all I will say. May Allah look over you and guide you in your quest. Have a safe journey."

With that interview over, I feel I have my answer. The city of Abbottabad is where we will be going. Osama bin Laden is in – or near – Abbottabad.

No doubt some people reading this and some of the other tales in this book may still look upon me as being a bit crazy for undertaking these trips into the Northern Territories. I will concede that the nickname "Crazy Texan" is probably well deserved. Some people have asked me if I have a death wish. In reality, I'm in no hurry to die. Since I remarried a few years ago, I have re-discovered how very sweet life can be.

However, my trips to Pakistan have brought the reality of the daily human struggle home to me in a way that none of my other experiences have done. By being here, I have come to see the grand scheme of life more clearly and to better appreciate it, and to gain a better perspective on the changes that have taken place throughout the ages – as well as the things that have not changed.

I came to Pakistan to be of help to those who most need it, hoping that I could also become a part of life as it is lived here – at least to the extent that this is possible for an outsider. But most importantly, I have come here in order to participate in improving that life. In the process I have met and shaken hands with the proud and the humble, the rich and the poor, with reasonable people who want to understand the world outside of their experience, and religious fanatics who seek to impose their visions of life on everyone else. To me they are all human beings, just trying to make their way in this life in the best way they know how. And when it comes right down to it, I am here in Pakistan because I have had a good life, and would like for these people to know that they can have a good life as well.

It is really as simple as that.

The Search for the Sheik Begins…

My crazy desire to meet and interview Osama bin Laden has grown stronger over the past few weeks, and I have decided to take some bolder steps in that direction. Today I am on another road trip with Mohammed, Sultan, and Saleem. The morning's travels, with the old van bouncing along jutted tracks that pass for highways, have left all of us eager to find a place to rest, to share a meal, and most of all, to enjoy a brief reprieve from the day's ever-increasing heat. We enter a small village, and I tell Mohammed to stop the van across from a small teahouse whose customers don't look too threatening. There are just a couple of old men, sitting and drinking their tea as they watch a few small boys playing nearby. Judging by the men's age, as well as their vigilant protective gaze as they watch the boys, a Westerner would immediately assume that they were the boys' grandfathers, but in this region, it isn't particularly unusual for a seemingly aged male to have fathered young children with one of his much younger wives. At any rate, I feel that this teahouse will be a relatively safe place for us to rest and inquire as to a café where a group of travelers can find a good midday meal. Saleem and Sultan are not as convinced as I am, and tuck their pistols into their waistbands as we walk across the dirt road to the shop.

A few moments after we sit at a small table in front of the establishment, the owner emerges, offering his greetings and setting small cups before us. It would be stretching matters considerably to say that my command of Pashto, which is spoken widely throughout the region, is passable, so I let Saleem and Mohammed carry on the conversation with the proprietor. Saleem had warned me repeatedly that outsiders are frequently looked upon with suspicion, especially in the tribal areas, and I don't want to place us all at risk of being shot or kidnapped for ransom by declaring early on that I am an American. I am, however, able to pick up on enough of the conversation to follow the general content, and am shocked when the proprietor excitedly utters the phrase, "Dr. Angel." So much for remaining incognito.

As it turns out, rumor and stories of the "Crazy Texan" and his work in the tribal villages long ago reached this village, even though my previous travels hadn't taken me within a hundred miles of this place. Following the brief exchange with my companions, the owner embraces me as if I were a long-lost brother, filling my cup with fragrant tea, then scurrying inside his shop and emerging with sweet dates and flatbread. He sets the platter of treats before us, and only then sets about filling the others' cups.

Once we have all been served, Saleem asks him if he knows of a good café where we can eat and rest for awhile before continuing on our journey. It is at that point that one of the elderly gentlemen at the other table rises and comes over to speak to us. He introduces himself, and Saleem informs me that he is a *Maulana,* and holds a place of great prominence in the village. The *Maulana* tells us that we should come and be his guests at his family's mid-day meal. I instruct Saleem to thank him, but to tell him that I cannot impose upon him and his family, especially at such short notice.

The *Maulana* laughs, then turns to me and says, in surprisingly fluent English, "Nonsense! It is an honor to have Dr. Angel in my home. It is not far from here. Let us finish our tea while the women prepare." It is obvious that the decision has been made, and the *Maulana* sends the boys running home to tell his wives that there will be guests, and to prepare a meal for them. When Saleem translates the *Maulana's* instructions to the boys for me, I am reminded once again of the incredible generosity I have so often observed and been the beneficiary of in my travels here.

As we sit, drinking our tea and exchanging small talk, I tell the *Maulana* of my fascination with the Sheik bin Laden, and he immediately puts his finger to his lips, and says that there are things better discussed where there are fewer ears listening, despite the fact that few of those who might be listening could understand English. I take the hint, and the conversation returns to things such as the condition of the road we have just traversed, and the varying quality of tea at different shops in the region. A little while later, the boys come running back, excitedly chattering. Saleem informs me that this is the announcement that the meal will be prepared shortly. We rise at once, and I tell Mohammed that Saleem, Sultan, and I will walk with our host, and Mohammed can drive the van, with the boys leading the way.

The *Maulana's* home is about a hundred meters away, and we resume our small talk as we walk together. I can tell that Saleem and Sultan are still not completely certain of the *Maulana's* intentions, as Sultan's hand remains discreetly on the butt of his pistol as we walk. I, on the other hand, feel absolutely safe, though I'm not certain whether to attribute that to my highly-developed intuitive abilities, or to a naiveté that has somehow survived many journeys in this perilous land. Either way, I enjoy the walk, and as the *Maulana's* compound grows closer, the aroma of meat grilling on an open fire fills my senses, reminding me that I am famished, and leaving little room for caution, much less fear.

Once we arrive at the compound, I spend a few minutes in the bathroom down the hall, washing the day's dust from my face and beard. One thing that never fails to impress me is just how refreshing it is to simply wash up after many hours spent travelling in the desert of the Himalayan foothills. We in the West take for granted such things as air conditioning, closed windows, and ice-cold drinks. But here, in the sands that blanket the top of the world, the contrast of a cool stream can be exhilarating, and the act of washing up can feel like a profound rebirth. All the while, as I refresh myself, I am continually assailed with the delicious smells that emanate from the kitchen. I have never personally experienced the sense of starvation, but the aroma, combined with the fact that I have eaten only a few small strips of flatbread and a handful of dates all day, leaves me more ravenous than I had ever been back in Houston. So it is that, when the *Maulana's* son comes to the door to tell me that the meal is ready to be served, I almost bolt past him in my rush to be fed. He senses my excitement, and laughs as we stride toward the large central room. I think he knows that his father has brought home a most appreciative guest.

We gather in a semi-circle, seated on soft pillows in proper fashion, with our feet tucked beneath us, the *Maulana* at the head, and I, seated to his right. The boys come in with cups and a large pot of fragrantly steaming tea, handing a cup to each of us and filling it so excitedly that I am certain a spill is imminent. Somehow, though, not a single drop falls anywhere that it isn't supposed to, and in a flash, the boys are gone. Before we even have a chance to drink our tea, a young girl, whom I assume to be the *Maulana's* daughter, enters and sets plates before each of us, and in the center, a large woven-reed basket filled with dates, almonds, and pieces of flatbread. Behind her comes another girl, slightly older, bearing a large platter, piled high with what I think to be more than enough steaming grilled meat to feed us all. Next come platters of vegetables, still sizzling from the grill, and a bowl of fragrant rice. Truly a feast fit for an honored guest, even if that guest is a crazy Texan and his friends.

As is the custom, we scoop the food using pieces of flatbread, and had the women been in the room, I'm certain they would have interpreted our enthusiastic eating as the compliment it truly is. The lamb is seasoned in a manner similar to that which I'd had before, with the exception that it is savory to the point that a sweat breaks out on my forehead as I eat. I am oblivious to the heat of the spices, however, and have to acknowledge that it is one of the most delicious things I have ever tasted. And in perhaps thirty minutes, the great mounds of food have all but disappeared, and all that is left is the sweetened yogurt that does a wonderful job of soothing the heat of the spicy dishes.

After the dishes are taken away, Mohammed and Saleem excuse themselves to wait outside, knowing that there are questions I want to ask the *Maulana*, and which he will likely feel more comfortable answering without too many ears listening. The *Maulana* and I end up chatting for what turns out to be a long time. We speak at first of things that are of great concern to both of us, as well as of trivial matters, as is the way of old friends. We talk about the children whose lives have been changed for the better in the clinics that our medical teams have attended. Eventually the subject changes to the conflicts that constantly arise, even among fellow countrymen, and this leads us to a discussion of the long history of the *Maulana's* own tribe. We also discuss how the dwellers in the tribal lands and villages feel about the conflict that is constantly going on all around them.

After an hour or so has passed, it becomes obvious to me that my host is tiring. I feel that it is time for me to ask one last question, the one that has increasingly consumed me as I've traveled through the tribal areas.

Looking the *Maulana* directly in the eye, I blurt out, "I would like to meet with and interview Osama bin Laden. Can this be arranged? According to the information I have obtained, he is in Pakistan, and most likely in Abbottabad."

There is a prolonged silence as the *Maulana* considers my words. I try to reassure him, saying that I understand his concern, and the concerns of others to whom I have made the same request. "As Allah as my witness, we do not intend to bring any harm to him or his family. I have become fascinated by the Osama bin Laden movement. Osama bin Laden has become a hero to millions in Pakistan and throughout this part of the world. Giant posters of him hang everywhere. Pictures appear in store windows and taped on the side of passing trucks and cars. He has not appeared in public for a long time, nor have any tapes or telecasts been broadcast by Al Jazeera or other world news such as the BBC. Some claim that he is dead. Others say he is too ill to lead. I don't know whether any of the rumors are true or not. All I know for certain is that I want to interview Osama bin Laden."

As I utter the last sentence, the room grows so quiet you could hear the proverbial pin drop. The *Maulana's* head is slightly bowed, his eyes closed. I wait. I have learned to be patient. Finally he opens his eyes and looks intently into mine. "It is possible," he says. "Osama bin Laden resides in Pakistan. Where do you travel to from here?"

"We plan to go north to Charsadda, and from there to Mardan and possibly through the mountains in the Malakand area."

He looks at his hands and says, "I suggest you continue east toward Sawabi, and then north to the City of Abbottabad. He will know you; there will be a messenger if it is allowed." We hold each other's gaze for several moments, and then a smile comes across his face.

I stand to leave and say, "I would like to leave some funds to help with school supplies, food, and clothing for the children in the *madrasa*."

The *Maulana* smiles and says, "I would like to present you with something, as well. Please wait a moment." He leaves the room, and upon his return he presents me with a copy of the Qur'an. I thank him for his gift. And then, as the other *Maulanas* have said before him, the *Maulana* says to me, "*You can look for Osama bin Laden, but it is he who will find you.*"

He escorts me through the courtyard and to the front entrance. As I turn to leave, I tell him that we are not going to go directly north into the Malakand area. This is the area that Sir Winston Churchill wrote so elegantly about nearly 115 years ago. After Churchill had participated in the Malakand Military Expedition, on his return from the Northwest Territories, he gave a clear warning to all who would venture into the region to stay out of the Afghanistan and Pakistani tribal areas. Unfortunately, our military leaders and politicians have failed to heed his wise advice. In any case, my companions and I will be taking the M1 Route west, and from there we will continue north to Abbottabad City.

I know that the *Maulana* has given me some good and sincere advice, and I am going to follow it. I return to the van, where I relay his instructions to the others. I tell Mohammed that we will continue north by northeast toward the City of Mardan, and then continue onto Sawabi, which we should reach by mid-afternoon. If Mohammed is not too tired from driving by then, we will proceed north to Abbottabad. This will not take us too far, and will keep us in the tribal areas where I also want to take more photographs. Taking this route will allow us to move north to Abbottabad City and on to the Karakoram Highway, which climbs through the Himalayas into the City of Gilgit as we approach the northern Pakistan/China border. All of us are excited and pleased with the information the *Maulana* has given me, and our adrenaline is pumping. We are eager to get on with our journey and my quest. Mohammed puts some popular music on his little disc player that he had taped to the dashboard, and we all begin to sing along. We feel, for the first time, that my wish to meet with bin Laden will really come true.

The Clash of Cultures

*P*akistan is a divided country – politically, socially, and economically. But most significantly, it is torn between two forces: a culture that has changed little, if at all, in centuries; and a modern world thrusting in upon it with computers, cell phones, email, iPads, and a social imperative that is diametrically opposed to the ancient code that so completely permeates the lives of its people. The majority of the population is uneducated, and lives off the land, in a survival mode torn by religious dissension and by the clash of tribal and clan attitudes that are thousands of years old.

Where will this clash bring them? And what role should America and the rest of the world play? To date, we have been very unsuccessful in our attempts at nation building – at improving education and medical care, sanitation, electricity, and fresh water supplies. We have been equally unsuccessful at opening and freeing job markets. The main reason for our failure is that such improvements would deal a crushing blow to centuries-old corruption and allow the expansion of what is presently a minuscule middle class. Past efforts by any number of countries should tell us that attitudes that are many generations in the making cannot be molded by throwing dollars at the culture of the past. It takes "boots on the ground," and – most importantly – boots that offer genuine service, rather than attempting to abolish every manifestation of the existing culture. Most of the people neither want nor need iPads, and will summarily reject what we in more highly developed countries so arrogantly consider to be their salvation.

I think it is neither exaggeration nor idle boasting to say that in the past several years, I, along with a small team of doctors, have achieved more positive public relations results in the tribal areas of the world – from Peru to Pakistan – than have been accomplished with the hundreds of millions of dollars that have been squandered by various governments. Despite all the power of governments, those billions of dollars and the benefits they promised have reached only the pockets of the rich and powerful, simply because there has been no oversight.

And the waste continues, not because America is lacking in its generosity, but because of its failure to manage that generosity.

Still pumped from our lavish meal, and the visit with the *Maulana*, and fueled by a renewed sense of purpose and adventure, my three companions and I continue on our journey to Abbottabad, singing along with the music on the dashboard player. After a while, the music ends, and there are a few moments of silence before Mohammed pulls the disc from the player, declaring, "Allah will help us. He will give us strength. Truth is on our side. You need to believe it will all happen."

We drive on for a while without speaking, each of us lost in his own thoughts. I am suddenly awakened from my ponderings when I hear Mohammed yell something I don't understand. Seized by a sudden urge to call home, I remove the sat-phone from its protective pouch, punch the speed-dial number.... and wait. Nothing. I redial the numbers in the futile hope that the phone will send the call through, when it occurs to me that we are on the side of a mountain in a series of switch-backs, with snow-capped peaks towering twenty thousand feet above: a "dead zone" where no signals can penetrate. I think, "Maybe when we get closer to the top and out of this canyon..." I shut the phone off for now, not wishing to use any more of the battery's precious and finite resources.

We have followed every lead, rumor, and tip, and for the first time, *I have a very good feeling about the information we have received.* Osama bin Laden is in Pakistan, and we are heading in the right direction. I am at the right place at the right time... and I am in the right profession, it seems. Doctors are told many things in confidence that never reach the police or the intelligence agencies of the civilized world, despite all the latter's high-tech equipment and "professional" intelligence gatherers. To the highly sophisticated intelligence networks, Osama bin Laden has not been heard from in years. He has disappeared as completely as if he had dissolved into the mist that surrounds these mountains. Where better to seek refuge than right under everyone's nose, in a centrally located and well-populated area of North Central Pakistan, such as Abbottabad and its suburbs?

And yet I realize how little of my quest is really in my control, despite the precautions I have taken and all of the careful research I have done. The *Maulana's* words keep echoing in my mind: "*He knows you are coming. He will find you. You will not be finding him.*"

I find myself increasingly pleased with Mohammed's driving skills. My confidence in his abilities to handle this terrain is beginning to solidify. The white-knuckle syndrome I had experienced as I grasped the door handle and pressed myself back against the seat has all but disappeared. That said, we are now on the Grand Trunk Road, where you run the very real risk of being killed in the middle of a firefight with the Taliban. The Grand Trunk Road and the Karakoram Highway are two of the world's most formidable driving experiences. Evidence of the sudden rockslides, washouts, and crumbling roadbeds are seen in the numerous overturned vehicles and burned-out remnants that line the road or that had tumbled to the canyons below. Hanging out the window to take photographs, I look back and see the rear wheels of the van only inches from the edge of the cliff. As the tires struggle to gain traction in the gravel, rocks spin from the rear wheels, falling thousands of feet to the canyon floor below.

The others seem unconcerned, a testament to the distinctive style of driving and their faith that Allah is not yet ready to take their souls. Mohammed doesn't slow down on the hidden curves, and seems to be almost purposely engaging in a protracted and high-speed game of chicken with oncoming vehicles. I find that my white-knuckle syndrome has returned with a vengeance.

About halfway through our trip, we find ourselves crossing the Tarbela Dam, with the Indus River far below us. The Indus River originates in Tibet, and water from the melting glaciers adds significantly to the river's flow from multiple tributaries coursing through the canyons and over the ridges, then descending into the depths of the canyons below.

The river supplies the water to the valley that is the breadbasket of Pakistan – the Northwest Frontier Province.

The fastest way through the Hindu Kush Mountains takes us into the Wild West, where every male ten years of age and older is armed with an automatic weapon. It is an area very familiar to Osama bin Laden. The road is now lined with donkey carts, badly dented Toyota pickup trucks, bicycles, and buses spewing black clouds of diesel fumes. Herds of goats and sheep move freely across the road, paying little or no attention to the blaring horns of the vehicles whose drivers wait impatiently for the animals to move out of the way. The road is lined with shops and stores, attended by bearded merchants peddling prayer mats and *Misbaha* (Islamic rosary beads). The smell of spice grilled mutton and the local flatbread called *naan* fill the air. Goat cheese, apples, pears, grapes, and pomegranates are covered by swarms of flies, over which the merchants endlessly twirl multicolored scarves. One man is selling green and black tea and lassi. We pass the food market and come upon a group of shops with household supplies and clothing on display, including colorful tribal robes, hooded cloaks, linen shirts, turbans, and carpets.

The merchants and their young helpers are all male. The few woman walking through the marketplace wear full *burqas*, in accordance with Islamic law and in fear of both Taliban enforcement and of the Muttahida Majlis-e-Amal, or MMA. The latter is a hard-line alliance of several religious groups that control the provisional government in this area. The next section of the market we pass contains medicinal items, including henna paste for skin drying, and ceremonial circumcision hats. I set the Nikon to full open and with my telephoto lens I fire off picture after picture.

I laugh to myself as my driver maneuvers the van through a line of donkey-drawn carts. We are passing a series of shops that have rifles, automatic weapons, and handguns, with boxes sitting out front, filled with what appear to be hand grenades. Curved daggers known as *Janbiyas* in decorated holders hang on nails, gleaming in the sunlight. I ask Mohammed to stop, and though he is hesitant, he complies with my request. As we enter the first gun shop, there is a display of photographs of Osama bin Laden, with the title "The Lion of Islam" in bold letters underneath. As I enter the shop, I look down at the box that I had noticed as we were driving by, and I realize I had been right: they are hand grenades. I ask the price and am told that it comes to approximately one dollar apiece, but the shop owner tells me that he will sell a whole case of about twenty-five or thirty hand grenades for approximately twenty dollars. I am, quite frankly, awestruck.

He then tells me that the seemingly brand new Russian and American automatic weapons range from fifty to two hundred dollars each. I can't help but wonder why the U.S. Army is paying three thousand to four thousand dollars for the same products at home. I assume that these were acquired during or after the Russian/Afghan conflict. The others were probably stolen from American supply depots. Knowing we plan on traveling north through the tribal area and into Taliban country and then up the Karakoram Highway, with the ever-present threat of bandits, I decide that we should add more firepower to what we already have. Since these prices are so unbelievably cheap, I purchase the entire box of hand grenades and have Saleem carry them out to the van.

Meanwhile, Sultan and I examine and test the automatic weapons. Sultan selects two that he likes. The shopkeeper says that he has something special in the back that we might like. He dashes behind a curtain, only to return with an exceptionally fine looking day/night telescopic sight, offering to throw it in for two hundred dollars more. I know that sights like this one cost from four to five thousand dollars in the U.S. I guess my smile gives away the fact that I want it. Sultan shakes his head at me, and I know that the haggling is about to begin. We play good guy/bad guy, with the merchant trying to interest me in the purchase of the two weapons and the telescopic sight. Sultan is repeatedly shaking his head an emphatic no, and the price keeps getting lower and lower.

We finally agree on a price, but then I tell the shopkeeper he has to add a thousand rounds of ammunition. We settle on 500 rounds.

NOT my typical attire, but when in Pakistan...

Although we hope to never have to use the weapons, their trade value alone in the Northern Territories are well worth the purchase. There is a handshake to close the deal. Sultan pays the storekeeper, and we take the purchases to the van, wrap them with some blankets, and place them on the floorboard.

Our purchase concluded, I realize that I am very hungry, and assume that the others are, as well. We leave Mohammed with the van and the three of us – Sultan, Saleem, and I – walk along the road, purchasing some cheese, fruit, and bottled water. Osama bin Laden's image is everywhere in this marketplace. It appears in murals on the sides of the buildings, in photographs tacked to utility poles, and in the windows of every store and shop that we walk past. Under many of the posters are slogans that read, "Allah commands that we build the atom," and, "Death to foreign invaders."

Even though we are dressed appropriately and I think we blend in well, I am very aware that eyes are following us from shop to shop. I begin to have an uncomfortable feeling. I nod to Saleem and Sultan, and can see that they share my uneasiness. I turn and begin walking back toward the van in the street, which is lined with the donkey carts and rickshaws. I feel that I need to get away from the crowded shops. Saleem has my back – literally, which is a good thing. The streets are filled with bandits, who view all visitors as their own personal CARE packages, to be grabbed and held for ransom.

There is a group of young men across the street, probably from the local *madrasa* who seem to be following us with their eyes. I find myself hoping they haven't taken to heart the preaching of their *muftis* (Sunni Islamic scholars), that killing of all strangers, particularly Americans, is sanctioned, even demanded, by Allah. Perhaps my imagination is running away with me, but I notice that Saleem has quickened the pace.

As we approach the van, I see that Mohammed is watching the situation in the side mirror and has already started the engine. Saleem is the first to reach the van, and quickly slides the door open, and he, Sultan and I pile in. The van is already moving before we even get the door closed. I can see that one of the shotguns is sitting across Mohammed's lap, and the AK-47 is wedged between the two front seats and easily accessible. He swings around the oncoming donkey cart to the middle of the street. Luckily there are no other oncoming wagons or vehicles as he floors the accelerator.

I look out the window to see if anyone is following, and Saleem yells at me, "Keep your head down!"

Within minutes we have left the crowded market area far behind, the van skidding on the gravel as Mohammed makes a perilously sharp turn back onto the main road. We have all suffered a few bruises and jolts, but we can at last breathe a deep sigh of relief. I lean forward, tap Mohammed on the shoulder, give him a big smile, and tell him he can slow down a little bit. The last thing I want right now is to flip this van.

The most immediate danger behind us, we cross the Indus River and continue on our way to Tarbela. It is a good opportunity for conversation, and I take it.

I am traveling with men who practice the most traditional form of Sunni Islam. Now is a good time to pose a question to my companions that has been on my mind for some time.

I know that Osama bin Laden espouses an orthodox Sunni Islam, yet he has forged an alliance with Iranian-backed Hezbollah, which is based in southern Lebanon, despite their religious differences (Hezbollah is "Shiite"). Approximately eighty percent of Muslims worldwide are conservative Sunni Islamic, and the remaining twenty percent minority are Shiites. The two groups have significant differences. "They kill each other over those religious differences, Muslim versus Muslim," I say to my companions. "Both sects read the Qur'an, which is very specific in stating that no Muslim should ever kill another Muslim. Aren't both groups – and Sheik bin Laden himself – breaking Islamic Law by doing so?"

Sultan considers himself a religious expert, and is the first to respond. "There have been successful waves of dissent and schisms in our and other religions. Most of these differences are a result of political or social change. Early on, within a century of the Prophet Mohammed's death, Islam split into Sunni and Shiite branches. The Shiite felt that appointing anyone but a direct descendent of the Prophet would be a departure from the ideals of Mohammed, and thus a corruption of the Prophet's intents."

Mohammed joins in the conversation, saying, "But the problem is that the Prophet left no male descendent. Therefore, most felt a suitable candidate should be appointed Caliph, who would be leader of *Ummah*, the worldwide Muslim community. The Caliph would have no inherent religious authority, but would be vested with significant political and military power."

Sultan adds, "Division deepened, and over time, those divisions became enshrined in religious doctrine."

I jump in at this point, saying that my readings have led me to believe that the split was both political and personal, and some even say it has ethnic origins, with divisions between Arabs and Persians. As the religious gap widened, each accused the other of preaching a radical doctrine of hatred, one for the other. I muse, "The Shiites accuse the successors of Mohammed of foregoing his true message and therefore being complicit in the corruption of Islam. But with all due respect, it seems to me that the Islamic clergy on both sides are self-serving. The clergy are seen by many of their own followers as elitists who cannot be trusted, and whose influence over the lives of their followers is almost totalitarian." I add that it seems that this influence is underestimated by Western governments and political analysts.

My companions nod, and Sultan asks, "Doctor Joe, have you ever heard of Taqi ibn Taymiyya?"

"No, I can't say I am familiar with him."

I am about to get a brief history lesson. Sultan explains, "Taqi ad-Din Ahmad ibn Taymiyyah (1263-1328 CE) lived during the times of the Mongol invasions. He is often cited as the spiritual father of today's radical revolutionary Sunni Islamic activism. Though he lived so many centuries ago, his influence is still felt."

Sultan asks me, "Have you ever heard of the Assassins?"

"Yes, I had read that they were a radical Shiite Muslim sect – I think from the eleventh and twelfth centuries, as I recall."

Saleem nods and says, "Some consider them the first group in history to use terrorism in an organized manner as a means of destroying more powerful enemies."

We ride on a while in silence, once again lost in respective reveries. I am thinking about all I have read and heard about the long history of religious and ethnic turmoil in this region – despite the fact that the warring peoples have many more similarities than differences. The devil is in those differences, which may seem trivial to the outside world but are anything but trivial to those embroiled in the conflicts. I wonder if peace will ever be anything more than a distant dream.

The Birth of Terror

ased in the remote mountains of northwestern Persia, the Assassins were probably the most famous of the suicide warriors, a radical Shiite Muslim sect that was established by Hassan iben Sadah. Some suggest that these early martyr warriors, similar to today's Al Qaeda suicide bombers, sustained their courage by fueling themselves with an excess of hashish, rather than with religious zeal alone. Further credence is given to this notion by the fact that the word "assassin" comes from the early word, *hashishiyun*. In any case, the Assassins were secretive, pledging their allegiance to each other and to their leaders, and they became strong in their shared beliefs and practices.

As the old saying goes, if we do not study the past, we are sure to repeat it. And here we have but another example. Obvious comparisons can be made between the Assassins and today's Al Qaeda. Al Qaeda demands absolute allegiance, and places a great emphasis on the effective use of martyrdom to reach its goal through jihad. Like Al Qaeda, the Assassins were small radical groups, outnumbered and outgunned in their seemingly doomed war against the Sunni. With their reputation of willingness – even eagerness – to die for their beliefs, suicidal killers acquired a level of power disproportionate to their numbers and armaments.

Like Al Qaeda, the Assassins chose public places, preferably during festivals or holidays, where the maximum number of people would succumb during their attacks. This also ensured that they would get plenty of publicity due to the sensational nature of their attacks. In addition to directing their attacks at public gatherings, they fought to topple governments by assassinating leaders, and successfully killed the Vizier to the Shah of Persia. As such, Muslims have had the longest and most sustained record of using suicide attacks over the centuries. It is certainly not uniquely a Muslim tactic, but Muslims have engaged in suicidal jihads more than any other group, not only against the West, but throughout Europe, Asia, India, northern Sumatra, and even the Philippines. Lacking the military capacity to effectively engage their enemies in what we consider "traditional combat," the assassins used homemade devices that could wreak the greatest possible level of destruction or kill as many of the enemy (Sunni) as possible, before inevitably being killed or killing themselves.

Like the early Assassins, Osama bin Laden's Al Qaeda holy warriors and the Taliban hide in the rugged mountainous terrain of Afghanistan and Pakistan, and have trained in the caves of Tora Bora. And like Al Qaeda under Osama bin Laden, the Assassins waged a systematic terror campaign against their enemies (mostly Sunni), as well as any Christians who entered their territory.

Using only the simplest of implements, their well-planned, fierce, and fearless attacks against what were generally considered to be well-armed and secured targets inevitably ended in their own deaths and martyrdom. Despite preventive attempts to protect their intended targets, the Assassins' tactics almost always proved successful. By attacking organized defenses with what amounted to military chaos, the assassins forced their enemies to devote a great deal of money, time, and effort to securing and protecting themselves from a very asymmetric war.

Unfortunately, we are seeing history repeat itself, and the world is now reliving this kind of warfare. Despite what many modern observers might believe, suicidal jihads are not unique to the Muslim culture. The U.S. faced a similar situation during World War II, in the form of the Japanese kamikaze raids, which, having numbered over three thousand during that war, still hold the record for the largest number of suicide missions.

During the Vietnam War, suicide bombers were again employed by the Viet Cong. They strapped explosives to their own bodies and rode bicycles into U.S. military camps, or drove stolen vehicles to their targets, detonating the explosives that were strapped to themselves. During the Tet Offensive, suicide bombers would enter U.S. bases and blow themselves up in a large crowd of U.S. military personnel. Perhaps most insidious was the practice of attaching grenades to the bodies of young children and threatening to punish them if they didn't walk up to a group of American G.I.s and pull the pin.

The Viet Cong also used specially trained suicide bombers to go after high-profile targets.

It should be noted that unlike the Al Qaeda attacks, those waged by the North Vietnamese and Japanese were directed at military targets and personnel, rather than the public. Following the Vietnam War, suicide missions were almost unheard of until Iran began employing so-called "human waves" of young martyrs – including women and children – during their war with Iraq.

Then, in the 1980's, Hezbollah began employing suicide bombers against American and French troops. It wasn't long before Al Qaeda turned to suicide missions. Their trademark tactic was to send truckloads or boatloads of explosives to be detonated in close proximity to U.S. targets.

It is interesting that suicide is considered a sin by Christians, Jews, and Muslims alike. As we understand it in the West, suicide is even less acceptable in the Muslim culture than in the Judaeo-Christian. The incidence of suicide in Muslim countries is actually the lowest in the world. In the West, suicide is usually a solitary and private affair. It is looked upon as a desperate and selfish act by someone who sees no value in life, and thus embraces death as a better alternative. Since suicide is unacceptable in all religions, and particularly in Muslim society, it is essential that the prospective martyr be convinced that his (or increasingly, her) act is not merely suicide, but a self-sacrifice for a noble religious cause in a legitimate jihad. It then becomes an act of martyrdom, rather than a sin borne of desperation.

This rationalization is based upon the prophet and his followers having historically displayed a willingness to die for Islam. The Qur'an describes being killed by the enemy or sacrificing one's life in jihad as the highest expression of martyrdom, and the only act in jihad that promises eternal life. The Muslim belief is that those who have sacrificed themselves in the cause of Allah are living eternally with their Lord. Al Qaeda and most radical clerics have taken the position that the only means by which they can prevail in their objectives is through jihad, with suicide attacks being an essential strategic tool. Thus, the taking of one's own life is rationalized as the lesser of evils, and thereby not only forgiven, but canonized.

Where "suicide" in its most literal definition is a solitary, self-destructive act, the sacrifice of one's life in the service of jihad consists of suicide attacks planned and carried out by groups of people acting together. The members of the group support each other by working together as a team to plan and complete logistical tasks, and they maintain expansive social interaction because of their shared purposes. It is not in itself looked upon as a self-destructive process; martyrdom is a deeply religious and politically motivated undertaking. The martyr feels the act is useful and benefits the larger society. Within their society, the suicide bombers are admired and applauded by their peers, which is why all too many aspire to martyrdom, hoping to be regarded in death as an honored *shahid*, a witness who has sacrificed his life out of passion for truth.

It is interesting that Osama bin Laden, in his declaration for jihad against Israel, Americans and other countries, declared that "due to the imbalance of power between our armed forces and the enemy forces, a suitable means of fighting must be adopted." He was referring, of course, to the suicide bomber, praising his martyrdom and reminding his followers of the promise that the martyr will enter Paradise when he dies. He spoke of martyrdom as the most effective tactic of inflicting damage against the more powerful opponent, and the least costly in both expense and casualties to the *Mujahideen* (guerrilla fighters).

The number of enemy casualties inflicted by suicide attacks is many times greater than the number of casualties inflicted by a single individual during conventional combat operations, especially in cases where the enemy has a numerically and technologically superior force. As a result, Al Qaeda inflicts the maximum number of casualties with a minimum loss of its own personnel, and at a far lower per-casualty cost than its better-equipped opponents. For example, in the attacks on the World Trade Center and the Pentagon on September 11, 2001, there were 155 victims for each suicide attacker. In many Muslim countries, an act of martyrdom receives popular support and admiration because it is perceived as the only weapon available in the face of superior military capabilities.

And, of course, there is the *Intifada of the shahid*, the uprising or rebellion that some have predicted and hoped will ultimately result in Muslim world dominance. The *Maulanas* in the mosques preach that Allah is great, for he has given to the poor and weak something that the strong and the wealthy who lack commitment do not possess – the ability to turn their bodies into bombs and thereby enter Paradise. They preach that this is an act of self-sacrifice for a noble cause, and part of a legitimate jihad.

Despite what is generally assumed in the West – and even by some in the Middle East, including my friend Sultan, as you will see – the act of sacrificing one's self in pursuit of martyrdom is not limited to any particular social class, cultural predisposition, or level of education. It is, as mentioned before, a religious and political act, using a weapon that is almost impossible to prepare for, and once activated, is almost impossible to prevent, particularly when the assailant is not only willing to die, but is actively seeking death. The harsh reality is that when an individual is willing, even eager, to die for a cause, the attack is almost impossible to deter. There are few means of intervention that are capable of thwarting the outcome.

Where the *shahid* willingly gives up his life to inflict death on others in the process, Osama bin Laden and his *Mujahideen* see the American soldier and the Soviet troops that they fought in Afghanistan as weak and cowardly. They see the reluctance of most U.N. and U.S. troops to die for a cause as weakness. This cultural misconception serves as effective propaganda, reinforcing the jihadists' assertion that Allah stands with them in their noble Holy Cause.

The U.S. soldiers and their European allies are the best-trained and the best-equipped to do the job expected of them, any place in the world. But there is a dramatic difference in religious philosophies in play between the two opposing forces: While the jihadists seek martyrdom because it guarantees them a place in heaven, the Western soldiers knowingly risk their lives for something they believe in, but actively seek to preserve their own lives, so that they can enjoy their victory here on earth.

* * * * *

As we continue on the road to Abbottabad, our conversation resumes. I want to talk about jihad. Our theologian Sultan says that the Sunni community is divided when it comes to the concept of jihad. "Mainstream Sunni Muslims do not support the propaganda espoused by Al Qaeda," he says. "Muslims killing Muslims is not acceptable. The killing of women and children is not acceptable. The killing of civilians, regardless of ethnic group or beliefs, is not acceptable. The Qur'an espouses the use of reason before force. Most important, bin Laden is not a religious authority. He is not in a position to declare fatwa (a legal opinion or ruling issued by an Islamic scholar), nor to declare jihad."

Mohammed interjects, "The suicide bombers are not military. My friends who are in the military are opposed to abandoning conventional warfare in favor of suicide bombings, and they adamantly despise attacks on civilians, hospitals, mosques, and public places."

My companions continue their discussion for a while, but I see fit to sit silent and listen to them. They each reject the atrocities that are committed in the name of the religion they hold dear, but it is apparent from listening to them that they have different ideas as to how the tenets of that religion are twisted, to the point that even devout believers can be convinced to perform acts that must surely offend any

God, no matter how He is described. I find their different perspectives quite enlightening, and though I am fascinated by their exchange, I eventually succumb to the heat and the monotony of the van's rhythmic rocking and swaying, and fall into an uneasy sleep.

The Price of Saying No: Mari's Story

The autorickshaw driver is obsessed with the attractive young female doctor, Maria Shah, whom many fondly call Mari. For many people in their small village, Dr. Mari is a hero, someone of whom they can be proud for everything she has accomplished. But to the young rickshaw driver, Mari is nothing more and nothing less than the woman who has done the unthinkable: she has rejected him. Her family had originally hired him to drive her to school when she was studying to be a doctor. He had fallen for her and had asked her to marry him. She had said no, but he was not satisfied and has asked her again several times. As always, the answer is: "No."

He broods constantly over the fact that she will not accept any of his overtures, and he feels as if the whole world is aware of her rejection and his humiliation. It would seem that this is the case, for he has been ostracized and rejected by the other autorickshaw drivers, and cannot accept the teasing and taunting from those he thought were his friends. But most of all he is haunted by his obsession for Mari. Increasingly he is driven by one thought: *If I can't get this girl, no one else will.*

Feeling more and more isolated, he goes into seclusion, and finally, out of desperation, he decides on a plan that he feels will restore his own self-respect and the respect of his peers. He makes an appointment at the clinic where Dr. Mari works, telling the woman who answers the phone that he is having stomach problems and is in pain. He knows the clinic will not refuse him, and he knows that since Dr. Mari is the only physician available, she will be there to treat him.

Before going to the clinic, he drives his autorickshaw down the back streets, constantly looking over his shoulder to see if any of his tormentors might be following, and repeating in his mind, *I have to do this or I will lose all respect.* Speeding past a group of black-bearded men leading ponies from the corral at the rear of the market, he keeps his head down as he passes through the largely untraveled narrow side streets and alleyways on his way to the bazaar. He thinks to himself that nothing can make each breath sweeter than redeeming himself in the eyes of his peers.

He realizes he is driving his autorickshaw very fast, and hopes that no one, especially a child, opens a door and steps out into his path, for he knows he would not be able to stop in time to avoid hitting them. He makes a sharp turn to the right and continues past the pens where the animals are kept. The market here smells like musk from the sheep, mingled with the damp odor of the rattan roofs that cover the stalls, lavender incense from the shops, and diesel fuel from the autorickshaws, taxis, and mini buses. He drives frantically on until he approaches the central portion of the market, and the heavier traffic and crowds force him to slow down.

The market is packed with women in saris with *dupatta* draped over their heads and covering the lower portion of their faces. All of them are jockeying for position at the small wooden stands, looking for the freshest of vegetables and fruits. The driver has to stop and pull to the side of the road while a herd of sheep and goats is driven down the street by several young boys in dirty, stained clothing. The boys continually whip the animals with small switches, trying to prevent the strays from stealing carrots, cabbage, and other fruits from the vendors' stands. Other shoppers stop where they are until this not uncommon disturbance passes them by. They then return to their leisurely pace of completing the day's shopping.

The driver restarts the autorickshaw, narrowly avoiding several pedestrians who cross in front of him, and again he steers to the center of the street. He continues through the vegetable

market to the area in which household supplies, farm implements, and plumbing and electrical parts can be purchased.
His mind is not on his driving, and he barely avoids an Asian
man carrying baskets of flatbreads and sweet pastries. A squad
of soldiers, in full uniform and with automatic weapons slung
over their backs, walks leisurely in pairs through the market.
They are easy to spot, unlike the I.S.I. and members of the
Special Frontier Force, who are always present, but not in uniform. The rickshaw driver is nervous in their presence, feeling
a vague uneasiness. *What if they know what I plan to do? What
if they recognize me later?* In reality, the soldiers and secret police don't even notice him, and even if they were capable of
knowing what he plans, it's unlikely they would respond. He
has been humiliated. By a woman. And they would certainly
understand.

Today, the market is relatively calm, and the locals move
freely about, quietly doing business with the merchants. The
driver's eyes constantly dart back and forth, and he frequently
looks over his shoulder, watching for an enemy who might be
present. He tells himself that he needs to remain calm and act
natural, just another rickshaw driver hoping that a passenger
will flag him down and need a ride from the market to their
home with their purchases. But he knows that he is here to
make a purchase, to take back his honor, and to punish the
woman who has dared to humiliate him.

He would have preferred to do this after dark, but his

appointment at the clinic is this afternoon. He empties the carrier and makes his way between the stalls that contain household supplies. He finds a small space between several pushcarts where he can leave his rickshaw unattended for a few minutes, and begins walking toward the household and plumbing supply stall. Amid all the seeming chaos, the market has its own internal order. Even the supposedly antagonistic and highly competitive merchants go quietly about their business.

The rickshaw driver is nervous, and can taste the bile welling up into his throat. But he has been careful. He has stayed away from the main streets, and this particular shop is tucked far down an alleyway off a narrow side street. The alley is a dead end, with a high brick wall about a hundred feet away. He is so fixated on what he is doing that he almost bumps into a tall, broad-shouldered man who hesitates for a second on his way out. The rickshaw driver steps around him as the other customer retrieves a pack of cigarettes from under his *shalwar* and uses the butt of his remaining cigarette to light the next one. He looks at the young rickshaw driver for a split second, then moves on about his business. As the rickshaw driver is about to enter the shop, the shopkeeper emerges from the shadowy depths and greets his new customer with a broad smile. "*Asalaam Aleikum.*"

This startles the rickshaw driver, who looks up and sees the shopkeeper, an obese man of about 5'10" with short black hair and a multi-colored prayer cap centered over it.

"What are you in need of? Can I help you?"

"My father sent me. The drains in our kitchen are obstructed. My father said I need to purchase something that will alleviate the problem and that you would be able to provide that."

"Yes, yes, the pipes in this city are old and they all obstruct. Everybody comes to me eventually for help with this problem. Wait here, please."

The shopkeeper disappears behind a curtain at the back of the store, and it seems to the young rickshaw driver that he has been gone far too long. He imagines that the shopkeeper knows what he is planning, and has notified the police, who will, of course, be here any second. As his paranoia builds, he paces nervously in the outer portion of the shop, absentmindedly picking up some of the plumbing items and examining them without having any idea what they are for or how to use them. Finally, the shopkeeper reappears with a jar containing a dark green liquid, but before handing the jar to the driver, he warns him, "Do not get this on your hands, and be particularly cautious not to get this near your face or eyes. That will be fifty rupees."

His heart racing and pounding in his chest, the driver pays the shopkeeper, takes the jar containing the highly caustic acid very gingerly from his hand, and proceeds to leave the shop. He is so nervous he almost trips over the doorjamb as he exits the premises. He walks over to his autorickshaw, places the jar into a small basket in the rear where the passengers usually sit, and secures it with bungee cords. He knows better than to attempt to drive and hold the jar of acid at the same time.

He carefully maneuvers the rickshaw from between push-carts, navigating down the narrow alley considerably more slowly than he had before. He retraces his path much more deliberately this time, still keeping to the less-traveled back alleys behind the market, not wishing to be seen. Remembering what the shopkeeper had said, *Everybody comes to me eventually for help with this problem*, he stops near a trash bin, where he finds an old newspaper to wrap around the jar before going into the clinic. He knows he can't just walk into the clinic carrying a jar of acid, which someone is bound to recognize.

As he is leaving the bazaar area, a man struggling with several packages tries to flag him down, but he is not interested in a passenger and pretends that he doesn't see him, quickly turning away from the bazaar and heading toward the main road. Traffic is getting heavier, but it is not as bad as it will be later in the day. He allows a truck piled high with hay to pass and maneuvers behind it, proceeding in the direction of the medical clinic. He stays close behind the truck, not wishing to be seen or to have would-be passengers try to flag him down. The nearer he draws to the medical clinic, the more unsteady he becomes. His hands are shaking, and he grips the rickshaw handlebars so tightly that his knuckles turn white and his fingers feel as though they are frozen in place. When he reaches the clinic, he drives the rickshaw through the gravel-covered

parking area to the rear, where he parks. Slowly and carefully releasing the bungee cords, he retrieves the jar of corrosive
green liquid from the basket.

He wraps the jar in the newspaper and proceeds to walk
to the front of the clinic. As he approaches the entrance, he
carefully removes the cap from the jar. Extending his right arm
to full length and holding the jar behind him, he adjusts his
shawl so that it conceals the jar, and he then enters the clinic.
His heart is pounding, his mind racing. All he can think of is,
If I can't get this girl, no one else will. He steps up to the counter,
where a small sign on top of the counter reads, "Registration/
New Patients." *If I can't get this girl, no one else will.* His fingers
tighten around the jar at his side.

The tension continues to build, to the point that he wants
to run screaming from the clinic, his quest a failure. He knows
he has to act quickly, or he won't go through with it. At that moment, the doctor steps from one of the examining rooms and
walks toward the registration desk. He moves quickly, his left
hand reaching up and pulling his shawl to one side. His right
hand thrusts forward as he takes several quick steps around the
registration desk. For a mere fraction of second, they make eye
contact, and Dr. Mari knows from his stance that something
bad is happening. She instinctively turns her head away to protect her face, but it is too late; she feels the shock of cold liquid
splashing onto her, striking her face, neck and left shoulder,
and soaking into her sari, running down her chest, breasts,

abdomen, and thighs. In seconds, she knows full well what has just happened, as the highly corrosive acid burns through her flesh, sending waves of agonizing pain through her body.

Her screams can be heard throughout the clinic as her attacker runs toward the exit, hurling the glass container to the floor as he flees. Others in the clinic come running, and several of the women scream when they see what has happened to her. She dashes toward the examining room, pulling her sari away from her dissolving skin, and immediately feeling the burning in her hands as they came in contact with the acid-soaked garment. She knows that regardless of the pain, she has to get the sari off and away from her to stop as much of the acid as she can from contacting her skin. Two of the nursing assistants rush to her side, and through her screams of pain she is able to tell them they need to rinse her with water as quickly as possible to dilute the acid and prevent it from burning her any further.

Her father accompanies her to the clinic most mornings, and it is his habit to sit and mingle with the patients, sometimes gossiping and teasing with the assistants, or just sitting and reading the newspaper. He stays a few hours and then goes home. She had thought he had already gone, but he is just leaving the medical clinic when he sees the young man dash outside, and hears his daughter's screams from within the clinic. He is torn between running after the fleeing rickshaw driver and tending to the needs of his daughter, but quickly realizes that it is more important to see to her well being. He and his family know who the young man is, and the father tells himself that he will be quickly found and apprehended. He rushes to the examining room to help fill basins with water, while the two nursing assistants begin to bathe the doctor's burns to reduce the effects of the acid.

The acute pain fades as the doctor drifts into a state of shock, and a merciful numbness engulfs her. She is vaguely aware when someone grabs her right arm and pulls it outward. She can smell the alcohol and feel the person rubbing it across the skin at the crook of her arm. Then she feels the prick of a needle, which actually offers a welcome respite from the burning pain that is beginning to return and envelop her. The needle is taped into place, and she turns her head, looks up, and sees an intravenous bottle is being hung.

She hears the keys unlocking the cabinet on the far side of the room where the antibiotics and pain medications are kept. The nursing assistant grabs two bottles and carries them to the examining table, then opens a sterile syringe and fills it with a narcotic, which she injects into the I.V. The doctor almost immediately feels warmth come over her, and the pain quickly begins to subside. The nurse quickly turns, peels the plastic covering off the second syringe, fills it with antibiotic, and injects it into the intravenous solution.

Burns are a common occurrence in this part of the world. Usually they occur when someone sleeps too close to hot coals and clothing catches on fire. Other times, they occur when someone brings hot coals into a tent to keep warm at night, and the entire tent goes up in flames. Then there are the acid burns, horrific attacks on women by men who feel their manhood has been insulted by a girl who has rejected them. It is the insane, male-driven compulsion of *if I can't get this girl, no one else will* that so frequently leads to beautiful young girls' lives being destroyed by an easily obtainable, inexpensive, and highly caustic acid being thrown in their faces. Often they are blinded. And even if they are lucky enough to maintain their sight, their faces are eaten away by the acid, leaving them severely scarred for the rest of their lives.

The young doctor's quick thinking in turning away from her attacker saved her eyesight, but she has still been horribly wounded, including facial wounds. The medication has had several minutes to work, and is doing its job. Her heartbeat has slowed, and her eyes feel heavy. She just wants to close them, grateful that the previously searing pain has subsided, leaving only a mildly painful burning sensation. All she can think of is that that they need to keep rinsing the acid away, diluting it and preventing it from burning any further into her flesh. They continue soaking towels in the basin of water and wringing them out over her skin, and applying wet towels and compresses to her neck and breasts. She sees her father moving back and forth, quickly refilling the basins as the nurses apply the wet compresses. She realizes that she is in the acute management phase of an acid burn: dilute it and remove it.

Thirty minutes pass, and the nursing assistants are satisfied that they have washed and soaked the affected areas enough to dilute and remove the caustic material from the doctor's body. They return to the locked cabinet and remove some tubes of topical antibiotic ointment, which they begin applying to the wounded areas. Over this they place soft cotton dressings. They know that she needs much more than they have done, but there is no further treatment that they can provide in this small clinic. She will need to be transferred to one of the major hospitals that have the staff and supplies needed for burn care.

Unfortunately, even the larger hospitals can provide little more than what the clinic has already done. The only burn center in the entire country is the Civil Burn Unit at Dow University in Karachi, hundreds of miles away. An air flight in Pakistan will not be possible, and the roads out of Shikarpur are narrow, gravel covered, pot-holed paths that would be impossible to navigate should it rain. The closest local hospital with doctors is in the city of Sukkur, and will require a journey north into the Punjab. There are no ambulances in Shikarpur, so a request will have to be made, a phone call placed to the Sukkur Hospital requesting that the one and only ambulance be sent to the Shikarpur Clinic to pick up the doctor. Hopefully, the ambulance will not be in use and a driver will be available. Hopefully, there is enough government funding to provide the ambulance with sufficient petrol to make the trip. The rains that cause the Indus Valley floods have ended several weeks ago, so there is a good chance that the road has not been washed out. And hopefully, there will not be caravans of lorries stalled along the road, trying to take supplies north to the flood victims in the Indus Valley. So many factors rely upon hope, a commodity that is in short supply in this region.

The staff at the clinic all know that they have done what they can for the moment, and that the doctor's acute care has been properly completed. The nurses go to the front desk in the waiting area to discuss their options and the possibility of obtaining an ambulance and transferring the patient to Sukkur. In the clinic there is only one patient who seems to be acutely ill. They take her back to the other examining room, and ask the other patients to leave and return tomorrow, explaining that because the lone doctor is now a critical patient herself, the clinic is effectively closed.

After several tries, the nurse at the front desk reports that she has been able to make contact with the hospital in Sukkur. Allah is looking after them. An ambulance and driver are available, but it will take the driver two hours to get to the clinic and another two hours to take the doctor from the clinic to the hospital in Sukkur. He will be leaving immediately, but the nurse can do nothing for now but return to the examining room and stand there, gently squeezing the doctor's right hand.

She wants to let her know that they are all with her. The doctor slowly opens her eyes and smiles, saying, "I taught you well. You did everything efficiently, quickly, and very professionally. I never thought I would be the one you would be looking after. Thank you. Thank you."

The nurse chokes back tears as she speaks. "You moved quickly. You saved your eyesight. I prayed to Allah for that. Your wounds are all manageable. You are young and healthy and you will do well. You've been working very hard here at the clinic, taking care of everyone else. But now, you get a vacation, and we will all take care of you."

The doctor thanks her again, and the nurse squeezes her hand tightly, saying, "We have called the Civil Hospital in Sukkur, and an ambulance will be here shortly. You will get good care there. Just close your eyes and rest until the ambulance arrives. I will be here with you all the time. If you need anything, just tell me."

Mari's father is now kneeling in the center of the clinic, his hands clasped in prayer. The nurse comes in from the examining room and gently puts her hands on the grieving man's shoulders, silently comforting him. After a moment, she tells him, "The acid did not blind her. She was very lucky. She has wounds on her face, chest, abdomen, and legs, but these can be taken care of at the Civil Hospital in Sukkur." The father looks through tear-filled eyes at the nurse, nodding his silent gratitude. For him, however, there are no words, and he doesn't have the strength to speak at the moment anyway. He knows he needs to save his strength for the task ahead: to go home and tell Mari's mother what has happened to their beautiful daughter.

Saving Mari

All Mari's father can think of at the moment is that he needs to get home to his wife and his family. The driver, who was told what had happened, nervously works his way through the traffic as the young doctor's father closes his eyes to his surroundings and shuts out the noises of the street. He begins to reminisce, speaking silently to his absent daughter as if the wind could carry his thoughts to her across the miles. It is all he can do now as she lies in pain, struggling for her life.

"When I first held you, my Mari, who would have thought you would become a physician? In our family, the girls do not receive a higher education, but you wanted to be a doctor. I remember your mother saying, 'That's out of the question. Go to the kitchen and begin cutting vegetables.' Then you came home one day with a stethoscope and said you had found it and were intrigued by it. You insisted you were going to become a doctor.

"I am not a highly educated man. I am just a shopkeeper. I sell spices. My house is small and consists of only three rooms. Yet we have seven children, a sick grandmother, and a paralyzed grandfather to contend with. How hard it must have been for you to deal with all of this and your studies. How difficult it must have been for you on all levels. Yet, you never complained – not once. You helped your mother in the kitchen, you tended to the sick grandmother, you helped with your paralyzed grandfather, and you never gave up hope.

"You attended the local public school, which was attended by boys and girls. You were an excellent student and passed all of your examinations. You entered the local high school, which was for girls only, and continued to be an excellent student. We deprived ourselves – and the other children – of many things so that we could save money and send our Mari to medical school. The entire family was so proud of your achievements.

"We ate more vegetables and less chicken and mutton. We did not buy new clothing items, but cleaned and stitched and passed them on to the younger children. When the time came for your final exams, we were all very quiet and tried not to disturb you or ask you to help with chores around the house. We were more nervous than you were as the examination date approached. Even during your studies, you took time to visit the homes of poor and sick people. And then you returned to your studies. You were such a good girl, and religious too. You always wore your burqa and a scarf when you were in public. When you returned from your final exams, you had a smile on your face and were very confident. You said that you did not find them difficult, and felt you had done very well.

"Then came the waiting. It would be several days before the results were known. We all prayed for you. The entire family had endured hardships over these years for our Mari.

"The day arrived when you would have the results of your examination and the determination of your future. We all awoke early that morning and we made a simple breakfast for the children, but your mother and I could not eat. School had closed for the younger children, and they went to visit friends or play out front. You left with the autorickshaw driver to collect your papers and the results of your examination.

"It was a work day, and I had to unlock the spice shop and prepare for my customers. I was still at the store working when you returned home and threw your arms around your mother, claiming that you had been accepted to the medical school in Larkana, and would be living at the dorms while you attended school and worked at the hospital. Your mother gathered up all the children *and rushed to the spice shop to tell me the good news. It was one of the happiest days of my life.*

"And now, this vengeful acid attack on my daughter, the doctor."

The taxi screeches to a stop, sending sand and small stones flying. The father jumps from the seat before the air has even cleared, and rushes into the house. His wife is tending to one of the grandparents. When she looks up and sees his face, she knows immediately that something terrible has happened. Her husband stands there shaking, tears streaming down his cheeks and falling in little droplets onto his chest. His lips are quivering, and he can hardly speak. Finally, words come, and he tells his wife what has happened, repeating over and over, "A vicious attack with acid! A vicious attack with acid! A vicious attack with acid!"

His wife grabs a scarf and quickly places it over her head, and as she takes her husband's hand, the two run from the house. The taxi is still waiting to take them back to the clinic from which he has just come, where they will await the ambulance that will take them all to the Sukkur Hospital.

The ambulance seems to take forever, but when it finally arrives, the nurses slowly and carefully help move Mari into the vehicle with her parents. It is obvious that despite the shots she has received, she is still in a great deal of pain. Even so, she puts a smile on her face and thanks the clinic nurses again for their help. The ambulance attendant slams the rear doors shut and turns the handle to lock them in place. He then climbs into the seat adjacent to the driver.

Word of the attack on the town's doctor has spread quickly, and the hospital and street has filled with several hundred townspeople. Some are shouting prayers for their doctor, while some of the men are waving sticks and bellowing that they will find this rascal and kill him. In order to navigate the now-crowded streets around the clinic, the ambulance driver turns on the flashing lights and siren. Some of the people they pass are weeping, and others are screaming in anger as the ambulance winds its way through the dusty narrow streets and onto the main road to Sukkur.

All of us on my medical team have heard of Dr. Mari and how she had overcome almost insurmountable obstacles in her quest to become a physician and care for her fellow townspeople. We have heard especially of her excitement at being able to work with the American medical teams to improve her skills and techniques. But I had no idea that our first meeting would be under such terrible circumstances.

* * * * *

The Civil Hospital in Sukkur is a small institution but is capable of providing the initial clinical care that Mari will need. However, it is not in any sense of the word a burn center, and is not equipped to treat burns, especially a severe burn caused by industrial acid. The only burn center in the entire country is in Karachi, and if Mari is to receive adequate treatment, once she is stabilized, she will have to be transferred there as soon as possible. Unfortunately, it is impossible to predict how many days it will take to process the necessary paperwork and obtain an ambulance for such a long trip. Karachi is hundreds of miles away, and there are no life-flight helicopters or other airlifts in Pakistan. She will have to endure a full day's ambulance ride on these primitive roads.

The next day, all the members of her family – her parents, her brothers, and her sisters – are gathered at her bedside in the hospital. The brothers are plotting their revenge on the family of Mari's attacker. If they cannot find the rickshaw driver who threw the acid on their sister, they swear they will go after the young girls in his family and attack them the same way that Mari has been attacked. This is very much a world in which people believe in an eye for an eye.

Their father, however, is a very humble, religious man, who, both hurt and frightened by their talk, screams at them, "No, no, no! You cannot right a wrong by doing another wrong. If you take your revenge out on the young girls in the other family, then they will want revenge on our family. I have three other daughters, and I don't wish to see any harm come to them."

This discussion is taking place at Mari's bedside, and she quickly intervenes, saying, "Father is right. If you take revenge on the other family with acid or guns, then our three sisters are in danger of being attacked. Please listen to Father, he is right about this."

Frustrated, Mari's oldest brother asks, "Then what are we to do?"

Her father tries to reassure them. "The police know what happened, the entire town knows what happened."

"The police do nothing!" they scoff. "The courts and the lawyers do nothing in Pakistan. We looked for the autorickshaw driver before we came to the hospital. He has already disappeared. People are saying that his family has given him money and that he has left Shikarpur and has already gone into hiding."

The father knows that it is best to offer his sons some hope of justice for their sister, and tells them, "He cannot stay in hiding forever. The police will find him. We will have to be patient. What is important now is that our Mari gets well and returns to the family and her beloved clinic. There will be no revenge, there will be no retribution from members of this family. We will not bring shame to this family or endanger the other children."

Meanwhile the big task at hand is to complete the paperwork and arrange for an ambulance to take Dr. Mari from the Sukkur Hospital to the burn center in Karachi. Her care in the Sukkur hospital is the best they can offer, but it is marginal at best. She is growing significantly weaker and malnourished, and barely hanging on to her life, being maintained with I.V. fluids. Antibiotics are hard to come by, and pain medication is very limited as well. The question is: will she be able to tolerate the long and difficult trip to Karachi? Will she live, or will she die?

Later, as I am sitting with Saleem and Mohammed and telling them Dr. Mari's story, I find tears once again welling up and threatening to flow again, as they have so many times in the past. Perhaps to console myself and stem the flow, I mutter to myself that her attacker will be brought to justice, and that his punishment will deter others from committing such crimes.

Apparently, Saleem's hearing is very acute, because he hears my mumbling, and quickly responds, "No! No! We live in a country where such things are commonplace. Murder is everywhere and highly visible. Women are beaten and sometimes even stoned to death. Women are scarred with the knife or accosted by having acid thrown in their faces or on their bodies. Who has not witnessed the slaying of someone close to them? Who has not witnessed an attack on a woman who is not properly covered, or who is alone on the street or alone in the market? She is brutally punished for sitting in the front seat of an automobile with her driver, or is disfigured with acid because she has rejected her suitor. It never ends. These occurrences are highly visible and everywhere. We have all witnessed these acts."

His voice grows a little softer and I see what looks like the beginning of a tear in his eye as he concludes, "If this is what we see and allow to occur and reoccur, what are we teaching our young people? They do not see an individual's life as something to be cherished, and they learn that their own lives are disposable!"

I am beyond stunned by his outburst, but know him too well to doubt the truth of what he says. I think at one level I have known it for a long time, known that these brutal "punishments" are not aberrations but rather are entrenched in the culture.

I fall silent, and both of them know to leave me to my thoughts. How can this be possible, for so many women to be tortured and disfigured every day, and even worse, for their families and the authorities to simply turn a blind eye to their suffering and accept it as if it were a natural part of life? As much as I have come to respect and admire the people of the Middle East, at this moment, I see them as the barbaric monsters so often described in the writings of racist bloggers in my own country. My tears are dried, replaced with a rage that I almost never feel, and always strive to avoid. Sometimes, however, rage is the only appropriate emotion.

Lives Without Value

When I meet her, the first thing that comes to my mind is that Dr. Mari Shah is a survivor, and that she is tough. Even so, I know she has a long road ahead of her. The caustic acid has caused significant chemical burns on her face, chest, abdomen, arms, hands, and on her legs as well. She is in great pain. I am told that when she was finally allowed to see her face in a mirror, she cried, and despite her earlier concurrence with her father's command that no revenge be taken against her attacker, she said, "I want acid thrown on his face and body. I want him to suffer the agony I have." It is an understandable sentiment, considering

153

all she has been through. Still, she is young and strong and determined to get past this adversity so she can return to her medical clinic and her hometown patients.

At least she is fortunate enough to be transferred to the Burn Center in Karachi fairly soon after her attack – sooner than many of us had thought was possible. An ambulance is sent from the burn center to transport her. Along with my team of surgeons, I have operated and taught at this burn center, under the sponsorship of my Children's Foundation and Hashmat Effendi's House of Charity from Houston, Texas. In fact, Dr. Mari had been looking forward to working with the team on our upcoming visit, and had been in contact with us by email. Now she is the one who will be receiving care.

Upon Mari's arrival at the Burn Center, emails are sent to Hashmat, who is in Karachi at the time working with some burned children who are to be transferred to the Texas Medical Center and the Shriner's Burn Hospital in the U.S. for their care. Hashmat is also seeing to the distribution of donated equipment that has recently arrived at the Port of Karachi. Hashmat has done a world of good for the children of this region; I'll explain more about her and her work a little later in this book.

Hashmat visits Mari Shah at the hospital over the next few days, and is pleased to see her continued progress now that she is in the burn center. Hashmat goes to the Pakistani authorities and the American Embassy and arranges for Dr. Shah's passport, and I write letters in support of her being transferred to the United States for the continued care and treatment of this unprovoked, dastardly, caustic chemical burn. Mari's brother and even a local politician have tried to expedite matters too.

Hashmat and I have spoken out on numerous occasions throughout Pakistan about these unprovoked acid attacks on women. We have even attended a meeting with the local press club to further publicize this problem, and have brought it to the attention of the minister of health and others in the Pakistani government. Our hope is to have a law passed to control the distribution and sale of these caustic acids.

As I have mentioned, these attacks on women occur every day, not only in Pakistan but also throughout many of the Muslim countries. *It seems as though these women already have a noose around their necks in utero, which is only tightened further upon their birth.*

With Hashmat Effendi at the Jacobabad Press Club, in support of women's rights to education and to call a halt to acid attacks.

Under the care of the well-trained and excellent doctors at the Civil Burn Hospital in Karachi, Dr. Shah continues to improve each day. Hashmat and I visit with her every day, and are pleased not only with her improvement from a medical point of view, but also with her mental attitude and her desire to return home and resume work in her medical clinic in Shikarpur. Yes, she has moments of bitterness and anger at her attacker – and again, all of this is completely understandable. But it seems clear to us that she is looking beyond her own suffering and is very eager to get back to her life.

While Mari Shah continues to recover, several more patients with acid burns have been admitted to the Burn Center. As I have indicated elsewhere in this book, they are only a few of the thousands of women that receive caustic acid burns in Pakistan – to say nothing of the rest of the Muslim world.

Surprisingly, none of the people at the hospital has ever seen a man with acid burns. I once saw a man who was similarly burned, but it turned out that he was actually the perpetrator of one of these despicable attacks. Unfortunately for him, he had been stupid enough to place the acid into a small plastic bag. When he squeezed the bag to force the acid up and out onto the young girl he was attacking, a significant portion of the acid splashed back on him, resulting in burns to his neck, chest, and arms. He was admitted to the Burn Center in

Karachi, as was the young lady he had attacked. In fact, it was within the Burn Center that she identified him as her attacker. That was one of the few occasions where the police were called, and the attacker was arrested in the hospital and taken away. But this is the only case I am aware of where a male was burned by acid. Compare this to the thousands of young women who are attacked in this manner each year.

As you can guess, I have met with many of these young women, and asked them to describe the circumstances that brought about their attacks. What I learned from these discussions has shocked and enraged me, to say the very least.

In Pakistan, as well as many of the other Muslim countries, a man is entitled to have four wives. It is customary for the husband to discuss with his present wives – especially his first wife, who usually assumes the status of the senior woman of the household – his desire to take on another wife. The wives may object for any number of reasons, but it is ultimately the husband's decision to make. The wives' objections are often founded in the husband's inability to support the wives and the children they bear. Especially in cases where the family is already poor, it would seem unfair for the husband to take on the obligation of yet another wife, but fairness where women are concerned is not a particular priority in that culture. In cases where the older wife feels threatened or displaced by her husband marrying a younger woman, the husband might retaliate by throwing acid into her face, effectively removing her from the equation.

Numerous women have told me of being teased in public and virtually stalked by young men in whom they had no interest, and whom their families did not consider to be acceptable suitors. When these women rejected the men's overtures, the men responded by attacking the women and burning them with acid. Other women told me that it was simply their refusal of a man's proposal of marriage, and the man's dog-in-the-manger attitude that resulted in their having acid thrown in their faces. Once again, it is a case of the man rationalizing that if he cannot have this woman, no one will. This was apparently what happened with Mari and the autorickshaw driver who attacked her.

Then there are the women who were better educated and more outgoing, and whose sense of independence led them to defy their husbands' or fathers' desire to keep them at home. They would venture out in public without a male family member in attendance, and as a result, one of their own family members would throw acid on them. There were also several women I spoke with whose only "offense" was that they had attempted to help a family member, a neighbor, or just a close friend who had been the victim of an acid attack. As a result of their efforts to help other unfortunate women, they were attacked themselves, and had acid thrown on them.

Recently, a teenage girl had acid poured over her head, and the acid flowed down her entire body. It was done simply because she had looked out her window one too many times at a young man walking by, after her father had repeatedly told her that watching the young man dishonored him and the entire family. This girl had never so much as met or talked to the young man, and didn't even know him beyond seeing the image of him through her window. The father ordered his wife to pour the acid on her own daughter, and the woman actually obeyed his command. As if this weren't horrible enough, the father demanded that the daughter be kept in the house in horrible agony, with the acid continuing to eat away at her flesh, for a full 24 hours before allowing her to be taken to the hospital. Somehow, the international press got wind of the girl's story, and thanks to today's electronic media, the grisly details were spread worldwide.

Often a younger man will marry an older woman who has come from a more affluent family, and who brings to the marriage money and property that the man wants. Such a man will often throw acid on the older woman to keep her "in her place," while he does whatever he wants. She will be so disfigured that she becomes completely dependent upon the man's "kindness" and willingness to keep her around. If that "kindness" isn't there, where can she go? Nobody else will take her in and risk bringing scandal into their home. What often happens is that she begs him to keep her, and turns her property over to him so that he will not discard her, only to be thrown out of the home or even murdered. And even then, nobody comes to her aid. Nobody demands that the man be punished.

One of the more recent events involved a Pakistan International Airlines flight attendant who had suffered severe acid burns. She told of having a frequently flying passenger who flirted with her repeatedly, and after a recent flight he came up to her and proposed marriage. She laughed when he made his proposal, assuming that the man was merely joking with her as he had in the past. Whether he was joking or not, the would-be suitor was offended by her rejection. He took the time to find out where she lived, appeared uninvited and unexpected at her home one day, and threw acid on her. It goes without saying that she is no longer employed by the airline.

There are many instances when a mother-in-law to be feels that an upcoming marriage is not in the interest of the family. Convinced that it will not be a good match, and seeing it as her job to protect the family's inheritance, the prospective mother-in-law sometimes convinces one of her younger sons to throw acid on the prospective bride. In some cases, the would-be mother-in-law does it herself. Either way, the marriage doesn't happen, and the discarded fiancée's life is ruined.

The staff at the Karachi Burn Center treats the women injured by these acid attacks, and hears the stories that led up to these terrible incidents, on an almost daily basis. When you consider that this is the only burn center in Pakistan, and that most of the victims never get taken even to a small village clinic for treatment, the sheer scale of the problem starts to sink in a bit.

Most of the victims of these attacks are women who are uneducated, who come from families with little or no education, and who are poor or middle class. In most cases, the attacker is male, and even though there are usually witnesses to the attack and the perpetrator's identity is known, he almost never faces punishment for his crime. In contrast, if such an attack were to befall a member of an upper-class family, there would be immediate and severe consequences for these actions.

Then there are those who are just innocent bystanders, casualties because they are just in the wrong place at the wrong time. One case in point is Ambareen Sheikh (not to be confused with another acid attack victim with a similar name, with whom my colleague Hashmat Effendi has worked). At the time I talk to her mother, Ambareen is twenty-four years old, and over the course of the past sixteen years, has undergone fifty-six surgical procedures for her burns. And she was not even the intended victim.

Ambareen was only eight years old when she was severely burned by caustic acid. She was playing outside in front of her home with other children when a woman ran past her, screaming, with a man carrying a jar of acid in hot pursuit. He ran into little Ambareen, tripping over her and spilling the acid onto the innocent eight-year-old.

Ambareen's father had died several years before, and her mother, devastated by her husband's early and untimely death, was faced with raising and supporting eight very young children. They were not a poor family, but there was never enough money for anything beyond absolute necessities. All eight children had been delivered at home, since they could not afford to go to the hospital. Besides, Mrs. Sheikh told me that many women choose to have home deliveries because they fear that after several pregnancies, the doctors will tie their tubes, even without permission. And now, with no husband to help with support, Mrs. Sheikh certainly couldn't afford to take Ambareen to a hospital to be treated.

Ambareen was playing marbles with her brothers, sisters, and cousins in front of the house when Mrs. Sheikh heard screaming and loud noises. She ran outside to investigate and saw people running and pushing each other. The older children had stopped playing marbles and ran towards Ambareen.

Ambareen was small for her age and slow to respond to what was taking place. She was pushed aside by the fleeing woman and had fallen down when the man who was chasing the woman tripped over Ambareen and spilled the acid over her.

There is a deep anger in Mrs. Sheikh's voice as she says, "Anyone can purchase this acid for as little as five to ten rupees." (This is the equivalent of 50 to 80 cents U.S.)

She continues, "It is intended for and sold to be used for flushing out sewer systems and cleaning bathrooms. The problem is anyone can purchase it." She pauses for a minute as tears well up in her eyes. She takes a deep breath, looks back at me, and continues, "There should be laws to control the distribution of such a harmful product."

I ask her, "Was the person who did this apprehended?"

"I am a mother alone with eight young children. There is no male figure to support or represent me. I was afraid to pursue it. People who throw acid are known to take retribution upon those who have reported them or stood as witnesses against them. I did not want any of the other children in my family harmed. I have very little money and no education. I could not pay the authorities. The authorities – the police – are very corrupt. The guilty could bribe the authorities, get released from jail, and then return to harm my other children. I did not want this to happen, and therefore would not cooperate with or involve the authorities."

"I have heard this many times before," I respond. "I have also seen other victims who have been attacked with acid out of retribution and revenge."

The mother repeats, "If the perpetrators are reported to the police and jailed, they pay a bribe and are released and disappear for a while. The police then lose interest and the perpetrators return to the neighborhood as if nothing had happened. They then are free to seek revenge on other family members." As she says this, her tears again begin to flow, and she uses the corner of her scarf to wipe them away before continuing. "What is a single mother to do? Women alone have no rights, and are not listened to. A family needs a male figure in a

Muslim country in order to survive. These stories are frequently depicted in the newspaper and on the television. The press may report it, but nothing will happen."

Little Ambareen suffered significant acid burns to her face, eyes, ears, neck, shoulders, upper arms, and breasts. If anything in her story can be considered good fortune, it would be that this happened in Karachi, and that she was immediately taken to the Civil Burn Hospital in the city. However, even though the child was admitted, the Center at that time was adult-oriented and not well equipped to take care of young children. The mother states that she was told that they would take care of Ambareen's acute problem, but there was a very long waiting list for burn reconstruction.

What Mrs. Sheikh is telling me is that if you are poor and have no money, you are not going to get medical care in Pakistan. As my good friend and ABC-TV news commentator, the late Marvin Zindler, always said, "It's hell to be poor." That's true no matter what country you live in – it is certainly true in the U.S. as well – but in Pakistan, medical care at the government-run civil hospitals is supposed to be free of charge.

Unfortunately, it really doesn't work that way. Most of the physicians in Pakistan could not earn an adequate living just working at a government hospital, so they hold two jobs. In the mornings, they usually go to the government hospitals, sign in, show their faces, have their tea, chat with the nurses, see a few patients so they can collect their government check, and then leave to attend to their private practices. Those private practices are, of course, run on a cash-only basis. This way, the Pakistani doctors have the best of both worlds. They get a government check that comes on a regular basis, and then they collect cash from those who can afford their services in their private practice of medicine.

Ambareen's mother continues with her story. "As a single mother, and having little money, I returned again and again to the government hospitals, only to be told that we were still on the waiting list. You can't imagine how a mother feels knowing her child needs care and she cannot provide it. All I had left was some gold jewelry, which I sold. I even sold my wedding ring. I then took Ambareen to a private clinic in Karachi. But again, as a woman alone, and with limited ability to pay, I was treated badly. Pakistani doctors control their patients. *They actually want their patients to beg them for their care!*"

But Ambareen's story was not over. A Dr. Faiz finally accepted Ambareen as his patient. Ambareen's mother thought her daughter would finally receive the care she so desperately needed, but it was not to be. "Dr. Faiz dressed very well, had long hair, and as I later learned, he was referred to as the 'playboy surgeon,'" says Mrs. Sheikh. She goes on to tell me that he exerted Mafia-like control over surgery in three hospitals and many clinics in the area. Other doctors worked for him and openly feared him. They were his "yes-men." Mrs. Sheikh quickly learned that if you went to another hospital and complained about Dr. Faiz's care and treatment, his yes-men would turn you away or insist that you return to Dr. Faiz.

"They actually scolded me for my actions," she tells me.

It was then, she acknowledges, that Hashmat and I entered Ambareen's and Mrs. Sheikh's lives. Ambareen was sponsored by Hashmat's House of Charity and my Children's Foundation to go to Houston for her burn reconstruction surgery. There, she went through many extensive surgical procedures, some of which were required to re-do the failed procedures that she'd had at the hands of Dr. Faiz.

Once again, Mrs. Sheikh wipes her tears away as she continues, "Dr. Faiz took what little money I had and said it was not enough to even give Ambareen a room. He even refused to provide a bed and a room for her after surgeries. She was placed on a blanket on the floor of the hallway. There was also the pain she went through after these operations. I blame myself!" At this point, Mrs. Sheik begins sobbing uncontrollably, and has to pause for a moment to collect herself.

After a few minutes, she regains her composure enough to continue, "This all changed when she went with you and Mrs. Effendi to the Medical Center in Houston for her treatment. The people there not only took care of her burn injuries, but they also recognized that she was very smart and talented. While she was undergoing her recovery in Houston, they taught her to speak English, and trained her in secretarial skills. Ambareen had no life when she left. No confidence. No trust in people. Now my Ambareen is happy. She is well groomed and outgoing. She has a goal in life."

"More tears on the sand," I blurt out without thinking.

Mrs. Sheikh smiles at me through her tears, saying, "First they were tears of sorrow, and now they are tears of joy."

I wish I could say that Mari's story had as happy an ending as that of Ambareen. But it is not to be.

I am unable to stay with Mari because I have so many other obligations. But I leave her with the hope and prayer that the tedious paperwork and passport issues will soon be straightened out so she can be transported to Houston to get the treatment she really needs.

I am shocked when I learn later that Dr. Mari has died, and that the official cause of death was an infection secondary to the burns she had suffered. I am appalled that no one would have told me right away, but even more appalled at the supposed cause of death. I think to myself, *There's no way she could have died of an infection!* The overall infection rate in even the smaller hospitals is infinitesimal, and is virtually nonexistent in the Burn Center in Karchi. Besides, it is highly unusual for burn victims like Dr. Mari who have received immediate treatment to get an infection, and almost unheard of for them to die as a result.

Something is badly amiss, and I suspect that I know what it is.

What I think is more likely is that her attacker, Aslam San-jrani – or someone working to protect him – came into her room at the hospital unnoticed, and either smothered her with a pillow or poisoned her. I have heard various contradictory ac-counts about Sanjrani's fate. Some of the accounts say he was taken to court but no punishment was given. Some say he was in jail for a while for his own protection, but that his family was able to obtain the support of high-level authorities. But I am told there are still many people who are fighting for justice: a real trial, and real punishment befitting the atrocity he has committed.

With his victim dead, however, Sanjrani pretty well assured himself that he would face no legal action as a result of his at-tack on Mari. In addition, Dr. Mari's death at his hand – or at his bidding – probably sent a clear message to the doctor's family, warning them and others not to dare pursue the matter any further. And given the typical response to such crimes in Pakistan, the family would naturally have taken the warning to heart, letting the matter drop, and mourning the loss of their beloved Mari in silence. Maybe I am totally off base with this theory. But then again... maybe not.

I simply cannot begin to express the outrage I feel, not just for Mari Shah, but for every woman and child in Pakistan, for I know that even those who are spared the agony of such a mindless and brutal attack live in fear. Fear of being attacked themselves, or of having their loved ones' lives either ruined or ended. And all because of some stupidly barbaric "code" that demands subservience to those who have even the slightest power over others. That power can be purchased for eighty cents, the cost of a jar of caustic acid. It can be wielded at no cost whatsoever, simply because of the cultural bias against anyone who might fall victim to another's insane rage.

I had originally thought that my most important accomplishment in this life would be to help cure the afflicted, to bring healing to the victims of war and ignorance. What I have come to realize, however, is that no matter how many people I might cure, and how many more might be cured because I taught my skills to other doctors, the flow of victims will continue unabated until such time as the ignorance and hatred that fosters violence is purged from the society itself.

Suicide Bombers

Rattling along the bumpy road to Abbottabad, I find it impossible to sleep for very long. I awaken to a spirited discussion between Mohammed and Saleem. They are talking about the suicide bombers again. I am all ears. Saleem forcefully expresses his opinion, shared by so many in the West and even some in his region, that the suicide bombers fit a specific demographic. "They are mostly young men, unmarried, uneducated, unable to obtain employment, poorer than average, and socially isolated," he says. "The typical suicide bomber is a loser and a loner, easily influenced by the irrational rants of the jihadists

He spends too much time at the mosque, and is convinced that all he has to offer is to martyr himself. And some are obsessed with the promise of being received by the Houris, the virgins that each martyr will receive in paradise. Such a man believes that in paradise, he will drink of milk and honey. These people are depressed, simple-minded, desperately poor, and uneducated." [1]

I am appalled by Saleem's statements, and have to speak up. "According to my research, you are dead wrong. It is a widely held misconception that all suicide bombers come from any one type of social background. Martyrs are as likely to come from the elite, well-educated families as from poverty stricken ghettos. They've all seen and experienced what you have mentioned, but psychologically I would say they are pretty normal."

Mohammed laughs and says, "No, that is not possible."

Saleem agrees with him. "I don't believe that."

"It's true," I respond, "and furthermore, they are not mostly young. Their ages vary widely. Some are definitely young children as you say, who you see as being easily manipulated, but most of them are in their twenties and thirties. Some are even older." I go on to explain that in general, the martyrs are

---

[1] The popular notion of "72 virgins" greeting the male martyr in Paradise is really a bit of a myth. To begin with, most Muslims don't believe in any specific number of virgins. In addition, Houris of the appropriate gender are promised to both male and female believers, and not just to martyrs.

educated, and come from families in the middle or upper class. Most have jobs with good incomes. And while it is true that most come from a civilian population, there are also some who have been recruited from the military in Pakistan and other countries.

"Apparently the other misconception is that you just wake up one morning and decide to become a suicide bomber," I add. "That is just not true. There are training camps for suicide bombers, and only the most suitable candidates are selected for a specific task."

Saleem concedes that point, and says, "I have heard of training camps in Pakistan and Afghanistan for those who wish to become martyrs."

Mohammed chimes in, "Well, the one thing they do have in common is that they are all religious zealots, who are told that martyrdom assures them a life in Paradise. Your typical martyr may feel this is the only way he can reach Paradise. I know they don't all volunteer, but there is a growing trend of these people to embrace jihad. Not just here, but in Europe and America also."

I feel somewhat strange lecturing my friends on their own culture, but believe it is important for them to understand what is really transpiring in their world. "Those who have been apprehended do seem to have one other thing in common," I say. "They all speak highly of Osama bin Laden and say that he was an inspiration for their undertaking jihad.

They were stirred by bin Laden's taped speeches and the Sheikh's writings, and wanted to be 'one with Osama.' They felt they could only accomplish this by being a martyr and performing jihad."

I add, "They all believe they are not really going to die. They believe they are going to a better life, a new life. They all seek the personal reward of a paradise." I explain that their political motivation is also critical, but the extent and significance of that motivation varies from individual to individual. Individual personal experiences influence political motives.

"There has to be a balance between religious and political goals," I muse. "At the training camps, religion is apparently used to shape and support political convictions." They feel they have an individual duty as Muslims to restore the rule of Allah by confronting the infidels. They see themselves as members of the *Ummah*, or Muslim community, and believe that by committing themselves to the jihad, they bring all Muslims one step closer to re-establishing the dominion of the Caliphite."

Saleem ponders this for a moment, and says, "You know, the Internet is full of videos that honor the martyr and his family, glorify his actions, and are designed to convince others to do the same. I think these videos have an immense impact on young minds. I have seen a lot of car and truck bombings on the videos, many with music and song on the soundtrack."

I interrupt him, saying, "That is interesting, considering musical instruments, singing, and dancing are frowned upon by the Salafi – the fundamentalist Muslims – and punished by the Taliban."

Saleem responds, "Yes, yes, you are correct."

"I guess when it serves their purpose it is allowable."

"The videos depict personal salvation of the individual, while inflicting mortal damage on his enemy. They are liberating themselves when they go to Paradise and in turn they are liberating their people," says Saleem.

Mohammed adds, "Some of them get paid."

Saleem laughs, "They don't get paid, they're dead."

"I think he means the family receives some compensation" .Mohammed grows impatient, adding, "I heard they get a lot of money."

Saleem elaborates, "The rumor was that they got $10,000 to $20,000. That's a lifetime of work. Financial compensation in these amounts were reported early on. This type of compensation is not available anymore, because transactions and money transfers have been monitored, and as a result, are significantly restricted."

We are beginning to lose daylight, with the sun beginning to disappear and then re-appear as we pass through the canyons on this desolate road. I don't want to be traveling on these roads at night, and neither do my companions. There is enough risk of getting killed here in the daytime; at night it becomes almost a sure thing. I tell Mohammed that we will be approaching Havelian at sundown, and perhaps we should look for a place to sleep and eat there.

"We can get up early and go on to Abbottabad in the morning," I say. "Sheik bin Laden is, by all accounts, somewhere in this area. If I am going to get my interview, we need to make inquiries, and since Havelian is almost a suburb of Abbottabad, I think we should inquire here on the street, in the market, at the mosque, and at the restaurant when we have dinner."

Mohammed looks worried. "You are gonna get us all killed."

I chuckle and try to assuage his fears, saying, "I believe it's all in how you ask and the perception you create."

He, however, is not convinced, and repeats, "You're gonna get us killed."

Still trying to lighten the mood, I respond, "If you die in the search for Osama bin Laden, do you still get to go to Paradise, drink honey and milk, and enjoy seventy-two virgins – or however many you want or believe you deserve?"

They all laugh at my comments, but Saleem is quick to point out, "There are no virgins left. Who wants a virgin? Give me an experienced woman any day."

We are all laughing now, and the tension of the moment has passed. Sounding much cheerier, Mohammed says, "We are only thirty or thirty-five kilometers from Abbottabad. The road in this area is not good, but much better than the portion we've already traveled. Let's continue on."

I think to myself that we should easily traverse that distance in the next hour, and accommodations and restaurants will be plentiful and superior in Abbottabad. I ask everyone to vote, and the decision is unanimous.

"See, we can be a democracy." A democracy of four, anyway.

There is more laughter, and we are all in a good mood. We have had our share of close encounters, but everything has gone well. It is onward to Abbottabad.

As we drive, I amuse myself by snapping pictures of the scenery as we pass. I am a little worried because we are in Taliban territory, and they have decreed that my hobby of photographing people is an affront to Islam. I have been warned not to photograph any women, but the men actually seem to enjoy having their photos taken. That said, it is only common courtesy to ask first. At least that will keep you from getting shot. Maybe.

The ban on photography is but the latest in the long list of Taliban decrees, and the only one I had been particularly worried about. I am already a target, and being caught taking photographs would give the Taliban justification for administering a severe public punishment. They have also banned television, music, dancing, kite flying, and even the playing of soccer, which had once been considered the national game. To top off the list, they have forbidden the presence of females in schools, as well as the office and workplace.

There is nothing in the *Qur'an* that says females cannot attend school or work outside the home. In fact, a very high-ranking *Maulana*, who was to Muslims what the Pope is to Catholics, had actually written a decree on parchment, declaring that women could be educated, but that the classrooms should be separated for boys and girls. This decree is obviously not satisfactory to many Muslim "men in the street," and certainly not to most of the religious leaders of the country. The only purpose of the Taliban's highly restrictive decrees is to intimidate and to maintain control over the local population. "Official" enforcement might be limited, but there will still be victims who will be beaten, and others who will actually lose an arm or their head for even minor infractions.

Saleem also points out that you cannot be seen in possession of paper bags, on the remote chance that the paper is made from the recycled pages of the Qur'an, and the Taliban has decreed that only plastic bags or cloth may be used for carrying supplies or groceries. As he speaks, an odd thought crosses my mind. I fear having a hand or arm chopped off as punishment far more than I fear being beheaded, since the latter would be quick and rather final. In the latest example of Taliban atrocities in their efforts to control the local population, they take people whom they deem to be sinners to the roof of the highest home in the area and throw them off. They have also decreed in northern Pakistan that once you step off the road, you are now on tribal property, and subject to arbitrary tribal laws and "tribal justice."

Since tribal wars rather than the larger Pakistani war prevail in this area, we welcomed the escort that the Pakistani regular troops offered to us at the last checkpoint. Even with the troops' protection, I'm still glad that we had taken the opportunity to purchase more weapons when we stopped at Darra. (I hate to say this, but I couldn't pass up the bargain for the weapons. Like my wife Terry, I love a good sale, and besides, the price was right, and the purchases were duty free.)

I am a physician, sworn to reduce suffering, but I am also a human being, with a fully developed survival instinct. As such, I have come to accept the fact that if push comes to shove, I am going to go down fighting alongside my trusted companions.

Osama bin Laden's Financial Network

I look up as we continue our way along the pothole-riddled dirt road that they have the audacity to call a highway. Just as we pass the sign that says "Foreigners Prohibited Beyond this Point," Saleem tells me not to worry about it. "I have obtained the proper papers, and we can enter Swat Valley in the Northern Territories. We will have to show our passports and sign at the checkpoints, they will go through our papers, and we may even have to leave some money with the officers, but we will be allowed into the Northern Territories."

As we pass through a small village, I notice that there are some shops with sheep tails attached to the wooden posts out front, blowing in the wind. "Saleem, what's with the sheep tails?"

"They indicate there is hashish for sale."

"Is it really so commonly available?"

"Oh yes, you can buy it at any place. It is of a very good quality."

Mohammed misunderstands the intent behind my question and adds, "We can also get *khat* to chew on if you would like." He is referring to the centuries-old habit, in this region, of chewing the leaves of the plant *Catha edulis*. Though it can have euphoric effects, its everyday use seems to be chiefly as a stimulant, on the order of coffee or tobacco – although it is not as addictive as tobacco. I, however, am only interested in the fact that where so many things are forbidden, drugs are sold openly, apparently with little concern for reprisal. "Tell me more about it. It seems the Taliban have a ban on about everything else, but not on the use of narcotics!"

Just at that point we hit a particularly large pothole and my head strikes the unpadded metal frame on the top of the van. "That hurt," I grumble. I fully expect Mohammed to lose control as he swerves to avoid another rather large and deep gash in the road. And, as I look up, I see that there is another vehicle in the distance bearing down on us as we career along, still on the wrong side of the road.

I tap Mohammed on the shoulder, just to make sure he sees the rapidly approaching vehicle, and he nods his head, saying, "No problem," and actually speeds up, still in the lane of oncoming traffic. I can see that the other side of the road is riddled with large potholes, but he is playing chicken with the oncoming vehicle, which I can now see is an eighteen-wheeler that is making no indication of changing lanes. The rules governing which side of the road you drive on are an absolute mystery to me, and seem to be determined by the size of the holes and the fallen rocks that litter the road. Rules notwithstanding, with neither Mohammed nor the driver of the oncoming truck giving way, I am starting to get anxious. It seems that those traffic "rules" are dictated in equal parts by the amount of *khat* the driver is chewing (or how much hashish he smoked at the last stop) and the holes in the road. The headlights are almost upon us when Mohammed swerves to the right, barely avoiding another crater in the road. I can feel the wind from the tank truck as it shoots past us, never once slowing down. After eight hours of perilous mountain passes, switchbacks with no guardrails that dropped thousands of feet, and now this latest incident, I feel like a cat that has already used up its nine lives. It even crosses my mind for a moment that I might need to smoke some of that hashish if we're going to take many more of these country drives.

I take a deep breath and reiterate my question, "Are drugs really that readily available?" I know that the Taliban has always controlled narcotics, making them cheap and easily obtainable, but I also know that growing the poppy was officially banned in Pakistan and Afghanistan, and that the U.S. has been trying to introduce other cash crops to the farmers to help sustain them. Despite all the "official" efforts, however, the poppy has long been the best cash crop they have. Moreover, the illicit industry is being overlooked, not only by the U.S. military, but also by the Afghani and Pakistani governments in their attempts to bring the tribal areas and farmers under control.

Sultan is nodding off, but Saleem is warming to the subject and is quick to offer a lesson in recent history to help me understand how the drug trade has flourished. "In the late nineties, Osama bin Laden was in Sudan, where he had spent a large portion of his funds building roads, for which the Sudanese government never paid him. In actuality, the Sudanese government did not have the ability to pay for the project that bin Laden's company undertook, in particular the building of the 'Defense Highway' linking the Port of Sudan and Khartoum. In fact, the Sudanese treasury was empty. In addition to the road projects, Osama bin Laden had obtained some large land holdings, upon which he had built farms, where he was growing wheat and corn and raising thousands of head of cattle. I have friends who were at the camp where he had his administrative facility, and where he established training camps for Al Qaeda fighters. He was eventually forced to leave all of it, with a value of $200-$250 million behind. At about the same time,

I read in the newspaper that the Saudi government had closed a number of Osama bin Laden's businesses in their country."

I nod, telling him that in my travels, I have found that there is always a source, always someone who will do pretty much anything for political gain, money, or other favors to them or their family – in particular, for someone like bin Laden, who can pave their way to a new or more affluent life.

Saleem replies, "There are many who would trade everything they had for that. Sometime in 1997 or 1998, when bin Laden was forced to return to the area around Jalalabad, Afghanistan, he was penniless."

Perhaps the heat and the rough ride are wearing on my patience, and I respond testily, "Sorry to interrupt, but what does this have to do with the growing of poppies and the availability of narcotics?"

Saleem says, "I will get to that. Let me give you the history of what happened and how the drug trade becomes a part of the equation. Bin Laden was not affiliated with and did not trust the Taliban, but now he was penniless and isolated. In addition, the Mujahideen and other tribal fractions were fighting with each other for power. Bin Laden agreed to meet with *Maulana* Omar, and gave his pledge of allegiance (*bay'at*) to the *Maulana*. To support this pledge, he sent some of his men in arms to *Maulana* Omar in order to help him in his fight against the anti-Taliban Northern Alliance. There was also a rumor that bin Laden arranged a marriage between one of his daughters and the *Maulana*. We don't have any way to confirm this, and it may be just that – rumor. If nothing else, the gesture provided security for Osama bin Laden and Al Qaeda."

He gives me time to absorb that, and then continues, "Bin Laden's next move was to obtain a fatwa demanding the expulsion of U.S. forces from Saudi Arabia. This he obtained from Afghani and Pakistani scholars. In cooperation with his second in command, Dr. Ayman al-Zawahiri from the World Islamic Front, bin Laden successfully pushed for jihad against the U.S., Jews, and other international crusaders. Bringing everyone under a single umbrella for jihad was a particularly good political move. But there was still one huge obstacle to be overcome: how to finance the alliance."

Growing even more impatient, I blurt out, "Saleem, please get to the point. Tell me what this has to do with growing poppies and the production of narcotics."

He laughs off my impatience and continues, "I'm getting to it. But first, you need to know and understand the history. Osama bin Laden's resources had largely disappeared, his accounts in Saudi Arabia were frozen, as were all his funds in other countries in the Middle East and Europe. A large number of his dedicated followers and hardcore Al Qaeda soldiers were rendered inoperable due to this lack of funding. Osama bin Laden is smart, clever, and practical, and above all, he will seize any opportunity that presents itself.

"Bin Laden knew his ability to attract experienced militants and willing neophytes to his cause depended on the financial resources he could provide. Guns, bullets, and bombs are not the only way to fight a war."

Mohammed speaks up, saying, "I have heard of the Fatwa of Hezbollah. It states that if we cannot kill the infidels of Europe, Israel and the U.S. with bombs and guns, we will kill them with drugs. They say they are growing poppies to produce narcotics for Satan, the Jews, and the Americans. I have read this."

The proverbial light bulb flashes on in my mind. "I read something about this, as well; that the Afghanis and Pakistanis are selling 7 to 8 billion dollars worth of narcotics to the U.S. and Europe each year, and that bin Laden and his people are involved in the growing, processing, and shipping of these drugs to the west. My God! When Americans buy these drugs, they are funding his war!"

Saleem, looking relieved that we have caught up, says, "That's what I am getting to. I know people who grow the poppy, and young men who have been unemployed because of the war who have found employment in drug factories producing the narcotics that are being shipped to the U.S. That is how Osama bin Laden re-established his fortune and funded Al Qaeda and his holy warriors. I have heard that his estimated share of the 7 to 8 billion dollar per year drug trade is 2 to 3 billion dollars. I know the words, but I do not know how many dollars this is. Billion is a number I cannot perceive.

"American drug users are traitors to their country. They are unconcerned that they are funding the jihad, and that through their purchases, they are responsible for the next terrorist attack on America."

The light bulb in my head burns brightly now, and I exclaim, "So this is the dirty secret behind bin Laden's new billions... it's not his inheritance, it's not money from his construction company, nor is it the gifts from wealthy Saudis and other Middle Easterners who support his goals. These new billions are not coming from his investments in manufacturing, shipping, or oil, but from Americans and Europeans who are purchasing illegal narcotics."

I am so incensed by this that I feel like screaming, but manage to express my anger in a voice barely above a whisper. "Most Americans – if they knew this – would believe that heroin addicts in the U.S., and anyone who sells, processes, or participates in the manufacture or shipment of the drugs should be found guilty, not of breaking drug laws, but of high treason! And in a time of war, treason carries the death penalty."

Mohammed asks a simple but loaded and pertinent question, "Do you really think the U.S. has the balls to stand up to the drug trade with a death sentence?"

My anger turns rapidly to disgust at his words. "Even if it can be viewed as treason, our politicians or judges do not have the stomach to try those who are involved in the drug trade as traitors and sentence them to an immediate death before a firing squad. I know it might be politically impossible, but the only other choice would be to register the users and to regulate and tax the distribution the way it is being done in the Netherlands. This would serve to eliminate the ridiculously high profits, and slash billions of dollars from what we now spend on ineffective enforcement." Now I am getting warmed up to a topic that I think is worthy of serious consideration. I muse to Saleem and Mohammed that legalizing and regulating the drugs would save countless lives and significantly lower the incidence of crimes, since more than half of all criminal acts are driven either by the need for money to obtain drugs, or by conflicts arising during drug deals.

"As a physician," I continue, "I don't advocate making drugs more readily available, but it is something that needs to be looked at again. As I said, the only other reasonable choice would be to consider anyone who utilizes drugs or is involved in the drug trade a terrorist, and to proceed with a firing squad. There are some countries that have taken this approach, and by doing so have eliminated their drug problem. But we have to ask ourselves, at what cost to our society's commitment to freedom?"

It is Saleem's turn to grow impatient. "Please let me continue. You have not heard the whole story. We in Pakistan are part of the problem. A double standard now prevails within the Pakistani and Afghani governments. The religious police or Taliban, sticks and whips in hand, patrol the streets looking for violators of Islamic laws. Yet they walk right past the stalls of opium dealers, who are conducting business on every corner. Osama bin Laden and the drug lords become rich beyond imagination, and can be seen with their bodyguards in their expensive Land Rovers with bulletproof glass, driving through the streets with their entourage around them. Meanwhile the Taliban and religious police busy themselves with Islamic law violators, dragging them to the squares in front of the Central Mosques, amputating hands and beheading the imbeciles, but ignoring those involved in the drug trade. The Taliban, and its unification with Al Qaeda, see themselves uniting under the white flag of Islamic purity, with the aid of the pure white powder."

Mohammed adds, "Sheik bin Laden is looked upon as a great hero of the Holy War. He engaged in combat with Soviet soldiers and conquered them. He fought openly in many battles. It is said that the Sheik was struck by shrapnel and has earned his place under fire, not in the safety of the board room or conference room, as many generals do. Osama bin Laden actually took part in the conflict and risked his own life.

"What's more, he has used his own finances to recruit and supply thousands of fighters for the cause. It is well known here in Pakistan that bin Laden uses his engineering abilities and his construction equipment to build fortifications along the Pakistan border and dig tunnels that stretch through the Pakistan and Afghanistan mountains. In many people's eyes,

Sheik Osama bin Laden can do no wrong, and is becoming the greatest of the drug lords. What better way to poison the West than with these drugs? It is just another weapon in his arsenal."

I begin to truly understand the genius behind bin Laden's efforts. An evil genius, to be sure, but effective beyond the imaginings of his enemies, to say nothing of the average citizens who are his targets. Between the devastating effects of the drugs themselves in destroying lives in the United States and the unbelievable amount of money that filters back to him – money that he uses to finance the equipment and arms and training camps for those who attack the U.S. and our Allies – bin Laden wields an arsenal of weapons that inflict grave wounds that we don't even recognize. I find myself so overwhelmed by the realization that all I can say is, "WOW!"

Saleem brings me back to the discussion at hand, saying, "Heroin is openly distributed, and they even call it 'Bin Laden.' The package even has an advertising logo on it that has the crescent moon. You know this is the traditional symbol of Islam."

"I never put the two together: heroin packets with the crescent moon are prevalent throughout the United States, on college campuses, street corners, professional office buildings and definitely at rock concerts."

"What do they sell for in the U.S.?" Mohammed asks me.

"I heard as little as $20 and as much as $200, but they are sold in what are referred to as recreational packets of ten at a slight discount."

Mohammed is stunned, adding, "That's more money than most Pakistanis see in an entire year."

"That's why Osama bin Laden has billions of dollars."

Saleem and Mohammed look at me for further comment, probably wondering about the puzzled look I have on my face. I have to admit that some of what I have heard is new to me, but it is also congruent with information I already know. I have read articles and seen some mention of the U.S. forces trying to control the poppy growing in both Pakistan and Afghanistan. Their efforts have apparently met with little success, since the alternative crops they have tried to introduce to the local farmers don't bring anywhere near the kind of income they can make by growing the poppies.

Truly, I don't have an answer for my companions. All I can think of saying is, "The American public has not been made aware of the significance of the poppy growing and drug trade from Pakistan and Afghanistan to the U.S. and Europe, nor are they aware that the purchase of these drugs by Americans is funding Osama bin Laden and Al Qaeda."

But I know my response to my friends doesn't scratch the surface of this huge problem. It doesn't do justice to the awful reality that we as Americans are funding, however unwittingly, the insurgents who are killing our young men and women, and plotting destructive terrorist acts in the U.S. and abroad. Invariably our conversation turns to 9/11 again. I say, "Shortly, we will be observing yet another anniversary of September 11, and honoring those who have lost their lives and those responders who came to the rescue in New York City. I know this is an unpopular view in the U.S., but we Americans brought this upon ourselves. People in all areas of the drug trade – and yes, even the drug users – made it possible for this to happen. Not to mention the United States' long-time bumbling of our Middle East policies... There needs to be a wake-up call. Is our government really that dysfunctional?"

Osama bin Laden is a hero to many in this part of the world, but he is also a metaphor for the failed policies and arrogant shortsightedness of the Western world. It is almost incomprehensible that one man, intent on waging war on the Judaeo-Christian world, could finance such a massive undertaking. The Saudi government had revoked bin Laden's citizenship. The Saudi government and other countries around the world froze his assets. He had lost hundreds of millions of dollars and was expelled from Sudan. He relinquished any chance to claim all of this when he "disappeared" from the sight of the civilized world.

Bin Laden was beyond experiencing a severe financial crisis. He was broke. This should have been the end of his terrorist organization. But the U.S. and other Western countries funded him with billions of dollars through his drug trade. The call to jihad came not from minarets or mosques, but from the white powder borne from colorful poppy fields. Like everything else, he planned from the beginning to offer only the best. In this case, "best" means whatever will cause the greatest problems in America, while at the same time funding a war machine that kills the highest number of American troops throughout the Middle East. And bin Laden has been very successful, on both fronts.

Building a Heroin Network

Going with what little money he had left and could borrow, Osama bin Laden established labs that would produce high-quality heroin. Through his contacts, he formed a worldwide production and distribution network, availing himself of the services of local poppy growers, highly-trained but out-of-work and desperate Russian chemists, established Turkish drug dealers, and even Sicilian drug bosses. He knew that his first need was cash, as well as people – not Mujahideen soldiers, but trained chemists.

The first step was to gain some control over the poppy growing areas of Pakistan, Afghanistan and Iran, which had long been under the control of warlord Gulbuddin Hekmatyar. Because of the war, Hekmatyar had been forced to abandon many of these fields, and he gladly offered them to Osama bin Laden, on the hopes that the fields could once again be made productive and profitable for him. To keep his promise to the Turkish drug dealers and Sicilian mafia, bin Laden had to stop producing low-quality grade 3 heroin and construct sophisticated labs utilizing his Soviet chemists to produce Grade 4 heroin.[1]

The process of making tar heroin from poppies has been known for hundreds of years, but the final stage in converting the grade 3 tar heroin to the fluffy white Grade 4 powder was a more recent innovation, and is in great demand by the international drug market. That the process required sophisticated refinements and the talents of highly skilled chemists was no real obstacle for bin Laden, who had willing and capable individuals more than ready to assist him in addressing all aspects of the process.

To fully appreciate the enormity of the problem, it helps, I think, to understand what goes into producing heroin. Harvesting opium is a labor-intensive process, done by hand and requiring a degree of knowledge passed down by opium

---

[1] For a detailed description of the heroin production process, check out the United Nations Office on Drugs and Crime (UNODC) web page at http://www.unodc.org/unodc/en/data-and-analysis/bulletin/bulletin_1969-01-01_4_page002.html. The information is somewhat dated, having initially been published in 1969, but it describes a process that has gone virtually unchanged for centuries, and remains accurate in its representation of the growing and initial stages of the refinement process.

farmers for centuries. The preparation begins approximately two weeks after the petals fall from the poppy flowers, exposing an egg-shaped seed pod that darkens in color from green to brown. Once the seed pods are collected, each must be carefully scored to a precise depth, using a specially-shaped knife with three or four parallel blades.

At first, the extracted sap is a cloudy, white liquid, which turns dark brown and sticky when exposed to the air. The opium is now a resinous gum, still more water than actual opium, which is allowed to evaporate in the sun for a few days until it turns into a sticky, dark-brown, semi-solid "goo." As the evaporation process continues, the gum is hand-beaten into a stiff dough and formed into bricks that, when properly wrapped, can be stored for extended periods. The bricks harden and become more stable and potent as they continue to dry. Many of the farmers crush some of their harvested pods and soak them in warm water, which is then simmered slowly, producing a very crude form of opium that is kept for their own consumption, rather than being sold.

The opium that is to be sold is made by adding the extracted sap to boiling water, filtering the impurities and debris through a sieve, and then boiling it for a time to let the water evaporate. As the evaporation process continues, the substance becomes what is commonly called liquid opium. The process continues until all that is left is a thick, brown paste – Grade 2 opium, ready to be smoked. The opium is then pressed into molds and allowed to dry in the sun, eventually hardening into a brick that is easily transported for sale to addicts all over the world, or, in bin Laden's business model, ready to be further refined by his chemists.

Once in the chemists' hands, this opium is subsequently boiled in a mixture of lime and water, which causes the white morphine to rise to the top, whereupon it is siphoned off, simmered in ammonia, filtered, and re-boiled until it turns into a fine brown paste. Once this paste is dried in the sun, it becomes Grade 3 heroin. The final step involves mixing the heroin with ether and hydrochloric acid, a process that can – and frequently does – produce a violent explosion. When this happens, not only is the heroin lost, but so too are the laboratory facility and the lives of anyone nearby. It is at this stage of the refining process that the expertise of those Russian chemists becomes absolutely necessary, but despite their expertise and care, such explosions do occur frequently. In the drug trade, such losses are viewed as merely a cost of doing business.

The final steps consist of mixing the Grade 3 opium paste in glass containers with acidic anhydride for approximately six hours. This process turns the paste into diacetylmorphine. After six hours, water and chloroform are added to precipitate any impurities. Sodium carbonate is then added, which causes the heroin to solidify and sink to the bottom of the container. The sediment of heroin is further purified utilizing activated charcoal and alcohol. Then the alcohol is made to evaporate by applying heat. If this process doesn't cause another explosion (and it often does), what is left is the pure white Grade 4 heroin powder, which demands a price a hundred times greater than the Grade 3 heroin paste. Enough to fund an empire... or a multi-front war.

Osama bin Laden was a well-organized businessman, and within a few months of his decision to enter into the heroin business, a number of sophisticated production facilities were up and running. Bin Laden would rapidly become the biggest supplier of this highest grade of heroin powder in history, not only in Pakistan, but in the entire world as well. His many laboratory facilities would be kept busy twenty-four hours a day, seven days a week. It became well-known that bin Laden paid top dollar for the raw opium, and often offered bonuses to the opium farmers to sell only to him. As a result, many farmers stopped growing other crops altogether, and planted their fields in opium poppies. It was estimated that more than three thousand kinds of raw opium were being produced as the result of Osama bin Laden's incentives.

Osama bin Laden's income from his massive growing, production, and distribution network has been conservatively estimated at $10 billion to $15 billion in a year, making the few billion dollars he earned through the bin Laden Construction Company over many years almost insignificant by comparison.

And where did this money come from? It came mostly from the U.S. and Europe. The American and European addicts essentially became the primary sponsors of bin Laden's efforts to arm and train the holy warriors who battle the American and Allied soldiers in the Middle East, as well as funding his terrorist activities against the U.S. and other countries.

Statistics have shown that Europeans consume more than fifteen tons of heroin a year, roughly twice the amount that is consumed by American addicts. The average new addict spends approximately two hundred dollars a day to maintain his habit. To maintain this habit, many drug addicts turn to crime, further increasing the cost in dollars and lives on American and European citizens. The unexpected outcome of the attack on the World Trade Centers in Manhattan on September 11, 2001, which left bin Laden penniless, was that he was forced into a new business endeavor. And this was one that served his purposes more fully than his former activities ever could, by supplying him with a military budget – and the capabilities such a budget buys – that was greater than that of most countries.

As my companions and I discuss these matters, my mind is reeling at the enormity of the whole thing. Then Mohammed interrupts my thoughts, saying that although the transportation of the heroin is a risky job that takes one through the dangerous mountain roads, it pays exceptionally well. He shares how he and some of his friends had decided to make some quick, easy money by joining a truck caravan from Pakistan through the Afghan mountains, and then north into Iran. Once they had arrived in Iran, they were escorted by members of Hezbollah into Turkey, and from there they proceeded, either individually or in small groups via different routes, to Sofia, the capital city of Bulgaria.

In Sofia, Mohammed tells us, the drivers met with local agents who negotiated deals with Turkish merchants. Their actions were done right out in the open and with blatant disregard for authority, leading Mohammed to assume that they had official protection.

Mohammed says he was astonished that the dealers resided openly in Sofia, maintained flamboyant lifestyles, residing in beautiful villas, and could even be found as guests in government-owned housing. One of the favorite gathering places for the drug dealers, he tells me, was the posh Hotel Botschaft, where they could routinely be seen, openly negotiating deals in the opulent lobby or over dinner in the adjacent restaurant.

Mohammed continues, "My friends and I drove the Abkhaz heroin route, through the mountains from Pakistan to Afghanistan, then north to Tajikistan, continuing on to Osh in Kyrgyzstan, and ending in Chechnya. Some of the trucks in the caravan did not make it, and can be found in the bottom of some mountainous ravine, because they often exploded when they hit the rocks, and disappeared into the fast moving streams below. This is not the end of the trip for the heroin or its drivers, but it was definitely the most dangerous and difficult part of the journey.

"I watched them in Chechnya as they loaded the heroin into Mi-6 helicopters and Abkhaz trucks. The helicopters landed in the port city of Sukhumi in the Georgian province of Abkhazia. It was openly loaded onto Turkish ships that took the heroin to northern Cyprus.

"I did not continue on, but I have been told by friends that it is in Cyprus that the packaging plants operate. The bulk cases of heroin are broken down into small, more manageable packets that can be easily distributed throughout Europe and the United States."

I wonder aloud why anyone would want to become involved in such a perilous enterprise, but I already know the answer. Mohammed says, "Drivers are paid more money for a single trip than you could earn in years in Pakistan." But obviously it is not for the faint of heart. Mohammed adds, "Once your load was delivered, you were then on your own to find transportation home. I was one of the fortunate drivers to make it through the treacherous mountain roads to Dedensky Rayon and into Chechnya. At times on the journey, I gripped the wheel so tightly that the muscles in my hands and arms went into spasm. I kept downshifting and gently pumping the brakes, never knowing if a tire would rupture or the brakes would fail and I would lose control and fall to the canyon floor below. But the money was good!"

I say to him, "You could have taken all that money, bought a nice little home or farm or opened a shop and retired quietly."

Mohammed says "I was young and foolish, and after risking my life, spent the money foolishly. And now, I am your driver."

Our conversation returns to the larger problem. The drug trade has become a multi-pronged weapon for Osama bin Laden and Al Qaeda. In the eyes of Al Qaeda, Europe and the United States have become victims of their own decadence and corruption. The sale of the drug effectively undermines the enemies at home. Heroin addicts are not only self destructive, but are also the source of more than fifty percent of all crime, committed to maintain the several hundred dollars a day they need to fund their habits. This creates a long and ever-increasing cycle of problems, whose costs are beyond most people's imaginings. The ultimate outcome is that it provides the finances Osama bin Laden needs to become the greatest warrior in the world, and the most likely since the time of Saladin to unite all of Islam.

Saleem says, "Many believe that Osama bin Laden is well on his way to creating world Islamic domination and to bringing about the triumphant day of Islam, when it is said that all creation will fall in submission before Allah's judgment. With the billions of U.S. dollars, English pounds, and euros, Osama bin Laden could once again re-establish his training camps, and set up and control world-wide terrorist cells."

And some would say that there is an even more sinister twist to the story. In order for Osama to achieve his ultimate goal, the Nation of Islam would have to become a nuclear power. In the same manner that he was able to locate Russian chemists and entice them to supervise his heroin labs, bin Laden went first to his Russian connection to reach his next goal: to obtain several nuclear bombs, or the materials and scientists needed to make the bombs. More than fifty nuclear devices – both nuclear suitcase bombs and dirty bombs – had apparently disappeared during the fall and reorganization of the Soviet Union. It is thought that a number of these bombs found their way onto the open market, available for purchase by anyone who had the necessary finances. And thanks to his heroin operations, Osama bin Laden now had the money, and was eagerly seeking to purchase the bombs.

Mohammed tells me, "It is said that at least twenty of these suitcase bombs have been smuggled into the United States, and are in the hands of members of sleeper cells that have been told to marry non-Muslims, to use their skills to obtain well paying jobs, and to live like their neighbors in the inner city or in spacious homes in the suburbs. In order to fit in, they are told to attend Christian churches, and to be active in worship services. In addition to working as professionals, others have led exemplary lives in the American armed forces. They are told to respect their neighbors and abstain from tobacco, drugs, and liquor. If nothing else, Osama bin Laden and his secret cells nationwide have patience. There is no question of that. The American government must know about this, but won't make the information public, because it would cause widespread panic."

I am stunned by this revelation, and find my anger rising again. I say, "The fact that these nuclear devices have made it to the United States is merely another example of the failure of U.S. intelligence officials to follow up and share information. The nuclear devices are in the United States. The doomsday clock is ticking, and it's only a question of time before we learn the where and the when of our next September 11."

Mamoona's Story

I am haunted even today by a teenage girl I treated, named Mamoona Ghaffor. Mamoona, through no fault of her own, received severe acid burns to her face and upper body She was only thirteen years old on the 13th of August, 2002, the day before Pakistani Independence. She had gone to the market to purchase flags and some small colorful accoutrements with which to decorate her family's house in Korangi Town, a very poor suburb of Karachi.

Mamoona's father earned his living as a vegetable vendor. Each morning before the sun rose, regardless of the weather, he would push his wooden two-wheeled cart to the wholesale vegetable distributor to purchase vegetables. He would then maneuver the high-wheeled, heavily laden pushcart over the rough, unpaved streets, swerving to and fro to dodge the heavy traffic. Horns were always honking, and the autorickshaw drivers were constantly screaming at him, but he kept his head down and shoulders pressing forward as he moved along the street, back to his own neighborhood. It was a difficult life, with temperatures over 100 degrees in summer and near freezing in the winter.

During the rainy season, Mamoona's father would cover his cart with a plastic tarp, secured at the corners with elastic, and cover his head and neck with a rough woolen shawl. He would take off his leather sandals, placing them under the protective cover with the vegetables, and walk barefoot through the mud covered streets, trying to avoid the deeper potholes. He would roll up the bottom of his *shalwar kameez,* to his thighs, in an attempt to avoid soiling it with water and mud. When the days grew cold, he would drape a tattered lightweight woolen shawl over his shoulders to his waist. His was an arduous life, pushing the cart up and down the local streets where he had established many regular customers. He always greeted everyone he met with a friendly smile, in hopes of finding new customers and establishing long-term relationships with them. He desperately needed to continually increase his number of customers, as he had nine people in his family, in addition to his wife and himself, all living together in a two-bedroom house, with the boys and men sleeping in one room, and the girls and women in the other. The children were getting older, and the food, clothing and school supplies he had to provide were getting more expensive all the time.

Mamoona's family had held a family meeting, and it was agreed that they would rent one of the rooms out to provide some much-needed extra money. They knew the prospective tenant, and felt comfortable with the situation. The tenant was a pleasant man who paid his monthly rent on time. After living there for a time, however, the tenant told Mamoona's father that he was having some difficulty and would be unable to pay the rent that month. Being all too familiar with such difficulties, Mamoona's father told the tenant he could stay until the next month and pay his rent then. Two months passed, and then a third without being paid, at which point the father told the tenant that he would have to vacate the room at the end of the month.

The renter vacated the room, but not without taking unwarranted revenge upon the family who had been so patient with him. Before he left, the tenant repaid their kindness by throwing acid on thirteen-year-old Mamoona. Unfortunately, Mamoona was looking directly at him, unaware of his intentions as he suddenly shot the acid at her from a plastic squeeze bottle. The acid splashed not only across her face, but also in her eye, rapidly dissolving the delicate tissues and destroying the sclera. Her agony was unimaginable to most people, and as she screamed at the top of her lungs, the tenant quickly fled. Mamoona's father went to the police and reported the incident, but to no avail: the tenant had left Korangi Town for parts unknown.

Mamoona was taken to the National Institute of Children's Health (N.I.C.H.) in Karachi. Word spread quickly in Korangi Town of the attack on Mamoona Ghaffor, and a women's rights group that was particularly interested in trying to stop acid attacks on women focused on Mamoona. Group members came to the hospital to visit with the teenager and tried to bring her things to make her more comfortable. They were very supportive of the family, and had helped Mamoona's father report the attack to a policeman, who took down the information. The group's involvement generated a short-lived media blitz, in which newspaper reporters, as well as television and radio commentators, visited Mamoona at the N.I.C.H. and reported her story.

With this story now in the public's eye, the local politicians were not going to risk losing their own place in the limelight. Local representatives, and even the mayor, came to visit Mamoona at the hospital. Typical of politicians, they promised everything, then left and nothing was done. Mamoona's father had to return to work to support the family, and she was left to spend most of her time alone at the N.I.C.H., while her family had to return to their daily struggle to fend for themselves.

The National Institute of Children's Health is chronically over-crowded and understaffed. Patients typically line the hallways, and equipment and medications are at a minimum. Pain medication – when available – is always given to those with the worst burns, and what is left is administered to others with less serious injuries.

Because of her facial burns, and particularly the injury to her eye, Mamoona was brought to our attention upon our arrival at the N.I.C.H. in Karachi. On examining her, it was obvious that she had received little treatment other than the cleaning of the wounds and the administration of a woefully inadequate amount of pain medication. I immediately recognized that if there were to be any hope of saving her eye and treating her facial injuries, she would have to be brought to the Texas Medical Center in the U.S.

Through the House of Charity in Houston and with my support, Mamoona received a passport and was brought to the Shriner's Hospital in Galveston, and placed under the care of Dr. Robert McCauley. Immediate intensive and extensive care was provided, but her eye had been too badly damaged, and couldn't be saved. Ophthalmic and plastic surgery procedures followed, including replacement with an artificial eye which, even on close examination, was difficult to distinguish from her real eye. With that treatment completed, the limitations on her visa required that she be returned to Pakistan. For the time being, Mamoona had received the ultimate in plastic and reconstructive care. As she got older, perhaps in one or two years, she would be a candidate for additional procedures.

Dr. Agris with Mamoona, after she had multiple surgeries and the fitting of a prosthetic eye at the Texas Medical Center.

Upon Mamoona's return to her home in Karangi Town, her poor uneducated family was preyed upon by a group of people posing as representatives of a Human Rights Organization. They told Mamoona's family that they could take her to doctors in Germany for further treatment, but that she would have to turn her passport and valid U.S. visa over to them before they could make the necessary arrangements.

This of course is not necessary, and the request immediately raised questions as to the group's legitimacy.

Mamoona's friends and family and everyone in her neighborhood advised Mamoona and her parents against doing what this "human rights workers organization" requested. One neighbor said, "Do not close the door on your daughter by aligning yourself with these people who are posing as human rights supporters."

Mamoona's family members were even more adamant, telling her, "These people are imposters. They seem very convincing, but once they obtain your visa and passport, they will disappear."

The House of Charity and the medical team kept in touch with Mamoona and her family, as we try to do with all our patients. We too were immediately suspicious when we learned about the supposed human rights group and their demands. I have no doubt that this group would have taken what little money Mamoona's family had to offer and disappeared.

Because of her daughter's extensive head and neck burns, Mamoona's mother was told to shave her head to facilitate her treatment, as well as the healing process. Being bald only added to Mamoona's despondency. As one would expect, Mamoona was very miserable and spent most of her days isolated in her home, crying.

Her suffering was not limited to the physical pain resulting from the burn and her surgical procedures. People who suffer such injuries also feel devastating psychological effects. Being burned by the acid was bad enough, but being shunned by relatives, friends, neighbors, and schoolmates, and even the members of her own family, had to be overcome as well.

But Mamoona was a smart young lady with a very strong will, and she was determined not to let the burns destroy her life and rob her of any hope. In her heart, she knew she had to overcome this tragedy and move on.

Finally, her wounds had matured and she was ready for reconstructive surgery. Hashmat, through the House of Charity, brought Mamoona back to the Texas Medical Center, where she could be offered the reconstructive procedures that were not available to her in Pakistan.

By the time she came to Houston, Mamoona's hair had grown in. While she was undergoing her reconstructive procedures, she was taught to use makeup such as Cover Mark, and was provided with clothing that she could never heve been able to afford at home. At the same time, she was acquiring skills that she knew would help her to rebuild her life, among them learning how to speak, read, and write in English. This was particularly enjoyable to her, and she learned quickly, having a particularly good ear for languages.

Reconstruction of the facial area after a burn such as Mamoona had suffered is a demanding, multi-stage procedure, requiring planning, patience, and the very special skills of a dedicated plastic and reconstructive surgeon. As the procedures progressed, Mamoona's outlook on life improved greatly. Emotionally, she was a changed person, and she began looking beyond her disfigurement to a productive future.

Mamoona told me, "I want to continue my studies. I want

to become a nurse and help others who have suffered the way I have. I feel I have a special insight since I am a recovering burn patient myself."

Mamoona returned to Karachi, Pakistan a new person. Her stay with us in Houston went far beyond the surgical reconstructive procedures. While there, she regained her confidence and developed an outgoing, *I can do it, and nothing is going to stop me* attitude.

Mamoona is now enrolled in a three-year nursing program at the Indus Hospital in Karachi, Pakistan. A suburb student, she gets along well with her classmates and teachers, and at this writing, she is beginning her second year at the top of her class.

Mamoona has learned to speak English fluently, and writes to us all the time, telling us that she wants to join our program after she graduates. She hopes to devote her life to helping her fellow Pakistanis receive the kind of respect and care they so desperately need and deserve, but have for the most part been unable to get. She now sees a future much brighter than she – and so many others like her – would have ever dreamed possible. And I cannot even begin to express the pride I feel in her persistence, or the renewed sense of hope that her success has instilled in me. She is proof that under the right circumstances, tragedy can be turned into a "happily ever after" story.

If only it were possible for the stories of the many thousands of other girls who suffer such attacks every year to have the same kind of happy endings, or even better, for the attacks never to occur in the first place, and the joyful endings not be precipitated by suffering...

Unfortunately, the vast majority of young ladies who have found themselves the targets of acid attacks spend their days at home isolated, miserable, and crying. Being confined to the home, these burn victims are often relegated by their families to positions typically reserved for common maids, forced to do all the housework, cleaning, and cooking. Ashamed to appear in public, many acid burn victims will never get an education. Shunned by family, neighbors, and former friends, they have no future to look forward to, and no chance of getting married.

The attacks destroy not only the victim's own life, robbing her of any hope for something better, but also the lives of her entire family, which also finds itself in the position of outcast because of the "scandal" that led to the attack.

Far too many other young girls who have had their faces horribly disfigured develop into otherwise beautiful young ladies with very attractive figures. These young ladies are often sexually abused by predatory males in their own community or even their own family, and find themselves molested by former friends and acquaintances, or even their own fathers. Many of them eventually become pregnant and will have an illegal abortion performed. often dying as a result.

I am filled with outrage at the knowledge that such an end might actually be the most merciful outcome these young ladies can expect. I wish there was something more I could do for them. I think that a loud public outcry against such brutal attacks is what is needed, and we have worked toward this goal by holding numerous public press conferences. Education is an essential tool in overcoming the ignorance in which such attacks are based, and in elevating the status of women to a more reasonable standard of respect.

Under the right circumstances, tragedy can be turned around and a happily-ever-after story emerge from one of ignorance and hate. Mamoona's story is an isolated one, and I am incredibly proud of what she has done, but there remains much work to be done before the kind of tragedy she has overcome finally ceases to exist.

Khat:
Better Than Food?

ohammed, Saleem, Sultan, and I are traveling up the Karakoram Highway on our way to attend to patients in the tribal villages of the Northern Territory. A man named Saleh and his young assistant, Bashar, have hitched a ride with us. They are two men who are part of a culture within a culture that most people in my part of the world never hear about.

Saleh is a forty-six-year-old truck driver, a squat man with large, deep-set eyes and a hawk-billed nose. He is missing several front teeth, leaving a black hole that is prominently displayed when he smiles, which he does often. His hands are rough and stained with engine oil and grease, for he does most of the mechanical work to keep his forty-year-old lorry running. His gray vest and beige robe are in dire need of washing, and the top of his head is wrapped by a soiled and dusty looking black *keffiyeh*, the cotton headdress worn by many Arabic men. He is a man of the road, a truck driver and proud of it. He speaks Urdu, Pashto, some Arabic, and even Mandarin Chinese. He has a deep voice and usually talks slowly, but at times he slurs his words together in rough, rapid bursts that even my interpreter finds slightly incoherent. Before long we realize that this is because the truck driver's mouth is stuffed with *khat*.

After many hours on this rough and dangerous road, Saleh tells us that his home is in the canyon ahead, and asks if we can take him and his assistant the short distance off the highway. We agree, and decide to rest here, since it is one of the few places where we can maneuver our vehicle off the Karakoram and into the depths of a canyon, through which runs a swift and frigid stream of glacier melt. The canyon is lined on either side by nearly vertical granite walls, and there is no way out except upward along the narrow switchbacks that must be navigated slowly and cautiously to avoid suffering the same fate as the many smashed vehicles that litter the bottom of the canyon.

We stop beside the stream, and all of us pitch in, filling plastic water bottles from the river and pouring them into the overheated engine's radiator. After this is accomplished, we sit in the shade of the van, whereupon Saleh brings out a velvet pouch of small, soft *khat* leaves with reddish stems. Mohammed explains to me that the size and color of the leaves determine the drug's sweetness and potency, and that the *khat* that Saleh has is of the highest quality. Mohammed goes on to explain that a small pouch of this size costs the equivalent of twenty-five dollars, and can be consumed in a single night's chew.

Bashar takes some of the leaves, presses them between his fingers to form a ball, and stuffs the ball into his cheek. Saleh offers the pouch to Mohammed, Saleem, Sultan, and me, saying, "*Khat* is much better than heroin or hashish because it keeps you working. It gives me energy when I chew it. It keeps me happy, and if I don't have something to eat, there's no problem, as long as I have my *khat* to chew. All the drivers chew *khat* to keep awake and to alleviate their fears on this dangerous road. It keeps you alert and working."

Mohammed says, "But it is very expensive."

"Yes," Bashar concedes, "it takes up a substantial part of my income. I always ask myself, do I drive this dangerous route in order to afford the *khat*, or do I need the *khat* in order to drive this dangerous route?"

* * * * *

Khat – also called *quat, qat, gat,* or *miraa* – contains an alkaloid called cathinone that is released when the leaves are chewed. It mixes with saliva to form a chemical closely related to adrenaline, and produces an adrenaline-like high that keeps the user going, even when exhausted. In addition, it gives users a general sense of well being and increased sociability. With chronic or excessive use, however, users tend to become less sociable and restless, and often suffer from acute nausea.

For the lorry drivers like Saleh and Bashar, the greatest incentives for chewing *khat* are that it keeps them awake and alert, allowing them to drive these dangerous roads for longer hours and complete their journeys sooner. At the same time it provides them with a sense of well being that dulls the tension inherent in traveling through such a dangerous area.

In Pakistan's climate, it is possible to reap two harvests of khat a year, from which each acre will yield the equivalent of roughly four thousand dollars, approximately five times the country's per-capita income. Surprisingly, the attitude toward growing and using *khat* is very different from that which is typically felt about the cultivation and use of poppies and its derivatives. Few in the region are against the growing and use of *khat*, in marked contrast to the intense campaign to eliminate poppies altogether.

The official efforts to discourage the cultivation of *khat* have been limited to the offering of subsidies for the voluntary substitution of other crops. The program has been ongoing for well over a decade, with no success to speak of. In fact it wouldn't be an exaggeration to say that it has been a complete failure.

Bashar asks us, "What brings you to these narrow canyons, mountain ranges, and dangerous, inhospitable territories?"

Sultan looks up, finishes taking a sip of water from his plastic bottle, and says, "We are escorting Dr. Jousef Mohammed (my alias) to the villages, towns, and medical clinics in the Northern Territories."

Bashar warns us, "You need to be careful. There are deep divisions between the different tribes of the Northwest Territories. They fluctuate quickly between periods of seeming unity and being on the verge of war with each other."

Sultan reassures him, "The doctor has forged ties and received assurances from twenty-four warlords and tribal Sheiks as well as pledges of loyalty and safe passage."

Saleh nods his approval, saying, "The doctor must be a very rich man to be able to purchase that type of loyalty from the warlords."

"No! No! You don't understand. The doctor has operated on and treated thousands of children from the tribal areas, even from across the border in Afghanistan. The surgeries, treatment, and medicine are free. The doctor does not accept money for his services."

At this statement, Bashar and Saleh begin speaking rapidly together. Their chatter ends as abruptly as it began, and Saleh turns toward me, crosses his legs under him, and with outstretched hands he proclaims, "Dr. Angel! You are Dr. Angel! Everyone has heard the stories, but most of us do not believe."

Mohammed returns to the van and brings back several photo books with before and after pictures of the children from the Frontier Medical Center, as well as from the hospitals and clinics in Abbottabad, Jacobabad, Lahore, Lachine, Haripur, and other areas. As Mohammed turns the pages and explains the medical program to them, Bashar retrieves the pouch from his belt and places more *khat* leaves into his cheek. He then passes the pouch to Saleh, who in turn offers it to us. We politely decline and sip our water as we look through several of the photo books with them.

At first, I think that Saleh is settling into a state of euphoria from the *khat*, but as he speaks, I realize that he is actually engrossed in his own quite lucid thoughts. "This route takes you through dangerous, tightly knit tribal areas. They have arsenals of weapons and jealously guard their territory. They do not abide by the Central Government's court system or rulings, having their own tribal laws that rule on everything from property disputes to murder. Many say that with education and exposure to the outside world via the Internet and other electronic devices that are being introduced, tribal influences have weakened, and that some tribesmen have gradually rejected the idea of the supreme Sheiks' unquestionable authority. They say that the people's demands for individual basic rights and freedoms are growing.

"But this is propaganda spread by the Central Pakistani government. Do not let that fool you. Young men with AK-47s man roadblocks, looking for any excuse to use their weapons. They can be bribed with *khat*, money, and tradable merchandise. One of the drivers was threatened only a few days ago by several of these teenage separatists. He shot them. He and his assistant then removed the boulders blocking the road and continued along the Karakoram to Gilgit."

Bashar joins in, saying, "Islamist gunmen dressed in black patrol the region in trucks. Black banners fly from short poles on the backs of their trucks, proclaiming, *There is no other God but Allah*. On this route, you have Al Qaeda, the separatists, and tribal factions to deal with. Do not travel these roads at night, because doing so places you in great danger of being kidnapped, stalked by mercenary tribesmen, or shot at by Al Qaeda insurgents."

I uncross my legs and get up, stretching. "Thank you for that information. We stopped at a teahouse not long ago where everyone inside was dressed in black and armed with automatic weapons. Interestingly, a Pakistani military patrol also stopped at the same teahouse. The men in black remained inside while the military patrol ate outside the teahouse. When we stopped, the military patrol warned us that this was not a safe place. The situation changed when I showed the same photo books that you are now looking at to the men in black. Thirty minutes later, we were all drinking tea together."

Bashar responds, "Pakistan is a state of anarchy, torn by tribal, ethnic, and religious conflict. Its population is young and growing. There are many unemployed youths, which poses a threat to the country's stability. In addition, there are many Afghan immigrants who have fled their country to Pakistan and only add to the burden. Al Qaeda is still strong, and is recruiting new followers with promises of money and glory if these young men will take up the fight against the U.S.-backed Pakistani regular army.

"The attacks they wage are still common and can occur anywhere. Protests are frequent. We know there is collaboration between the tribes and Al Qaeda. There is always someone trying to mediate between the Islamic militants, the tribes, and the Central Government. Al Qaeda has demanded that the government withdraw troops from the northern provinces and Balochistan and enforce the law of the land – Sharia."

"Where Pakistan is concerned," I say, "it seems that many people are fighting a losing battle. After all, it is the *Islamic* Republic of Pakistan, a country founded on a religious constitution, not a democratic one. I think many people forget that, especially those in the United States State Department. Pakistan was not founded as a democracy, is not a democracy now, and it will not be a democracy in our lifetime." (I sense that I am about to get on my soapbox again, but once I get started, there's no stopping me.)

"In addition," I continue, "you have the strict social codes that regulate and control Pakistani women. Most women in Pakistan are uneducated, and are not given any choice. The only people we see on this road and most roads throughout Pakistan are men.

"I have spent five years traveling through Pakistan and it is my opinion that the majority of women fare poorly in regards to education, health, and economic opportunity. Fifty percent or more of Pakistani women are illiterate. Marriages are arranged with girls as young as twelve and thirteen years of age. Unlike men, women cannot get divorced. They have limited property and inheritance rights. Al Qaeda thrives in this environment. In addition, unmanned American drone attacks on suspected militants have killed many civilians in these villages. This has inflamed sentiment against the United States, and served to entice many young men from the tribal area to join Al Qaeda."

Saleh interrupts excitedly, exclaiming, "Yes, yes, you are right. The people see them as heroes. There will be a revolution here, and I think it will happen very soon."

Saleh and Bashar both have a limited education. They have not attended high school, much less a university. On the other hand, they did not grow up attending *madrasas* and therefore do not have significant religious convictions. What seems clear to me is that they are very knowledgeable about today's world.

Saleh says, "We work hard, provide for our families, and do not get involved in protests. My father made me promise him that I would not. My father speaks passionately for the need to eliminate government corruption and patronage, and to guarantee rights for women."

I smile as he speaks, knowing that this is what is in the hearts of many in the region, even if they keep their thoughts to themselves for fear of reprisals. "Your father is correct. You should abide by his wisdom and wishes."

Mohammed stands and stretches his legs, and appears somewhat anxious. "We really need to be going. I agree with the advice that Saleh has given us to be off this road before it gets dark."

We all shake hands, say our good-byes, and Mohammed, Saleem, Sultan, and I get into the van.

As we pull away, Bashar shouts, "Keep in low gear on all of the switchbacks. You will live longer that way."

He laughs and waves as we proceed up the road that will take us back to the Karakoram. And once again I think to myself how interesting it is that despite my having spent many years of my life in formal education and training, I've received some of the best education from some of the least likely and most poorly educated people in the world.

Attack: Terror on the Karakoram

I am visiting at the home of one of my patients, a small girl whom I have just treated. She lives just north of Mansehra, and I have brought her back to her home. Her family is deeply grateful for the care she has received, and they have graciously extended their hospitality to Mohammed, Saleem, Sultan, and me.

As I sip my tea in the single room that serves as sitting area and bedroom, the simplicity of the home and the lack of possessions only seem to reinforce the tight-knit family relations, and the love and caring, that I have seen expressed all around me. It isn't that the humble surroundings are lacking

231

in warm touches of color here and there. The wooden bed with the typical woven rope top is covered with a colorful quilt and a brightly colored blanket in red, yellow, and black with a white fringe. My little patient has pulled it all the way up to her neck and is clutching the small stuffed teddy bear that I had given her at the hospital. Her older sister is sitting on the bed next to her, gently running her fingers through her sister's hair and chatting. My patient is looking up at her sibling wide-eyed, and with a radiant smile. She is at home now with her family, and obviously feels safe in her familiar surroundings.

Saleem, Sultan, and Mohammed are having a lively conversation with the girls' father, uncle and several of the other men. But I feel like taking a walk, maybe taking some pictures. As I finish my tea, I place the cup and saucer on the small table to my left, pick up my camera, and walk outside the open door of the mud brick home. I take several deep breaths of the fresh mountain air as the cool evening breeze begins to build, chasing away the oppressing heat of the day. This remote site is off the Karakoram Highway, about one hour north of Abbottabad. I stop and gaze up at the mountains, watching the sun as it sinks in the west, casting a reddish glow on the terraces and ramparts of the snow-capped mountains. I can't help but wonder what this world looked like a thousand years ago, and then I realize that in the place where I am standing, the vista has probably not changed for the past thousand years.

Looking upward at the few stars whose numbers will soon grow rapidly in the darkening sky, I am lost in my own thoughts, when I am suddenly pulled from my twilight dream by Mohammed, who has been standing behind me. He gently places his hand on my right shoulder, bending his head low and whispering in my ear.

"We don't want to be on these roads after dark, it's much too dangerous. They have invited us for dinner, but we really need to be leaving as soon as possible. It's not safe to be traveling these mountains at night."

I think it odd that he worries less about the dangers in his work, which is fraught with the ever-present and very real likelihood of encountering gunmen in the mountains. This is a dangerous place, day or night. The thought is fleeting, however, and I know that he is right; it is time to leave. Together, we turn to re-enter the home to say our good-byes.

While Mohammed enters the building, I follow the narrow path to the left and turn the corner, where I untie the drawstring of my *shalwar*, exposing the large fanny pack that I have stuffed with a two-inch-thick bundle of well worn 100-rupee notes, my passport, and several credit cards. I am struck by the irony of carrying the cards, which of course are of no use in this part of the world. Perhaps they offer me a sense of familiarity, a reminder of the world in which I live when I am not wandering in this strange place. There is a second pouch in the pack, which is filled with coins. I count out twenty of the 100-rupee notes, and I roll them tightly in my hand. I know that this roll of bills is more than our farmer host can earn in several months. I carefully zip the pouch closed and tuck it back into the *shalwar*, pulling the drawstrings tight and securing them in a snug bow. Then I retrace my steps along the narrow path, returning to the entryway of the house.

Mohammed, Sultan, and Saleem are shaking hands with the men, apologizing for not being able to stay, and promising that we might be able to return at the end of the week. I shake hands with the uncle and cousins, and as I turn to shake hands with the father, he grabs me in a bear hug and kisses me on both cheeks. Returning his embrace, I discreetly press the money into his left hand.

He immediately throws up both arms, saying emphatically, "*Jee nahee-nahee*" – a respectful "I cannot accept!"

I hold the money out and say, "This is not for you, but for the child and for the medication she will need." He continues to refuse, protesting that I have done enough already.

In keeping with tradition, I hug him and kiss him on both cheeks, then ask his permission to say good-bye to my patient and thank his wife and the other ladies for their hospitality. He says he has no objection.

I walk several feet to the bed where the child is now lying next to her sister. I kiss her gently on the forehead and tuck the covers in and around her. She looks up with her big beautiful eyes and smiles. Her hands quickly fly from under the covers, and she gives me a big hug around the neck. I take this opportunity to press the money into her little hands and fold her fingers around the roll of bills, and then to place her hands back under the covers. I press my fingers to my lips, letting her know that this is our little secret. I tuck the bedding around her and with a conspiratorial wink to her and her sister, turn to leave the room. As I turn, I hear her whisper very faintly, "*Shukriyaa*." ("Thank you.")

I quickly wipe away the tears that are welling up in the corner of my eyes and I exit the room, walking carefully along the edge of the narrow path to the adjacent buildings. There are six women and two young girls sitting cross-legged on the dirt floor. A small wood fire crackles beneath a kettle, scorched black from many long years of use.

I lean into the doorway, smile at them, and say, "*Shukriyaa-mehrbaanee*." ("Thank you; special thanks.")

They are all dressed in colorful saris, and while most of them have their heads modestly covered, their smiling faces are exposed. The eldest woman, whom I assume to be the grand-mother, is looking at me as I hold up my camera and point it at the women, waiting for their permission to photograph them.

There is a short conversation among them, and the elder turns to me and gives her consent. This is an honor and a rare opportunity, to be allowed to photograph the ladies, especially since they have their faces uncovered. I take several photos and thank them.

I turn from the doorway and walk down the narrow path that winds its way along the edge of a small lake. Mohammed, Sultan, and Saleem are already standing out front, and they begin their descent, repeatedly looking back to make sure I am not having trouble climbing down the narrow steep path that leads to the first terrace below the dwelling.

As we come out onto the first terrace, the path becomes much flatter and easier to navigate. I pass a small herd of goats that only look up for a few seconds before returning to their grazing as I continue making my way down the path to the next terrace. I turn and look back up the path, and see the entire family standing along the ledge in front of their home. The father is holding my little patient, and they are all waving. I wave back, then pull the camera from my shoulder one more time and take several pictures.

I cross the next grassy terrace and come to an irrigation ditch. There is a line of rocks in the ditch, which I assume are intended as stepping stones, but I can see that they are wet and slippery, and I decide that it would be better if I just jump across. Beyond the ditch, the narrow path continues sharply downward. There are several mud huts along the path, with a group of children laughing and playing outside. I wave to them, they wave back, and we continue our hike downward across the terraced fields to the dirt road below, where the van is parked.

* * * * *

We are in Taliban country, and Mohammed, Sultan, and Saleem repeat the warning that we need to be out of the mountains and onto the Karakoram Highway before the sun sets. New and even harsher edicts have been issued recently by the Taliban – among them, a decree forbidding men to measure women for clothes. All fashion magazines are to be destroyed, and women are not to be allowed to use paint on their finger-nails or toenails. In addition, it is forbidden to take snapshots of friends – particularly women. Even inviting a foreigner to one's home for tea will give rise to suspicion, and could result in far-reaching consequences. Interestingly, the only exception is for medical care, and everyone in this village knows that I am the doctor – not just a doctor, but the "Crazy Texan" / "Dr. Angel." Still, I don't want to take any chances.

Moreover, we are in the Northern Territories, in the tribal area of the Pashtun, who follow a different social code than that which the Taliban is trying to enforce. The Pashtun give the tribal *jirga* or grand council the authority to make judgments based on their traditional laws, especially in situations regarding medical care, the treatment of strangers or guests, ownership of land and cattle, and so forth. This unwritten code of ethics is referred to as *Pashtunwali*, and has been followed for hundreds if not thousands of years. The line between *Pashtunwali* and Sharia law has always been blurred, with variants of the two codes being followed in greater or lesser degree across the Pashtu belt. Unlike the Sharia, however, *Pashtunwali* does not aspire to govern the practices of other ethnic groups. The Taliban's desire to force Sharia law on the Pashtun has only served to deepen the ethnic divide between them.

Sultan lags behind to make sure I am okay, as Mohammed gets into the van and starts the engine. Saleem is already riding shotgun when I reach the side of the van and plead with him to sit in the back with Sultan, so I can photograph the mountains as we descend to the Karakoram Highway below. We have had this conversation many times before, and I know he has my safety in mind. As he has done on previous occasions, he partially acquiesces, saying that after we descend the mountains to the Karakoram, we will trade places before continuing the long ride back to Abbottabad. I nod in agreement, and the four of us ride in silence the rest of the way down the steeply graded road, until we reach the bottom. Just as Mohammed opens the door so we can change places, a huge Pashtun tribesman suddenly appears from the bend in the road. He has enormous feet and hands, a long thick nose, black eyes, and a bushy, unkempt black beard that extends to his abdomen. His sheer size and imposing manner would generate fear in anyone.

He stands on the side of the road looking up at us, a carved wooden staff in his left hand. Suddenly two small children in colorful tribal outfits appear, and it is apparent that they are picking wildflowers along the side of the road.

Saleem, the ever-alert bodyguard that he is, has already moved toward the front of the van and assumed a protective stance. I sense that Sultan is on full alert as well, ready to spring out of the van at a moment's notice. I step to the right of Saleem, flashing my best smile and pointing to the children. The tribesman smiles back. As the children look up, I wave to them and point to my camera. The tribesman scoops up the little ones in his huge hands and turns towards me with a big smile, saying, "A *salaam Aleichem*." ("Peace be with you.")

Saleem answers him back, "Peace to you as well."

I again point to the camera. The Pashtu tribesman says, "*Pakhair*." ("Welcome.")

We exchange a little small talk, and then he asks where we are headed. I tell him we are headed to Abbottabad and the Frontier Medical College, and again I point to the camera.

He says, "*Khey*," which means, "Very good."

I then take some photos of the children and tribesman in their colorful outfits. I press the buttons on the back of the camera and show them the series of photos. The children giggle and point to the screen as I run through the photos for a second time. Then I thank him and we exchange polite goodbyes.

Mohammed is waving at me to get into the van, and Saleem is already sitting on the back seat next to Sultan; both men have their weapons across their laps. I slide into the front seat and out of habit reach for the seat belt, which of course is not there. The door rattles as we start down the mountain, so I open it and slam it shut, but I am still not sure that the latch has actually caught. Not wanting to risk falling out of the van as it hurtles down the mountain road, I shift my weight toward the center of the vehicle, away from the door.

Plumes of white dust rise in the air along the narrow ribbon of the battered mountain road as we make our way down to the Karakoram Highway that runs from Mansehra in the north to Abbottabad in the south. I shiver a bit in the chill of the evening air, and wrap my recently-purchased woolen shawl around my shoulders. I place one of the cameras on my lap and the other at my feet.

And then...I don't know why...a cold chill that has nothing to do with the evening air suddenly goes through my body. I lift the M-4 rifle from the floorboard and place it across my lap. I feel marginally better.

As we continue down the mountain, I catch the image of a young boy sitting on a stone a wall, apparently doing his homework. I tap Mohammed on the shoulder to get him to slow down a bit as I take some photographs through the open window. As we continue further toward the valley, we come upon an open field where about a dozen teenagers are playing cricket. I again place my hand on Mohammed's shoulder, and when he slows to a crawl, I lean out of the window and spend several minutes photographing the cricket game. Then we proceed down the road once again.

A bit further along, Mohammed gears down for a rather steep incline to the main highway. I adjust the M-4 on my lap so it will not slip, and place my Nikon with the 200-millimeter lens on top of the weapon. The terrain levels as we travel west, approaching the floor of the Kaghan Valley. The road intersects with the Karakoram Highway just north of Mansehra. We turn south where the Karakoram Highway skirts Mansehra. The road is only one lane in each direction, filled with a seemingly endless procession of small buses, donkey wagons, and motorized three-wheeled rickshaws that skirt in and out of traffic with no apparent regard for the presence of other vehicles or pedestrians. We also find ourselves sharing the road with severely overloaded sixteen-wheeled lumber trucks coming from the Northern Provinces and as far away as China – all headed for Abbottabad and areas further south. I can see from Mohammed's face that he is not happy with the traffic, but secretly I am pleased because it forces him to drive slowly, giving me the opportunity to take more photographs. I keep thinking that Mansehra, with its rich mix of Pashtun, Punjabis, and Kashmiris, will be a great place for people watching.

We continue south along Shinkiari Road, passing through Old Town and the Bazaar area. In the slow-moving traffic, Mohammed is able to get directions from a local rickshaw-taxi driver, who tells us to continue past the mosque, and we will eventually connect with Abbottabad Road. We are told that there will be another mosque to our left as we continue south.

Other than the large library and bazaars, Mansehra is little more than a major transportation junction along the Karakoram Highway as it winds its way to Abbottabad, Rawalpindi, the Kashmir, and the Swat Valleys. Saleem informs me that there are three granite boulders on the north side, known as the Ashoka rock, upon which the Mauryan King Ashoka had ordered the carving of fourteen edicts in the Third Century B.C. E. The inscriptions were written an ancient Kharoshthi script, and dealt with morality, moderation, tolerance, compassion, and the leading of a respectful life. I find myself wondering at the interesting dichotomy between the ancient teachings and the present state of warring mountain tribes and recently imposed Taliban influence.

We pass the Kashmir Bazaar, where almost anything can be purchased, then slowly cross the bridge along Jaffar Road, which passes the smaller but older Neelam or Jerah Bazaar. The pungent smell of charcoal fires and roasting meat begins to fill the air, stirring my appetite, but common sense tells me that this is not the time or place to be stopping. We are still determined to continue south and reach Abbottabad before the sun has completely set.

About a kilometer further south, we enter the Karakoram Highway and leave the traffic of Mansehra behind for an open road where the traffic moves much faster. I decide to pass the cameras back to Saleem so he can put them back in their protective cases and drop them into the storage area behind his bench seat. As I am handing him the cameras, I glance out the back window and can see flashing lights moving very fast behind us and gaining on us rapidly.

I tap Mohammed on the shoulder and he nods and points to the mirror, indicating that he has seen them as well. Sultan shouts over the noise that it is a military transport convoy. I holler for Mohammed to find a spot where he can pull over to the side of the road as quickly as possible. He nods, saying, "I see a wide place in the road, just before the curve that is coming up."

Mohammed begins to slow down, and eases the van onto the outer edge. I am nervous and anxious. I click the M-4's safety, then pull back and release the slide, chambering a live round. Wrapping the M4's sling around my right hand, I take my shawl and drape it over the weapon so it will not be visible when the convoy passes. I can hear Saleem and Sultan in the back seat doing the same with their weapons.

The lead vehicle is a Jeep with a .50 caliber machine gun mounted in the bed. As it speeds by, I can see two men in the cab and four men sitting on either side in the back, their shawls wrapped over their heads and around their faces. Only the eyes are visible, protecting them from the wind and the chill of the evening. Several large canvas-covered trucks with camouflage paint suddenly appear and thunder past, kicking up gravel with their large deep-treaded tires. The canvas drops covering the rear of the trucks are flapping in the wind, and I can see men sitting on wooden benches inside as they pass. There are also stacks of crates full of what look to be ammunition or explosives filling the trucks, almost to the tops of the canvas covers. Every truck in line is tailgating the truck in front of it, with only a few feet separating each one.

Mohammed has only just pulled the van back onto the road when another Jeep with its .50 caliber machine gun comes alongside of us and then zooms past. Mohammed downshifts, grinding the clutch. The wheels spin, spraying gravel until we reach the more compact roadway, where we can get up to speed.

At last Mohammed says, "This is good. We have a military escort. They are going into one of the many military depots in Abbottabad, and we can follow them." He increases his speed until I can clearly see the Jeep that is bringing up the rear of the convoy. At this point, my earlier worry deepens.

"Mohammed, I don't think this is a good idea. They could misinterpret our intention and think we are attacking them. Also, if the convoy is attacked, we are so close now that we will be just another target and won't have a chance to escape. I realize that being close to the convoy could work in our favor, but I'm not comfortable with it. Please slow down and drop back a few hundred meters."

From the back I can hear Saleem say, "The convoy is good. This is the most dangerous road in the world. Where Karakoram meets with the Grand Trunk Road outside of Abbottabad, more people die every day. The convoy is a good thing!"

Nodding, I reply, "Okay, the convoy is a good thing, but let's be safe and drop back so that we don't give the wrong impression, and so we'll have time to respond should the convoy be attacked."

Mohammed begins to slow down, and I am intently staring out the front window for any sign of trouble. It looks as if we are in the middle of nowhere. The only signs of civilization are a row of several dark mud huts to our left and a rutted buggy path beside the road. A wooden donkey cart rests against one of the huts, and several donkeys are tied to a stake beside it, eating their evening meal from a large bucket.

We are passing through a narrow gap in the mountains, which are actually rolling foothills that lie beneath the peaks. On the left, the lane is flatter and more uniform. The wind whips relentlessly, scattering a gray mix of powdered dry sand and salt across our windshield. As I look further down the road, I feel sorry for the men sitting in the open Jeeps being subjected to this.

I glance over at the speedometer and see that we are moving quite fast, a mile a minute. We are now about a hundred yards behind the convoy. Suddenly there is an explosion up ahead that nearly blinds us. And then there is another, so close that it rocks the van. The sky begins to glow red, and the redness grows brighter and brighter until it literally overwhelms the daylight. I can barely see the road. We are still moving at more than a mile a minute and closing the distance between the convoy and us much faster than I like.

Mohammed begins tapping the brakes so that the gravel will not cause us to spin off the road and careen off the side of the mountain or into the ditch on the other side. As the dust clears, we can see flames reaching towards the sky, illuminating the road ahead. The van is beginning to slow, its tires digging in noisily as it gains a grip on the loose gravel road. A machine gun begins to fire, and is answered by flashes from small arms fire from the hills to our right.

We are now within fifty feet of the Jeep, which is slowly moving forward. The men in the back have thrown off their shawls and are preparing their machine gun for action when another IED detonates, lifting the Jeep off its wheels and flipping it into the ditch at the side of the road. And that is the last memory I have for the next few minutes, as the blast is so strong that it throws me against the door, which gives way, whereupon I am flung violently to the road, landing on my shoulder and right hip.

From there, I can see our van tipping on its side – still moving forward – and I can hear the sound of metal grinding on the road. The exposed undercarriage of the van is facing me as it continues along the road, its outer wheels spinning in mid-air. The van finally comes to rest about twenty yards south of where I lie, wheels still spinning erratically. All I can think of is Mohammed, Sultan, and Saleem, who are still in the vehicle... and the sound of heavy machine gun fire echoing through this narrow valley. I realize that the lead Jeep with the .50 caliber machine gun is answering the attack.

We are not the target, but we were too close to the convoy, and hurtling along at sixty miles an hour, we couldn't stop quickly enough. We came right into the field of fire. It was the blast of the last IED that had flipped our van on its side.

The flashes are all coming from the west, leaving me exposed in the middle of the road: not a good situation. It is really only then that I fully realize that I have been thrown clear, but the M-4's sling is still wrapped around my right forearm. With my thumb, I press the safety to off. I can see flashes along the hillside, but the attackers are well hidden in gullies and behind rocks. They are not after our van, and I think that perhaps by avoiding conflict we can get out of this alive.

I pull my shawl over the M-4 and lie very still. It occurs to me that there might be a sniper with a scope in the hills, and if I get up, I will be an easy target. Then I quickly remember that the small groups of rebels are not trained as snipers, and usually rely upon IEDs and small automatic arms to disrupt the local military and convoys such as this one.

I wiggle my toes, move my knees, and arch my back slowly to determine whether I have been injured, and if so, how badly. Everything seems to be working. I am sore from the jolt of being thrown from the van to the road, but that is wearing off as well.

Just as I am planning my next move, a machine gun opens fire from the roof of one of the mud-huts on the west side of the road, strafing the overturned vehicles. Bullets are bouncing off the undercarriage and then multiple explosions follow as the ammunition that the truck was carrying detonates. The canvas top is aflame and the tires are burning. A think black plume of acrid smoke fills the air, and as the wind gusts through this narrow passage, it blankets the road. I hold my breath with each gust, for the smell burns my nose and throat, but as each cloud of smoke clears I take another breath.

The clouds of smoke are actually working to my advantage. As they blanket the road, I gradually begin to move myself towards the rear of the van by digging in my heels and pushing myself along with my elbow. I am still afraid to get up and make a run for it, lest I expose myself to the continuous small arms fire that comes from the west side of the road. Explosion after explosion tears into what is left of the supply trucks, and flaming pieces of canvas and hot metal fly through the air. The ground shakes as I inch my way across the road toward the rear of the van. The sound is deafening, and the sand and dirt are kicked up along the road only inches away from me as the machine gun to my west begins strafing the road again. I do not return fire as I do not have a target, and don't want to draw attention to my position, exposed as I am on the open road. I say a prayer, not just for myself, but for Mohammed and Saleem and Sultan as well, and continue to inch my way across the road toward the rear of the van.

Then I hear two explosions back to back; they are different from the sounds I've heard from the ammunition in the supply trucks. Perhaps, I think, it is a hand grenade or a rocket grenade. After that there is silence – no firing from the heavy machine gun mounted on the Jeep that was the lead vehicle in the convoy. There are no more flashes along the hillside to the west. The flames shoot skyward, and there is black smoke still blowing along the road with each gust of wind.

The sun is setting now, producing an eerie glow. Then, as if on command, small arms fire begins to strike the vehicles in the road. Dust and sand are kicked up all around me, and suddenly I feel a hot burning sensation in my lower abdomen. I have been hit. The pain is sharp at first, and then everything seems to go numb. I reach up under my shawl and press my hand against my abdomen; I am bleeding. I maintain the pressure for several minutes and then withdraw my hand, surprised that there isn't more blood present. I move my feet and wiggle my toes. Everything seems intact and functional. Notwithstanding the pain and sudden feeling of nausea, I am more alert than ever, my adrenaline pumping.

I begin to think that maybe it wasn't a direct hit after all, but just a ricochet. Concerned with my own condition, I am not paying much attention to my surroundings, until I suddenly realize that all is quiet again. The firing from the hills and the rooftop to the west of the road has ceased. This is more worrisome. I have seen too much in my time in Pakistan, and have heard too many horror stories, to be reassured by the sudden stillness.

My mind reeling, I shout out for Mohammed, Sultan, and Saleem, but there is no answer. Perhaps they escaped the van, but the explosions still coming from the supply trucks have prevented them from hearing me. Maybe they are still in the vehicle, injured or unconscious. Based on all of the reports that I have seen, I know our attackers will be coming, and soon. And I know what they will do.

They will shoot the wounded and rob the dead of money, rings, watches, and any weapons or supplies they feel they can use. They will even remove clothing. Mutilation of the bodies and beheadings have been reported as well, and I know these are possibilities – not pleasant thoughts at all, but this is reality.

My nausea passes, but the burning sensation persists. I reach down with my left hand and am surprised that there is still a minimal amount of bleeding from my lower abdomen. At this point, that is the least of my concerns. I dig my heels into the gravel and, using my elbows, I continue to inch my way across the road and toward the rear of the van, which, though lying on its side, appears to be intact.

Though it seems like hours, all of this has taken place in just a few minutes.

I see a group of men moving toward me, walking along the road, outlined by the flames from the burning vehicles. My weapon is still covered with the bloodstained shawl; I double-check that the safety is still off. I lie motionless, playing possum. I can now hear voices and laughter; the men are celebrating their success. Another gust of wind arises, and a black cloud of smoke passes over me. As it clears I can see three men walking down the road in my direction.

They are young, perhaps in their twenties. The man to my right has his weapon slung over his shoulder. The one in the middle is a few steps in front of the other two, almost skipping down the road, showing off to his comrades. He is waving a sword and making slashing motions as he prances down the middle of the road. The third man, relaxed to the point of complacency, is carrying his weapon casually in his right hand, extended at his side.

Now they are about fifty yards away. The sun is at my back and low, which means that it is glaring right in their faces, almost blinding them as they approach me. This is very much to my advantage. I don't move, but just let them continue in my direction in their jubilant, acting-out manner.

Then I hear the crunching sound of footsteps on gravel in the ditch to my right, where the Jeep had gone off the road during the attack. I am hoping that some of the soldiers in that Jeep have survived and are working their way from the ditch to the road now that the attack has ended.

And then I see him. He is not a friendly. He is probably checking the status of the soldiers who were in the Jeep when it was blown from the road, and most likely scavenging their bodies for money, watches, and anything else he can find. He is slowly and carefully moving along the ditch, and I can only see him from the waist up. Then he steps out of the ditch onto the road, turning his head towards the other three, who are just a few yards behind. He is facing away from me, and I notice the .50 caliber machine gun sitting on his left shoulder. The tripod is still attached and visible in the front. His left hand is gloved, but the fingers have been cut away to allow for dexterity, while the gloved palm protects his hands against the heat of the weapon. He is holding the barrel.

Typical of the Taliban, his *thobe*, or gown, is cut short above the ankles, and he wears a black headdress, secured by a rope ring. I can see his face clearly; his mustache is nothing more than a shadow across his upper lip, but his beard is full and extensive. The Taliban has adopted this way of dress and grooming because it is said in certain Hadiths (traditions) that the Holy Prophet was similarly attired and trimmed.

Above all, these men are utterly fearless and brutal in battle, having no qualms about shooting the wounded, beheading their enemies, and removing other bodily parts. These are all fear tactics, and they work. The Taliban fighters are notorious for giving no quarter, sparing neither young boys nor old men: they are veritable messengers of death from whom no one escapes. And they are known for being completely fearless of death, believing that in death they will join Allah in Paradise. And so, not caring if they fall, they dance upon their enemy with only one goal in mind – annihilation.

The man I am watching now is apparently signaling to the group that is approaching him from the south. It is now clear to me that he has looting on his mind, for in the hand that is not on his weapon he is holding up several wristwatches and a satchel, which he must have removed from the men in the disabled Jeep. While his attention is thus diverted I move my head slightly so I can take in the road and the hills on the west side, from which the convoy took fire. I do not hear or see any others. Surprisingly, no other traffic is on the road; I am wondering if the road has been blocked at its northern or southern ends so that other travelers, upon seeing the flames and explosions, might have a chance to turn their vehicles around. I am hoping someone has reported the attack.

Now the men are talking loudly among themselves and not paying any attention to me. I shift my eyes rapidly from right to left, taking in as much as I can as quickly as possible, but there are still only four men on the road. Occasionally the younger man glances back over his shoulder, but none of them seems particularly concerned. Their pace is leisurely and relaxed.

The man with the machine gun on his shoulder is short, with broad shoulders and dark hair. I surmise that he is in his late thirties or early forties, and is easily the senior of the group. I can now see that he wears narrow frameless glasses propped halfway down his angular nose. He seems to be the one in charge. He has a lean face, and even though he is relatively young – and in a more privileged world would be considered to be in his prime – his face is lined and hardened by life. On his feet he is wearing what appear to be tan sneakers, or possibly a stolen pair of combat boots.

The young man closest to him is not more than twenty years old. He has a short beard and mustache with a ruddy, pockmarked complexion. His dark gray *shalwar kameez* is dirty and stained, and he wears sandals. The young man who was twirling the sword is thin and tall, with a narrow face and deep-set, narrow eyes. He is wearing a dirty light-colored *shalwar kameez*. Now he is speaking loudly and gesturing with his hands, capturing the attention of the others, who periodically laugh at his antics. The one who keeps looking over his shoulder is the youngest and shortest of the group, and is also very thin.

The men continue talking to each other and begin moving leisurely forward, now glancing at our van, which of course is still lying on its side, its wheels occasionally spinning as the wind gusts down the narrow confines of the road. They are entirely too interested in the van for my comfort.

My abdomen is burning, the adrenaline still pumping as I contemplate my options. But all of my contemplation ends abruptly when sounds of movement come from the van. The group turns as one towards the vehicle, and I immediately roll onto my right side, pressing the M-4 against my shoulder and digging my elbow into the dirt for additional support. I am painfully aware that if that one fellow gets the machine gun off of his shoulder, I won't have a chance.

There is no time for thought. I must act, or I will die.

Aftermath of Attack on the KKH

As the man with the machine gun manages to get the weapon off of his shoulder and begins to raise it into firing position, my chosen action is immediate and instinctive, and supersedes any intellectual or moral constraints I might have. I know that if I hesitate for even a split second, I won't stand a chance, and neither will my friends. I fire a three-round burst into his chest, and then shift towards the closest of the three Taliban. He takes several lunging steps towards me, with his sword taking the full blast from the M-4. The youngest man has his weapon in his right hand and is bringing it to his shoulder when I fire, taking him

257

down. The remaining combatant is attempting to un-sling his weapon from his shoulder, and is simultaneously turning as if to flee. I swing my weapon in an upward arc as I fire; my three-round burst hits him first in the chest, then in his neck and head, and he crumples lifeless to the ground.

My eyes scan the road, the ditch, the mud huts to the west, and the rolling hills, fully expecting to see more enemies bearing down on me. When there is no answering fire, I breathe a sigh of relief. The adrenaline is pumping madly as I take the chance of pushing myself up onto one knee and fire a series of bursts into each of the fallen combatants. At this moment, I am not Doctor Angel, but a messenger of death. I will escape this ambush injured, but alive.

Using the M-4 as a crutch, I work my way over to the van and pound on the back door, yelling, "Saleem!" "Mohammed!" "Sultan!"

I am filled with relief when Saleem shouts, "The door is stuck. I will try to kick it open, stand back." I move to the side away from the door, still scanning the surrounding hills and roadside for movement, but seeing no one. The sun has almost set, and there is no moon. The road is dark, save for the flames still shooting skyward from the two burning trucks. The van door bursts open, and I have never been as glad to see anyone as I am to see Saleem lying on his back and kicking the door free. I reach in and pull him forward, helping him and Sultan out of the van. Both seem confused, but I can see no sign of injuries. Saleem looks at me and sees the blood stain on my *shalwar kameez.*

"You have been injured."

"I have been shot. It hurts like hell, but it's superficial, and the bleeding appears to have stopped. Do you have your cell phone?"

"*Da. Da.*"

"Call the hospital and tell them what happened. And call the police or the military."

Saleem fidgets, trying to pull the cell phone from his pocket. Retrieving the phone, he flips it open and rapidly dials a number. The call goes through, and he begins screaming loudly into the phone. I tap him on the shoulder to get him to lower his voice and to slow down. "Tell them we are about two kilometers south of Mansehra on the KKH." He relays our location, and I continue, "Tell them there was a military convoy and it was attacked. There are many injured and dead. Tell them we need four or five ambulances. And tell them to notify the police and military in Abbottabad and Mansehra."

After a few moments, someone comes back on the line, saying there is a military patrol in the area, that they have seen the flames, and that others had also reported gunfire. The person says that they should be here in a few minutes, then terminates the call. A few minutes later, the phone rings, and the caller says that ambulances are on the way from Mansehra and Abbottabad, but that it could be thirty minutes to an hour before they arrive.

I hear movement coming from the front of the van and tell Sultan to check and see if Mohammed is okay. He runs to the van, just in time to help Mohammed out the back door. Mohammed is holding his head, and his face and hair are covered with matted blood. There is a large gash across his forehead where he must have struck the steering wheel or the frame of the van as it flipped on its side. He seems lucid, and other than complaining of soreness, he doesn't think he has suffered any broken bones. I take my knife from my pocket and tell Saleem to cut a strip from the bottom of his *shalwar*. I then wrap the strip of material around Mohammed's forehead several times and tie it snugly.

The adrenaline has been keeping me going up to this point, but now I am beginning to feel nauseated and light-headed, and I lie down on the ground. Mohammed comes to my side, whereupon he notices the bloodstain on my clothing. He takes the knife from Saleem and cuts through my clothing to examine the wound. Mohammed says, "It seems as though the bleeding has stopped. You are very lucky." He then cuts the belt holding my large overstuffed fanny pack and removes it. "You have three abdominal wounds."

The fanny pack contains a wad of several hundred rupee notes, almost three inches thick. Behind that are my passport and credit cards. The secondary pouch is filled with coins. These layers have apparently acted as a surrogate for an armored vest, blunting the force of the bullets that struck me and reducing their penetration. Mohammed was correct; I have taken three bullets in my lower abdomen. Because of the minimal bleeding I assume that they are buried in the fatty tissue or surface abdominal muscles, but haven't penetrated deeply enough to hit any major organs. Suddenly, I begin to shake and feel very cold. Saleem runs to the van, and pulls out one of our sleeping blankets and wraps me in it, while Mohammed folds one of the shawls and presses it to my abdomen. I wince at the pressure, and gently admonish him, "Easy! That hurts!" He smiles broadly and chuckles at my histrionics, but doesn't let up on the pressure.

From the north, we can see flashing lights approaching. A Japanese-built two-door pickup truck with flashing lights over the cab, and a stripped-down trunk at the back that is opened to the elements, comes to a screeching halt only a few feet away from us. Several men with automatic weapons jump from the back, and the driver and his companion walk toward us. The others move along the road, scanning the area. The driver asks us, in good English, what happened. I explain that we were returning to Abbottabad when the military convoy had just passed us, and was assailed by IEDs and small weapons fire. The driver looks over at Saleem, Sultan, and Mohammed, who assure him that they are all right, but that I have been shot, and seem to be going into shock, and need to be transported to the Frontier Medical College in Abbottabad as soon as possible. As we are all talking, we see more flashing lights rapidly approaching us.

Mohammed kneels at my side and I tell him, "See if they can push the van back onto its wheels. See if it will start. That will get me to the hospital faster than anything. We don't need to wait for the ambulances, they are an hour away." He hesitates, knowing that the danger may still be awaiting us, and obviously preferring to remain in the protective company of the military men. I sense his hesitation, and implore him, "Go! Go!"

Saleem and Sultan remain at my side as Mohammed stands and speaks rapidly to the commanding officer, almost shouting at him. The officer quickly disappears down the dark road, returning with eight men. They take positions along the side and back of the van, and with one good push set it aright. Mohammed immediately climbs in and turns the key. The motor strains, but after several tries, it is running. We have transportation! One of the officers comes over to me and asks how I am doing. With teeth chattering, I tell him that I am in pain, but feel that I'll be all right. I inform him that I am a doctor, and have a good idea as to the extent of my injuries. He asks me for my name, and when I respond, he exclaims with a broad smile, "You're the Doctor Angel! What are you doing here?"

I tell him that we had taken one of our patients back to her home just north of Mansehra, and we were returning to the Frontier Medical College in Abbottabad when the attack occurred. He nods thoughtfully, then responds, "There are four dead Taliban along the road only a few feet from here."

Looking down and seeing the M-4 next to me with its flash suppressor and scope, he asks, "This is yours?"

I look up at him, and with a broad smile that I would prefer to suppress but cannot, I answer, "*Da. Da.*"

My smile must be infectious, because he returns it as he says, "I will need a full report, but that can wait until later."

I say again, "*Da. Da.*"

Still smiling, he continues, "You did good. We have some wounded, and you have probably saved their lives as well."

Now that my adrenaline overload has passed, his statement reminds me that there might be others who are wounded as well. "Please let me know how they are doing when you come to visit."

"I will do that, Doctor, but for now, we need to get you to the hospital." He calls several of his men over, and they lift me and carry me, still wrapped in my blanket, to the bench seat in the back of the van. Sultan comes along and gets into the van behind the driver's seat, and Saleem, grabbing the M-4, jumps into the seat next to Mohammed. Then we are off, making our way south toward Abbottabad.

Only one of the headlights is working, and several soldiers with flashlights guide us around the burning trucks and onto the highway. Plumes of black smoke fill the air, almost completely blocking our view as we pass the burning trucks along the narrow ribbon of the ancient and battered highway. After many years of war, the highway is deeply rutted by the constant passage of heavy war machinery, and dotted with the craters left by artillery shells and IEDs. My body is reading the tortuous history of this road, with every bump and jolt feeling like hot knives being plunged into my flesh. Sultan looks back at me lying there grimacing and asks if I am okay. Mohammed and Saleem, up in the front, are obviously wondering the same thing. I can see the concern on all of their faces. I look up at Sultan, force a smile, and say, "Don't worry. I'm not going to die on you guys." Then I close my eyes and pass out, the loss of blood and onset of shock finally catching up with me.

When I open my eyes again, I am in a nearly bare room at the emergency facility of the Frontier Medical College. Mohammed and Sultan are hovering over me. Saleem is nowhere to be found. I look around me, and spot an orderly, leisurely mopping at the floor. I ask him, "Where is the doctor?"

"No doctor."

"You need to call and get the doctor, a general surgeon, and an anesthesiologist here immediately."

"They home sleeping."

"There are many wounded men from the convoy. They will be coming here. Who will take care of them?"

"No come here. Go to military hospital. Many doctors, many surgeons at military hospital."

Relieved at the news, I remember that I am badly hurt, as well, and bark at the man, "Then take me to the military hospital."

"Impossible. We wouldn't get through the front gate, much less to the hospital. Also they would be too busy with their own people."

This is getting us nowhere, so I ask, "Are there any nurses working tonight?"

"*Da. Da.* Two of them. On the post-op ward, second floor."

"I want you to go to the second floor and bring those two nurses to the emergency room now. Run!"

As the orderly leaves, Saleem appears in the doorway, and I call out to him, "Saleem! There is a storage room on the second floor outside the operating room, where my sterile equipment, medicines, and antibiotics are locked. I need you to find someone to unlock it and bring the equipment to the emergency room." The urgency in my voice is clear, and Saleem dashes out of the room, just as the two nurses, Fatima and Nayab, arrive.

I turn to Fatima and ask her, "Are the post-op children doing well? No problems?"

"They are all doing fine. Most are sleeping."

"I need an IV. Can you get me 500/1000 cc of saline, some tubing, and a needle?"

They both nod and hurry from the room as Saleem returns. There is a slight panic in his voice as he says, "The room has a padlock on it, and I can't find anyone with the keys."

"Who has the keys to the operating room and the equipment storage locker?"

"He goes home at night. He will not come until 7:30 tomorrow morning."

"Do you have someone here that does maintenance or repair?"

"*Da. Da.*"

"Where is he?"

"He sleeps at the hospital."

"Wake him up and bring him here. This is an emergency."

Just at that moment, the nurses come in with the IV. I put my left arm out toward them and they apply the tourniquet, insert the needle, and attach the IV, which hangs on a metal rod above me. I tell them, "We need some IV antibiotics."

Nayab shakes her head. "We don't have any."

"Yes, we do. I left several bottles of Ancef and Gentamycin on the anesthesia table in Operating Room Number One. There may also be some left over in Room Number Two. Please go upstairs and check the anesthesia tables, and bring any you find back with you."

Fatima leaves, and Nayab puts a blood pressure cuff on my right arm. I think to myself, *So this is emergency medicine in the Northwest Territories. If you are part of the military, there is a facility available. If you are a civilian, it's likely you are going to die.* Saleem enters the room, pulling an elderly and obviously half-awake gentleman with him. I ask, "Is this the maintenance man?"

Saleem nods.

"Saleem, you need to interpret for me, slowly and carefully. Does he have a bolt cutter or a lock cutter, or a pair of heavy clippers that can cut the lock from the equipment room?" Saleem translates this several different ways before the maintenance man comes out of his drowsy stupor enough to indicate that he understands what we want. As they leave the room, I yell after them, "Saleem, stay with him until till you find the equipment. And bring it back quickly. Please!"

There is nothing to do now but wait. I feel reasonably comfortable, and close my eyes. A few moments later, Mohammed, who along with Sultan has not left my side, pats me on my shoulder, and I open my eyes. Fatima returns, holding some bottles of medication in her hand. I motion for her to bring them closer, and I see that she has four bottles of Ancef and two bottles of Gentamycin.

I can see that she is nervous, so I flash my best smile and say quietly, "We'll start with two grams of Ancef. Save the others for later." She lays the bottles on a tray on the far side of the room and strips the packaging from a syringe and needle. She then draws up the two grams of Ancef and injects it into the 500 cc's of saline solution, gently shaking the bag to mix it evenly throughout. Once the Ancef is sufficiently mixed with the saline solution, she re-hangs the bag and increases the flow.

I smile at her again, and she seems to have gotten over her bout of nerves. I thank her as Saleem walks into the room again, dragging the old maintenance man by the sleeve of his wrinkled and stained *shalwar kameez*. As he enters the room, I glance down and notice for the first time that the old man is barefoot. Saleem has obviously been following my instructions closely, and has not let this old man out of his sight. He holds up a heavy pair of metal shears that should be more than adequate to cut through the small lock on the supply cabinet.

I nod my approval, and tell Saleem, "Take him to the second floor across from the operating room and cut the lock off the supply room door. Inside, you will find two large black plastic bins, one of which will contain the sterile surgical instruments, and the other will be full of medications and supplies. We need both of those down here immediately. Mohammed, you need to go with them and help them carry the cases." I can tell that Mohammed does not want to leave my bedside, but I look up at him and say, "This is important. We need these supplies now. Go."

I feel the blood pressure cuff compressing on my right arm as Nayab takes another reading. Turning toward her, I see Fatima standing at her side. I tell her, "Go back to the operating room. Next to the sink where the surgeons wash, there should be some surgical soap, Betadine, and some scrub brushes. Bring them down here now." She leaves, and Nayab, who has finished the blood pressure reading, follows. I lay my head back down, close my eyes, and wait. As I lie there, I hear the sound of motorcycles outside the emergency room, and hope that they are not accompanying patients in need of care, knowing that I'm just not capable of treating anyone else right now.

Much to my relief, Hassan and Ali charge in. These are the two surgical residents who have been working with me this past week in the operating room, and they are quite proficient with their surgical procedures. A rapid conversation takes place in Urdu as Mohammed tells Hassan about the attack on the convoy, the shoot-out that followed, and my subsequent wounding.

As Mohammed finishes with his recounting, I open my eyes and look up at Hassan and Ali and say, "Everything is going to be okay. Here is where you get to show me how well I taught you. You are going to open these wounds, clean them out, and hopefully remove the three bullets that are someplace in my abdominal muscle. Then you're going to have to suture Mohammed's head wound as well."

Mohammed says, "My head's not so bad. You take care of the doctor first."

As Mohammed finishes his sentence, Fatima returns from the operating room with the Betadine solution and scrub brushes. Right behind her is Saleem, followed by Nayab, who is carrying the equipment boxes of sterile instruments and supplies. I tell them, "You have all worked with me for a week now. You need to set this room up just like we do in the OR. Everything will be sterile technique. Fatima, wash, put on sterile gloves, and you will set up the surgical tray with Nayab. And Nayab, you will open the sterile packages of instruments and supplies so that Fatima can arrange the surgical tray. Now Ali, go scrub and put on some sterile gloves. And Hassan, remove the bandages the military applied and scrub out the wounds, then bring me a 50cc bottle of the Xylocaine anesthetic, a 10cc syringe and a 25 gauge needle."

Saleem, eager to reassure me, says, "Everybody has been called. Many people will come to help. It should not be very long."

I know better. There will be more casualties here soon, I am sure of it. "Saleem, the military hospital may not be able to handle all the casualties. When the general surgeon and the anesthesiologist arrive, you need to set up OR Number One and Number Two to handle any overflow they may send us. I have a feeling that we are going to be very busy in a very short time." Saleem nods, looking at me intently.

"Also, Saleem, contact the military hospital and tell them we will have two operating rooms ready, and can handle their overflow. We have the equipment to deal with the burn patients in particular. The hospital administrator lives on the grounds across from the emergency room. If he has not yet been informed, knock on his door, wake him up, and explain what has happened. He will have the contact telephone numbers for the personnel we will need. Now go! Go!"

Hassan strips off the pressure bandage and begins scrubbing my lower abdomen. This is very uncomfortable, but I know it is necessary. When he is finished, Fatima brings me the syringes containing the local anesthetic, and I prop myself up on my elbow and inject each of my wounds, which almost immediately dulls the pain and makes me much more comfortable.

Ali takes the opportunity to scold me, good-naturedly but firmly. "That is our job. We are now the surgeons. You need to lie down and let us do what we need to do."

Ignoring him, I hand the last of the syringes to Fatima and say, "Give the anesthetic a few minutes to circulate in the surrounding tissue, and then you need to make an incision over each of the bullet wounds and remove any cloth or paper that was dragged into the wound. After that, we will try to remove the bullets." Looking over at Fatima and Nayab, I think how they have rotated through the operating room and learned their tasks very well. They have set up the sterile tray and instruments quickly and efficiently. I smile at my staff, all gathered around me, for the first time looking at me as their patient rather than their colleague.

I tell them, "It's show time!"

I can see by the expressions the faces of both Hassan and Ali that they are feeling very anxious about operating on me. I reassure them as best I can, though I can certainly imagine what it is like, not just to have your procedure observed by your teacher and colleague, but to actually be operating on him.

"You're both good surgeons and you can do this. Take the forceps and the hemostats and remove any of the cloth, paper money, or other debris that was pushed into the wound from the fanny pack, then scrub it out again. After that, have the nurse bring in a bottle of peroxide from the equipment locker and just pour it into the wound."

They go to work cleaning and debriding the wound. Thanks to the local anesthesia, I am relatively comfortable, and I lay my head back, close my eyes, and allow Hassan and Ali to do their jobs. After a few minutes, Hassan touches my arm and startles me, making me realize that I must have drifted into a twilight sleep. He tells me that the wounds are clean. I ask him, "Have you ever removed a bullet?"

He shakes his head sharply. "No."

"Well, it's time to learn. You need to extend the wound using the scalpel, then spread the wound open with the right angle retractors. Once that is done, let Ali hold the retractors. and using the large clamp, explore more deeply into the wound until you feel metal contacting metal. Then grasp the bullet with the clamp and pull it out quickly. Can you do that?"

Hassan and Ali both nod and assure me that it will not be a problem.

Hassan picks up the scalpel and begins to make a transverse incision across the bullet wound on my right side. I remain propped up on my elbows with a pillow against my back, observing. Hassan is hesitant, and barely cuts through the skin. "Press harder. You're not accomplishing much." I can feel him increase pressure on the scalpel slightly, but he's still holding back. This isn't working. I grab the back of his hand and push the scalpel through the skin onto the surface of the muscle, then withdraw my hand.

Hassan looks at me, obviously concerned. "I'm hurting you."

"No, no, do your job."

Finally, the wound is sufficiently opened, and Ali places the retractors as I'd instructed. Hassan picks up a clamp and begins exploring the wound. After a couple of seconds, I hear and feel the clamp making contact with the metal slug. With a sigh of relief, I tell Ali, "It's not very deep; just into muscle." As I make this statement, Hassan withdraws the clamp that holds the first of the bullets.

Hassan seems not just relieved, but proud of himself as he holds up the slug. Then he says, "I will suture it..."

I interrupt him in mid-sentence, "No, no. You need to irrigate it, then pack it with sterile gauze and leave it open so it can drain. That will reduce the chance of it getting infected."

Hassan pours peroxide in the wound, thoroughly cleans it, and packs it with the gauze. Moving on to the second wound, he picks up the scalpel, more confident this time, and cuts through the skin to the surface of the abdominal muscle in one easy motion. Ali places the retractors, and in less than a minute, Hassan locates and removes the second slug. Then he cleans and packs the wound.

I'm feeling better about the procedure now, and decide to let Ali gain some experience, as well. "You did a great job, Hassan. Now trade places and let Ali remove the last bullet and clean the wound while you hold the retractors." I may be the patient, but this still is a teaching situation, and I know that both of them need to have experience in a procedure they will inevitably have to repeat many times in their professional future. I'm reminded of an old adage I learned during my internship: *See one, do one, teach one.* Ali is very dexterous, and obviously feels more confident, having observed how well the procedure went on the first two wounds. In the next few minutes, he has the wound opened and the third bullet is removed. He irrigates and packs the wound, then applies a pressure dressing over my abdomen with an elastic bandage.

I remember that I have several donated abdominal binders in the medical equipment locker, and instruct Fatima to get one to place around my abdomen for additional support. I am relatively comfortable but I know that in a few hours, when the local anesthesia wears off, there is going to be significant pain.

I look up at Mohammed, who has remained by my side through the entire procedure, and tell him, "It's your turn. They are going to clean that forehead and scalp wound and suture it, and I expect you to behave yourself." He shakes his head at me, unwilling to accept treatment until he knows that mine has been completed. Saleem and Sultan are still in the room, and I call them over and tell them both to help move me from the operating table to a chair on the other side of the room. Mohammed still stands adamantly beside me, feet planted like the devoted friend he is, refusing to leave me even in the safety of this room.

I tell Hassan and Ali, "Don't listen to Mohammed. Get that filthy head dressing off, clean out the wound, inject the local anesthetic, and suture it. Then give him an injection of one gram of the antibiotic. You're in charge here, not him. He is the patient." Fatima and Nayab are already clearing away the instruments and setting up a new sterile tray. Hassan and Ali close Mohammed's head wound, applying more than twenty-five sutures and applying a sterile pressure dressing.

Just as they are finishing, we hear sirens in the distance, probably on their way to the military hospital. Then the sounds grow louder. They are bringing wounded here. The screech of tires outside the hospital entrance confirms my suspicion. The wounded soldiers have arrived on our doorstep, and at this point, I have no idea how many there are. One thing is certain: wounded or not, my turn as a patient is over.

Surgeon to Patient... and Back Again

Saleem leaves the emergency room, returning in less than a minute to let us know that there are two burn victims in the ambulance. Nayab announces that Operating Rooms Number One and Two have been prepared, and that everyone is ready to proceed. Hassan will be the acting surgeon in Operating Room Number One, and Ali will take charge of Operating Room Number Two. The injured men have to be brought from the ground floor to the second level via the stairway, because the elevator isn't working. Saleem, Sultan, and Mohammed join the ambulance team to help bring the stretchers up to the second floor, placing the injured on the operating tables.

277

I grab the railing with both hands and try to stand up. As I struggle to rise, my knees begin to shake, and I feel a searing pain in my abdomen. Despite my discomfort, I can't escape the thought of the injured men lying on the operating tables. I need to be there. I take one halting step at a time, the injured nerves in my stomach radiating a sharp, burning sensation through my thighs to my calves. As I reach the first floor landing, I have to stop and rest, wondering whether I'll be able to make it to the second floor. While I stand here debating the risk of proceeding, the decision is made for me when Sultan and Saleem arrive, each assuming a position on either side of me, placing my arms over their shoulders and helping me up to the second floor. Mohammed follows closely behind.

As I arrive at the surgeons' scrub room, I kick off my sandals, and Fatima places a surgical cap on my head, helps me into my surgical scrubs, and ties the mask behind my neck. I enter Operating Room Number One, and Mohammed fetches a metal swivel stool from the corner of the room and brings it over for me to sit on as I work. The anesthesiologist, Dr. Abdul, has already started the IV and is administering pain medication directly into the patient's vein. Hassan has a pair of scissors in this hand and proceeds to cut off the wounded patient's uniform.

Upon my initial observation of the patient, I can see the typical effects of a blast injury, evidenced primarily by second-degree burns. As the patient's shirt is cut off, the back of his hands and forearms exhibit a combination of second and third-degree burns. There is a similarly affected area across his upper chest and neck as well. The remainder of his torso and lower extremities show no evidence of injury, and there does not appear to be any evidence of broken bones.

I tell Hassan, "Check his eyes and apply some ointment to them if it's needed, then begin debridement and cleaning of the wounds, and apply the Silvadene topical antibiotic."

He responds, "We do not have that medication here."

"I brought several one-pound jars, Hassan. They are in my medical supply kit." I ask Fatima to get the Silvadene and some clear topical antibiotic ointment for him, whereupon she leaves for the supply room across the hallway. Everything is proceeding well, and I'm pretty certain that our patient is going to be just fine. Turning to the other patient, I tell Dr. Abdul that there is a bottle of Ancef on the anesthesia tray, and tell him to inject 1 gram of the antibiotic directly into the patient's IV.

Dr. Abdul smiles at me, saying, "I've already drawn up the syringe with the antibiotic, but was waiting for your okay before injecting it."

I'm once again reassured as to these people's proficiency, and tell Dr. Abdul, "Do it now, thank you."

I feel a sudden shudder go through me, but it ends just as quickly as it began. I take in several deep breaths and exhale a sigh of relief. The local anesthetic is wearing off quickly, and the pain is increasing, but I need to get to Operating Room

Number Two to triage the patient and organize his care. With a grimace, I brace myself with my hand against the wall and cross the thirty feet to Operating Room Number Two. The cold tiles feel good against my bare feet. Wincing with every step, I feel the pain resonating not only down my legs but up into my head as well.

Saleem steps up beside me. "I saw your face. You are in a lot of pain. Maybe you should lie down."

"I can't just yet, Saleem. I need to see the other patient." As I enter the second operating room, Ali is busily cutting the burned soldier's clothing away. His IV has already been started and he has been given some pain medication. Nayab is standing at the head of the table talking softly to the injured man, who is responding to her questions and seems reasonably comfortable. He is a young man in his twenties, clean-shaven, with wide-set eyes, black hair, and a sharp nose with a bump on it. Nayab is shining a light into his eyes, checking for signs of trauma, as well as neurological problems. The patient is responding to her commands, and I am pleased to see that he has suffered no eye injury. His face and neck are burned, but the burns are mostly second degree with some mild blistering, most notably around his mouth area and lips. His cheeks are a little sunken. His burns are mostly to the right side of his body, including his arms, shoulders, right chest, and upper thigh area. He has some bruising on his hip and leg, but there are no broken bones. I give the same orders: pain medication, antibiotic, and nasal oxygen, followed by debridement and cleaning of the wound, and the application of topical antibiotic cream.

Ali proceeds quickly and efficiently with the help of Nayab, who continues to speak to the patient. This proves particularly effective, as he gradually calms down and finally begins to smile. The operating room has large windows along one wall, something we do not see in the States. The moon chooses this moment to clear the mountains and cast its light upon us, further illuminating the room. The wounded soldier raises his left hand and points toward the moon, saying something that I can't interpret.

Dr. Ali translates for me, "Patient said that it's a good sign, that he has always been a lucky man. Things always go his way, just like they are breaking his way now."

With Ali continuing to translate, the patient thanks all of us, and then he points to me and says, "I know that man. I saw his picture in the newspaper. He is our Dr. Angel."

I start to chuckle, but my abdomen reminds me of a lesson we were never taught in anatomy classes: that the humor bone is directly connected to the exact spot where the bullets hit me. I settle for a wan smile and tell him, "Unfortunately, this angel has a broken wing tonight."

Mohammed shakes his head and looks at me with a broad smile. "You've been shot. There's a big difference between target shooting and combat. I recall my coach that taught fencing. He explained that the mask hides your opponent's eyes, but in war, it is different when you meet the cold gaze of the men who intend to kill you."

"You can say that again," I murmur.

Mohammed continues, "You have spent your life saving lives, but tonight you were placed in a different position. The sight of your own red blood being spilt changed things for you. You saved your own life, but also our lives, and the lives of these soldiers we are now caring for." Before I can respond to that, he is off on another track, and it is apparent that he is really getting wound up now as he says, "What have they gained by taking some lives and injuring others? What did their enemies gain by selling terror? They are madmen! Lunatics!"

I consider what Mohammed says, but think he is missing something. "Mohammed, whoever planned this attack was remarkably methodical. This was not an impulsive attack. This was planned meticulously. If it is madness, it is madness with control and purpose."

To my surprise, our patient speaks up again, and Ali translates: "They are Anarchists. They are trying to sell terror, because it is through terror that the Taliban controls the population."

I have to agree with what he says, and I nod and reply, "The Taliban are certainly achieving that in the Northern Territories. Maybe we need to think like a radical or an Anarchist or madman to counter the insurgents. Imagine what it is costing in terms of young men's lives – not to mention money, and the overall economy."

I look out the window again at the moon and stars, and am filled with confidence and a rare sense of pleasure in knowing that I am going to be able to help these young men. Perhaps it is the excitement I feel, given the circumstances, at realizing that I too am still alive, and ambulatory. I don't want to even think about the endless and much less pleasant alternatives. Right now, at this moment, everything is going well in both operating rooms, and I know that my own injuries will heal.

The sense of satisfaction I feel is interrupted somewhat by the pain that once again begins to radiate from my abdomen into my legs. I wave Mohammed and Sultan over, and putting an arm around each of their shoulders, I say to them, "Take me across the hall to the recovery room; I need to lie down for a short while."

Mohammed and Sultan help me to the recovery area. I sit on the bed and rotate my hips as Mohammed supports my back and lifts my legs, helping me lie down flat. I close my eyes. I haven't slept in twenty-four hours, but despite my exhaustion, sleep eludes me. My mind is racing. I hear more sirens approaching and I wonder: *Are they bringing injured to the military hospital, or are there yet more wounded who are being brought here for care?* I know that if the latter is the case, I'll get the job done somehow. I have a pretty cool head under fire, if I do say so myself. I am determined to make the best of this situation, and to provide care for as many patients as need it.

* * * * *

I close my eyes again and try to make some sense of the attack that has taken place. The road from Mansehra to Abbottabad is not known for this type of attack. There are many more terrorists both north and west of this area, but few operate in the heavily guarded town of Abbottabad, what with the many military divisional headquarters located here, as well as the Pakistani Military College.

The Taliban seems to be doing its best to catch up to their Muslim brothers in the mountains to the west. In that region, there are more mountains and forests to hide in, making it a major conflict zone. The Abbottabad-Mansehra-Muzaffarabad triangle is much more urban. But the location of tonight's attack, halfway between Mansehra and Abbottabad, splits the difference.

In my mind, I begin to replay the attack, this time in slow motion, with each minute detail falling into place. Wooded hills surround the area, with a tight cluster of vacated mud brick dwellings lining the dirt roads. Each road has a deep trench on the side to drain the rainfall into the river below. The spot was well chosen for the placement of IEDs. The few buildings located on the hill across from the road, consisting of what appear to be a feed shack, several small single family dwellings, and a storage building and outhouse, could serve as effective cover for an ambush. To the right of this is a baked-brick, tin-roofed shed, where a farmer might be expected to store a tractor and wagon. From his position on the roof, a sniper could clearly see every corner of the road as it curves through this passage of low rolling hills before it turns south toward Abbottadad.

Thinking about it now, I realize that this was a perfect place for the machine gun that sprayed the vehicles and the road. It allowed the gunner to lie flat on the roof, hidden by the two-foot-high lip that traversed the front of the building. Now that I am lying here with my eyes closed, I can better appreciate what has just happened. The warning signs were there, but we missed them. I go over them in my mind and see every detail with perfect 20/20 hindsight. A donkey stirring uneasily. Several dogs barking as we approached. A bleating goat tied up in front of the mud hut. All of these signs had been very much out of the ordinary. As the sun was setting, the animals should have been bedded down and quiet.

The IEDs were not on timers or attached to cell phones, but were triggered by the pressure of the vehicles as they passed over them. That meant that the men who called themselves Jihadists had been close enough to have a clear view of the road. They detonated the IEDs as the truck passed over them, dealing a deathblow to the vehicles and their passengers. The attackers' plan and implementation had been almost flawless, and they had been in perfect position to flee unseen into the virtually impenetrable mountains to the west – mountains that they knew as well as the contours of their lovers' bodies.

More and more details are coming back to me. I recall that as we approached the area, the dogs had already been reacting, apparently to the movement of our attackers. Growls from a large sheepdog had started a chorus with other animals from around the buildings. They were already alerted to the Jihadists hidden on the roofs and ensconced behind large rocks and in the hollows. We should have taken notice when the barking turned into a sustained chorus, or even when a few of the animals had begun howling. After all, we had previously passed through many small villages in the evenings, and they had all remained very quiet, the only smell in the air being that of food cooking on outdoor fires.

I recall now what I saw after the IEDs had taken out the two supply trucks. I remember seeing the man in the tailing Jeep standing in the truck bed and beginning to fire the .50 caliber machine gun in the direction of the muzzle flashes from the small arms fire that had erupted nearby. I remember that I thought at the time was that he was shooting blindly into the dark. It had only lasted a few seconds when incoming gunfire from the rooftops answered, tearing through the metal and glass of the truck. The gunner had been struck in the chest, and even now I can see him, spewing blood as he heaved for the last time, tumbling off the side and down, rolling down into the muddy ditch on the side of the road to die. Just then another IED had exploded, sweeping the Jeep off the road and into the ditch. It was this explosion that flipped our van and flung me onto the road. The small arms fire continued, and the machine gun was spraying the road, setting off the ammunition in the supply truck and dispensing death to anyone nearby.

It is all coming back much more clearly now.

In my mind, I can still hear the sound of the booming explosion and feel the reverberation off the surrounding hills and against the valley walls. Echoes of each salvo had assaulted my ears as the sound waves bounced back and forth through this narrow passage along the KKH. Time had ceased to exist as the adrenaline was pumping through my body, and the severity of my own injuries didn't even register. I remember feeling significant abdominal pain and a dull ache deep in my brain, as well as a sharp pain across my forehead. The tension of the moment had extended to my arms, and my shoulders had felt as if they were in spasm.

A flash of light shining in my face makes me recoil, and I slowly begin to realize that I've been in some kind of twilight dream or vivid memory. I realize that I am actually lying on the bed in the post-op ward, looking into the beam of a flashlight in Nurse Fatima's hand. In her other hand are two syringes. Using the flashlight beam, she locates the port to the IV line and injects the next dose of antibiotic. She then shines the light back on my face and says, "That was your second dose of antibiotic, and I have some pain medicine as well."

"I think I'm ready, Fatima, but give me only a half-dose this time. I want to be functional if other patients arrive and I'm needed in the operating room."

She says, "The two soldiers are doing well and have been taken to the post-op ward. We are cleaning the rooms and sterilizing the instruments in anticipation of other casualties."

Coming more fully out of my mental fog, I ask her what time it is, to which she replies, "The sun will be coming up soon. Close your eyes and try to get some rest. You need it."

As she leaves the recovery area, my thoughts return to the ambush. Had they not been greedy, had not wanted to scavenge the bodies for money and other valuables, or additional weapons and ammunitions, the attackers could have easily fled through the hills and safely escaped the area before help arrived. They had been over-confident, feeling so secure and successful in their attack that they thought they could plunder and possibly mutilate the wounded and dead. That had turned out to be the last mistake they would ever make, the mistake that had turned me from being a healer into a killer. I can see their deaths – at my hand – in my mind's eye, as clearly as if all of it had just happened. I find myself wondering whether the images will ever go away, or at least diminish with time as everything usually does. But I know that I will never be totally free of them, and the thought fills me with a deep sadness.

It occurs to me that Osama bin Laden, living in a compound in Abbottabad, would not want any attacks along this section of the KKH. He would not want the increased security that such attacks would bring, which would only jeopardize his hideout in Abbottabad. This attack had probably not been sanctioned by him or any of the other Jihadists' groups in the area. It had more likely been carried out by a small independent group of *Mujahideen*, perhaps borne of a personal grudge by one of the warlords in retaliation for an attack on his village or compound in the area. It just hadn't fit the usual pattern. The motive for the attack could be as simple as the acquisition of weapons, explosives, and the valuables that would be stripped from the wounded and dying. Or it could be something else entirely. In truth, I still have no idea what had motivated this attack, so close to the military bases of Abbottabad and the compound of Osama bin Laden.

There will be no celebrating this as a victory, not in my mind. The others are already saying I am a hero, but their praise leaves a bitter taste in my soul. It occurs to me that it is impossible to think when you're upset and mad, and doubly so when you're mad at yourself. I chide myself for allowing the memory to upset me so, and tell myself to calm down.

And then I remember that we have a full surgical schedule ahead of us, and that brings a smile to my face, and chases away the ghosts, at least for now. I can already hear the mothers and children in the pre-op wards only a few feet away, and it is with gratitude that I remember the real reason I am here. Sleep finally claims me, if only for a little while.

* * * * *

Rising from my bed a little later, I cross the hall to the recovery area adjacent to Operating Room Number One. With Nurse Fatima's help, I remove my dressing, replace the packing, and then grab a bottle of local anesthetic, a sterile needle, and a syringe. Fatima stands there, looking with wide eyes as I inject my lower abdomen with the anesthetic. "Fatima, snap out of it. Get me some clean dressings and help me re-apply the binder." She hesitates for a few seconds, then applies the sterile dressings and pulls the binder closed. I tell her, "Tighter! I need pressure on the wound and support so I can stand."

She says, "If I make much tighter, you won't be able to breathe."

I tell her, "Then it will be a lot quieter around here." She begins to laugh, and I laugh with her.

The support tightened to my satisfaction, Fatima turns aside and leaves the room, saying over her shoulder, "I'm going to have them make you some hot tea and bring you some naan."

With the thought of a cup of hot tea and some food, I realize that I am famished, and my appreciation for her increases even more. "I would like that."

As she disappears down the hallway, Nurse Nayab enters the room. Looking at me, she asks, "Did you or any of the others get any sleep last night?"

"Perhaps an hour."

"Good. After the pain medicine knocked you out, several more burn victims arrived. We worked through the night. It was like a MASH unit here, and they are all doing well. I just made rounds with Dr. Abdul and Dr. Ali. They are having some tea, fried eggs, and naan right now, but they will be in the operating room shortly to start this morning's schedule. But you, Doctor, are a patient today, and you need to eat. There is some food for you in the doctors' lounge." I'm not going to argue with her. I go to the medical supply closet, unlock the storage unit, and remove some antibiotics for myself, then proceed to the doctors' lounge for tea and naan. And then my day really begins.

The first child with the simple unilateral cleft is being placed on the table, and Dr. Abdul is preparing to administer the anesthetic. It has been a long night, and now it looks as if it is going to be an even longer day. But the doctors and nurses have no intention of disappointing these children and their families. They have waited months in anticipation of the American team's arrival to provide care for their children. They have slept on benches and stood in line, hoping they would be selected for treatment. It brings to mind what a good friend once said when we were doing a mission trip in Russia. He had been giving a television and radio interview, and announced, to everybody's astonishment, "This is a medical lottery."

One of the reporters had asked him, "Could you explain that further?"

To which my friend, the late and much-missed Marvin Zindler, responded, "If your child is lucky enough to be selected, then you are a winner. If for some reason the child is not selected, then you've bought yourself a ticket to the lottery by investing travel time, sleeping on the bench at the hospital, and waiting in line to see the doctor... but your child will not be treated. So you've lost. In some cases, if you lose the medical lottery, you may lose your life."

The reporter had asked him, "What determines who is selected? Who wins the lottery?"

To which Mr. Zindler replied, "If the child is sick, he or she is not a candidate for anesthesia. If the child is malnourished and has a low blood count, he or she will not be a candidate for surgery. If the degree of the defect exceeds the equipment and facilities available at the small hospital, then you lose the lottery. It is truly *a medical lottery*."

I don't know why this comes to mind at this time, except for my realization that if we don't move forward according to schedule, twenty or more children will lose *their* medical lottery. With this knowledge weighing on our minds, we will all work all day. We are all still bone-tired, but there will be time enough to sleep tonight.

My thoughts are interrupted as Hassan appears, having finished his meal in the lounge. I tell him to scrub up and start the first case in Operating Room Number One. I ask him, "Where is Ali?"

"He is on his way."

"When he arrives, tell him to start the next child, who is in Operating Room Number Two. It is a difficult double cleft, and I'll start scrubbing up so I can help him with it. Fatima, I need you with me in OR Number Two. Please have Nurse Nayab help Dr. Hassan in Number One."

It suddenly hits me that I have not talked to my wife Terry in two days, and I know she will begin to worry if I don't call her. How do I explain to her what has happened? I have avoided discussing some things with her, especially when I've been on these dangerous mission trips in the Northern Territories, but I have never lied to her. After so many years, I have finally met the girl of my dreams and have made a friend for life. I feel I am the luckiest man in America. I am deeply in love with Terry, and try to show her that in every way. I want ever so much to tell her what has taken place in the past twenty-four hours...but then I wonder if it couldn't wait a little while longer. I vacillate between wanting to drop everything and find a phone to call her, and simply concentrating on the task at hand.

I try to look at the situation from Terry's point of view. She too is aware of our great good fortune of having discovered each other, and I want to believe that she would not let my hesitancy to tell her the whole truth about what I've been through come between us. I feel that some type of compromise is in order, but have to admit that I have my own hands full – both literally and figuratively – right at this moment.

I walk over to the scrub sink and begin washing, but I am still thinking of Terry. Things have settled down, I think, so maybe it would be better to have one of the others explain to her what has happened. No, if she doesn't hear it from me directly, she'll be even more worried and upset. The best course of action will be to just explain what happened and reassure her that everyone is okay. But then I think, *When did that ever work?* "Yes, *dear, I got shot. No, you don't need to come over here. I'm fine. Heck, I'm even back in the operating room, and not on the table. So you see, it's really not that bad.*"

My thoughts are interrupted when I hear Ali calling to me from the operating theater. I rinse off my hands and walk the thirty feet to the OR. It is time not only to change this child's life for the better, but also the lives of the immediate family, the distant family, and the friends and relatives who will look differently upon him after the surgery is completed. Gloves on and head down, my own physical discomfort – and my personal dilemma – become minor details by comparison.

Getting Closer to Finding the Sheik

The words of the Maulanas have played over and over in my mind. "When you go looking for Osama bin Laden you won't find him, he will find you."

I have made many trips to Pakistan to tend to the medical and surgical needs of the children in the tribal areas, but on this trip, I have been driven by another burning goal, as well. As may be abundantly clear to you by now if you have read this far in the book, I also want to meet with Osama bin Laden, to get to know the man who is so adored by some, and reviled by others. I want to know how he justifies the murder of innocents in the name of a peace-loving deity: a paradox that is seemingly beyond comprehension. I know that he is not a god himself, as some believe, but neither can I picture him as do so many Westerners – a demon bent upon the destruction of entire races and cultures. Perhaps I am naïve, but I genuinely want to believe that there is some goodness in him, even if that goodness is horribly misguided and incomprehensible to most of the world's population.

My interest in Pakistan was sparked in 2006 or 2007, when I met Hashmat Effendi, who is mentioned in the narrative about Shakira "the thankful one," as well as in the story of Mari Shah, elsewhere in this book. I cannot say enough good things about Hashmat, who is the founder and C.E.O. of the House of Charity (http://www.houseofcharity.com), a nonprofit organization based in Houston. Through this organization, Hashmat provides medical care and other necessities of life for children in need throughout the Middle East, India, and Central America. In that sense, the House of Charity is much like my own Children's Foundation (more information about that is at the back of this book).

In addition to medical care, both groups support educational programs and help provide needed school supplies, and we are also both very supportive of women and women's rights. Each organization brings its own unique approach to these problems and issues. Some of the issues with which we are both deeply concerned include the use of kerosene burning and acid attacks on women; restricted educational opportunities for girls and women; and the general suppression of women in these areas of the world. We are also concerned about child labor issues. It was a natural for Hashmat and me to decide to work together to help address these problems.

Hashmat and her people, along with our medical/surgical team from the Children's Foundation, helped to provide medical care to the hordes of Afghan refugees who were pouring across the Pakistan border. I was amazed by what I witnessed in the tribal areas, where medical care was virtually nonexistent. The sheer magnitude of the need for humanitarian efforts was beyond my comprehension, much less my ability to describe. The scale of suffering the medical team encountered was mind numbing. We saw people dying from horrors ranging from diseases that are virtually extinct in the West, to the gravest of wounds, inflicted upon even the innocents who were unfortunate enough to be in the wrong place at the wrong time.

I have to admit, however, that it wasn't just the needs of the women and children of Pakistan that I found so compelling. I was also fascinated by Osama bin Laden, and equally fascinated by his second in command, Dr. Ayman al-Zawahiri. The United States State Department had been calling Osama bin Laden "the most significant financial sponsor of Islamic extremist activities in the world today." They also accused him of supporting terrorist training camps in Pakistan, Afghanistan, and other areas throughout the Middle East. And yet, to the many refugees who had fled the violence bin Laden's followers inflicted upon them, his image remained that of a savior to Islam, a loving yet terrible prince.

My quest to find the mysterious Saudi billionaire and, of course, my desire to provide badly needed medical care to the afflicted, might have been my primary driving force, but in all honesty, there were other things that called me back to such a hostile region, over and over. As may also be apparent by now, I had discovered a culture and a way of life that has existed virtually unchanged for over two thousand years, but which remains totally foreign to the Western world. I fell in love with the Pakistani people, particularly those in the Northern Tribal areas. As I have expressed elsewhere in this narrative, I began to see – and, to an extent, understand – a way of life that has survived the test of time beyond measure. It is a world where less is more, where people are humble and charming, yet can be incited to extreme violence. They are people who are firmly opposed to any American presence, yet have greeted me – and my medical team – with loving, open arms. My curiosity aroused by the paradox that these people's lives presented, I have had little choice but to return to them again and again in order to explore, and try to understand, their attitudes, their way of life, and their religion.

* * * * *

The Pakistani and American military intervention in Afghanistan paved the way for a decade-long effort to bring down the Taliban and launch the so-called global war on terrorism. By the time I have become engaged in my quest to meet bin Laden, circumstances are such that defining the bilateral relationship between the U.S. and Pakistan has become nearly impossible, and is riddled with glaring contradictions. The Pakistani military and government sources repeatedly – and inaccurately – have asserted that Osama bin Laden is still hiding in the mountainous regions across the border inside Afghanistan. This has led a naïve United States to continually search along the Pakistan/Afghanistan border area, needlessly spending millions of American dollars and man-hours in a search that has no possibility of success. The misinformation and downright lies perpetrated by the ISI – the Inter-Services Intelligence, which is Pakistan's premier intelligence agency – as well as other high-ranking political and military figures, have resulted in this fruitless effort being continued for years.

In countless meetings, various political and military leaders from within the U.S. and Pakistan have tried to identify the problems and break the logjam that has resulted from American military actions on Pakistani soil. Those actions have produced significant civilian casualties without actually eliminating the "high-value" targets at whom they were supposedly directed, and as a consequence there has been a string of international scandals that have turned public opinion in Pakistan – and the rest of the world – against American involvement. This has forced the Pakistani government to withdraw its support of the U.S. In reality, the actions that the Pakistani government has taken have been aimed at undermining U.S. efforts, rather than assisting in those efforts. There is also a continuous upheaval due to the significant control that the Pakistani military maintains, which actually prevents the government in Pakistan from playing any role in establishing security policy for the country, or even in determining the role that foreign intervention should play.

Collaboration with the U.S. has therefore become extremely unpopular in recent years. The fact is that Pakistan's government continues to be a personality-centered affair, with a very narrow base for authority. And even though Pakistani President Asif Ali Zardari had allowed an influx of thousands of American CIA operatives and other Special Forces personnel into Pakistan by secret arrangement, Osama bin Laden and his family have remained as elusive as ever. At the time I am embarking on own mission to find and speak with bin Laden, it remains to be seen how – or if – the civilian establishment and military leaders will re-engage with the United States in a cooperative effort. Suspicion and mistrust are rampant, and the general public in Pakistan sees bin Laden as an invincible force, a national hero, and a protector of the faith.

Of course, this all works to my advantage in my quest for an interview with Osama bin Laden. There is a rumor of the Sheik's whereabouts that continues to haunt me, because it has continually re-emerged as we have traveled the Karakoram Highway from Haripur through Abbottabad and into Mansehra. The fact that the rumors are in direct conflict with "intelligence" reports doesn't particularly concern me, as I have seen first-hand just how accurate such "intelligence" really is, and how well-informed so many of the people in the tribal areas seem to be. If the rumors are true, Osama bin Laden and his family are actually located between Haripur and Abbottabad, far away from the search efforts.

Our group has been told again and again that Osama bin Laden has an obsession for Pepsi Cola. My driver Mohammed was told that bin Laden had cases of Pepsi Cola strapped to the backs of donkeys and brought across the Pakistan/Afghan border into the caves of Tora Bora. And now, as Mohammed, Saleem, Sultan, and I travel along our route in the southern Swat Territories and into Abbottabad, we are hearing repeated stories of a "special" customer with a Pepsi Cola addiction. I have to admit I am finding the issue more and more intriguing.

Feeling refreshed from a short nap in the bouncing and swaying van, I open my eyes, gently rub them, reaffix my glasses, and sit up. "Mohammed, Saleem, Sultan, I have a question."

This startles them, because they thought I was still sound asleep on the bench seat in the back. They don't realize that my eyes may have been closed but that my mind has been going a mile a minute.

Saleem, sitting in the front, smiles and says, "Mohammed, this sounds like trouble." Sultan, seated right behind Mohammed, laughs.

"No, no. I just want to know your thoughts about the rumors regarding bin Laden's addiction to Pepsi Cola. Why not Coca Cola?"

Saleem responds, "Coca Cola has a very big franchise and thousands of outlets, in Israel as well as in Pakistan. Because of Coca Cola's franchise in Israel, Osama bin Laden will have nothing to do with their products. Since he has the money and the wherewithal, he can bring in Pepsi Cola, and does so in large quantities so a supply is always available."

Mohammed and Saleem say that they have heard the rumors again and again, and are inclined to believe them. Sultan nods his agreement. I suggest that as we pass through the towns and villages in this narrow corridor where we feel bin Laden is being housed, we should keep our eyes peeled for any merchants selling Pepsi Cola. And when we stop in the markets, we should ask the merchants where we can purchase Pepsi.

What I honestly don't understand is, if there is any credence to the rumors, and bin Laden's desire for Pepsi is common knowledge, then why aren't others following up on the information in their search efforts? And yet, knowing how the U.S. Secret Service and other intelligence finding operations work, I can see how they might disregard such information as being nothing more than idle gossip, and ignore it entirely. These "sophisticated" intelligence services often seem so enamored of their own state-of-the-art techniques that they ignore the value of information gathered by local people who blend in and speak the language, who know the right questions to ask and how to ask them without raising suspicion.

My impression is that the CIA and other intelligence agencies are so focused upon what they believe to be significant electronic surveillance that they are totally oblivious to the value of plain old human intelligence in locating the Sheik and his family. We have narrowed down our quest to a very small area, and all I can think of is what the *Maulanas* and numerous others had told me: *"You do not find Osama bin Laden. He will find you."*

So now that we are seriously and officially on my quest, we want to make this as easy as possible, and to locate ourselves as close to the bin Laden family compound as we can. This will allow his people to check us out, establish contact, and see that we have no intentions other than what we have declared: an interview for a book I intend to write and publish. It is my hope that bin Laden will want the world to know his motives beyond what the world's intelligence communities and media portray, but I also suspect that he hopes to establish his place in history as a great warrior for Islam. Great warrior, reviled terrorist, or something altogether different, it is obvious that bin Laden's ego has played a significant role in his actions, and I hope that such an ego might inspire him to open himself up to me in a way he could not with other people.

We feel we have made exceptional progress on this trip, and that what had once been considered only rumors are now being proven to be true. There are very few hospitals in the area, and because of my years of work here, I have full access to all of them. While Saleem, Sultan, and I are checking the hospitals and birth records and questioning the nurses as to any unusual happenings, Mohammed is driving to the small towns and villages looking for anyone who is stocking Pepsi Cola.

One bright sunny morning as the four of us are driving through the streets of Abbottabad, we strike gold. Or perhaps it would be more accurate to say that we strike aluminum. We pass a narrow alleyway, and just past the alley is a store that appears to sell groceries, electronics, and household appliances, along with assorted other goods. There is a fruit and vegetable display right outside the store. Suddenly a bright light in the alley catches my eye. The winds have briefly blown up the corner of a tarp, which covers what appear to be cases of Pepsi Cola. The light that caught my eye was the sun reflecting off of the aluminum cans. Pepsi is something that I did not expect to see here, and I excitedly scream, "Stop, stop!"

Mohammed looks over his shoulder at me and says, "What is wrong?"

"I need to go into that store – now!"

"It's just another store," says Mohammed, who obviously did not catch the glimpse of Pepsi cans in the alley. "There are many of these small shops. There are others that are much better where we can stop."

"No, we need to stop here. Turn the van around and park on the opposite side of the street."

Now everybody is looking at me strangely. Apparently Saleem and Sultan didn't see what I saw either.

"That store sells Pepsi Cola products," I insist.

"How do you know?" asks Saleem.

"They're stacked in the alleyway between the two buildings, under a tarp."

"If they are under a tarp how do you know they are there?"

"The wind blew the tarp up for a moment and I could see the cases closest to the ground as the tarp fluttered up and back." I am a little exasperated that I have to waste time explaining my reason for wanting to stop.

Mohammed is already making the U-turn and coming back on the other side of the road. He finds a spot where he can avoid the ditch that parallels the road, and maneuvers the van into a place where it will not block traffic.

I slide the door of the van open and jump out, with Sultan and Saleem quickly following behind me. Mohammed stays in the van and keeps the motor running.

As we approach the store, Sultan puts his hand on my shoulder and says, "Let me do the talking."

I agree, since I am so excited that I will most likely say the wrong thing. Sultan seems calm and up to the task, so I let him pass through the entrance to the shop while I stay outside with Saleem and look over the fruits and vegetables.

Sultan comes out only seconds later to tell me the owner says he has no Pepsi Cola in stock. "I think we'd better leave," he says, obviously not convinced that I'd really seen what I saw. I point to the alley where the tarp-covered stacks are sitting. At that moment, as if on cue, the wind blows up a corner of the tarp again, and now Sultan and Saleem can also clearly see the Pepsi logo on the cans.

We have a quick huddle to discuss the situation. Should we remove a can from the exposed case and confront the shop-keeper? Should we bring the merchant outside and ask him if the cases of Pepsi belong to him? Or should we inquire at the business establishment on the other side of the alleyway from the shopkeeper? The other choice would be to purchase some fruit and just leave without raising any suspicion.

Sultan says he will purchase some fruit and then begin a conversation with the shopkeeper. He says he will ask if the cases of Pepsi Cola that we saw perhaps belong to the merchant in the adjacent shop, and he'll ask if we should inquire at that store. We agree on this tactic, and Sultan suggests that Saleem and I return to the van across the street and wait there.

I hate not being part of the action, but I agree that this is the best approach. Sultan re-enters the shop while the three of us wait breathlessly in the van. When Sultan returns with his purchases, he waits until we are driving before relaying what happened.

He tells us that he made his purchase of fruits and a few vegetables, then casually raised the question as to the ownership of the cases of Pepsi Cola in the alley. The merchant said, "Oh, *those* cases. They are for a special customer and have already been paid for – they are not for sale."

Sultan says that he didn't want to raise any suspicion, so he matter-of-factly asked, "Well, then, do you have any Coca-Cola or orange drinks?"

The merchant said, "Yes, yes, come back here." He led Sultan to a shelf stocked with orange, grape, and apple drinks. Sultan purchased several of each and then left the store.

His voice is trembling with excitement as he is telling his story. He repeats, just in case we didn't get the significance the first time: "The merchant said he had a *special customer* and that the Pepsi Cola products were already paid for and he could not sell them."

Of course, we are all aware of the probable significance of that statement, and to say that I too am excited would be a huge understatement.

We praise Sultan for the great job he did gathering this intelligence, and the van lumbers on through the streets of Abbottabad.

Now it seems more apparent than ever that Osama bin Laden is Abbottabad and, I presume, very close to where we are right now. He is very likely living behind one of these large walled-in homes that we have just passed. I can just feel it.

The question now is this: Do we wait patiently and take the passive approach that has been repeated to us all along our route from Peshawar to Abbottabad? In other words, do we wait for Osama bin Laden to find us? Or do we take a more proactive approach and stake out this grocery store to see where the Pepsi Cola products are delivered?

Of course there is a third choice. We could do both.

I'm sure there will be a lengthy debate tonight as the pros and cons of each of these ideas is presented, visited, and revisited. And indeed, after dinner Saleem, Sultan, Mohammed, and I all meet in my room and discuss the possibilities. It is decided that we will drive to the area again in the morning and see if there is a vantage point from which we can observe the grocery store while the van remains hidden.

Meanwhile, we agree, we will not vary our routine very much from day-to-day attendance at the mosque for Morning Prayer, and then to the market. We will also continue to stop at some of the teahouses in the central part of the city; they are always a good source for information.

The next morning we return to the area, parking the van blocks away from the store, in a location where it won't be immediately visible from the street. Then we continue on foot to ascertain the best surveillance spot where the grocery store can be discreetly observed.

There is a lot of traffic on the road, and at one point we are nearly run down by some children riding bicycles. As we walk, I scan the shops and homes, looking for a sign – any sign – that the Sheik may be near. I don't know quite what I am expecting to see, or even if the sign I am expecting is something mundane or mysterious. But I can clearly imagine that somewhere nearby is the tall bearded man I have been seeking. I can almost feel him. Maybe he is watching us, even now.

I know that I am now doing everything I can to find him. I have taken all the necessary precautions – or at least I think I have. And yet, at this moment, I am beginning to wonder if it will all come to fruition, because in the end, everyone knows I am an American. And this is a part of the world where Americans are distrusted, often taken advantage of...and sometimes killed. But somehow, this makes me even more determined to continue on my quest.

I would be lying if I said I am not an adrenaline junkie. And the adrenaline has been pumping overtime since yesterday's discovery of those Pepsi cases. Our subsequent plans to follow this lead – the most solid one so far – really quickened my pulse, and I stayed up most of the night thinking about it.

Ernest Hemingway once said that there is no hunting like the hunting of men, and I have to agree with him, even though he was talking about war, and in my case I am only "hunting" in order to get an interview. Now I will have to live by my decisions, and hopefully no one will die by them.

I have always considered myself an optimist, and I have been able to use this trait to my advantage. I've always been the "never-say-quit" guy; it is something I have been taught nearly all of my life. Even though my optimism has sometimes been severely tested while leading medical teams around the world, I have never quit. I've never allowed myself to get discouraged because of setbacks due to bad weather, poor transportation, equipment failures, or anything else. All of these situations have just left battle scars that, in my opinion, have made me even stronger. Those scars have served as a reminder to me that there is a larger purpose for my life, and that giving up just because of a setback or two would be selfish. If I were to give up I would be letting myself – and everyone else – down.

If you join a medical mission team for selfish reasons, you're setting yourself up for personal failure and possibly professional failure as well. I have had doctors, nurses, and ancillary personnel join my teams over the years, only to be placed on a plane back home before the mission was completed. Their hearts are not in it, and they never achieve what they could have achieved. What has kept me going is my desire to make a difference, a desire based neither on jingoistic ambitions nor glamorous ideals. I am not trying to be a hero or a saint, and I am not trying to impose "Americanism" on anybody else. What I really want to do is help people who need it, and at the same time help to change the image of the "Ugly American."

I remain forever haunted by the statement I've heard more than once in this region: "Americans come here only to kill us." I have desperately wanted to change that image of Americans. Just doing that would make me feel good – it would make me feel as if my efforts were worth something.

I do feel that as the years have gone by and my medical teams and I have completed more mission trips, we have made a significant change not only in the health and well-being of those we have treated, but just as important (or even more important), we have also helped change their attitudes towards America and Americans. I certainly think we have made a difference for our military when they came to the towns and villages where we had preceded them. So far – knock on wood – no U.S. or U.N. military force has been fired upon in any town or village where our medical team came before them. I would like to think that we had some influence there. So my missions have always been about more than just direct patient care.

I also love teaching many of the other physicians and nurses who have been part of the team. That's one of the most rewarding aspects of my medical career.

I know that we will not be able to stay in this region forever. But those whom we have taught will continue our work into the future, and they will be our spokespeople, perhaps telling others that the Americans made it all possible. To me, that is the best legacy I could leave.

I am lost in my own world, ruminating about these matters as we amble along the side of the road. Thank goodness for Saleem, who grabs me and pulls me away from the road just in time for me to avoid being plowed over by a monstrous oncoming truck. Long tails of desert sand and dust follow the truck as it bounces over the pothole-strewn dirt road. Then we see that this is the first of a caravan of jingle trucks – the customized vehicles common throughout the region – and they are moving quickly in our direction. The trucks are colorfully painted and adorned with pieces of rugs, festooned with chimes and all sorts of other dangling metal cutouts. They create quite a racket as they bounce along the gravel road, headed for the next village. It's easy to see – or rather hear – where they get the name "jingle trucks."

The jingle trucks are typically used by locals to transport goods, including cattle, rice, wheat, timber, and building supplies. They are almost always overloaded, and it is not uncommon to see a truck jacked up on the roadside having its axle welded. Many of the trucks travel south from China on the Karakoram Highway, but they also travel east to west through the mountain passes, where some have become vehicles for smuggling drugs and weapons across the Pakistan border into Iran, Afghanistan and beyond. The smugglers bury weapons and packages of drugs within stacks of firewood or under piles of rugs.

Two to three men usually accompany each truck. The drivers are experts on negotiating the mountainous roads, and usually there's a younger man too, who serves as the mechanic and can improvise and maintain the truck in running condition. It is not uncommon for one or two of the crew to be armed with automatic weapons; it all depends on the cargo and the route they are taking.

The drivers know every back road, valley, and mountain pass by memory. They know how to avoid checkpoints, and they know exactly where they can cross the borders undetected. They also know that with small amounts of cash or some of the goods they are transporting, they can buy passage through the Northern Territories and tribal areas.

Occasionally, however, a team of younger and more inexperienced infantrymen will come upon a jingle truck and will attempt to search the load. It's all in a days work for the drivers, who stand on the side of the road, wrapped in their woolen shawls smoking, while their younger assistants sit cross-legged on the roadside in the sun.

In my travels I've seen many roadside search-and-seizure scenarios. Well, to be accurate, there's often more searching than seizing involved. The truck drivers accept the annoyance as part of doing business, and the military often find that their efforts yield no contraband. Since the contraband is always buried deep in the interior of the truck, finding it would require a full day's work unloading – and it just isn't worth it.

I love these colorful trucks and I have hundreds of photos of them. No two trucks are the same; the colors and designs represent tribal, religious, political, and personal experiences. They are literally a rolling history.

In any case, seeing several of the trucks traveling through Abbottabad is unsurprising. As the last vehicle passes, we see a man posted twenty feet above us, perched atop some hundred-pound sacks of grain in the back of the truck. His rifle is pointing up and leaning against his shoulder, and as he glances down at us, I wave to him. He waves back and then is lost to my vision in a swirl of sand and dust.

The dust finally settles, and we decide to make our way back to the area across from the store with its stash of Pepsi. There is a one-story brick and mud building that had earlier caught our eye. The building is wedged between a warehouse filled with sacks of grain, and a ten-foot-high wall that is losing its stucco façade. Shards of broken glass line the wall's upper edge, apparently to prevent an intruder from attempting to gain a handhold to climb over. There is no activity, and the building looks abandoned. As we walk past, Mohammed taps me on the shoulder, makes a circle with his hand, and then leaves the group. The rest of us continue casually along the shoulder of the road as Mohammed circles around behind the grain depot to look at the building more closely and determine if it is indeed abandoned.

As Saleem, Sultan and I make our way down the narrow dirt street, we come to a spot where the street is walled on both sides by mud-brick dwellings with rusting natural gas tanks on concrete blocks in the front. The familiar laundry lines span the alleys and backyards with clothes, as always, fluttering in the light breeze like flags. Another one of the brightly painted jingle trucks lumbers by, its tires kicking up enough dust to obscure the entire street in its wake. We push through the dust clouds whipped up by the truck, making a hard left down a small alley to get away from the sand and dust. As we continue in the direction of the bazaar, the alleyway funnels into an even narrower passage between high mud brick walls paralleling an open sanitation ditch. Reaching the bazaar, we see that the shops are all open and the merchants are out in full force, as are crowds of purchasers. It is clear that the locals buy, sell, and trade here, and once again I find myself captivated. As we walk along the crowded street I peer into each of the shops, scarcely realizing that Saleem and Sultan are moving in closer to me, as if on high alert. As usual, I am lost in my total enjoyment of the sights, sounds, and smells of the bazaar. All too soon I will be profoundly grateful – once again – for my bodyguards.

At once, the crowd around us begins to scatter. It takes a moment for me to realize what is happening: the shopkeepers have spotted a Toyota pickup truck moving quickly through the crowded street, trying to avoid the rickshaws and donkey carts. The truck is not completely successful at this, but continues at race-like speed, and I can see merchants and customers alike quickly retreating towards the back of the shops.

Saleem and Sultan grab me by the shoulders and push me towards an alley behind several large wooden crates. The Toyota pickup flies by and I can see that a machine gun has been welded into the bed. There are several men in the cab with automatic weapons, and the ones in the back are standing up, holding on to a roll bar and waving flags.

They are Taliban.

The truck screeches to a stop at the next intersection, about fifty meters ahead, just as several donkey carts are crossing. Two of the Taliban jump out, with automatic weapons slung over their shoulders and flags in their hands. They are screaming and hitting the donkeys on their rumps to get them to move across the road more quickly.

I fully expect to see and hear automatic weapon fire any second, but instead, something entirely surreal happens. I try to move from behind the crates with my camera, but Saleem and Sultan have other ideas, and push me back. But I am still able to observe what is happening.

What we see are the people – shopkeepers and shoppers alike – forming a human barricade around the truck, as well as around the two men who have jumped to the street. The vendors begin shouting and waving their fists, and from what I can discern, they are yelling for the Taliban to get out of the bazaar. I manage to pull free from Saleem and Sultan, and move carefully along the stalls under the covered awnings. Saleem and Sultan, realizing they have no choice, follow me, but I am moving too quickly and they are soon lost in the crowd. As I draw closer to the melee, the crowd grows, with the shouts becoming louder and the fist-waving becoming more forceful.

The men from the truck stand as if transfixed, their weapons still slung on their shoulders, and they seem confused as to what is happening. Clearly they are not accustomed to this level of defiance – or any defiance at all, for that matter.

At that moment someone comes up behind me and taps me on my shoulder. My adrenalin is pumping so high that I feel as if I might jump out of my skin. Whirling around to face what I fear is a new threat, I see with relief that it is Mohammed.

He has returned from surveying the building and was drawn to the excitement. He gently directs me toward the doorway of the shop and pushes on my shoulders, urging me to assume a crouching position. From here I have a good view of what is taking place, and my camera is clicking away.

An elderly man dressed in a long gray robe with black trim emerges from the shop across from me. He wears a plain black turban and what appear to be brand-new sandals – at least new in comparison to the tattered, dust-covered flip-flops worn by the locals who are surrounding the Taliban truck. The man has a long white beard with some flecks of black still visible. He is either the local *Maulana*, one of the village elders, or a tribal landlord and clan leader.

The man holds both hands high, and the crowd begins to calm down. As he speaks in Pashto to the crowd, Mohammed, standing behind me, whispers translations into my right ear.

After addressing the crowd, the elder turns to the Taliban and announces, "I own many of the shops in the bazaar and most of the land around here. I will not allow you to harm anyone in this town. I have treated these people well – much better than the central government. You will *not* come here and attempt to shatter that alliance."

The old man stands in front of the truck, not moving. He then slowly begins to stroke his beard, as if in deep thought. Finally he says, "Now, show me your faces, and I will talk to you."

I rest my Nikon on the corner of a nearby fruit stand and continue to photograph the scene. I notice that the two Taliban men in the street have turned anxiously toward the driver – perhaps the leader – as if for guidance.

Once again the crowd begins to stir, their voices rising, and they begin pounding their fists on the truck again. Mohammed, now shouting in my ear so I can hear him above the noise, tells me what the crowd is saying. Some are yelling for the Taliban to leave them alone and others are just shouting for them to leave.

The truck is now trying to back up slowly, for going forward is currently impossible with the donkey carts still occupying the center of the street. But the crowd continues to push in, and the two men who had abandoned the truck turn and dash back through the throng, heading in a different direction. Some of the young men who were standing behind the truck run off after the fleeing Taliban, which allows the vehicle to back into an alley and make a U-turn to escape.

I really am not sure why the men had chosen to run. Maybe they don't quite trust the citizens either. Suddenly one of them crosses right in front of the shop where I am kneeling down. His face is partially covered with a black bandana. He glances at Mohammed and me for just a second, and I'm sure he has noticed the camera, but he continues on his way, moving as quickly as he can from the crowd. I can see him fleeing down a side street leaving the bazaar.

The truck has now completed its turn, and with its wheels spinning, dust and sand are flying everywhere. I look up, my eyes itching from the dust storm. Then I turn and walk further into the back of the shop, waiting for the cloud of dust to settle.

There is a smell of sweet meat cooking, and I can see a small kitchen area to my right, with a work table and several fresh flowers in a small vase. A woman is cowering behind that table and cuddling a young girl to her. There is also a small boy, maybe nine or ten years old, in the corner. The eyes of the mother and daughter are bulging as they see us, and the little girl begins to weep. The boy runs towards his mother, and she pulls both children close to her.

As I continue to look around, I see that in the shadows to the far corner of the room there is an older man with his back to the wall: the father, no doubt. He has a well-trimmed beard, a turban, and long sideburns that seem very Western to me. He puts his fingers to his lips, and with an outstretched hand he opens his palm, indicating that we need to stay low and keep our heads down. We have no argument there.

I somehow feel as if we are intruding on this family, and I start to make a move towards the front of the store, but the father holds his hand up again, indicating that we should not go forward yet. He comes around the table where his wife is still clutching her children, and as he does so he pats the young boy on the head. Then he peers intently towards the front of the shop, and after a while says something softly in Pashto. Mohammed grabs my arm and raises me from the floor, saying, "It's all clear now, it's safe to go out to the street again."

I pick up my camera and sling it over my shoulder. Shifting to the left side of the room, I begin moving toward the exit, with Mohammed behind me, and we step outside the store. The family is following closely behind. I glance back at them, and although the mother shakes her head in disapproval, the girl and boy seem fascinated by me – or perhaps by my camera. I point to the camera and then to each of the children. Their eyes grew wide as big smiles appear on their faces, and the little girl's weeping has all but stopped. I move out from under the tattered awning over the front door, and as I turn back, the entire family is standing there beside the front entrance. I again point to the camera, and the father indicates that it is okay to take the family's picture.

The lighting coming through the tattered awning and the front door is less than optimal, so I set the flash and take several pictures. I then turn the camera around, and the children run to me so they can view the photo. I take some hard candies out of my pocket and look at the parents to get their approval before offering them to the children.

"Its okay," says the man in English, surprising me. "I know who you are. You are the American 'Dr. Angel.' I'm glad you have come to Abbottabad to help us."

"Where did you learn your English?"

He grins widely. "It's a long story and now is not the time. Come visit us again, and we can sit and talk. I have heard you have other interests here in Abbottabad – and perhaps I can help you with that."

I smile broadly, then nod my head towards the wife and children, and I place my hand over my heart in the typical expression of "Thank you." I have made some more friends today, and for that I am truly thankful.

There is still a lot of dust and sand blowing along the main street. I raise my sheath to conceal the lower portion of my face, and again I nod to the family as Mohammed and I leave their shop. We start down the main street of the bazaar, and Saleem and Sultan soon join us, admonishing me for my little adventure. The excitement has died down, and the bazaar is already returning to its normal activities. Everyone has started back towards the shops.

We spot the village elder with the black turban walking under the canopies on the far side of the street. A small crowd has gathered around him, and an active conversation is taking place. But he pushes through the group and continues on his way.

I turn to my own small group and ask if there is anything we need to purchase at the bazaar before returning to the van, but nobody can think of anything we really need. When reach the edge of the bazaar where the van is parked, Mohammed unlocks and swings the side door open. I suddenly realize that I have a raging thirst, and the first thing I do is grab a bottle of water. The others follow suit.

Mohammed starts the engine and we turn down a side street. He is very excited and speaks rapidly in Urdu to Saleem and Sultan, explaining what took place in the shop where he and I had hunkered down. And then looking at me as if suddenly realizing that I might not be able to keep up with everything he is saying, Mohammed switches to English. He explains to Saleem and Sultan that the shopkeeper recognized "Dr. Angel," and knows that the doctor is hoping to meet Sheik bin Laden for an interview. Word travels fast in the tribal areas. Mohammed says that one of us needs to return to that shop and have further conversation with the merchant. We agree that this is a good idea.

I then ask Mohammed what he discovered in the building across from the grocery store that was selling the Pepsi product. After all, that was the original reason for our outing today: to case the area and determine the best spot for surveillance.

Mohammed says, "It is apparently an abandoned wood-working shop – or at least I believe it is abandoned. I saw no sign of recent activity. Some of the equipment is still there but it doesn't look very functional. There are some remnants of un-finished wooden furniture and everything is covered with dust.

I think that it will make the perfect spot to observe the grocery store across the street."

We nod, taking this in, and then Mohammed continues, "One of us needs to move in to that building after the grocery store closes, and we can each do an eight-hour shift – myself, Saleem, and Sultan. I'll be happy to take the first one this evening. No one will miss one of us if we rotate. But they would probably miss the doctor, so I guess he gets out of surveillance duty."

We all laugh and agree that this is a good plan. Saleem volunteers for the second eight hours, leaving Sultan to take the morning watch after the early call to prayer. We don't even have to debate who will do what, and when. Everybody is in agreement with the plan, and is willing to do his part.

We continue on the narrow back road out of town, because we still want to get a better feel for the area. We pass fields with haystacks and scattered herds of large black water buffalo. As the van moves on through the countryside, I am lost in thought. Today was very encouraging in more than one respect.

First, it was profoundly heartening to witness the townspeople's angry defiance when the Taliban truck came through. Though the Taliban's intent was to intimidate the people, it backfired, and the Taliban were forced to retreat.

Secondly, I am more convinced than ever that my quest to meet with Osama bin Laden will finally bear fruit. I am also more convinced than ever that despite our clever surveillance plan, it is he who will find me, rather than vice versa. But I feel it will only be a matter of time before we are contacted by one of his people.

First Meeting
with the Sheik

As it turns out, we aren't kept waiting very long before we are contacted by one of bin Laden's group. Sitting in a small teahouse, we are talking about everything and nothing at all when a man whom I would guess to be about thirty years old walks over to our table and greets us. Since my Pashto is less than fluent, Saleem translates for me. The young man says that he has heard talk of my own thirst for Pepsi Cola, and informs us that he might know where I can obtain a small amount, if I would like to do so. Mohammed warns me that this might be a trap, an attempt to kidnap a rich American for ransom, but my gut feeling tells me otherwise.

The stranger tells me that his boss would like to extend an invitation to join him this evening for a cold glass of the soda we both seem to favor, and for a bit of friendly conversation. I tell Saleem to thank him for the invitation, and to ask him for the address and time. The man's response is strange; he says that I should return alone to this same teashop at eight o'clock this evening, and that he will then take me to his employer's residence. He stresses that I must be alone and can bring only a pen and notebook. Nothing more. Once I have accepted his instructions, the man bids us goodbye, turns, and abruptly leaves, disappearing into the crowd in the marketplace a short distance away.

Mohammed, Saleem, and Sultan are still not convinced, and they try to talk me out of returning later tonight, but I've made up my mind. We spend the rest of the afternoon in idle, if nervous, chatter. As the sun begins to set, and darkness falls upon the city, I climb into the van, and Mohammed drives me back to the tea shop, which has closed for the day. Despite Mohammed's insistence that he remain behind and go with me to the meeting, I sense that if I am not alone when my escort returns, he will drive on by without stopping, and my chance at having a meeting with bin Laden will be lost.

It also crosses my mind that if my armed driver is sitting at the table with me when the man returns, there is a good chance that we'll both be shot and left to die in the street, yet another instance of a foolish American who wandered where he should not have. Suggesting the potential for this last – and very possible – scenario, I am finally able to convince my faithful driver to leave me. He begrudgingly climbs back into the van and, with a final disapproving look back at me, drives away to pick up Sultan and Saleem. And then I am alone.

I sit at the table for what feels like a long while, thinking I must look rather foolish loitering in the dark outside a long-since-closed teahouse, on a seemingly abandoned street. Looking at my watch for what must be the twentieth time, I realize that I've only been here about fifteen minutes when I hear a vehicle's engine in the distance. The sound grows louder, and after a moment or two, I see a small pickup turn the corner onto the street where I'm sitting. As it draws nearer, I can see that it is an old Toyota, its body dented and rusting in places. Then, with tires sliding in the gravel, it skids to a halt directly in front of me. The driver is the same man who had approached us earlier, and his greeting is terse and commanding. "Get in."

I reach for a seat belt, only to realize that if there had been one at some point, it is long gone. The driver produces a large woolen sack and places it over my head, his intent quite clear: I am not yet worthy of his trust, and therefore am not to be allowed to know the location of my meeting. We depart, and I am immediately relieved that this driver doesn't have Mohammed's love for scaring his passengers. The route he takes is obviously and intentionally circuitous, and after just a few turns, I am at a complete loss, not only for where we are, but even for the direction in which we're headed.

I estimate that we have been driving for about fifteen minutes or so when the truck finally comes to a halt. At my driver's whispered word, I hear what sounds to be a large, ancient gate opening, and the truck once again lurches forward. As we come to a stop, I raise my hands to remove the hood, and the driver (or is he my abductor? I will have my answer soon enough, I reason) grabs them. "Not yet!" He gets out of the truck, and quickly comes to my side and opens the door, pulling me roughly from my seat. He leads me by the arm, and after we've walked about thirty feet, he removes the hood. It takes a few seconds for my eyes to adapt to the bright light, whereupon I see that we are in a portico of sorts, the entryway to what looks to be a large house directly in front of us.

Before entering the house, the driver motions for me to remove my sandals and leave them by the door. I am then ushered into a large central room with no furnishings save for a row of large cushions along the far wall. With the wave of his hand, I am directed to sit. I walk to the far side of the room and sit cross-legged with a cushion at my back. When I look up, the room is empty. True to the instructions I have been given, I have brought only a notebook and pen. I have no electronic equipment, not even my cell phone. I am hoping that as these interviews progress, and I develop a rapport with the

Sheik Osama bin Laden, I will be allowed to use a recorder and perhaps even obtain some photos. My other thought is to request that the Sheik provide the camera and the recorder if that makes him more comfortable... but that is for the future.

I don't know why, but I have the feeling that I am being observed, even though I can't see anyone. As time passes, I find myself becoming anxious, and think this might be some type of test. I need to do something, so I open my notebook and begin to sketch the room. Minutes pass, and I try to remain calm and concentrate on my sketch. Finally, a young man enters the room carrying a small tray with some hot tea and dried fruit, which he sets on the floor next to me. I look at him, and for a few seconds we make eye contact. I smile at him, saying the Urdu word for "Thank you," but he doesn't respond. As he straightens up and turns to leave, I say the Pashto word for "very good." This gets me a smile. The young man stops for a second, and in very good English says, "You are welcome. You are the American – the Angel doctor everyone is talking about."

His command of English startles me, but I reply in Pashto, "Yes. You may call me Joseph."

He nods and responds, "Peace be with you."

He points to the tea and the small basket with the dried fruit and cheese, then turns and leaves. I sip the tea and nibble at the fruit as I return my attention to sketching the room.

I don't hear him enter the room, and don't know what causes me to look up, but when I do, I see a very tall, lanky gentleman standing a few feet from me. His face is thin, making his cheekbones seem more prominent and accentuating his large, deep-set eyes. He has a book in his left hand that I assume to be the *Qur'an*. He is barefoot and dressed all in white, and his beard extends almost to his waist. His sudden appearance has startled me, and I move to stand. He holds his hand out, palm down, indicating I should remain seated, and in a soft, pleasant voice says, in Pashto, "Peace be with you."

I respond, also in Pashto, "And to you also."

Sheik Osama bin Laden sits across from me, looks over at my notebook, and smiles at my sketch. I turn the book so he can see it better. As he looks at my drawing, the young man who had served me the tea and treats enters the room and sits next to the Sheik. He will serve as our interpreter. Osama bin Laden is an educated man and almost certainly has a working knowledge of English – in fact, his English is probably much better than my Pashto – but for many reasons he prefers not to use the language. So we will keep up the masquerade by using the interpreter.

I nod respectfully in the Sheik's direction, saying, "You do me a great honor allowing me to interview with you."

He smiles and responds, "I have heard many good things about the Angel doctor from Texas, and it is my honor to have you in my home."

I decide to get right to the questions without further pleasantries. "Sheik bin Laden, how long have you been living in Abbottabad?"

"About three and a half years."

"You are living here with members of your family? Your wives?"

"Yes."

"When you were nineteen years old, you married your Syrian cousin, Najwa Ghanem Najwa, correct?"

He replies, "Actually, I was only seventeen years old when I married Najwa. However, several years ago, when we were living in the Sudan, in Khartoum, Najwa left with my eldest son Abdullah and returned to Saudi Arabia, where they are still living. At that time we lived under very austere conditions without running water and proper toilet facilities. Abdullah did not favor this lifestyle. He wanted to return with his mother to Saudi Arabia and rejoin the family business. He and I had discussed this on many occasions. Abdullah said that Allah had blessed the family with wealth, and that his mother Najwa and he had the right to enjoy it."

I press on, "Your other wives are from Saudi Arabia?"

"Three of my wives are from Saudi Arabia, and the fifth and newest member of my family is from Yemen."

"So you have four wives living with you now?"

"No, my second wife, Khadijah Sharif, also divorced me when we were in Sudan, and she returned to Saudi Arabia with my son and daughter. I have not seen them for several years now."

I pause a moment to collect my thoughts, but before I can ask another question, bin Laden continues. "I married for the fifth time in the summer of 2000 to Amal Ahmed Abdel-Fatah Al Sada, who as I said is a Yemeni woman. This was an arranged marriage, and she was only seventeen years old at the time. She is twenty-seven years old now, and is at the house with me. My close friend Abu Jandal arranged our marriage, and the Al Qaeda leader arranged for a wonderful wedding celebration. But for a while, before Khadijah Sharif and Najwa returned to Saudi Arabia, all my wives and children lived together happily with me."

"How many children do you have?"

"I have eleven sons and thirteen daughters. We all live together, with the exception, of course, of my eldest son Abdullah and of my son and daughter from my second wife."

The Sheik's voice is normally soft, but now I can hardly hear him. He has a wan, faraway look about him, and I think I actually see a tear in his eye, which he seems to try to conceal by staring intently down, as if studying his cup of tea, searching for some unknown secrets it might hold. He takes a sip of his tea, and the room seems suddenly very quiet. He looks up and continues, "Abdullah could never seem to tolerate the simple and austere life that we led. We are all different. Allah has made no two of us alike."

"You are saddened by this."

"I feel he has been disrespectful to his father in choosing an affluent lifestyle, and disobedient in leaving his family behind."

I can see in his eyes that he is deeply hurt by having his eldest son leave him, perhaps more so than having his wives and the other two children leave. I can understand. It is very easy to imagine myself in his place, and I find myself empathizing with him, what with my own son having left Houston, Texas to pursue a life in New York City. But that, as they say, is another story. I ask him, "So in addition to your fifth wife, your other two wives are also well and with you?"

"Khairiah Sabar and Siham Sabar are both well. We have been separated from time to time due to circumstances that I could not completely control, and the need for me to be moving rapidly from place to place. However, they are both here with me. Amal was in Pakistan, but returned to her family in Yemen for a while. With the help of family members, I arranged for her to be smuggled out of Yemen and brought to Pakistan so she could rejoin me."

I find myself wanting to steer the conversation away from the subject, which is obviously a painful one for him. "As a physician, I would like to ask about your health. There have been numerous reports that you suffer from multiple serious conditions. Some of the accounts go so far as to indicate the need for dialysis as a result of diabetes or other serious afflictions."

He chuckles at this, and responds, "These accounts of course are fanciful. I am in excellent health. I do not require or take any medications. I have always enjoyed walking through the mountains, especially in the early morning after prayer, and I miss my horses and the pleasure of riding out across the desert. The past several years, however, I have confined myself to this walled compound, but for my own safety and the safety of my family, and not because of health issues."

Now I feel it is time to get to more serious matters. "The CIA and other foreign intelligence agencies are still spending millions of dollars looking for you in Afghanistan and the Northern Tribal regions, and yet, here you are, in Abbottabad, in the safety of this beautiful home. I would think that you would have to have gotten help from the Pakistan Government, the military, or the ISI to acquire this compound, much less to have been here so long, undetected and in relative safety."

He nods, saying, "I have connections within the ISI who have made it possible for me to secretly come to Abbottabad, and later to bring members of my family here as well."

"You are telling me you have friends in the ISI and other high places of the army or the Pakistani government."

"Yes, yes, special, very personal relationships that go back to my days in Afghanistan when we were fighting the Russians and receiving support from the ISI. These are deep-rooted relationships that go back many years. Like family, these allegiances are never broken. Perhaps they are even stronger than family."

I find myself feeling emboldened, and begin down a path that I realize could have serious repercussions for me, if I have misread this man, "You remind me in many ways of a British man named T. E. Lawrence, better known as Lawrence of Arabia, who fought for the Arab cause. With a small, determined group of fighters, he accomplished what the British at that time thought to be impossible. His exploits made him a hero of that generation.

"Similarly, many people have great admiration for what you were able to accomplish, especially against the Russian forces in Afghanistan. They have respect for you because of the austere life that you have chosen for yourself and your family, even though you come from one of the wealthiest families in the world. They have tremendous respect for you, for you have not bowed to the enormous pressures from within the Muslim community, nor from some of the world's most powerful leaders. Yet, your own family members have disassociated themselves from you because they do not approve of the violent attacks that have occurred around the world and have been attributed to you.

"Yet I see your picture in store windows, emblazoned upon T-shirts, etched into the back of cigarette lighters, and on stickers on school children's backpacks. I have worked in hospitals through the Indus and into the Northern Territories. More than half of the baby boys born in these hospitals are being named Osama. This is happening not just in Pakistan, but throughout the Muslim world. This is a testament to your popularity, and to the admiration and respect you inspire. It is my experience that Sheik bin Laden's popularity extends far and wide, and even though you have expressed contempt for the Saudi Royal Family and describe them as Infidels, you too have deviated from true Islam. You are especially popular in Saudi Arabia, perceived as the voice of the Muslim nation and a fighter on its behalf."

I allow a few moments for my words to sink in. I realize that I am stroking the Sheik's ego, and hope that by so doing, I will earn some degree of tolerance from him as the discussion progresses in directions that he might not find so flattering. Finally I continue, "I think the Western media have played a role in portraying you as a Superman to the Muslim World. Even as they revile your tactics, they have elevated you to the status of folk hero to non-Westerners – the David to a larger and more powerful Goliath. They have spun it into a story of bin Laden versus the U.S.A., the epic battle of the century, if not the millennium.

"The Western press has latched onto the idea of Osama bin Laden as a villain, unwittingly giving you and your cause credence and popularity by promoting an image that is reviled by the West, yet adored in the Muslim world. I don't think it is an exaggeration to say that the press has done more for the Muslim cause and bin Laden in particular than any single entity. They have done things for you that you could never have achieved yourself. They portray you as a warrior who displays no fear of death as you advocate for the Muslim cause worldwide. What we in the West see as horrific, such as the attacks of 9/11, many Muslims see as your first steps in the return of the Muslim empire. Thanks to the press, the people of this region perceive you as the most famous Muslim warrior of our time, and the man who just might be able to achieve the goal of Muslim world domination. My question to you, Sheik bin Laden, is this: Do you see *yourself* as the Prophet that the Muslim world has been waiting for?"

The young man who has been interpreting for me intervenes, speaking in rapid English. "He is the awaited and enlightened one. He is the soldier of the Apocalypse that was promised. The Hadith has foretold his coming. Osama bin Muhammed bin Laden is the promised one. The rightly guided Caliph who has been sent to us. It was foretold that he would arrive from Arabia and that he will be called from the depths of the cave by Allah. He will be the Savior of all true believers."

The Hadith is the collection of sacred teachings supplementing the Qur'an. Essentially it is a collection of the sayings of the Prophet Mohammed. It is obvious that our young interpreter believes passionately that bin Laden is indeed the chosen one.

The Sheik himself does not respond to this outburst, however, so I go on. "I have read the Qur'an and portions of the Hadith. The writings foretell that the long-awaited one will be a descendent from the line of Muhammed. I wasn't aware that the Sheik bin Laden was a descendent of Muhammed through his daughter Fatima. It is also said that he will have the name of the Prophet. Is that why the Sheik now signs his name on his correspondence as Osama bin *Mohammed* bin Awad bin Laden?"

The room is suddenly very quiet. As I look from my young interpreter to Osama and then back again, I am beginning to feel very uncomfortable. Perhaps I have overstepped my bounds and found too soon the limits of bin Laden's tolerance. I am, after all, a guest in his house, and perhaps I need to soften the tone – if not the direction – of this conversation. I look directly at bin Laden, and then lower my head, saying, "I think of myself as educated and well-read, but I am not a scholar of the Qu'ran or the Hadith. I do recall from my readings that the Enlightened One will appear at a time when Muslims are oppressed throughout the world. Oppression has many faces, however. There are social restrictions that lead to the oppression of women throughout most Muslim countries. I am not directing this at your household, because I know two of your wives have doctorate degrees. One has a doctorate in Arabic languages, and the other has a doctorate in Sharia Law."

At this, bin Laden smiles and nods.

I continue, "They have been with you through difficult times in Tora Bora, Afghanistan, and Yemen, and have returned with you here in Abbottabad. This is loyalty I can appreciate and understand. However, women throughout the

Muslim world remain uneducated, and are treated with little respect. Most are restricted to the home, and not allowed to travel beyond the walls of their family compound. I would like to discuss this and hear your comments, for in my humble limited studies of the Qu'ran, I have read nothing that says that a woman cannot be educated, nor is there anything that I have been able to interpret that requires them to wear the *burqa*.

"But let us return to the question at hand. You have taken the name of the Prophet Mohammed. Men bow before you and greet you as the Awaited Enlightened One. You have peers throughout the Muslim World who have been unduly oppressed; you have united an army of religious Muslim believers as foretold in the Hadith. You have successfully fought off the vast army of the Soviet Union – the oppressors. The non-believers. The army of the Infidel."

Bin Laden is now smiling again. His eyes are focused on me, and he is gently nodding in agreement. I continue, "The Hadith foretells that the Long Awaited One will be tall, will have a distinctive forehead and a prominent nose, and will also have a black mole on his face. You fit this description, and now you have taken the title of Mohammed. Are you the *Mahdi*? Are you the *Mahdi* who will be restoring justice to the world by imposing Sharia law on all nations? Are you the *Mahdi* who brings forth the Day of Islam for all people – believers and non-believers alike – and causes them to submit to the will of Allah?"

My interpreter answers, "He is the *Mahdi*."

Bin Laden turns and looks sharply at the young man, silently but effectively scolding him for his outbursts. The young interpreter pushes back from our small circle and lowers his head in submission.

Turning his attention to me, bin Laden finally speaks, "There are those who have given me the title of Enlightened One – The *Mahdi*. Only Allah knows if this is my true destiny. I am but his humble servant. The One God, who has sustained with one of His helping Hands, and saw fit to allow us to defeat the Soviet Empire, is capable of bestowing upon me this great task. Allah is capable of sustaining us again, and of allowing us to defeat the non-believers at home and those abroad. I believe that the defeat of America is achievable with the permission of God, and with God on our side it will prove to be easier than the defeat of the Soviet Empire. There is a great aura about America. It uses this to scare its enemies before it engages in battle. Our brothers, the true believers, will overcome. God has ever cleared the path for them by the Muhajadeen. God will sustain us with His Helping Hands to break America, for with God, we are capable of that."

He pauses, running his long thin fingers down his scraggly beard. His shoulders are hunched and rounded. His face has countless wrinkles, each bearing testament to a life spent beneath an unrelenting desert sun. And of course, there is the distinctive black mole. Though middle-aged, he appears at this moment to be much older. He slowly sips at his tea, as if searching for his next words in the depths of the cup.

After a few moments, he lifts his hands into the air and says, "The American military organization will also fail because of its extravagance in leadership and the inability of its soldiers to endure the hardships that we live with every day in this part of the world. I and my soldiers of God take the proud stance against all global disbelievers, and I affirm our steadfastness on this path. God will replace the people of this Earth for those who love Him, people who are humble towards the believers and hard on the disbelievers, and who strive in conflict with God's way without fearing anyone's reproach. Such is God's favor. He grants it to whoever He will. I will follow that will. You asked, am I the Enlightened *Mahdi?* God in his wisdom will show us the proper path and the people themselves will also determine this."

He reaches forward and takes another sip of his tea, smiles and nods in my direction. I recognize this as an indication that our session is over. I take a last sip of tea and thank him for the opportunity to speak with him, and for extending to me the hospitality of his home. But there is so much more that I want to know and understand, and I ask him, "Will we meet again tomorrow?"

"One week from tonight, as the sun sets, be outside the mosque which is located near the Sarafa Bazaar. We will find you. After the evening prayers we will talk again."

With that I stand up, and the young man walks me to the door and across the courtyard, past the guest house with the bodyguard. I stop, turning toward the bodyguard and salute. He salutes back. I feel safer if they recognize me and know who I am, especially since I am hopeful of being invited for additional visits to the compound in the future.

Two of the bodyguards come forward, slinging their automatic weapons over their shoulders. They slowly nudge the bolts from the door in the compound wall. They slide it open enough for me to pass through, then step to the other side to let me pass. I thank them in the customary fashion, placing my right hand over my heart, and quickly turn and depart. I walk in the direction of the Military Academy, knowing my driver Mohammed will be parked on one of the cross streets, awaiting my arrival. After I have walked several hundred yards a light flashes. This is the signal I am waiting for, and I hear an engine starting up as I approach the intersection. It is Mohammed with our van.

He looks at me, apprehensively and says, "It went well?"

"Very well. We have another meeting a week from now. I was told they would find me. I need to be in the vicinity of the mosque behind the Sarafa Bazaar when the sun sets."

I have no idea where this relationship, such as it is, will go, but one thing I do know: there is no turning back now.

Between Meetings...
Surgery & Reflection

I've been unable to sleep for the last several nights. The air seems so heavy I can hardly breathe, and it isn't just the hot climate that is to blame. All I can see when I close my eyes is the face of Osama bin Laden, again and again. Is this a man I am meeting with, or a monster? I close my eyes and attempt to get some sleep, but once again the face of the Sheik appears in my mind's eye. It has been an uneasy week for me, and the unease grows stronger as the time for the second meeting approaches.

There isn't any easy way to get over it or past it. I am here on a medical mission, and in a few short hours, I will have to be up, fully alert, and in the operating room. But my need for sleep is overruled by the constant replay of my meeting with the Sheik. A million thoughts run through my mind, chasing away any possibility of my getting the sleep I so desperately need. What type of man is this, and what kind of questions can I ask him and realistically expect to get truthful answers?

This trip has now gone way beyond just medical care. I can't help but wonder whether I've gotten in over my head. As a doctor, I have not only taken an oath, I have also made a pledge to myself that my patients would always come first. Now, however, I find myself in a situation where the events of my own country and the larger world are on a collision course with that pledge. Will my intrusion into the events of that larger world – one very unfamiliar to me – cost me my life? And if so, how will that affect my patients here, or for that matter, my family? My family knows how dangerous it is for me to be working the Northern Tribal Territories of Pakistan. My wife Terry hasn't taken it well – particularly when I finally told her about the attack on the Karakoram – but how could I expect her to?

On the other hand, she isn't surprised that I am where I am, since I have always gone into the areas where my team and I are needed most. The previous year, for instance, I had met with twenty-four warlords, and I never asked who was Taliban or Al Qaeda, but requested only that they respect my team's work and cover our backs. The warlords all pledged their allegiance to us, with the stipulation that we not bring regular army troops (Pakistani regulars or the Pakistani police force) into their towns. In my mind, it seemed to be a very simple and fair agreement – you help our children, and we will take care of you. You and your team are our guests, and we will see to your protection and comfort. On the other hand, they live in a society that believes in an eye for an eye, and I know that if we cause them problems or hurt them, they would not hesitate for a moment to kill us.

Over the past five years, a relationship of mutual trust has developed between the warlords and my team. Many of the people we meet don't even know my name, and refer to me as either Doctor Angel or the Crazy Texan. When I was in one village, I was given a donkey wagon, which is the most common local means of transportation. But unlike most who would sit in the wagon and trot along the rutted dirt road, I would stand up and drive it like Ben Hur in a chariot, holding on to my cowboy hat with one hand and the reins with the other, and with my white coat blowing in the wind. I can't imagine why they would refer to me as the Crazy Texan!

I have personally operated on almost five thousand children, and my team, working with the local physicians and surgeons, has performed more than twenty thousand procedures. I've studied Urdu, and try my best to communicate with my patients and staff in that language, and even try to use it in the market or street. I believe that my often awkward attempts to speak in their native tongue have served to further endear me to the people in the villages and towns. Still, I sometimes wonder whether all these efforts at establishing goo will might ultimately backfire if I make some little mis-step. After all, I am still an outsider, and an American one at that.

Since sleep is obviously not going to come, I figure there's no sense lying in bed staring at the paint peeling. I get up and turn the ceiling fan from medium to high, which makes an imperceptible change in the oppressive heat, if any at all. There is some bottled water on the small table at my bedside, and I snap open the cap and take a drink, pouring the rest over my head. I turn on and affix my battery-operated head light, pulling the straps snugly, then get out the diary that I have kept on all my trips for more than 25 years. "Diary" seems a bit misleading as a description. I have filled several hundred of these books, all dated as to time and place, and they fill a couple of large book-shelves in my home.

At least there is power tonight. But the still air hangs in the room, the whirring ceiling fan providing no real relief. My T-shirt clings to my skin, and the musty odor of the room hangs in the darkness like the remnants of some fetid ghost. The moonlight shines through the broken slats of the window shade, casting flickering shadows across my diary as I begin to write. My first meeting with Osama bin Laden has played havoc with me these past few nights, and I am anxious about the upcoming second meeting. I find myself hoping that returning to the operating room in a couple of hours will relax and calm me.

I continue to write in my diary, but after about an hour, I still feel the room closing in on me, so close that I feel as if I'm being suffocated. I rise and pull on my *shalwar kameez*, and slip into my sandals. I leave the head light in place and use it to navigate my way down the hall to the side door. At the doorway, I press the small button on the side of the light to switch it off and venture outside into the cool darkness, at once grateful for the absence of streetlights or other forms of illumination. I look up to the sky and see millions of stars, far more than anyone who lives anywhere close to a city ever gets to see. I amuse myself by locating the constellations I still remember from my time in the Astronomy Club at Asbury Park High School.

My thoughts are interrupted momentarily by the barking of dogs some distance away, but they quickly tire of their ruckus and I am able to return to my star gazing. As I look up at the sky, I find myself thinking of Terry and wondering what she is doing right now, on what is an early afternoon back in Houston. I hope she doesn't think I'm being selfish by spending this time away. A friend once said to me, "You work ridiculous hours. You are underpaid. And you are in an area where people are going to try to kill you." And I had answered him by saying that I love it. Every minute of it.

Despite the satisfaction I get from these journeys, right now, I can only think of how much I miss Terry and her radiant smile. I long to hear her voice and to see the light in her eyes that I find so intoxicating. I will have to find some special gift for her in the market. Something that will make her smile and remind her of just how much she means to me.

As I stand here thinking of home, the stars are beginning to dim before the slowly rising sun and the beginning of the new day. And at the end of that day, at sunset, I will be on my way to my second meeting with the Sheik.

Inasmuch as there is only one bathroom for all of us, and since I'm already awake, it seems only prudent to be the first to wash up and get myself ready for the day ahead. Once I finish cleaning up and dressing, I set to the task of assembling the photographic equipment and medical supplies I'll need to take to the hospital.

Within the next hour the atmosphere in the house changes dramatically, the stillness and silence replaced with the flurry of activity as the others awaken and begin their preparations for the day. Saleem knocks on my door, with the very pleasant announcement that breakfast is ready. Until this moment, I hadn't given any thought to eating, but upon hearing his words, I realize that I am famished. As I walk toward the small dining room, I am greeted by the most delicious of smells, and entering, I see that there are fried eggs, flatbread, and hot English tea set out.

Mohammed approaches me and asks, "I saw the light on in your room almost all night. You were worried?"

"Not worried. Anxious, and somewhat concerned, but not worried." With that, everyone at the table smiles and the atmosphere lightens considerably. I smile as well, and after we all wolf down our meal, I turn again to my driver and say, "Mohammed, get the car ready. We are leaving for the hospital. We have a long day ahead of us. And Saleem, Sultan, I have two heavy bags of medical supplies and camera equipment. Please help me take those to the car. The rest of you, please finish your breakfast. We will go ahead and set up the operating room and prepare the first two patients. You can join us when you are ready."

My colleague Dr. Nur nods quickly. "We will be there in about twenty minutes." I smile, glad that he is here and working with my team.

Dr. Nur, an accomplished otolaryngologist (ear, nose and throat surgeon) is a youngish man, in his forties. Slimly built and light-skinned, he has a full shock of dark hair and facial features that are both delicate and strong. When not in surgical scrubs, Dr. Nur is always immaculately dressed in elegant Western style suits that look as if they were tailor-made. He is impeccable regardless of the time of day, or the long hours he has put in with the medical team and me. He is full of energy and confidence, and carries himself well, walking with a strong, purposeful stride.

He is a hard worker and a quick learner, he learned the techniques to repair cleft lips and cleft palates very quickly. In fact, he ultimately got to the point where he did the best cleft palate repair I have ever seen, and that is saying something. I've been proud to have him as a student of these surgical procedures, and proud to call him my colleague. He has worked tirelessly with the surgical teams.

Because of his efforts and desire to learn more about the surgical techniques, we arranged for Dr. Nur to come to the Texas Medical Center as a foreign postgraduate exchange student. And now here we are together again in the OR at Shalama Hospital in Lahore, Pakistan, and Dr. Nur is giving back to the less fortunate people from his own country. Even after the American teams leave, he will continue his practice here, offering free surgical treatment for those in need.

Dr. Nur and others I have trained in Pakistan – and indeed, throughout the world – will train other local doctors in these procedures and techniques. They will use the equipment and supplies we have donated. So the care continues: a long-time medical and surgical tradition.

When we arrive at the hospital, we see that the perimeter has been secured, with guards stationed at the front entrance and along the hallways, all the way to the operating room. There are two guards at each of the clinics, all with automatic weapons slung over their shoulders. One of the guards in the hallway is smoking, and as I walk by, we exchange salutes and I give him the "evil eye." He immediately understands the meaning behind my frown and puts out the cigarette. I nod and smile, and he smiles back. The patients are already crowding the waiting area and into the halls. It is obvious from their impressively colorful tribal outfits and clan headwear that they are from the Northwest Territory and Tribal areas.

Saleem and Sultan help me bring the equipment into the operating room, and I tell them and Mohammed that they can have the day to themselves. I tell them it might be a good idea to take a walk through the markets, stop at some of the tea houses, and get a feeling for the atmosphere by listening to what is being said about the medical team's presence in the area. Mohammed says, "We have heard mostly favorable remarks. How should I respond to these people?"

"I respond like this," I say, gesturing with my hands toward the children who line the hallways, waiting to be seen. "We are doing everything we can to give back to this community. There will always be critics. Let the facts speak for themselves. If you want, you can talk about the children and their health, then acknowledge that they are your future generation, and must be cared for and protected.

"That's why it is important for this program to do well. They need to know I am here to help their people and to address the country's medical needs, and if anyone says anything else, it is a misrepresentation of what's in my heart. You can tell them we are not only helping those who need immediate care, but also teaching their doctors and the medical students and nurses how to provide that care for the rest of their lives."

I'm on a roll now, and find myself waxing philosophic about the state of medical care. "The current medical model is flawed, not only here, but in America as well. It is my hope to focus on preventive medicine through promotion of and increased access to medical services. This is a patient-centered approach. I am not trying to advocate a healthcare system for Pakistan or any country. I just hope the examples my medical team and I are providing will encourage all citizens in Pakistan – and throughout the Middle East, for that matter – to take a more proactive role in their families' health care.

"And if you want to get into it, you can explain that we tried to provide this help by working with other non-profit organizations to establish an exchange program where doctors can see what we have accomplished at the Texas Medical Center, as well as providing them an opportunity to study there. When they return home, they take these new ideas and develop them so as to best fit into their communities. I undertake these international medical missions with one purpose in mind: to help people live better and longer, especially the kids, who are our future generation."

I notice that both Mohammed and Saleem are looking a little...overwhelmed, and I laugh. "I'm sorry, guys. You got me on my soapbox, and once I get going, it's hard to stop. But I think you understand my feelings, and I think you are wonderful ambassadors, so go to the market, have lunch, visit the teahouses, and listen, listen, listen! Bring me back whatever news you feel is important. And above all, whenever anyone asks, be sure to let them know that everyone who feels he or she needs medical care is welcome, and that there are no fees. In fact, if anyone attempts to charge any of my patients, I want you to find out who it is and report it to me immediately." With that, I turn and step into the operating room.

I have explained before that each operating room contains not one, but two tables, that there are few amenities, and the operating rooms resemble a MASH unit more than a hospital facility. The basics are available, but not much more. The advantage of having two operating tables in the same room is that I can operate and teach at the same time. I select a case with which the local surgeon or resident is comfortable, and then a more difficult one for myself that might be beyond the proficiency level of the local surgeon. It works out well for everyone involved.

When the children come for surgery, they sit on a wooden bench outside the operating room, fully dressed, with their name and assigned number inscribed on their forearm with a marking pen. When their turn comes, they are asked to leave their sandals under the bench and are taken to the operating room in street clothes. The idea of removing your clothes and being placed in a clean hospital gown is not part of the routine here, since there are no such things as hospital gowns, anyway. The children are, to a person, very stoic. There is no acting up or crying. Many even try to climb onto the operating table without any help. An intravenous needle is placed quickly, without a tear or complaint. The children receive no pre-operative sedation, and frankly, don't need it.

I instruct the nurses to talk to the children constantly while prepping them – about family, friends, sports, anything that they can to keep the children talking and distracted. The children are very verbal, often communicating among themselves from one operating table to the other. The older children are all very supportive of their younger friends or siblings.

Once the anesthesia is given, the surgical site is scrubbed and the procedure is started. It always amazes me that in these hospitals, an entire patient chart consists of only two hand-written pages. One lists the patient's problem and the findings from the physical examination, and the second is left for the physician to document the diagnosis and treatment or surgical procedure, neither of which ever consists of more than two or three sentences. This is in stark contrast to where I work at the Texas Medical Center, where the average chart has more than thirty to forty sheets of paper before the patient even gets to the operating room, and often doubles in size within a day or two. It's sad that we have to go through this in the States, since 90% of what is in the chart is worthless information, included for the sole purpose of satisfying a litigious legal system and the ever-growing and seemingly endless bureaucracy of our hospitals.

Such obsessive documentation doesn't make patient care any better or safer. It has little or nothing to do with the patient's treatment or outcome. Over the past forty years that I have been a physician I have watched this phenomenon, this explosion of paperwork. Nowadays, the emphasis is on going to the "paperless" chart, which is actually a misnomer, since everything is initially put down on paper, and then you turn around and type it into the computer. I find this duplicated effort to be a colossal waste of time. And I know for a fact that it has a deleterious effect on direct patient care, because the amount of time you can spend with a patient and the number of patients you can see has been greatly reduced as a direct result.

This is particularly true when it comes to nursing care. When I make rounds and walk down the ward hallways, I usually can see four or five red nurse request lights on, where the patient's IV has run out, or a Foley bag is overflowing and urine is covering the floor, or the patient needs help to get to the bathroom, or the oxygen saturation level has dropped below the safety point and the monitor is going off... but no nurses are answering those calls because they are all in a back room, typing patient information and notes into a computer. Rather than sitting in a back room of the nursing station, typing in useless information, they should be with the patient.

Given this all-too-common situation, are we providing better care? Of course not. Do I blame the nurses? Again, of course not. While the vast majority of nurses are deeply committed to providing their patients with the absolute best care they can, they are under great pressure to perform a ridiculous amount of record keeping that benefits only the attorneys and hospital bureaucracy. Many nurses I talk to express their frustration at this, and some are even leaving the medical field altogether, rather than remain in an environment that fosters neglect of their patients.

In light of today's atmosphere in the healthcare field, I would advise anyone to do anything he or she can to stay out of even the best of hospitals, where you are just a number on a sheet that goes into a computer. This is particularly true in the larger university hospitals in medical centers. If you want personalized care, you need to be in the doctor-owned and doctor-run private facilities. Medicine today has become very impersonal and very expensive because of this bureaucracy-centric attitude, and I, for one, would rather be here providing needed direct care on a personal basis and not diagnosing my patient on a computer screen.

* * * * *

This morning, Doctor Nur is doing a unilateral cleft lip, and we are discussing the procedure. I glance over every once in awhile to see how he is doing and answer his questions. My own procedure, on a burn patient who required extensive skin grafting, is completed. The local doctors and students are amazed at the automatic staple gun I brought with me, as this device has reduced the time required for such extensive suturing of the skin grafts from several hours to just a few minutes. They have never seen a surgical staple gun, and all are anxious to learn how to use it.

As I mentioned in an earlier chapter, turnover time in the Pakistani hospitals – the time it takes to clean the table and bring in the next patient – is brief compared to what I'm used to in the States. On average it is about five minutes, whereas back in Houston at the Medical Center, it takes any-where from an hour to an hour and a half. This includes the time for nursing and operating room personnel to take their required, government-sanctioned breaks, and the inordinate amount of time spent going through the unnecessary paper-work that has nothing to do with patient care or safety. Then, when they are finally ready to bring the patient to the room, you find that the anesthesiologist didn't want to wait any longer, so he took his lunch break, and now we are all waiting again. On a good day in most American facilities, you might get two or three procedures done, whereas in the small hospitals and MASH units in the Third World countries, each surgeon is able to perform ten to fourteen operations a day. My team and I have done as many as five hundred procedures in two to three weeks. In the U.S., most surgeons don't perform that many procedures in six months, or in many cases, in a whole year.

What is also interesting (and again, another point I mentioned earlier, but I think it bears mentioning again) is our relatively low infection rate. Of the thousands of procedures that my team and I have accomplished under these limited circumstances, there have been few if any infections or unwarranted results, which is a better average than that which is achieved in most American hospitals, despite their stringent efforts to maintain a perfectly clean surgical environment.

In Pakistan and during other similar Third World medical missions, we try to keep the surgical cases moving efficiently, safely, and out of necessity, rapidly. As the final sutures are being placed, the anesthetic is stopped and the airway tubes are removed. Not having a recovery room, the child is placed at the foot of the operating table, where a nurse is stationed. Her job is to continue monitoring the children until they are more alert and responsive.

Meanwhile, two more children are brought into the room and placed at the opposite end of the table. Now there are four children in the room, two on each operating table. Two kids recovering, and two being prepped and put to sleep. This is the safest way to proceed, since the post-op patients are in the same room with the anesthesiologist and the surgical team until they are fully awake. They can then be taken to the intermediate care area, where observation is continued with a nurse monitoring the child, but where a family member can be present as well.

It takes less than five minutes to clean the table and bring in the next two children. The staff then brings in a sterile set of instruments, and their procedures are immediately started. Meanwhile, the two children at the opposite end of the tables are waking up from their anesthesia and being monitored. Close observation, safety, and personal one-to-one care. What a concept!

Before I begin my next procedure, I review the skin markings with the local surgeon, who is going to do his first syndactyly release. This is the separation of congenitally webbed fingers. This child's fingers were joined together at birth, giving the impression of a flipper, and they need to be separated to provide individual digital dexterity. Once learned, the procedure is not complicated and easily accomplished. It is best done with tourniquets applied to prevent blood from entering the fingers, so that the surgeon can see the small nerves and arteries, but they do not have any modern tourniquets in most medical facilities in Third World countries. These tourniquets look like blood pressure cuffs that can be inflated and the pressure electronically controlled to eliminate bleeding during the surgical procedure.

Necessity is the mother of invention, and one of the reasons I like to bring residents, fellows and young surgeons from the U.S. with me is so they can learn how to improvise. The best surgeons are those who were trained under conditions like this and those who have served as surgeons in the military, where their ability to learn and improvise makes the difference between success and failure – and life and death.

I show them how to use an elastic bandage, by wrapping it around the fingers and extending it to above the elbow, thereby compressing the blood in the child's arm. Once this is accomplished, the bandage is unwound from the hand to the mid-forearm and then tied. This provides the same compression effect as a $5,000.00 electronic pressure cuff, for the cost of fifty cents' worth of elastic bandage. This gives a surgeon an operating time of about one and a half hours, which is plenty, since this procedure usually takes about forty-five minutes to an hour.

Once the "tourniquet" is in place, I take a few minutes to go over the classic markings for separating the fingers, leaving enough tissue to close the lateral surfaces.

I then turn to my patient, sleeping only a few feet away, and I wash the child and place the sterile towels around his wound. He was injured on a threshing machine, an injury that is not uncommon in this agricultural area. His fingers are partially amputated. The treatment here is usually the complete amputation of the damaged fingers. However, with my magnifying loupe in place, I am able to see clearly enough to reattach the small tendons and nerves and save this child's finger and hand, so that he will be a productive member of society again. Under the harsh conditions he will face throughout his life, he needs his hand and fingers intact if he is to have any hope of surviving.

The team works straight through the day, without taking any breaks. Since there is no cafeteria, doctor's lounge, or vending machines, the only reason to leave the operating room is to make a quick stop at the bathroom and return. Lunch is usually around four or five in the afternoon, and consists of whatever the doctors' wives make and bring to the hospital. Each takes a turn cooking for the entire group. Some of the doctors help cook the meals the night before, which are then reheated and brought to the hospital the next day. The meals are homemade, wholesome – and most important: no one has ever gotten sick after eating them.

The more difficult cases on the younger children are always done early in the day, and today, the only remaining procedures are two minor surgeries, which the local doctors say they will do after lunch. Mohammed arrives and joins us, then reminds me that the sun is setting, and that I have a meeting that evening. When your hands are busy and you are enjoying your work, time goes quickly, and I am suddenly aware of how late it is.

As I walk down the hall toward the small closet-like room where I can change back into my "native" garb, two guards bearing AK-47s salute me, and I return the salute. I quickly change, and then meet Mohammed. Just as we pass through the front door, an old man whose beard falls in great white waves across his chest steps forward. He is wearing a tan robe and a brown matching vest. His turban is white and neatly wrapped, and his feet and sandals are quite clean. In his right hand, he clutches a Qu'ran, and I notice that little remains of his left hand, the fingers of which are partially amputated. Deep irregular scars stretch across the back of his hand and extend upward along his forearm. The wounds are old and healed, and I quickly determine that this is not an acute problem.

I greet him, saying, "A salaam Aleichem."

Smiling, he responds, "Wa Aleichem salaam."

The introductions are brief, with Mohammed doing most of the speaking. The old man tells Mohammed that his name is Wazir, and that he was injured about a year ago when a bomb had exploded. He says he is lucky to be alive, but that he has come to the hospital in hopes we can improve his hand's function and ease the pain he always feels. I think at first that he is a Pakistani, until I hear him tell Mohammed that he is a Pashtun from one of the local tribes. Mohammed tells him that we are finished for the day, but that we will be happy to see him first thing in the morning, and that he can register with the hospital now.

Wazir turns to me and says, "I was afraid to come forward because of the two guards at the front door."

In my painfully American manner, I tell Wazir, "They are there for our protection, and mean you no harm."

A broad smile appears on the old man's face. He purses his lips and nods. You have to respect the old man for his tenacity in the presence of his fears. His weathered blue eyes have most certainly looked upon deeper levels of tragedy in these mountains. I remove one of my appointment cards from my pocket, and give it to Mohammed. "Tell Wazir that this is his ticket to see me at the hospital in the morning. Tell him if he presents this to the guards, they will let him pass and he can register now or in the morning, and we will then examine him and make suggestions for his treatment."

Mohammed leads Wazir inside to the registration area, and quickly returns. When I get to the van, Saleem and Sultan are waiting. I ask about their day, and they report that they only heard good things at the market and teahouses. Sultan says, "Your reputation for doing good continues to grow."

"Any surprises?"

"Yes. I told them you were an American, and they could not believe that an American doctor and his team were here, or that you were the famous Doctor Angel of the Northern Territories."

"Is it safe to tell these people who I am?"

"Doctor Agris, you have the brown skin and clothing of a desert dweller, and you have grown a beard, but you're an American, and that is okay. Let me have my fun. The tribal leaders have your back. You have more respect for what you are doing than does the local *Maulana*, even though you're an American who speaks fifth grade Urdu with a terrible accent."

I break into a smile and everyone begins to laugh as Mohammed shifts the battered old van into gear and starts for the market... and to the meeting that has so consumed my thoughts.

Second Meeting with the Sheik

*I*f I had had any delusions that my first meeting with Osama bin Laden established an unassailable bond of trust between us, those delusions will be shattered on the way to the second meeting. If anything, my companions are even more concerned about this follow-up meeting than they were the first one. After all, bin Laden and those close to him have had time to mull over our conversations, and, given the distrust and uncertainty that must surely persist despite their regard for my work, they may very well have decided I have some secret agenda after all. My three companions have also had time to mull – and fret – and as we set out for the second meeting, the atmosphere in the van is quite tense.

The dirt road turns lazily to the right as Mohammed avoids some deep potholes that look as if they could swallow up the entire van. We pass a pair of modest-sized brick homes and several tents standing alongside them. Mounted on the roof of the larger structures is a pair of satellite dishes, and as we pass, I can hear the hum of diesel generators. It is a clear evening, and as I look out the window I can see hectares of tilled fields where local farmers grow their crops.

Saleem follows my gaze, and says, "They are growing shaftal, which is a clover that originated in Persia."

Along the side of the road there are some black water buffalo, as well as goats with ropes tied around their necks and fastened to a stake in the ground to keep them from wandering off. We had left the hospital on Pineview Road, going in a northwest direction toward Shimla Peak. The road intersects with Jail Road, and Mohammed turns back south toward the town.

Wondering at the route he has taken, I speak up. "This is the long way, Mohammed. You began by going away from the market, but now you are turning back towards it. Is there a problem?"

"No problem. Just being cautious. I wanted to see if we were being followed. I plan to come in from the west, passing through the wheat and vegetable market, and will stop at Masjid Road. You will get out there. You can walk north towards the mosque, and then turn in front of the mosque toward the

Sarafa Bazaar. Saleem will be close behind you, Sultan will go directly to the bazaar where you will be approached, and I will stay with the van."

As previously instructed, I am once again careful to empty all my pockets, leaving only my notebooks and two pens. I give my wallet, passport, cell phone, and other incidentals to Saleem to care for. Perhaps in time, I will be allowed to have a camera or even a video camera at one of our meetings, but for now I am following the Sheik's rules, and hoping to earn his trust.

I leave the van first, and walk towards the cross street that passes in front of the mosque. The bazaar is abuzz with activity: bodies moving, elbow to elbow, darting in and out of the shops and from beneath the canvas covers that overhang the myriad of items on display. Children play in and around the shops and under the stalls, peeking out curiously as prospective buyers stop to look though the merchandise and haggle for the best price. There is a continual babble of voices, and a strong scent of tobacco fills the air. Urdu is the common language, but others are speaking Pashto and Punjabi.

Once again I have the powerful sense that I have turned the clock back a thousand years, as I am certain that this scene is little different than it was in the days before Europe and the West had "discovered" this place. I am fascinated with the sights and sounds, along with the scent of meat roasting on open grills, and I find my mind drifting to the time of

Tamerlane – Timur – and Genghis Khan. I can't help wondering, and not for the first time, whether I have been born five hundred or a thousand years too late. I feel as if I would have been right at home in the time of Genghis Khan.

Sultan and Saleem had armed themselves before leaving the van, after which Mohammed took the van north towards a restaurant, and parked it behind the building. Sultan has two pistols, concealed under his vest. He moves quickly, circling the bazaar on its north side, entering east to west and looking for my approach. Saleem, who has concealed a small but deadly machine pistol under his wool shawl, follows about thirty yards behind me, and no doubt he can see that I am lost in my own thoughts.

I pass a small courtyard between the mosque and the jewelers in the bazaar, and looking down this narrow alley, I notice a group of grim-faced men sitting at a small tea shop. My eyes move rapidly from side to side as I check them out. The expressions on their faces, and their body language as I pass, bring me back to reality. One of the men abruptly gets up from the group and steps from the alley into the street, walking toward the bazaar. I have stopped to look at the handmade jewelry in the display in one of the shops, and out of the corner of my eye, I notice the man's sudden approach. I decide it is a good idea for me to remain at the shop, haggling with the owners over a beaded necklace and some bracelets, and periodically glancing to see what the suspicious gentleman is up to. He turns his back to me, and slowly – unnaturally slowly – lights a cigarette, while continuing to observe my movements.

Unbeknownst to me, Saleem has spotted him as well, and pulls out his cell phone to call Sultan, who responds by moving quickly through the crowds. Sultan is carefully looking for any other suspicious individuals of concern, but remains focused on the man who is so obviously watching me. My apparent stalker looks to be in his late twenties or early thirties, but his slight build and weathered appearance make him look older at first glance. His straight black hair is slicked back, with no sign of graying, and like most men in the region, he sports a short beard. He has an irregular scar extending from his right side-burn to his jaw, and seems to be missing part of his right ear. He is wearing a light blue *shalwar kameez*, and is wrapped with a stained brown woolen shawl. Judging by the unusual way the shawl hangs on his body, I suspect that underneath it, he has concealed an automatic weapon, most likely an AK-47.

At the same time, Saleem is again on his cell phone, talking to Sultan, saying, "I see him. I think you are right. This could be trouble. He is armed. He has stepped from the alley to the main street, and I think the doctor has noticed him as well. He is standing, smoking a cigarette, and looking over his shoulder toward the doctor, and doesn't seem to know what his next move should be. I am almost directly across the street from him. I will hold my position here, and see what he does next."

As I continue along the street, the feeling that I have entered a place that is stuck in the Dark Ages grows even more pronounced. Dust-covered vans that have long since ceased to function are parked in the streets, and bands of equally dust-covered children chase one another in and out of the alleys and around the carts, deftly avoiding layered piles of garbage and other debris. I am startled by the animated chattering of an elderly man's pet monkey, perched on his shoulder and loudly protesting the taunts that several of the children have been directing at the animal. Not far from me, a group of men and women are sifting through a relatively fresh-looking pile of trash, obviously in hopes of finding something they can use or sell. Their search – and the children's play – is interrupted by several men carrying AK-47s, who jostle their way through the crowded market area, indiscriminately shoving shoppers aside as they pass. Further down the street is an array of packed kiosks, each laden with wicker baskets piled high in neat pyramids of various fruits and vegetables, as well as open sacks filled with lentils, rice, and dried beans.

I am now aware that the young man with the scarred face is moving from shop to shop, openly following me as I make my way along the main street. He is apparently unaware of Saleem or Sultan's presence, a fact that I find quite comforting.

As I approach the far end of the market, I feel a tap on my shoulder, and turn to see the young man with the scarred face and deformed ear directly in front of me. He greets me with a disarming smile and firmly shoves me toward the alley at the end of the market. I can feel the butt of the AK-47 under his cloak pressing against my back as he continues to push me forward into the alley. I turn toward him and offer a greeting, not wanting to antagonize him. "As you wish," I say.

He responds civilly enough, with the traditional Arabic phrase that, translated literally, means, "Peace be upon you."

But then I ask him his name, and his response is anything but peaceful; in fact his only reply is to push even harder with the butt of his weapon, moving me further into the alley. This does not go unnoticed by Saleem and Sultan, who approach the entrance to the alley from either side, still trying to determine if they are dealing with only one individual or if he has accomplices nearby, waiting to assist him.

A young boy of eight or nine, wearing filthy tan trousers and a stained polo shirt, comes running down the alley, oblivious to what is happening. This gives me the opportunity to push back against the wall as the child passes between us. At exactly the same moment, Saleem and Sultan burst into the alley, startling my would-be abductor. Before he can respond, they have their guns pressed into his rib cage and back. Sultan reaches into the man's shawl and removes his weapon. At the same time, Saleem frisks him and finds a pistol tucked into his pants. I can see the fear in the young man's eyes, and quickly raise my hands to prevent the confrontation from progressing any further.

I move to within inches of the man's face, and in as gruff a voice as I can muster, ask him, "What's going on? What do you want?"

The man looks from me to my companions, and seemingly on the verge of tears, asks us, "Are you going to shoot me?"

Sultan presses his weapon harder into the young man's side and sneers, "No. We are going to roast you like that goat over there for treating the doctor in this manner."

The young man shifts his feet as though to sidestep around one or the other of us, but realizing that escape is impossible, and with Saleem and Sultan pressing their weapons tightly into his side, he closes his eyes and leans back against the wall.

Sultan asks him, "You want to tell us what this is all about?"

"I... I was told to bring the doctor to the Sheik."

Sultan smiles threateningly and says, "Then we can all walk together."

"No! I can only bring the doctor. If you show up, especially with weapons, we are... I am dead."

I offer a compromise. "How about we all walk out of the market quietly together, and proceed in the direction of the compound. Before we reach the compound, my two friends will leave us to continue on alone."

Sultan and Saleem are shaking their heads vigorously. They are dead-set against the idea, but seeing that my mind is made up, they keep their objections to themselves. Sultan continues to refer to the young man as dog meat and nods in the direction of a vendor across the alley who is cutting up raw chicken on a cutting board covered in dried blood, and wearing an apron that looks as though it has never been washed. The implied threat is clear. For several seconds, no one says anything.

I break the stalemate by putting my arm around the young man and leading him back down the alley, with Saleem and Sultan close behind. For twenty minutes, we wander together through the stucco-walled alleys, keeping away from the main streets, vendor stalls, and shops, while all the while following the young man's direction.

Scarface stops, looking over his shoulder at Saleem and Sultan, and announces, "You must leave us now. Only the doctor can continue forward."

When he says this, Sultan jabs him painfully in the ribs with the muzzle of the man's own AK-47, saying, "I expect you to treat the doctor with respect, or we will make good on our threat and roast you like that goat back there in the market. Do you understand?"

He agrees, but doesn't move. I turn to Sultan and tell him to give the man his rifle back. Sultan again shakes his head emphatically, refusing to do it. I reach out to take the weapon from Sultan. He holds on tightly to it for a few seconds, then slams it quite forcefully into the young man's chest, telling him that there will no more pushing and poking of the doctor.

The man's pain is obviously outweighed by his relief at not being killed by Sultan or sent to his death at the hands of the Sheik's bodyguards, and he spits out a joyful "*Shukriyaa.*" ("Thank you.")

As my "abductor" and I begin to walk off, Sultan and Saleem shout after us that the man is now responsible for me, and then, just for good measure, they repeat that if anything happens to me, they will find him and roast him like a goat. The fear returns to his eyes, but with a sharp nod in my direction, he lets me know that it is time to go. He motions with his hand that he will go first. We stay off the main streets, wandering erratically through the back alleys, which I assume to be an effort to disorient me and eliminate any chance that I will be able to lead anyone to bin Laden's location. I understand his caution; he has been pursued for years by the most advanced and highly motivated military in the world, and hasn't stayed alive by being careless. After a while, we reach a rather large, high-walled compound. My escort is recognized by the guards, who open the gates and let us in, albeit with their weapons at the ready.

Upon entering the grounds, one of the bodyguards puts me through the usual body check, and though he finds no weapons, he confiscates my journal, photos, and ballpoint pens. After the thorough pat-down, Osama bin Laden's son Hamza appears, along with the same young man, Ahmed, who had helped with the interpretation and discussion on my last visit. I immediately ask them, "May I please have my journal and the photos that I wish to share with the Sheik?"

The bodyguard is instructed to give the materials back to me, and I thank them.

The bodyguard stands firmly in place, his AK-47 at his right shoulder, staring intently at me. I feel very uncomfortable, which Hamza apparently notices, and, raising his voice slightly and looking at the bodyguard, he barks an order for him to bring tea to us. He then motions me forward into a large room to the right of the central hallway. There I sit cross-legged on the carpet. The interpreter follows suit, seating himself to my right. Hamza says he will fetch his father.

I look around me, trying to orient myself as to the layout of this place. The kitchen on the first floor is located directly behind the room we are sitting in. However, there are no connecting doorways. You have to walk along the long central corridor, and just as you approach the stairs, there are two massive iron gates. These gates prevent access to the stairs, which lead upward to the Sheik's personal apartments. As you approach these iron gates, there is a doorway on your right. This is the entrance to the first-floor kitchen.

I have been working for several days at the Frontier Medical College, which, as I will later learn, is just a short ride from the bin Laden compound. I spread a collection of before and after pictures in front of Ahmed as we sit there, and explain to him the kinds of medical problems from which our patients suffer, as well as the surgical corrections we have performed. No form of surgery offers the kind of instantaneous improvements that can be achieved with plastic and reconstructive surgery. These results are graphically portrayed in the before and after photographs he is looking at now. I can tell that he is suitably impressed, and he asks many questions and offers his reflections on what he sees, the last of which appears to be particularly significant to him. "They say you do not take any money for your work, whether poor or rich. You and your team of doctors and nurses do Allah's work."

I am surprised – and touched – by his statement. "Allah has blessed me with the education and abilities to perform these surgeries and change the lives of these children for the better. That is the only thanks that I need, and it gives me great pleasure."

"God has endless bounty and knowledge. He grants it to whoever He will. Such is God's favor, and I can see that He has favored you."

At this point, the Sheik, barefoot and wearing a simple white *shalwar kameez*, enters the room, his son beside him. He walks slowly toward us, and a broad smile appears on his face as I stand to greet him. Before I can reach out to shake hands, he embraces me with a big hug and a kiss to each cheek. "Peace be with you, and all God's mercy and blessings. I have been told you have been working at the Frontier Medical College, doing God's work. He loves those who love Him and who strive in God's way without fearing anyone's reproach. You are truly Doctor Angel."

He pauses a moment and then continues, "Today, I want to hear more about what you and your team have accomplished at the Frontier Medical Hospital. Then you will stay and we will eat, after which I will answer all of your questions on whatever topics you choose for this evening."

I respond, "I brought some photos of the children and adults that we have operated upon. I've been explaining a little bit about the procedures to Ahmed."

Bin Laden claps his hands sharply several times, and two young men arrive, one with a tray of small cups and pot of fresh tea, the other carrying a tray with several woven baskets containing pistachios, walnuts, and dried apricots. Both still have their AK-47s slung over their shoulders. As the first young man sets the tray with the hot tea in front of us, his weapon slides forward, and I see that it is about to knock the pot of hot tea over. I spring to my feet, grabbing the weapon as it slides off his shoulder. All of a sudden, I find myself in a very difficult situation, sitting next to Osama bin Laden with an automatic rifle dumped into my hands. The expression on the bodyguard's face immediately changes, and I have no idea what his reaction will be: to trust my intentions, or to leap to protect his master.

I put on my best smile and say, "*Shukriyaa, shukriyaa.*" Then I add, for good measure, "*Sab teek hai.*" ("Everything is okay.")

The Sheik smiles, and assures his bodyguard that everything is fine.

The tray with the hot tea has now been placed before us, unspilled, and the bodyguard eyes me suspiciously as I place the rifle back onto his shoulder. He quickly, and with a clearly-understood emphasis, pulls the weapon rather tightly into a safe position, and smiling a smile that communicates both embarrassment and threat, says, "No problem, no problem."

The two bodyguards almost run from the room, and I take my place between bin Laden and Hamza. I sip my tea and help myself to the freshly sun-dried apricots – one of my favorite foods – while Hamza and Ahmed discuss the surgical photos with the Sheik.

Picking up several of the photos, the Sheik holds them out and says, "God has challenged you with these children, and He has guided your hands to once again give them life, where all hope had been abandoned. I can see the difference in their faces from the before to the after pictures, and the joy in the faces of their parents."

I nod my appreciation for his kind words, and respond, "Correcting an injury or a congenital deformity such as a cleft lip goes way beyond the deformity itself. First, you have the immediate physical change, but with that change comes a feeling of mental and psychological well being. A child who may have never gone to school, a child who had even been ostracized within his own family, now begins a new life. The relationship within the family, between the parents and the child as well as between the siblings, changes for the better. The family comes back together, and the child is no longer an outcast in his or her own home. The next level is between distant family members such as aunts and uncles and cousins. There is a new acceptance, as if a newborn had just entered the household. Then there is the next level of acceptance, with friends and neighbors, schoolmates, and others within the community. The change for the child extends well beyond the physical."

Bin Laden picks up several of the photos that display the most dramatic visual evidence of these surgical "miracles," and he says, "Can you explain to me how this is possible?"

I reply, "I would like to invite you to the Frontier Medical College to observe surgery and meet with the children and their families. There, you could see for yourself how we operate, and how the lives of our patients are affected."

"If only that was possible," he says. "But in order to remain safe I have to take precautions and cannot do even the simplest things that most people take for granted. I have become a prisoner within my own house. Even your presence here is looked upon by some within and outside my household as a security threat. But I rejoice in the work that you are doing, and I do not fear any betrayal on your part. Still, there are many others who would betray me. Even so, I would like you to show me how you do this." He points to my journal. "Maybe you can draw some pictures."

"I would be glad to try," I say, and then decide to take this opportunity go out on a limb. "I have been taking notes in my journal throughout these conversations, and I hope that your trust in me is deep enough to honor my request to be allowed to bring a recording device for our next meeting. I would rather not trust the words of a man such as yourself to my memory or my scribbled notes."

Osama rubs his chin thoughtfully, looking into my eyes as if to read my soul. "I will consider this. Now please show me how you do this surgery."

I flip to a blank page in my journal, and begin sketching the anatomy of a unilateral cleft lip. I then draw in the structures of the muscle and the underlying bone. Not a bad sketch if I do say so myself. Next I make a series of sketches in a step-by-step fashion, each advancing the surgical procedure a step at a time, until the final result is achieved. As I describe the process I continue sketching, and bin Laden asks very pertinent questions as to function and sensation, all of which I answer as I proceed through the sketches. Ahmed and Hamza look on, obviously fascinated with the sketches and my explanation. As I continue to sketch and speak, one of Osama's other sons joins us and begins looking through the photos as well. Then the two bodyguards reappear, this time without their weapons, and hold a brief but rapid conversation with Hamza and Ahmed. As the bodyguards turn to leave, Hamza announces, "Dinner is ready."

The two young men help me gather the photos, which I place into the journal and set behind me. I keep reminding myself of the details of proper mealtime etiquette. I fold my feet tightly beneath me, so that the bottoms of my feet will not be pointing towards anyone in the room. I remind myself to use only my right hand when accepting the food and eating, and that there are to be no business, religious, or political discussions. Just to be on the safe side and avoid any chance of offending anyone, I decide it will be best to allow the others in the room to ask me questions or otherwise direct the topics we discuss during our dinner hour.

Half a dozen large pots are placed on the floor in front of us. They are uncovered, and steam gently rises from them, filling the room with a delicious melding of aromas. Large serving spoons are placed in each pot, and plates are passed to each of us. As a guest, I am expected to serve myself first, and using my right hand, I use one of the large ladles and take some of the rice and chicken, as well as a portion from a dish of vegetables with a spicy red sauce. I also help myself to a plate piled high with salad – all with my right hand. There is another plate, covered with a colorful cloth. Gently lifting the cloth, I see a stack of fresh *naan* flatbreads, and I take one of these as well. Once I have served myself, everybody else takes turns helping themselves. I watch the others as they balance the plates on their knees and begin eating, using the pieces of the flat bread to gather the food into bite size, taco-like rolls.

For the next few minutes, everyone is focused on eating, and nothing is said.

Then Ahmed breaks the silence and asks me, "Are you married? Do you have any children?"

Just as I am about to answer the question, a young man I had not seen before enters the room and places a large bowl containing a white liquid and a basket with pine nuts and almonds on the floor between us. I use the large ladle to spoon some of the mixture over the top of my rice. The liquid is *jameed,* or sheep milk yogurt, and is a most welcome addition to the dinner, as the food is spicy, and beads of perspiration are already forming on my forehead. The cool yogurt with the pine nuts and almonds sprinkled on it is very soothing, and makes for an excellent end to the meal.

I turn now toward Hamza and Ahmed to answer their questions. "I have had two wives." They stop eating, eyes widened and smiles across their faces. I have achieved a pleasant and unexpected response.

"I have a son and a daughter," I continue. "My son is an engineer and physician, and my daughter is a lawyer. They are both married, and I have seven grandchildren."

I break off a piece of *naan,* and forming it into a half circle – using only my right hand, of course – I scoop some of the rice and yogurt into my mouth. I repeat this, as do the others, occasionally adding some pine nuts or walnuts to the mix.

Feeling (perhaps overly) confident and comfortable, I begin to speak. "You have honored me with this wonderful meal, and I greatly appreciate the hospitality you have shown me. But I would be less than honest with you if I don't share with you some things that concern me deeply as I get to know more about your culture and your people. I hope you will excuse my impertinence, and not take offense at my observations." I can tell that I have aroused the Sheik's curiosity, as well as a bit of discomfort in the others. But I can't stop myself.

I continue, "Many of the women here have to cope with no food and with seeing their children grow sick from malnutrition. Women and children suffer from trauma, depression, and even hysteria because they don't know when the next unmanned drone rocket attack will come. How can these children relate to a mother's affection and discipline when they see adults killing each other and their families unable to protect them and provide them with their basic needs? There is so much turbulence and stress that children don't even trust each other.

"Parents don't know how to explain this to their children, and have stopped communicating with their kids. In some areas, more than seventy percent of the children have lost a family member to the war. The children that I have spoken with tell me about loneliness, nightmares, flashbacks, and worse, all caused by the rocket attacks. Many of the children are orphans, with no hope of having a family, education, or job except as soldiers, fighting in a war they don't understand. The warlords have used boy soldiers, some as young as ten years old. The Taliban, with their connections to the Pakistani *madrasas*, accomplish nothing more than the spread of religious hatred, and encourage thousands of children to enlist and fight. These children soldiers are also used as slave labor to carry ammunition and food supplies. The older ones end up guarding storage units and installations, and even fighting. The plight of women and children seems to get worse every day. Is this really the future of Islam?"

As I speak, I can sense a complete change in the room. A level of tension, if not hostility, has replaced the congeniality of a few moments ago, and I ask myself, *Have I gone too far? And will I leave this place alive?* But I have come this far, and my curiosity, fueled by my aversion to the suffering I've seen, drives me onward. Even if my words bring me death, they are words I feel must be said, and I know that I must continue, if not to get answers for myself, to plant questions in the mind of the Sheik.

Second Meeting: Getting in Deeper

I figure there is no turning back now. Osama is looking at me with an expression that is either amusement or the beginnings of anger. The others in the room just look stunned, and keep glancing at the Sheik to see what his reaction will be.

I continue, "I have read the Qur'an multiple times. According to the teachings of Islam, women are equal to men, and are to be respected. No woman that I have spoken to, not even the poorest or most conservative, wants the Taliban to rule. The Taliban's actions are actually turning people against Islam.

"There is no universal standard or tradition among the tribes. As you travel from one tribal area to another, there is extreme diversity in their levels of development, as well as in the cultural barriers that define a woman's role in each society.

"Take the Pakistani Pashtun. They were proud to send their girls to school and continue to do so, despite the Taliban's threats. Pashtun tribal leaders vigorously encourage female education, and even signed an edict demanding education for their girls. Yet their beliefs are not universally shared among the different tribes, where there seem to be as many different definitions of women's proper roles as there are tribes and nationalities. Many women with even a smattering of education have refused to wear the *burqa*, yet the Taliban have made such dress codes – including beards for men and the wearing of the *burqa* for women – compulsory. They have issued similar edicts ordering all Muslims to refrain from watching movies, engaging in sports, dancing, and even singing at weddings. The Taliban view many Muslims as impure and needing to be forcibly 're-Islamicised.'

"And if I may speak freely, my impression is that you share that view."

I stop a moment to take a breath, and then plunge right back in. "These attacks on woman are not rooted in Islam or the usual cultural norms, but rather in wholly arbitrary political beliefs and ideologies. You say that you want Islam to become a world religion, and for the *Ummah* to be restored.

Common sense alone would dictate that in order to achieve this goal, you must win the hearts and minds of the men and the women, for it is the women who bear the children and control the family's activities. Quite simply, the Taliban's policies are in direct conflict with reality. Any way you look at it, this is a lose-lose situation."

I pause a moment to try and gauge Osama's reaction. I don't have to wait too long before he speaks. "Compromise with the West would signal defeat. It would say that we were wrong all along. It is up to the West to moderate their position on universal human rights. The policies of the Western Infidel would give obscene freedoms to women which would lead to the same kind of widespread adultery you have in your country, and herald the destruction of Islam. Islam would be destroyed by the domination of the Western Infidels.

"The men of Islam would become like women, and women cannot defend themselves. The Holy *Qur'an* cannot adjust itself to Western requirements. People need to adjust themselves to the requirements of the Holy *Qur'an* and to the words of Allah."

He then reaches for an apricot from the basket between our feet. While his tone has grown more insistent – even harsh – I feel comfortable going on, albeit somewhat more cautiously. "I am a guest in your house, and this discussion is not meant to insult, but to enlighten and educate. I am seeking enlightenment and education for myself.

"I find it sad that many Westerners do not appreciate the significance of this devotion to Islam, when it is the defining feature of the daily lives of most of the world's Muslims. But I am trying to better understand. I have come to appreciate that Islam encompasses every aspect of Muslim existence: behavior, education, clothes, eating habits, and personal relationships.

"For centuries, Muslim scholars have interpreted, reinterpreted, and developed theological and ideological arguments around these concepts. In our time, this debate impacts the future security of the entire world. From our conversations, I can see that you believe that the global Caliphate can be re-established. This is definitely part of your charismatic appeal and influence throughout the Muslim world. You have become a figurehead for the resurgent Muslim identity, but most Muslims are middle of the road, conservative, hard working, and family-oriented. They believe in education for both boys and girls. Most Muslims are not extremists. They are not linked with a Salafi interpretation of Islam, and do not endorse the writings of Qutb." I am referring to the late Sayyid Qutb (1906-1966), an influential Egyptian author, poet, educator, Islamist theorist, and the foremost member of the Egyptian Muslim Brotherhood in the 1950s and 1960s. Although he had many critical words for the Muslim world, he was also severely critical of the United States, whose culture he considered vulgar and primitive, obsessed with sex and violence. Qutb is widely considered – at least by Western observers – to have shaped the views of the Islamists and Al Qaeda.

"Most Muslims are not fundamentalists," I continue, "and most fundamentalists are not terrorists, but most present-day terrorists are Muslims, and proudly identify themselves as such. You will excuse my impertinence when I say it seems to me that you do not represent Islam as most see it, and many of your statements and actions directly contradict basic Islamic principles. And so I sit here trying to understand your motives, goals, and ambitions."

Osama doesn't pause before responding this time. "The struggle against imperialism is neither glorious nor necessarily useful, but it does serve a purpose. My first duty is to establish God's law throughout the land of Islam and cause the word of God to prevail.

"For this to happen requires that Islamic Holy Law – the Sharia – be established as the law of the land. The ultimate struggle is not against the Westerner per se but, against the Westernization of the Muslim world. The first battlefield in my jihad is the extrication of Infidel leaders from within the Muslim nations, and their replacement by a perfect Islamic order."

I find myself growing a bit more agitated, and my tone becoming more confrontational at this point, but realize that if I cannot remain emotionally detached, I must still strive to at least appear pragmatic. "You are espousing the Wahhabi teachings and the radical writings of Qutb. This is militant

Islamic radicalism. This is nothing more than religious fundamentalism as a means to control women and the population in general. I do not challenge Islam or the Qur'an, nor the inerrancy of their basic dogma, but you cannot stop modernization. The gap will widen. And through the universality of the Internet, computer, and modern media, as painful as it may seem to you, receptive audiences and like-minded groups of Muslims worldwide will be changing.

"China tried to stop modernization several decades ago, and realized that although they are a communist country, if they were going to be a world power, they would have to become an economic and industrial force. That meant their population – both men and women – needed to be highly educated. In making knowledge more widely available, China opened the doors to more and more personal freedoms. In my humble opinion, Islam is going back to the dark ages. I again apologize for speaking this way in your home, but we are both entitled to our opinions, and I am eager to have you educate me further as to yours. I do not fear anyone except God, and I will very willingly declare that there is only one God, but I will not put any other name to Him. Although some of my women friends argue with me and ask why I assume God is a Him and not a Her."

With this, the Sheik and his sons begin to laugh, and finally the elder bin Laden responds, "Indeed, this principle is liable to be embraced by women if we do not place controls over them. The U.S., England, and Israel claim that they want to annihilate terrorism, but it is no longer a secret that their true goal is to annihilate Islam. I cannot ignore that, and neither can any true Muslim. And what have the ministers who govern the countries of this region done to resist this obviously hostile strategy? Nothing. Egypt and Saudi Arabia in particular increase their affiliations and trade with the Crusaders. They work with the Crusaders to fight against the Mujahadeen and make life difficult for the honorable preachers and scholars of Islam who are trying to alert our *Ummah* to the need to defend itself. They are preparing the region for Israeli expansion in the formation of a Greater Israel. The Crusaders want to incorporate the whole of Palestine and portions of Egypt and Syria and perhaps Lebanon and Jordan into this Greater Israel. What they have done in Palestine, courtesy of the Zionist-American alliance, they wish to repeat over the entire Middle East. Our people are living in constant fear and alarm, expecting death to come at any moment from missiles or bombs, destroying our homes and killing our women and children.

"The U.S. and its allies do not realize that God is sufficient for us, and that He is our great guardian. We belong to God, and to Him we shall return. He will bring action against the Jews, the Christians, and all treacherous rulers who attack us. We have no obligations to the Jews or Gentiles, and I want them to know it. I need to stop the Infidels' evil and save the Muslim world. I tell you, doctor, the only path to success is with our God. I am not bloodthirsty. I am not a tyrant, and I only want to put things right as far as I can. And I will succeed with God's help. I have always trusted Him and always turned to Him. Thus, I have declared a jihad for the sake of God, for it is the only way to stop the Infidels' evil. Doctor, you know better than anyone that you are accountable only for yourself. The work you have done in the Muslim and Christian world have shown that you have strong faith and are a believer. You who believe, if you help God, He will help you. The Day of Judgment is coming. We will outwit them and gain ascendancy over them."

"Sheik bin Laden, I am not a religious scholar, but from my readings of the Qur'an, it says that you should not harm another Muslim, you should not attack women and children, and that you should not kill, period. Yet, you have taken the lives of many Muslims and injured and killed many innocent women and children. I find this difficult to understand as the simple man that I am, much less as a physician."

Shaking his head, bin Laden says, "The Hadith of the Prophet states that the struggle against the enemies of Islam will be decided by fighting and killing. It has become a jihad for the sake of God. Muslims were victorious over the communist Russians, raising the self-confidence of our fighters. We are now ready to take on the great Crusader – the U.S.A. – as well as its English supporters, and the Jews. They do not frighten us, for we have shown we could defeat the great communist powers.

We outwitted them and gained ascendancy over them."

I'm not convinced. "That still doesn't explain the killing of innocent children and women and the attacks on civilians."

Bin Laden counters, "The Mujahadeen provided the amazing example of self-sacrifice with their Arab brothers from around the world. They smashed the arrogance of the Russians and inflicted defeat upon them. The Russians withdrew in disarray. They suffered a crushing defeat at the hands of a small group of believers. We stand firm and victorious under our God, who will now defeat the American and Israeli forces and any of their allies that intercede. Our strength and power is in our God. America and her allies will be defeated just as the Great Russian bear has fallen.

"And I am patient. This is not something that will happen next week, next month or even next year, but in decades to come, perhaps long after I have joined the glory of my God. During that time, the followers of the jihad will continue to prepare, and the cowardly Americans will eventually run away and hide. The American policies supporting the Jews and occupying Saudi Arabia must end. The Americans must move their bases from our cities and deserts. There will be a solid blow to the face of America, a blow that they will never recover from or forget. I will use whatever means God places before me. Explosives have become passé. Poisonous gases and nuclear devices will be used to strike down the disbeliever for their injustice towards us in the Islamic world. As the twin towers in

New York collapsed, things even greater and more enormous are yet to occur, an attack upon the Zionist-American alliance that they will never be able to recover from."

Thinking back to the words of Japanese Admiral Yamamoto after the attack on Pearl Harbor, I ask bin Laden, "Are you not worried that you will go one step too far and you will awaken the sleeping lion? America, Europe, and the rest of the world have been more than patient in the face of your attacks. If the sleeping lion awakens from its slumber, the American superpower, with its enormous military strength and vast economic power, may let loose its forces upon the Muslim world, and will destroy whoever and whatever crosses their path. Is there any doubt that they have the power to do this?"

Osama's son, Hamza, joins in, saying, "They will never use their nuclear arsenal. They do not have the will to do that again. But God is with us and has granted my father nuclear capabilities."

These words take me completely by surprise. The notion of a nuclear-armed bin Laden is beyond unthinkable to me, and I cannot help but wonder whether Hamza's declaration is true or just an exercise in bravado. For the sake of not only my own country, but of every living creature on earth, I sincerely hope it is the latter. Perhaps only time will tell, but for now, I desperately need to learn more.

The "Nuclear Family"

'm floored by Hamza's declaration that his father has acquired nuclear weapons, but given the heightened tension level in the room, I know I need to be careful not to make matters worse, and certainly not to give them reason to believe that I am their enemy. Still, I need to find out whether Hamza's statement is true. I look up at Hamza and Ahmed, shrug, manage to force out a reasonably off-handed smile, and say, "I would like to hear more about your nuclear capabilities."

I am, of course, well aware of the endless speculation, ever since 9/11, that Osama bin Laden has nuclear weapons or that he is intent on acquiring them, and that it will only be a matter of time before he has them. Thousands of words have been spoken and written about this matter – on broadcast media, in print media, and, especially, on the Internet. There have been countless discussions, arguments, and assertions, with some pundits, armchair experts, and a few real experts insisting that Osama does have nukes, others saying he doesn't, and others saying that sooner or later, unless he is stopped, he will almost certainly have them. This is a matter that has preoccupied my thoughts as well, but I have always tried to lean towards the more optimistic (from a Western perspective) view that Osama's organization does not have nuclear capabilities and will not have them in the foreseeable future. Yet I have always harbored more than a shadow of doubt about this hopeful view, wondering if I, like so many other Westerners, have just told myself the things that make me feel more comfortable. And now here is my chance to get the truth, straight from the source... or maybe not. But I have to try anyway. So I look at Hamza, waiting for him to go on.

Hamza states, matter-of-factly, "My father got these nuclear capabilities from the scientists and military men in the Soviet Union during its collapse."

"I'm not doubting your honesty, Hamza, but you will forgive me if I find that a little difficult to believe."

The Sheik interjects, with no small amount of obvious pride, "Let us say that with enough money, you can acquire almost anything. But now, it is quite late, the air is chilling, and we have gone far from our original discussion. Would you like a hot cup of tea before you leave?"

I say, "I would appreciate that." But the truth is that leaving at this point is the last thing I want to do. I have the sense that a colossal fuse is at the point of being lit, if it hasn't been lit already. I need to pursue the subject of a nuclear-armed bin Laden, even at the risk of alienating him. I know more than ever how essential it is for me to proceed cautiously. I decide that the best way to reintroduce the subject is by telling the Sheik that I had studied engineering before going into medicine, and that physics was one of my minors in college.

"My education," I begin, a little tentatively, "has not been confined to the study of medicine. I realize that you can go online and find the plans for making different types of atomic explosives, but you need lots of other things to actually make a nuclear weapon. Most, with money, can be obtained. Others, with experienced personnel, can be built. If you have the time and the expertise, it is not that hard. What's hard to get is the nuclear fuel for the process. If I remember correctly, only two types are suitable, uranium and plutonium. The problem is that you need highly enriched uranium in the form of U-235 or highly enriched uranium – HEU – to make a nuclear bomb. To create that, you need a manufacturing facility, big bucks, scientists, and enough time to build it undetected."

A young man brings in the tea and he pours some, first for me and then for the Sheik and his sons. I add some sugar and then slowly take a sip. Nobody says anything for a long moment, until I say, "Let me be very clear about this. We are not talking hypothetical here, are we?"

Osama does not answer me directly, but only smiles and responds, "You have an excellent science background, and your knowledge of the subject is surprisingly good. Perhaps you should be working for me!"

"Thank you for the compliment, but my heart is in medicine. As I said before, you can obtain most of the knowledge I possess online. I am sure you and your sons are very aware of this."

The Sheik is now obviously more interested in continuing the dialog than ending it, and says, "Doctor, let us pursue this further."

I find myself thinking, *Whatever it is that I've gotten myself involved in now is way beyond the hypothetical.*

The Sheik presses on, "And, what can you tell me about plutonium?"

"Well, you get plutonium-239 from enriching uranium. This requires a nuclear breeder reactor. What you are really doing is removing the plutonium-240, which is an abundant by-product, but which I understand would cause a nuclear weapon to fizzle or misfire. Such a reactor is impossible for the average man to purchase, and I don't know of anyone who would have a nuclear breeder reactor available for lease."

"With enough money you could get the fuel, correct? How about in the U.S.A.? How do they make it?"

I respond, "The only such plant that I know of is located in Paducah, Kentucky. Its purpose is to enrich uranium for fuel used in nuclear reactors that provide electric power... a totally different process."

"Could you modify the process so as to create the nuclear material necessary for a weapon?"

"As I said before, the Kentucky facility is designed to en-rich uranium for the use in nuclear reactors that produce electricity, not to build bombs."

"Where exactly is all this material going? How much U-235 would you need to build a bomb?"

"I have no way of knowing that. You would need someone with a lot more expertise than the superficial knowledge I possess, most of which I have obtained from reading *Scientific American* and other publicly-available journals." At this, I fin-ish my tea and stand up. "If you are willing to discuss this on my next visit, I would be interested in pursuing this topic and hearing more about your dealings with the Russian scientists and military men that you mentioned earlier."

With a nod of his head, Osama says, "Peace be with you, until we meet again. I am isolated behind the walls of this compound, and you are a breath of fresh air in my life. Hamza and Ahmed will show you out."

As we leave the house, we disturb some of the chickens, which begin to squawk and race away from us. This alerts the guards, who suddenly appear, each with an AK-47 at the ready. Hamza waves and shouts for them to open the heavy metal gate in the outer wall of the compound. Several milk cows are nestled against the wall; they are not at all happy to be disturbed at this time of the evening, and seem particularly resentful at being prodded with the barrel of the guard's AK-47.

Hamza embraces me with a kiss to each cheek, and I ask him to thank his father for the dinner and very stimulating conversation. "Tell him he hasn't converted me yet, but I do have a better appreciation of him and his motivations."

Ahmed pats me on the shoulder and says, "He will be pleased to hear that."

I want to make certain that there will be further meetings, and ask him, "You will contact me in the market sometime in the next few days?"

He says, "As usual."

The door is then opened just enough for me to get through, and is quickly closed as soon as I step through. It is a clear night with a slight breeze, and as I walk along the dirt road passing several other large walled homes, dogs begin to bark for a moment, then grow quiet again as I pass further along. The scent of freshly cut hay or perhaps oats reaches my nostrils as I come to the crossroad and turn toward the city, where I know Mohammed will be waiting for me. I spot the van about a hundred yards away and quicken my pace. I want to get back to the house as soon as possible and go through my notes. I sense that this evening's conversation was particularly important, and want to be sure that I have transcribed it accurately.

I am deeply concerned by the statements about Russian scientists, Russian military men, and their willingness to sell nuclear material. Especially their willingness to help bin Laden build nuclear weapons. The Sheik seems eager to learn all I know about obtaining the materials and the technology needed to make such horrific weapons. I find myself feeling deeply concerned, but have to admit that at the same time, my curiosity has been stirred.

As I approach the van, I tap on the window, which startles the dozing Mohammed. He rubs his eyes and takes a second look through the dirty window before lowering it halfway. It occurs to me that my traditional attire must be an effective disguise if even my driver doesn't recognize me immediately.

"You were sleeping, I'm sorry to have awakened you."

"I will open the door. Get in. We need to leave this area as soon as possible. There have been some police patrols out tonight."

After I climb into the van, Mohammed shifts into gear and slowly moves forward with the lights off. In fact he doesn't turn the headlights on until we come to the main road. He then turns north in the direction of the Frontier Medical College. I am surprised to see the number of shops open and the amount of traffic that is on the main road. I turn toward Mohammed and say only one word: "Ice cream." Well, two words.

His excited response reveals that he is delighted by the distraction. "Yes, there is an excellent place a few kilometers further along, on the left side of the road. It is very popular."

He drives a short while, then stops, waits for a break in the oncoming traffic, and then cuts across the road, slamming on his brakes in front of a small shop. There are no signs or displays that would indicate that they sell ice cream.

I have to ask, "How do you know they sell ice cream here?"

"Everybody knows."

By the time we exit the van, several other vehicles have pulled up alongside us. The occupants are mostly in their teens and early twenties, and they are laughing and talking loudly.

Mohammed whispers in my ear. "No talking. Point to what you like and I will order it." I am proud of my ability to speak Urdu, but Mohammed feels this is not the time or place for me to practice.

After looking over the impressive selection of flavors, I select pistachio and apricot, and Mohammed picks chocolate and some other type of fruit. The man behind the counter points to several different sizes of containers, and I point to one without saying anything. While he is packing the ice cream, I take some money out of the pocket in my *shalwar kameez* and try to slip it into Mohammed's hand, but he pushes it away. The clerk tells Mohammed it is twenty-five rupees for each container, or a hundred rupees total. That comes to about eighty cents U.S.

I grab a few small plastic spoons from a cup on the counter while Mohammed pays. We exit the shop, which seems to be getting busier by the moment. We return to the van, and I immediately attack the pistachio ice cream with all the zeal of a child. Mohammed, knowing my weakness for ice cream, begins laughing hysterically. He turns the van around, and it takes a few minutes before he can enter the main road, which is clogged by an endless line of three-wheeled motorized rickshaws, some taxis, and the occasional donkey cart, all of which he avoids with exceptional skill. We continue north toward the Frontier Medical College and Frontier Valley University. The further we get from the center of town, the fewer rickshaws we see, and Mohammed increases his speed until he is going faster than I am comfortable with. But rather than ask him to slow down, I reason that he has gotten us through places that are much more perilous than this road, so I just sit back and eat my ice cream and leave the driving to him. A few minutes later, I can see the white six-story buildings on the hilltops to my right. He slows the van and we take the turn-off into the small medical complex.

This road is closed to through traffic, secured by a metal gate that looks similar to that found at a railroad crossing, but manually raised and lowered using a counter-weight. We pull up to the guard station and two men come forward, each carrying an AK-47 on his shoulder and a pistol in his belt. With difficulty, I crank down my window. They recognize me. One of the guards runs to the opposite side of the road and pulls on a rope which drops the counter-weight and elevates the crossing bar. The old van gives a shudder as Mohammed gears down to ascend the hill. We enter on the flat surface above in front of the Frontier Medical College and turn right into a private parking area. I reach behind my seat and retrieve my notebook as Mohammed grabs the ice cream. At least for the night, we are "home," and safe. But somehow, safety is a distant memory to me now. The thoughts of nukes in bin Laden's hands, along with the threat that they entail, keep rolling over in my mind.

Life Goes On...

As we drive back from my second meeting with bin Laden, a deep uneasiness fills me. As far as I am concerned, the way his interest peaked when the discussion turned to nuclear weapons made it obvious that he has every intention of using such devices against America and any other country that he deems to be an enemy of "pure Islam." The only inhibiting factors are his ability to get the materials he needs, the availability of the expertise and facilities to actually build the bombs, and the means of delivery. Recalling what Mohammed and Saleem had said previously, I know that bin Laden has enough money to buy whatever materials and manufacturing are required.

As to the expertise, I am all too aware that his claims about desperate Russian scientists are more than wishful thinking, as there are plenty of out of work scientists from the former USSR who are bitter about the loss of their positions. And many of them blame capitalism – and by extension, the United States – for their troubles. The final piece of bin Laden's doomsday puzzle, the matter of delivering such devastating events, is already in place, according to Mohammed and Saleem. I have little reason to doubt their claims of sleeper cells being in place and awaiting their assignments. Yes, bin Laden could pull it off. How close he is, there's no way of telling, but I have no doubt that he moves closer all the time. And, I can't help thinking, we in America will continue to wait, relatively unconcerned, and blind to the menace that creeps ever nearer.

The delicious ice cream is a poor salve for the worry that fills me now, a transient distraction that does little to take my mind off the images of my country suffering an attack that dwarfs the one that shattered our sense of security on 9/11. After parking the van, Mohammed and I walk about a hundred yards on a stone-inlaid path that overlooks the city below. The path is lined with rose bushes in full bloom, and in the stillness of the evening, without even a hint of a breeze, the scent is particularly strong.

At the end of the path, we come to a series of steps that descend to a terrace cut out of the side of the mountain. To our left is a building that looks like a motel. It has eight rooms with sliding glass doors that open onto the terrace, overlooking the city below. The rooms are modern, clean, and very nicely decorated, with twin beds, built-in electric heaters, large built-in closets, hand carved furniture and colorful, thick woolen carpets. There are connecting doors between the rooms that can be locked from either side for privacy. There is even a modern Western-styled bathroom shared between two rooms, with an open shower facility and plenty of hot water. Mohammed and Sultan are staying in the first room, and two of the resident doctors who are working with me at the hospital occupy the second room. I have been given the third room all to myself. I say good night to Mohammed, thank him for waiting so patiently for me, and then retire to my room.

I kick off my sandals, put my notebook on the table, and open the second container of ice cream. The conversation with the Sheik ended on a very unexpected topic, and I want to be sure that my notes describe the exchange exactly as I remember it. I know from experience that the best time to review such documentation and make any additions or corrections is now, while it is still fresh in my memory. I am not sleepy at all. I enjoy my ice cream as I carefully go over my notes. I'm not certain at this point what I will do with the information I've gotten tonight, but I know that at some point, I have to try to get people to listen, and to be aware of, to prepare for, and hopefully to eliminate the threat that hangs over the world.

Once I'm satisfied that I have written an accurate accounting of the meeting, I take a wonderfully hot shower, slip the clean white *shalwar kameez* pajamas over my head, and set the alarm clock for 6:00 A.M., which will give me about four hours of sleep. Unfortunately, my thoughts jump from mulling over the unsettling discussion, to reeling with the plans for the following day. Those plans include a full surgical schedule in the morning, an instructional seminar during the late afternoon lunch/dinner break, and then a return to the operating room for the evening's surgeries. With all these thoughts battling for my attention, it takes a supreme act of will to get myself to sleep.

Years of experience have taught me that although I need very little sleep, my circadian rhythms demand that I rest from about one to about five in the morning. With four hours of sleep, I can operate at full capacity, but if I remain awake during that block of time, I can sleep for eight hours during any other time period and still feel exhausted. My last thoughts before I fall asleep are filled with the hope that all of the patients are doing well, and that I won't be awakened prematurely to deal with an emergency.

* * * * *

The alarm goes off precisely at 6:00 A.M., and for a few moments, I lie awake in my bed, confused and unsure as to exactly where I am. It takes me several minutes to become reoriented. I reach over and turn on the light above the night table, then I go to the bathroom to wash and dress. Sliding open the glass door, I step outside, drinking deeply of the fresh morning air. Closing the door behind me, I walk down the narrow path along the terrace, up the steps, across the gravel parking lot, and down the rose-lined path towards the hospital.

The doors to the hospital are still closed, so I walk around to the emergency room entrance and into the main lobby. There is a guard behind the desk, but he is sleeping soundly, and takes no notice of my passing. I cross the lobby to the staircase, since the elevator hasn't been working since our arrival, and from the looks of it, hasn't been working for a long time. I climb the stairs to the second floor and enter the children's ward. The nurses are already busy with their morning tasks, and barely look up, nodding at me as I enter, then returning to their duties. I examine the post-op patients first, and am pleased that they are all doing well. I leave instructions for the nurses on dressing changes, and leave the ward.

My next stop is the adjacent ward where the pre-op patients are. I pull the hand-written schedule off the wall, going down the list and making some adjustments to the schedule based on the patients' ages and the difficulty of the procedures to be performed. I replace the schedule on the wall with a piece of adhesive tape and start back down the stairs. As I enter the lobby, the guard is awake now, sitting at his desk, and he snaps to attention and salutes as I pass, nodding at him. The front door that had prevented my entry earlier easily unlatches from the inside. I proceed down the steps and back toward the main house.

Upon arriving at the main house I walk up the four steps to the open front door. Upon entering, I see that several members of the team are already there. I am mildly startled as the loudspeakers from Abbottabad call the worshipers to the mosque for the morning prayers. The front room of the house is almost overwhelmingly large, at more than a thousand square feet, with curtained windows that look out over courtyards and allow the morning light to fill the room.

I glance down at the intricate inlaid pattern of the stone floor, and suspect it must have taken the artists who created it months to conceive, and probably a year to actually complete. On the far side of the room, there is a fireplace, into which an electric heater has been installed. Interestingly, all the furniture, couches and chairs alike, are placed along the wall, leaving the entire center of the room open. At the far end of the room is the dining area, dominated by a table that can easily seat twenty people; the table is already set for breakfast.

Out of curiosity, I walk through the dining area and into the kitchen, where two men and two women are preparing breakfast. I pass through the kitchen and enter a tiny courtyard that is only visible from the kitchen itself. There are chickens running around, along with several very interesting, colorful birds that I am not familiar with.

One of the house servants steps outside and, pointing to these birds, says, "I take care of them. They are beautiful, no?"

"*Da. Da.*"

He proudly points to a small whitewashed two-story building with no windows on the first floor. "This is my house. I live here with my family."

I can see that he is proud of his home, and sensing that he wants to show it off, I point toward the doorway and say, "May I?"

Smiling broadly, he responds, "No problem."

The door is half-opened, and I can easily see inside. There is a chair and a small table in the corner, and a mattress on the floor. There are several articles of clothing hanging on hooks around the room, but no mirror, no photos, and no wall hangings of any type except for a small religious banner in black with gold print. That is all his family owns, and yet they are happy to have a roof over their heads, food to eat, and a small salary. When I turn back toward him, I see that he has a small basket full of grain in one hand, and is sprinkling the grain across the courtyard, where the grateful (and obviously hungry) birds gobble it up eagerly. I can't help but be humbled by the simplicity of his life, and the meagerness of his demands upon it. A rush of thoughts dances in my mind, a listing of the mundane and truly insignificant things with which we concern ourselves. I find that in a way, I am actually envious of the simple joy that so obviously fills him, and wonder why those of us with so much more often find that joy so elusive.

My thoughts are interrupted when one of the ladies appears in the kitchen doorway, beckoning us into the house. Breakfast must be ready.

As I turn toward the doorway, my new friend beams as he says to me, "She is my wife."

I turn to her, greeting her, "How are you?"

To which she replies, "Good, thank you."

I pass through the kitchen into the dining area, just as everyone is being called to the table by a woman I haven't seen before. She seems to be in her mid-fifties, of medium build, and dressed in a most intricately embroidered peach-colored silk chiffon. Her hair is shoulder length and neatly combed, with an elegant-looking little French braid in the back that hangs below the nape of her neck. Her head and shoulders are demurely draped with a peach silk chiffon scarf. Her nails are painted and her lipstick matches them. She is wearing very feminine gold sandals that accentuate her toenails, which are painted to match her fingernails. I assume by her appearance and mannerisms that she probably belongs to Pakistan's elite society, and upon being introduced, I learn that my assumption is correct, as she is the wife of the president of Northwest Medical College and Dental School.

Arrayed across the large table are fried egg omelets, beans, yogurt, a plate with thinly sliced tomatoes and cucumbers, and a platter of naan flatbread. The household help begin pouring English style hot tea for everyone. Conversation at the table is lively, revolving around yesterday's cases, today's schedule, and the progress of my recovery from being shot. After a few moments, our aristocratic-looking lady's husband, the president of the Medical College and Dental School, joins us. Dressed in a Western-style brown suit, he looks strangely out of place, since the rest of us are all dressed in more traditional garb. As he strides across the room toward the table, he asks one of the servants to bring fresh fruit and milk to the table. Taking a seat next to me at the end of the table, he smiles at me and and inquires as to how the wounds I sustained during the attack on the Karakoram are healing, and how I am feeling. Niceties aside, we resume our discussion of the plans for the day, including the surgical schedule. He says he has an early business meeting to attend, and tells one of the servants to inform the driver to have the car ready in about fifteen or twenty minutes.

We all finish breakfast at about the same time, thank our host and hostess, and leave for the hospital as a group. The sun is coming up over the mountains, and the sounds of traffic in the awakening city below dispel the stillness as effectively as the rising sun chases the darkness away. We walk briskly to the hospital and proceed up to the second floor. I enter the doctors' lounge area, change into my surgical greens, put on a cap and mask, and walk toward Operating Room Number One. I pass through the scrub area and then stop to observe the OR. The first child is on the operating table, and a new anesthesiologist named Abdul Al-Hassan is talking to one of my residents, Dr. Hasnain. I stand at the doorway, unnoticed, and I listen. It soon becomes apparent that they are talking about why I survived the recent ambush on the Karakoram Highway.

"A person could explain it away by saying it just wasn't his time yet."

"No! Doctor Joe did this himself. He dodged death on the battlefield. Other good men died that night. The doctor didn't."

I have been so busy and preoccupied over the past several weeks that I've actually had little time to dwell upon the ambush, let alone any deeper meanings behind my survival. While I am undeniably grateful to have lived through this experience, I've chalked it up to a combination of quick thinking, competent medical care, and no small amount of luck. Of course I had many emotions at the time the attack was happening, and certainly during the immediate aftermath.

But there was never really much time for me to obsess about myself, when so many other people needed my help. Within forty-eight hours of being shot, I was back on my feet doing a full schedule of surgeries. And of course the meetings with bin Laden have occupied the rest of my time and much of my thoughts. I have been constantly aware of my wounds – how could I not be? Despite being carefully tended, they have caused me no small amount of discomfort, which comes and goes. But there have been too many other matters needing my attention.

For the most part I have taken a philosophical approach and have simply accepted that I survived, and that's that. It is what it is. Now, however, as I listen to the conversation between the new anesthesiologist and my resident, I think to myself, *Maybe the simple explanation was not enough...not this time.*

And in an instant I have an epiphany, a deep sense that perhaps there was some "greater plan" at work during that attack – something more than just my own survival instincts, reasonably good reflexes, and sheer dumb luck. I'm not sure why I feel different in this instant, but I am struck with the profound feeling that my life has changed forever. I start thinking how my life has changed so much in such a short period of time. The experience of facing – and cheating – death such a relatively short time ago was both terrifying and exhilarating, and it suddenly comes back to me in a flood of emotion.

But once again I am pulled back to more mundane realities when Hasnain asks a question that I often find myself asking: "How much longer can he go on? The guy is what, sixty-five, seventy years old? He's more than twice my age, and I'm feeling the effects of everything we have been through in the past few weeks."

The anesthesiologist just shakes his head as he looks up from his patient. "No point in speculating how long he can hold up to this type of day-to-day wear and tear."

I cough as I enter the room, and both the anesthesiologist and Hasnain look up from the patient, startled by my presence. "For your information, I am nearly seventy years old."

Hasnain blurts out, "*Gandagi! Gandagi!*" ("Shit! Shit!")

I can't help but laugh at his embarrassment, and neither can the anesthesiologist. Glancing across the room, I notice that the nurse who had been preparing the instrument tray in the far corner is laughing as well. I walk over and put my hand on Hasnain's shoulder. "I am doing just fine. Let's see how well you will be doing at the end of the day. Now, scrub up and let's get this case started."

This child, our first patient of the day, has a burn contracture – or shortening of the musculature – of the foot and ankle area. He has difficulty walking because of the position in which he holds his foot. The plan is to do a double z-plasty or zigzag incision, which will release the contracture and add length by providing additional tissue in the area. This will allow him to hold his foot in a normal position when walking, and flex his ankle without difficulty.

I ask Hasnain, "Do you know how to do a double z-plasty?"

"Yes, yes."

Nurse Fatima hands him the small centimeter ruler and a marking pen. Hasnain begins marking the child's skin where the zigzag will be made. I approve his markings, and Hasnain asks Fatima to pass the scalpel. Initial incisions are made, and the first of the flaps are elevated. I nod my approval, saying "You're doing well, and can complete this with Fatima's help. I am going to Operating Room Number Two to help Ali.

Ali is working with Nurse Nayab, and Dr. Abdul has already started the anesthetic for this child, who has a double cleft lip. I review Ali's incision markings, then inject the upper lip with the numbing solution, which will reduce the bleeding and provide anesthesia during the procedure. It is the dental anesthetic xylocaine, and the lip will remain numb and painless for three or four hours after the procedure is completed. This will make it much easier to manage the child in the initial post-operative phase. It also allows the anesthesiologist to maintain the child in twilight-like sleep, rather than a deep anesthesia, which is a much safer approach and minimizes the chance of any complications.

Ali and I work together on this complicated double cleft lip, and once the tissue has been transferred and the defects closed,

Ali will finish placing the small delicate sutures on his own.

I remove my gloves, wash my hands, and then return to the first operating room. The procedure has been completed and they are already wrapping the leg. The next patient is sitting outside the door of the operating room, along with the other children who are awaiting their turn in surgery. They sit quietly on the wooden bench, without their parents, talking among themselves and playing games. There is no crying and no fussing. As I noted in another chapter, the hospital doesn't have gowns, so the children are in their street clothes, though their sandals have been removed. The night before, each of their mothers was given surgical soap and told to bathe her child. The children receive no pre-operative medication, simply because we don't have any.

Once a surgical procedure is completed, an orderly comes into the room and picks the child up in his arms, as the nurse carries the IV that is still attached to the child's arm. We don't have any gurneys with which to transport the children, either. The orderly and nurse carry the child across the hall and into the three-bed recovery area, where the child's mother is waiting. They then return to the operating room, which is cleaned and ready for the next patient in only five minutes – again, in marked contrast to the hospitals I've worked at in Houston.

There are other differences too. Not only are there no gowns for the patients, but sterile sheets and drapes are in limited supply as well. For all the facial cases here, we just place a single sterile towel across the chest and under the chin. In operating rooms back in the U.S., the patient would be wearing a surgical gown and covered with so many layers of sterile sheets that you wouldn't know there was a child underneath. There would be so many wires and monitoring devices attached to the patient that you would think we were operating on a robot. Not here. Only a single towel covers the area directly adjacent to the area where the surgery is being performed. But as I have noted, I have attended more than ten thousand cases in Third World countries under these MASH-like conditions without any problems, and with virtually a zero infection rate for our oral and facial cases.

Our antibiotics supply is limited, and what supply we do have is utilized on those cases that are most likely to incur infections, such as burns, hand injuries, farm implement injuries, and injuries that are the direct consequences of war. To our advantage, we are able to significantly reduce the dosages of the antibiotics because our patients have never been exposed to antibiotics, and a small amount goes a long way.

There are no antibiotic-resistant microorganisms or flesh-eating bacteria here, since the occurrence of such organisms is the result of decades of expensive and inappropriate antibiotic use in the United States and other developed countries.

In my opinion, the more developed countries' efforts to combat infections have actually had the exact opposite result, effectively increasing the likelihood that such infections will occur.

The next child in line has a unilateral (one-sided) cleft lip. The identification badge taped to his pullover says his name is Parveen. I introduce myself to him and take his hand. He doesn't complain, and walks with me directly to the operating room, whereupon I see a sudden change in his expression. I smile at him to ease his apprehension, and he smiles back, albeit somewhat wanly. The two orderlies immediately lift him to the table, and the anesthesiologist places a tourniquet on his upper arm and inserts an intravenous needle. This whole procedure takes less than thirty seconds. The anesthesiologist keeps talking to the child all the time about his brothers, sisters, family, school, and sports, diverting his attention as the intravenous sedative is administered. The child doesn't even have time to cry before he slips into that twilight state, and we are ready to start.

Everything is under control, so I take a break and go to the doctors' lounge, where there is always hot tea, and sit with my feet up for a few minutes before returning to the operating room. I am pleased that in the short time we've been together, we have formed a very smooth-running team. Fatima brings me the charts from the morning cases, each of which consists of only three pages: the physical, including the diagnosis, the laboratory report, and the operative notes which I am writing by hand and are rarely more than two or three sentences. I am struck again, as I often am, by the contrast between the rudimentary paperwork in this hospital, and the forty-page-long patient charts at the Texas Medical Center back home.

It's an issue that won't go away and that never ceases to raise my ire. I've long thought that the abundance of these required forms are the result of government mandates thought up by desk jockeys and hospital lawyers, primarily to justify their exorbitant annual salaries. Furthermore, hundreds of millions of dollars will be spent across the U.S. in hospitals and doctors' offices to meet the new federal mandate of a paperless system.

But it won't end there. These systems will require secure data storage facilities, frequent system updates, and ongoing maintenance. Hospital and office personnel will have to take training courses to learn to use the systems. Of course, the government will change the mandates - and the procedures - of the system on a yearly basis, requiring further changes by the computer companies and subsequent additional training costs. These costs will be passed along to the hospital and doctors, who will in turn be passing it to their patients.

So much for bringing down the cost of medicine.

To compound the problem, any remotely proficient hacker will be able to gain access to the system and obtain not only an individual's medical history, but all of his or her personal information, including social security number, credit information, and the like. And all the effort and expense that is poured into the system won't provide even a single patient with so much as one dose of a needed medication or a single dressing change. To put it bluntly, it is, in my opinion, clearly a lose/lose system, and the more I think about it, the better my retirement from direct care starts to look.

The charts completed, I leave them in the recovery room so they can go with the patients. I return to the operating room, where the next two patients are already asleep and waiting for me. The first child has large, severe burns to the chest, neck, and adjacent area. There are contractures, which limit shoulder motion as well as his ability to lift his left arm. This is such a large area that once the contracture is released, the resulting defect will require a skin graft, which we will take from the boy's thigh. We have brought an electric skin graft machine called a dermatome with us from Houston, and this is the local medical team's first opportunity to see it in action.

I look in on Operating Room Number Two, where there is a simple one-sided cleft lip to be repaired. Ali has done many of these with me, so once we review the procedure and the markings, I say to him, "Ali, if you need me, send Nurse Nayab to OR Number One."

He nods, saying, "Easy case, should be no problem. I am comfortable with it. I will send the nurse so you can come and look at it before I put the bandages on."

I go to the scrub sink, and from there I don a full gown and gloves for the grafting procedure and enter the operating room – only to find that a crowd has gathered, consisting of interns, residents, medical students, and several of the doctors who have completed their cases in other rooms. All are anxious to learn and see how the electric dermatome is used. I demonstrate the assembly and settings for the dermatome and set it aside on a sterile tray while a contracture is surgically released. The electric surgical knife is used. The bleeding is therefore minimized, so the wound is ready in minutes for the application of the graft. I think to myself, as I often do, "It's show time!"

I carefully explain each of the steps I am going to go through in obtaining the graft, first in English, and then I ask Hasnain to translate in Urdu. I pick up the dermatome, release the safety, and with a light touch apply it to the thigh, where it cuts a perfect graft. This thin sheet of skin is immediately transferred to the chest wall and the undersurface of the arm. The assembled doctors, residents, and nurses are expecting to see it sutured in place, but I have a surprise for them. I send one of the surgical assistants to the storage locker and ask him to bring back the stainless steel staple gun. Within a minute, the assistant returns to the operating room and removes the packaging from one of the staple guns. The graft is stapled into place in just a few minutes, a procedure that, if done with sutures, would take at least an hour to an hour and a half. One of the interns speaks up and says, "We don't have anything like that here."

I get to give them another surprise. "I have a case of these and will leave many of them for the doctors to use, and some for the interns and residents to practice with."

His excitement is contagious, and there is a chorus in the room of, "Thank you, thank you!"

I have to admit that their appreciation feels mighty good, but I try to go on matter-of-factly, "We have several other burns that will require grafts over the next few days, and those who wish to be in the operating room and observe or get some hands-on experience, please talk to me about it tonight after the surgical cases are completed."

As the daylight wanes and the line of children awaiting surgery grows shorter, I realize that despite all of the earlier talk about my stamina, my recent abdominal wounds have diminished it somewhat. In spite of the physical discomfort and increasing tiredness I am experiencing, I have to admit that this has been a good day, and all things considered, I feel pretty good.

And just for the moment, my worries about Osama bin Laden's plans have taken a back seat.

Sidna's Story

This is the story of Sidna, a bright and beautifully vibrant teenage girl, but it is really the story of thousands upon thousands of girls in Pakistan and Afghanistan.

Having finished her high school education, Sidna's family felt it was time for her to marry. The family was poor, and Sidna's father looked forward to being given a generous dowry in exchange for his daughter's hand. Basically, Sidna was going to be sold.

The father, who was a laborer, eagerly set himself to the task of finding her a suitable husband, as is still the custom of the region.

He looked for an older, richer man, and showed the candidates photos of his daughter, enticing the old gentlemen with stories of her beauty and intelligence for almost a year. Finally, one of the men asked to meet the girl. Sidna's father was jubilant, thinking only of having one less of his nine children's mouths to feed, and of the significant bride price his family would get. A bride price is somewhat like a dowry, but instead of being given by the family of the bride to the family of the groom, it is money that the groom pays the bride's family in exchange for her hand.

Sidna's father told his wife about the possibility of the upcoming marriage, and although she was not quite as excited as her husband, she realized that this was the way things had to be. They took Sidna shopping for a new sari, and attractive but inexpensive costume jewelry, and they paid a laborer who worked in a beauty shop to do her hair and makeup. Sidna would be her potential suitor's fourth wife, and they wanted to make the best impression possible. The inspection visit went well, the man agreed upon the bride price, and a day for the wedding was selected. The future groom's other wives, in particular the oldest senior wife, were not happy at all about this arrangement. They had teenage children the same age as the new wife who was being brought into "their" home. They knew, of course, that there was nothing they could do about it.

The wedding went on as planned, and Sidna quickly became the old gentleman's favorite. He lavished gifts and attention upon her, but her life in her new home was miserable. The older wives saw her as little more than a servant, and gave her every difficult and unpleasant chore. She complained to her new husband, but he merely laughed her complaints off, repeatedly telling her that things would get better with the passage of time. He did not intercede with quarrels and disagreements among the wives, who took his apathy as permission to continue and even increase their abuse. After a few months, Sidna felt she couldn't bear the situation any longer, and asked her husband for a divorce, pleading with him to allow her to go back to her family.

Unfortunately, although a Muslim woman can ask for a divorce, generally only the husband has the right to grant one. For the man, obtaining a divorce may be as simple as pronouncing the Talaq – the formula of repudiation – three times and clapping his hands, whereupon the divorce is final. It isn't always that simple; customs and laws vary from country to country and among different Islamic schools of jurisprudence (Shiite and Sunni Muslims have different rules for performing an Islamic divorce). But more often than not, Muslim women get a pretty raw deal in both marriage and divorce, particularly by Western standards, and especially in areas dominated by the Taliban. The newly-divorced wife is generally allowed to get a few of her personal things, and is then thrown out of the house.

However, Sidna's husband was unwilling to relinquish his young prize, and refused her request. She decided she would stand her ground and fight back, believing that her position as the fourth – but favorite – wife put her in a position of power. Difficult situations arose daily amongst the women, with the other wives openly expressing their anger and animosity toward this young interloper, but Sidna was determined to take advantage of her position as the old man's favorite wife. If she was not allowed to divorce, then she would take control.

She would soon find out that such power was an illusion.

The other wives – particularly the senior lady of the household – felt threatened by Sidna's defiance, and decided that she must be put in her place. The senior wife decided that the only answer was to remove this young upstart who was trying to take control. Having made her decision, she enlisted the other wives in a plan to rid themselves of Sidna. It would be a simple plan, one that is carried out countless times in the region, and the wives knew that it was nearly foolproof. This young girl was going to die.

Over the next several weeks, the senior wife was more pleasant than usual toward Sidna, demanding little of her, but it was all in an effort to put the troublesome young woman off her guard.

In the rear of the house was a storage room with only a single narrow slit of a window. The senior wife, with the help of the other wives, went into the storage room one evening when no one was around and removed everything of value. The senior wife then began to prepare the room for the culmination of her plan, placing a ball of yarn wrapped with straw and soaked in kerosene into the room, and dousing the floor and walls with kerosene.

That evening, while they were both in the kitchen, the older wife asked Sidna to please go to the storeroom and get some flour. This was not an unreasonable request, and since the senior wife had been particularly pleasant to her over the last several weeks, Sidna hurried off to the storeroom to fetch the flour. Placing the large, heavy key into the lock, Sidna entered the storeroom, noticing the heavy aroma of the kerosene, but thinking little of it. Meanwhile, the senior wife had kicked off her sandals and moved quickly and silently behind the girl. She approached the open door as quietly as she could, struck a match to the kerosene-soaked yarn ball, then cast the torch into a puddle of the flammable liquid, and slammed and locked the door, trapping Sidna inside. She found the muted whoosh of the flames quite satisfying.

Joseph Agris, M.D.

Sidna Saves Herself

*S*idna thought it curious for the door to slam shut behind her, but didn't give it too much thought. Almost instantly, however, as the flames from the small torch quickly ignited the kerosene the older woman had spread along the floor and walls, the room was engulfed in flames. It was only then that it occurred to Sidna that she was in danger. And when she first felt the searing heat, she realized that the senior wife was bent upon murdering her.

Many women had fallen victim to this too-common scenario of murder, but Sidna was smart and resourceful. Mustering every bit of her strength, she rolled the cask containing the flour across the room to the base of the window. She then climbed on top, and using the wooden flour scoop, smashed the pane of glass. The smoke from the burning kerosene was choking her. She wrapped her dupatta scarf around her face to protect her head and neck, then used the flour scoop to smash the remaining jagged edges of glass from the window frame. The window itself was nothing more than a narrow slit, but being thin and muscular, with the supple joints of a young teenager, she managed to squeeze an arm, a shoulder, and her head through, filling her tortured lungs with a desperately needed breath of fresh air.

With her right hand extended against the exterior wall, Sidna used every bit of her adrenalin-enhanced strength to leverage her body upward through the narrow opening, just as the flames began to reach her legs. She now had her shoulders through, and both hands against, the outside wall. She continued to wiggle from side to side until her hips cleared the window frame, at which time she tucked her head and dropped almost five feet to the dirt below, landing with a painful thud on her shoulders and back. She tore the dupatta from her face and neck and began breathing deeply of the fresh air as she ran from the storage shed, now engulfed in flames.

She never looked back, but instead ran as if her very life depended upon it, because it did. If the senior wife discovered that her attempt at murder had failed, she would surely try again, and this time, Sidna knew that the older woman would not fail. She ran through the fields until she reached an irrigation ditch, filled with cool running water. At first, she bathed her feet in the cool water, but after a few seconds, she just sat down in the shallow ditch, allowing the cold water from the glacier melt high above to flow over her legs and ease the pain from her burns. She did not know it at the time, but the cold water halted the progression of the burns.

As she sat there looking up at the sky, she contemplated what she should do and where she could go to get away. She had heard stories about other young girls who had been victims of kerosene burning, but had never met any. She had assumed that the stories were used by senior wives and mothers-in-law to frighten the younger members of the household and ensure their control over them. She now knew that these stories were all too real, and that the practice was not a myth, but a reality. She was hurting, but the frigid water had soothed her burns considerably, almost anesthetizing them. She was young, strong, and brave, and intelligent enough to realize that it would take every bit of her resolve and strength to survive. Her family's home was several miles away, but she knew she could shorten that distance by following the paths through the fields, where she would be less likely to encounter anybody. The one thing she did not want was to meet any neighbors or friends, because by fleeing – indeed, by merely surviving – she would be marked as having dishonored her husband and family, and she would likely be put to death.

By the time Sidna finally reached her family home, she was exhausted. The children were at school, and her father was at work. Several of the women, including her mother, were at the house. She quickly told them what had happened. One of the women went out to the main road and summoned an autorickshaw driver to the house, instructing him to take her to the hospital.

The driver tried to reassure them, saying, "She is fortunate. The American medical team is working at the hospital this month. I have driven other burn patients and children with various medical problems."

One of the women rushed to the door with a handful of Pakistani money and placed it in the driver's hand. "This is to pay the doctor. If you need more, tell them that the family will be there tonight."

The driver smiled. "The American medical team does not

accept money."

The mother scoffed at his ridiculous statement, saying, "Everyone accepts money, and doctors are expensive."

The driver responded, waving his hands for emphasis, "No! They will not take money. The treatment is free. Their senior doctor has been to many cities in Pakistan doing this type of work. We call him Dr. Angel."

The mother remained unconvinced, saying, "I have heard such stories, but who believes such things in Pakistan?"

The driver smiled reassuringly and handed the money back, "I will take her and speak to the director myself. You are a good family, and I have known you for a long time. And you don't need to pay me, either."

The motorized rickshaw started with a sudden lurch, the spinning tires flinging rocks and gravel as the driver shifted into first gear and sped away.

During the past several years we have seen many young girls

who said they have received kerosene burns. In my naiveté, and being unfamiliar with the practice of kerosene burning, at first I believed that the burns were caused by accidents involving the small kerosene stoves and, to a lesser degree, heaters that are used in most of the homes throughout Pakistan and the Middle East. After spending years in Pakistan, however, my naiveté has long since succumbed to the harsh reality that kerosene burning is a common means of disposing of a "problem" female. It is apparently as common a practice as is the throwing of acid on a girl's or woman's face and body to punish her for some purported offense that can be as minor as embarrassing a man, or being the subject of gossip.

Ironically, murder by kerosene burning is most often committed by mothers-in-law who do not like the young lady. The mother-in-law or other family member locks the young girl in a room and starts a kerosene fire, typically ending in the girl's death. The husband says nothing, and soon goes out and finds a new young wife, who may very well suffer the same fate at some point. There is usually no investigation, no prosecution, and no justice at all for the young women who, if they're "lucky," are horribly disfigured. Some would argue that it is the vast majority of the victims – the ones who die – who are the fortunate ones. And this horror happens every day. Only those few "lucky" ones escape. These are the ones we see in our burn clinic.

Sidna is one of those rare individuals who is truly lucky. She can thank her intelligence, resourcefulness, and quick actions in a life or death situation for bringing her to us. Upon her arrival at the hospital, we begin giving her intravenous therapy with antibiotics and pain medication. She is then taken to the operating room, where her leg wounds are cleaned, and topical antibiotic ointments and soft burn dressings are applied. Most of the burns are second degree, and will heal on their own. There are some small areas of third degree burns on her legs, but these are minimal and will be dealt with at a future date if needed.

I hope and pray that Sidna is not destined to live her life with a reputation for being "troublesome," and that she will not become a victim of another "accident." I fear that the next time, she won't be quite so lucky, and will end up dead or horribly disfigured, like so many other young girls in the region, a victim of an unreported crime that is as common as it is horrible.

Third Meeting
with the Sheik

We have finished the day's surgeries and have completed the evening rounds at the clinic, and all is well. I return to my room, take a hot shower, and put on a simple *shalwar kameez* with some gold trim on the collar. I slip into black sandals and place a nondescript gray topi – a Muslim prayer cap used in Pakistan – on my head. Stepping outside, I walk along the poorly lit path at the base of the mountain to the parking lot.

Mohammed is already at the wheel with the engine running, and Sultan is riding shotgun. Saleem will not be joining us tonight. I slide the van's side door back just enough

441

to step in and then I slam it closed, hard enough to make sure the temperamental latch takes hold. Even before I am situated on the bench in the back of the van, Mohammed puts the vehicle into gear and heads down the side of mountain toward the guard station. He slows down and salutes, and they open the gates. A few feet past the guard station, we come to a stop, waiting for a break in the brisk flow of traffic. As soon as there is a break in the line of oncoming vehicles, Mohammed darts onto the main road going south into Abbottabad.

In a few minutes, we come to the junction of Mansehra and Jinnah Roads. Mohammed maneuvers around several rickshaws and donkey wagons and swerves to the right, continuing on the Jinnah Road toward the market area. The Pakistan Tourism Development Corporation (PTDC) office is on our right, and at the next intersection with the Central Road, we have to stop to allow cross-traffic to pass.

When the British controlled this area, they had built a number of churches, one of which, St. Luke's Church, still stands at this intersection. We pass the Suburban Internet Café on our left, then a bank with a money exchange area, an enterprise which the Muslim religion frowns upon, as paying money for money or charging interest is considered taboo. Like everything else, they have found ways around this. We then pass several small cafés that are doing a bustling business. Just before we approach Gumani Road, which forms the northern border of the Sarafa Bazaar, there is a small, dark side street –

little more than an alley – where several other cars are parked. We pull over and add our van to the lineup.

There is no moon tonight, and without any streetlights to speak of, it is very dark. A light breeze is blowing, and Sultan wraps himself in a gray wool shawl as he climbs out of the van, but I think this is more to hide the automatic weapon he is carrying than to protect against any chill. I am unarmed tonight, as there is really no place to conceal a weapon in the clothes that I am wearing. After getting out of the van, I adjust the fanny pack I am wearing. It is secured in front over my abdomen, but under my *shalwar*. In it, I carry some money, my passport, and other important identification papers that I will need to show if I get stopped.

Mohammed drapes his own shawl, crisscrossed over his shoulders and across his chest. There is a noticeable bulge on the left side, which I assume is because he has armed himself with a pistol. Mohammed's and Sultan's job is to look after me, and as usual, they take it seriously. We emerge from the dark alley paralleling Gumani road and head towards the northwest corner of the Sarafa Bazaar, in the direction of the mosque where Mohammed wants to stop for evening prayers. It is the same spot where we had been contacted by bin Laden's bodyguards a few days ago.

The past several days have been uneventful, with no contact from the Sheik or messengers. And so far there is no sign of them tonight. It may be because we have come so late to the market area, having remained in surgery until almost midnight once again. We stroll casually along the crumbling mud brick structures, many of which have been equipped with electricity, legally or otherwise. On these buildings, one or two light bulbs hang from bare wires under the awnings and in the shops themselves. I find this hodge-podge web of electric wires, dangling freely from a wooden pole at the corner, oddly fascinating.

Behind the shops or on the floors above are the shop owners' living quarters, and peering down the central isle between stacks of merchandise for sale, it is not unusual to see the flickering illumination of a television set, surrounded by bare-legged children and the occasional chicken strutting among them. I stop at one of the shops and purchase a half kilo of fresh pistachios, and then continue along the main thoroughfare, passing a series of cafés, food-stalls, and assorted small shops selling fruit, vegetables, and confections.

Even at this late hour, the market is crowded and the shops are actively trading. When the day's work is completed and the men of the neighborhood return home after sundown, they go to the market. The streets leading to and around the mosque come alive with humans, animals, mopeds, rickshaws, and the ever-present handcarts. It is a combination of medievalism and modernity that has always intrigued me, and has given the central districts of Muslim cities their unique flavor. It is not until ten or eleven at night that the hubbub reaches its zenith, and the pace of activity doesn't begin to diminish until about two in the morning.

The market is particularly busy because of Eid, the last several days of Ramadan. The activity in the marketplace during that holy month can only be compared to the Christmas season in a shopping mall back home. The bazaar is packed shoulder-to-shoulder with people celebrating the holiday and purchasing special foods and gifts. The mosque is decorated with hundreds of fairy lights. Some stores have noisy gasoline generators sitting curbside to better light their establishments.

One store is emblazoned in green and yellow neon lights, suspended from the overhead awnings and bathing the carnival-like atmosphere in a ghoulish glow. Small wooden Ferris wheels are hauled into the streets, along with antique swings to occupy the children, whose laughter echoes through the alleyways and the shops. There is usually a charge of only a few pennies for a ride. Unlike carnivals in the States, all the rides are turned by hand, rather than electric power. Attendees are all dressed in their finest clothing, and the aroma of foods grilling on open fires blends with the fragrances of perfumed oil, filling the air and creating an atmosphere that can be found no other place in the world. Unfortunately, the spectacle is impossible to catch on film, and can only be remembered in the mind's eye.

I am enjoying myself immensely, trying quite success-fully to absorb and get lost in my surroundings. Unlike their gawking doctor (and fortunately for me), this scene is not new to Mohammed and Sultan, and they are probably more amused by my reaction than by the celebration itself. They are focused upon watching my back, and at the same time looking for our contact person. We approach a small outdoor café where there are several wooden benches and elongated wooden tables being shared by the patrons, who are sipping their tea and people-watching.

I notice Mohammed giving a sudden glance to Sultan, who nods back in response. They have seen something that I have not: two men in the coffee shop are not engaged in conversation as are the others around them, and are facing outward toward the road, their eyes scanning all those who pass. They focus on our small group and seem intent upon following us with their eyes. Sultan, who is to my right and slightly behind me, gives me a gentle poke to continue walking and to not make eye contact with our observers.

Not fifty yards up the road, we pass through a dirt parking lot filled to capacity. On the other side of the lot, beside a detached shed on the side of a two-story mud brick house, a young man in his twenties stands, watching us intently as we draw nearer. The woolen scarf draped across his shoulders and upper body fails to conceal the shape of the automatic weapon he carries. There is now no doubt in our minds that this young man, as well as the two men in the coffee shop, are spotters who have been purposely posted along this section of the market. Are they there to make sure that we aren't being followed before contact is made, or are they there for some other purpose?

In any case, Mohammed and Sultan have no doubt that we are being closely watched. After walking another forty or fifty meters, we come to an opening in the perimeter fence at the far end of the parking area. Two more men have been posted at this point, and as we pass, one of them dials a cell phone. I can't help but wonder what this is all leading up to, and whether something else is going down tonight. I am growing tenser by the minute.

The market is beyond crowded, overflowing with evening diners and bargain hunting shoppers. A heavy aroma of grilling meats, mixed with the smells of coffeehouses, wafts through the air. The smoke from hookah pipes drifts from the warren of small shops and awning-covered stalls of the bazaar and permeates the narrow, winding alleyways that circle the mosque. We walk past a sandstone stairway that leads to the courtyard in front of the mosque, where several gentlemen have removed their sandals and are washing their feet in preparation for evening prayer.

We cross over to Masjid Road, passing in front of the crowded and noisy meat and vegetable market, then wind our way along the west side of the bazaar, heading directly toward the mosque. Our pace is slow, and we stop occasionally to look at items on display, purchasing some confections and other sweets as we move through the sprawl of streets and alleyways in the old city.

These bazaars began life over a thousand years ago, serving trade caravans as they came from China along the Silk Road. The caravans would travel south to Pakistan along what is now referred to as the Karakoram Highway, and onward to what is presently called the Grand Trunk Highway to the Khyber Pass, which would take them into Afghanistan and ultimately onto the European continent. As we wander through the streets of the city, the ancient and modern seem to converge in the dim light of the evening, and it is easy to imagine an ancient marketplace, illuminated only by gas lamps and bonfires.

Dressed in wrinkled and often stained *shalwars*, merchants coax customers into their shops with offers of a small taste of a sweet or a handful of cashews or walnuts. There are groups haggling over prices on each side of the narrow thoroughfares, and we can hear the thin tinny beats of traditional music spilling from the adjacent coffeehouses. Along this section of the market, vendors sell everything from what they claim to be handmade silver ornaments, copper wares, and gold jewelry, to woolen and silk rugs and traditional sandals. Brightly printed T-shirts and American jeans are some of the few examples that remind us that we're in the twenty-first century.

The shoulder-to-shoulder crowd moving through these narrow alleys is composed of young and old alike, but there are almost no women to be seen in this part of the market, except for perhaps one or two very old women. A young man in his twenties pushes by the group, carrying a tin tray laden with pastries and tea. I notice that he has a nasty red gash with dry blood on his forehead. We all follow him with our eyes as he skillfully carries the tray above his head on one hand, maneuvering through the crowded alley, then suddenly disappearing into one of the tea shops on the left side of the road.

While I am observing this young man, Mohammed notices two others, and I barely have time to catch a glimpse of them myself before Mohammed ushers me into the nearest teahouse. We are now in sight of the mosque, the same location where contact was made a few days ago. I wonder about the urgency to slip inside the teahouse, and Mohammed whispers to me, "Those are the same two who were watching us from the parking lot. The younger one – the one with the gray woolen shawl – is definitely armed, and he is focused on us."

We take seats at a table and the waiter comes over immediately to take our order. Sultan orders tea and sweet cakes. The tea arrives within the minute, and the waiter pours it into small porcelain cups in front of each of us, then disappears. Mohammed slowly sips his tea, but maintains eye contact with the young man who is sitting across from us, but is positioned in such a way that I cannot see his face.

Another waiter, wearing what once was a white apron, but is now stained with coffee, tea, and confections, arrives with a tin plate of sweet cakes. His clothes are unkempt and don't fit well, and the topi he wears on his head is oddly tilted to one side. He nervously slides a folded piece of paper under the edge of the tin plate containing the sweet cakes, and hurriedly leaves us.

Mohammed takes one of the sweet cakes and bites into it, and with the other hand removes the note and begins to read it. He takes another sip of tea and sets the cup down. Without raising his elbows or forearm, but only moving his fingers and wrist, he motions for the young man across from us to approach. At the same time, Sultan slides his chair out from the table, and positions himself between me and one of the other well-armed men who had been following us. This also allows Sultan easy access to his weapon. The young man crosses over to our table, and Mohammed, still holding the sweet cake in his hand, motions for him to sit down.

Greetings are exchanged, and Mohammed reaches out and politely shakes the young man's hand, but it is quite apparent that neither he nor the stranger trusts each other. At that tense moment, I get my first unobstructed view of the young man's face. I had been altogether lost in my own thoughts and thoroughly distracted by the noise, smells, and colorful atmosphere of the bazaar, but with that first glance, I suddenly become aware of who has joined us.

He is Osama Bin Laden's son, Hamza!

I am immediately excited and relieved by the realization that of course, the Sheik's son would have to take unusual precautions in meeting us, including having us followed through the bazaar by several armed bodyguards. The waiter sets an additional porcelain cup on the table and fills it with steaming tea.

I gently push the plate of sweet cakes in Hamza's direction and greet him. He responds in kind, reaching out to shake my hand. The long-awaited contact is now realized. We eat our sweet cakes and drink our tea. It seems that everyone is worried about the potential dangers of these secret meetings – everyone but me, that is. As we finish the last of our tea and snacks, a nervous young man sitting at an adjacent table wipes the tips of his fingers on the sleeve of his *shalwar*. We recognize him as one of those who has been following us.

Hamza understands the unspoken message, and says, "We need to go. The Sheik is waiting." As we all begin to rise from our seats, Hamza holds up his hand and says, "Only the doctor."

Sultan responds, his concern clear in both his expression and his words, "We will all walk together as far as the mosque, and then you and your friend who is sitting over there will be responsible for the safety of the doctor. He is with you, isn't he?"

Hamza glances over at the man, "Yes, he is one of the body-guards from the compound."

Sultan nods. "I thought so. He's been following us through the market most of the evening."

Hamza offers no apology, stating quite matter-of-factly, "We need to be sure nobody is following you or us."

Sultan wants to let Hamza know that we too were watching things very closely, and that we were as aware of their presence as they were of ours. "We understand the need for security and we are in complete agreement with it, not only for your safety and your family's safety but for ours as well." It is obvious that Sultan also wants to put Hamza at ease, and is pleased when the Sheik's son smiles in response. Sultan is back to his typically calm self, standing there next to me, his even breathing indicating that he is once again feeling relaxed, the danger passed.

Mohammed raises his hand, palm outward, and looks directly at Hamza. With an unmistakably stern tone, he says, "The doctor is your responsibility now. He is in your protection now."

With that, Sultan and Mohammed leave us, and our group continues north on Main Bazaar Avenue. I will learn later that the bodyguard joined Mohammed and Sultan at the mosque for evening prayer, a good sign that tensions are abated and that a level of trust has been established. When we reach the mosque, Hamza and I circle to the east side of the mosque, continuing north on Club Road. Hamza flags down a motorized rickshaw driver, saying to me, "It's late. Let's ride to the compound."

I am all for that suggestion. With adrenaline still pumping through my veins, I board the rickshaw with Hamza, who turns to the driver to give directions. We pass several of the typical walled in homes that I recognize, and drive past some open fields. There is a hayloft to our right that I remember from previous trips, and I know we are very close to our destination, having become quite familiar with the route to the compound.

Hamza points to a house fifty yards ahead on the right and asks the driver to stop. He pays the driver and we get out. The rickshaw makes a quick U-turn in a bit less than its own length, and continues south along the unlit road. These three-wheeled vehicles' maneuverability is a big advantage in the downtown traffic area.

Hamza turns to me and says, "I apologize, but we have to walk the rest of the way."

"I understand," I respond. "It's the right thing to do, for everybody's safety." As we walk together along the dirt road, gusts of wind blow sand in our faces and whip at our clothing. We wrap our woolen shawls over our heads and across our faces to protect us from the blowing sand and the evening chill. There are no lights along the road, and the homes we pass are all dark. Within a few minutes, we arrive at the compound, which by now is familiar to me. Hamza withdraws a small flashlight from the pocket in his *kameez* and flashes it off and on several times in the direction of the guardhouse roof.

Shortly, there are several flashes from the guardhouse in response. He then places the flashlight in his pocket, and we wait. I hear the heavy metal bolts being withdrawn, and then the sound of iron hinges grating on each other as the heavy door is opened just enough to allow us through. It is immediately closed, and the bolts are slammed back into position. One of the guards now standing almost directly in front of me has an AK-47 slung over his shoulder. I raise my arms and extend them, expecting a pat down.

Hamza steps between me and the bodyguard, and with authority in his voice, says, *"Jee nahee,"* waving away the frisking.

I lower my arms, face the bodyguard, and say, "Peace be with you."

He responds in kind. "And peace be with you too."

My immediate instinct is to reach out and shake his hand, but I remember that in this culture, you don't shake hands with bodyguards and servants. Seeing my hesitation, Hamza smiles and indicates everything is all right. The bodyguard and the two men who had been closing the gates leave together, and I walk with Hamza across the open area, disturbing some of the chickens as we stroll toward the main house.

As we enter the house and turn to the right, we see Osama bin Laden, already sitting cross-legged on the floor in this room, with tea and dishes filled with some small pastries, walnuts, and pistachios arrayed before him. He waves his hand, inviting Hamza and myself to sit. A rapid conversation takes place between bin Laden and his son, and from the few words that I can understand, Hamza assures him that all precautions were taken in bringing me to the compound, and that we were not followed. He tells his father that my bodyguards went to the mosque for evening prayer and that everything was satisfactory. Apparently satisfied, bin Laden smiles and pours a cup of tea and gently slides it in my direction.

I take the cup and thank him. He passes his hand over the food, offering it to me. I know it would be impolite not to accept his offer and take something; besides, the pistachios and walnuts – my favorites – are superb, so as I sip my tea, I help myself to a handful of the nuts.

Hamza speaks up at this point, saying, "My father has talked of nothing but the discussion you had with him regarding nuclear weapons, and your understanding of these as an engineer. It is this subject he wishes to pursue with you tonight. He is willing to tell you about the bombs that he has been able to acquire, and in return, he would like for you to tell him what you know about nuclear material, because he does not know how to determine its efficacy or value and potential. Are you willing to discuss this with him?"

I think for a moment before responding, "It's been more than thirty years since I've been at the engineering university, and many things have changed since then, but I do have a basic knowledge. Nothing you could not pull off of the Internet today, but I would like to hear what you've acquired and what you are planning to acquire."

Osama says, "Let me start by giving you some background information and then we can build on that. First of all, we have already acquired!"

"Not to interrupt you, Sheik bin Laden, but I'm an avid reader, and several years ago the *London Times*, not to mention the *Jerusalem Reporter* and *Al-Arabi*, gave in-depth reports on the sale of Special Atomic Demolition Missions, commonly known as nuclear suitcases. They were purchased through military officials and former KGB officials from the Soviet Union at the time of its collapse. These suitcase-sized nuclear devices were not considered strategic weapons, designed to be used against the U.S. and its NATO allies. It was estimated that the Soviet Union produced more than 800 of these 'suitcases,' which of course were actually not suitcases at all, but measured approximately five feet by three feet, and weighed an estimated seven hundred to nine hundred pounds each.

"This was only a beginning. Over the next decade, they were miniaturized, and truly became suitcase-sized nuclear weapons, measuring less than three square feet in size, but still weighing a hundred fifty to two hundred pounds. These compact units were what I would call 'do-it-yourself kits.' But it was not as simple as throwing the switch, setting the timer, hitting the button, and the nuke would go off. It would take four or five highly trained individuals with specialized knowledge in the areas of electronics and nuclear materials to assemble the bomb and then to actually integrate the detonator with the nuclear material. Each of these compact suitcase bombs could yield a blast of approximately one kiloton, which, for example, would be enough to destroy twenty-five to fifty percent of Manhattan."

I pause to take another sip of tea and a handful of pistachios. After a few moments I continue, "I also know that the Russians were not the only ones working on miniaturized atomic devices. The U.S. produced similar items that they referred to as 'Davy Crocketts.' They were so compact that they were designed to be carried by Navy Seals as part of diving gear, and could be parachuted into a target area, as well. These nuclear suitcases weighed in the fifty- to sixty-pound range, and were about the size of a large attaché case. The units contained separate canisters of fissionable uranium and plutonium, with a new more simplified triggering mechanism that could be instantaneously activated or utilized with a timer. As a safety factor, both the Soviet and U.S. nuclear suitcases were designed with electronic locking mechanisms that were said to be impossible to override. Of course, with the right experts and technical know-how, nothing is impossible.

"Over the past two decades, things have changed considerably from the early techniques, which were unstable and very expensive. It has become an entirely new science. People had been feeling their way, through trial and error mostly, but after two decades of experimenting, a lightweight, attaché sized one -kiloton device has finally become available."

The whole time I am speaking, the Sheik and his son are nodding. They are obviously fully aware of everything I am saying, and from their expressions I can tell that I am adding nothing new.

After a little hesitation, I draw a deep breath and say, "I have dedicated my life to working with those less fortunate and to saving and preserving life, but I haven't forgotten the ways of the world." I pause again, wondering if I should take the conversation in the direction that I've tried to take it before. I am still trying to understand the man who sits before me. I continue, "You are at the core of powerful Islamists, a man among men of a darker age. You and your followers have come together to produce an interesting phenomenon, to both fulfill an ancient religious prophecy and amass an unlimited amount of cold, hard cash. In so doing, you have been able to purchase influence in all facets of government, to acquire information from spies in the corridors of power and informants through-out the world. With your unlimited funds, you could obtain information about anyone or anything. It is yours for the asking. Here I sit with a powerful man, wondering what he hopes to obtain from a surgeon whose interests lie not in power or politics, but in healing. So I must ask you, Sheik bin Laden, what is it that you want from me?"

And unspoken, I cannot help but wonder whether I could live with myself if I actually give him what he wants.

An Unsettling Exchange

Our gazes – the Sheik's and my own – are locked. On the surface, this would seem to be either the intellectual parry and thrust of two unlikely acquaintances, or the confrontation of the mongoose and cobra. I have no delusions about who holds the power, and who would prevail if the confrontation were to grow hostile. Once again, however, I must confront my obsession with understanding this greatest of human paradoxes, an obsession that causes me to override my caution. I ask the Sheik, "What is it that you want, and what do you want from me? I am a surgeon, not a political player?

"Some have said that you wish to become the Muslim's caliph, yet Islamic prophecy states that in order to establish the new caliphate you would need to have originated from the Quraish tribe as well as be the direct descendant of the Prophet. If my research is correct, and I believe it is, you are from Hadramaut, and this tribe is not from Quraish."

Bin Laden says nothing, and I continue. "You have stated numerous times in your broadcasts that you are a man who wishes to die in the service of God, but nevertheless you have contrived to remain alive, continually changing your tactics and strategies, moving secretly not only from city to city, but country to country and exhibiting an extraordinary flexibility. Now I ask you again, why am I here and what does Osama bin Laden want?"

He raises his shoulders and sits straighter, to his full height. Without breaking eye contact, he finishes his cup of tea, sets his cup down, and and raises up his hands as if to beseech some divine audience. "Say O Allah! Thou originator of the heavens and the earth! Thou who knowest the unseen and visible. What is calamity? And, what will convey to you what the calamity is? A day when humankind will be scattered like moths and the mountains like corded wood, And for those whose burden is heavy, they will be in a contented life; and for those whose burden is light, their place will be an abyss. And, what will convey to you what it is? Raging fire."

He pauses for a long moment, as if to let me absorb this dramatic passage from the Qur'an, and he never takes his eyes from mine. After a while he continues, in a less histrionic tone, but one that I find considerably more disturbing, "A nuclear suitcase! New York, Boston, and Houston would each become a nuclear wasteland. Approximately half of the exposed population would die of the radiation effects over the following months. The area would become an uninhabited wasteland. Hotspots of radiation would persist for perhaps hundreds of years. The results would be nightmarish beyond comprehension, even for a small one-kiloton tactical nuclear attaché.

"Depending on the density of the population, fifty thousand to one hundred thousand would die within seconds, and the killing blast would travel for a half mile. Nearly anybody and everything within its path would be incinerated. In a major U.S. or European city, millions would be affected and ultimately die.

"Those who survived the initial blast would be exposed to radiation that would ultimately destroy their immune system. Some would be lucky enough to die within days of their radiation poisoning, while those not so lucky would wither slowly over the course of months. It would be impossible to send in rescue workers, for they would be doomed by the highly lethal fallout that would follow the blast. The radioactive contamination that would carry on the prevailing winds could extend for five or ten miles from the blast area. The number of victims traumatized and wounded would be beyond your government's ability to count, much less treat, resulting in an unprecedented healthcare crisis that would be beyond the capabilities of even an army of Doctor Angels.

"There would also be long-term financial and cultural effects of such an attack. Millions would be without work. Fear would prevail throughout the country. Airports would close. Major ports and shipping would cease and ultimate stagnation would result. The great and powerful nation of America would be brought to its knees, and the rest of the world of infidels would follow.

"The great tyrant, America, has made many accusations against us. It charges that I'm carrying out acts of terrorism and that these are unwarranted. If inciting people to do what you refer to as terrorism really is terrorism...and if killing those who kill our sons is terrorism...then let history be witnessed that I and my comrades are terrorists. Every Muslim from a young age learns to hate Americans, Jews, and Christians. It is part of our belief and our religion. Since I was a boy, I have been at war with and harboring hatred for them.

"I have used my money. I have used the Infidel's money, given freely to me by the greedy and the addicted in your society. With that money, I have purchased portable nuclear weapons from the Russian mafia and from ex-military personnel. I have retained the services of scientists that have worked on these projects. And I have been helped by the

Chechnya mafia and the Pakistani Secret Service – the I.S.I."

As he speaks, I feel my stomach tighten as once again, I am reminded that Americans are indeed funding his efforts to kill us. We are killing ourselves in more ways than one – directly, by killing our bodies and our spirits with his heroin, and by giving him the incredible amounts of money he needs to feed his killing machines throughout the world. Along with these undertakings, bin Laden has established an unbelievable number of websites throughout the Muslim world, with each calling for a jihad, his Muslim call to arms and declaration of war. And there are plenty of receptive ears in the Muslim world, listening and eager to join him.

I wonder if the Sheik is even aware of me now, for he has a faraway look in his eyes as he continues, as if addressing a crowd of followers. "My Muslim brothers of the world, your brothers in Palestine and in the land of the two Holy Places of Mecca and Medina are calling upon you to take part in fighting against the enemy – your enemy and their enemy, the Americans and the Israelis. They are asking you to do whatever you can with your own means and ability, to expel the enemy, humiliate it, and defeat it and drive it out of the sanctities of Islam."

Listening to him now, it strikes me once again that even though Osama bin Laden is not an ordained religious leader, by issuing and signing this *fatwa* as Osama bin Mohammed bin Laden, he has established himself in a new light in the eyes of his followers. Thus does he reveal his vision of an Islamic utopia, and of establishing himself as a leader of a global *Khalifa*. Under the green flag of Islam, he dreams of the union of all true believers into a single Islamic state, which, in his vision, will arise from the ashes of the Judaeo-Christian civilization and the destruction of the United States and Israel.

Bin Laden turns his attention to me again. He goes on to say that he has paramilitary cells in fifty-five countries throughout the world, and that if one cell is located and destroyed, another one will emerge to take its place. He claims that twenty-two of these cells already have suitcase-sized atomic bombs. He boasts that several are in Europe and Canada, but the majority are in major cities in the United States.

"I have made a declaration to kill the Americans and their allies, both civilians and military. It is every Muslim's individual duty to make and fulfill such a declaration, in any country in which they reside. I order all non-believers to remove their armies and personnel from the land of Islam. This is in accordance with the words of Almighty Allah. We will fight the pagans until we establish Sharia law, a prevailing justice and a worldwide faith in Allah."

The threat that is so explicit in Osama's statements, not to mention his sudden swing from pragmatic discussion to barely contained rage, is making me very nervous. I realize that my anxiety must be showing, as I notice that I am eating large handfuls of walnuts and dried apricots at an unbelievable rate, and clinching my teeth with each bite. I know that for my own peace of mind, if not my immediate physical safety, I need to change the direction of this conversation.

Trying to break the tense mood, I smile at him and say, "I would like some tea, please."

Hamza jumps up and shouts from the doorway, telling the servants to bring the tea. I can see from his expression that he is probably as relieved as I am to bring this conversation to an end. I don't know if the Sheik's verbal rampage is actually over with, but at the very least, I welcome the break. I glance back at the Sheik; his shoulders are now slumped, his head down and eyes closed as if he is in prayer, and he is suddenly looking much older than his years.

A young man enters the room with the tea, but the Sheik doesn't raise his head. I nod at the young man, and he pours tea for all three of us. He then places the pot on the floor between us and hurriedly retreats from the room. Hamza takes his seat to my left. As we sip silently, I weigh what bin Laden has just said, and remember that terrorism, by definition, is a form of asymmetrical warfare that does not require significant sums of money. The introduction of nuclear suitcases to the terrorism equation changes things dramatically.

Wanting to resume the dialog, I begin cautiously, "Please indulge me for a minute. You're spending hundreds of millions of dollars for nuclear material. How do you know that the traffickers are actually delivering uranium-235? Aren't you taking a big gamble of being cheated?"

"It has been a difficult process, and the cost has been great. And yes, unfortunately, I have handed over significant funds to traffickers who claimed they possessed atomic material, but did not. They posed as atomic engineers and sold uranium and other nuclear products that were unusable for nuclear weapons without significant additional processing, which require facilities we do not have. It was what you call a scam. I understand the Russian traffickers who sold this material to me also managed to sell some at extravagant prices to the Iraqis. As a result, these Russians are no longer with us.

"I know I'm not in a position to produce fissionable material, nor are we able to construct nuclear weapons. So we turned our interests to the purchase of small portable nuclear devices that have already been built and whose efficacy has been established. I will admit that we have had problems upgrading and replenishing these nuclear devices so that we can detonate them in the future. I have now obtained the expertise of Pakistan's nuclear engineers, with the help of the Pakistani Secret Service. I have also turned to former Soviet scientists, Chinese nuclear scientists and technicians, and others who could be persuaded to our cause for monetary or religious reasons. Greed is amazing. If you offer enough money, there is always a taker. The group we have brought together has done its work well. Our attempts to obtain these powerful weapons of mass destruction have been successful.

In time, and with God willing, we will represent a significant threat."

Hoping to keep the Sheik talking, I compliment him, "You have done your research."

"I have learned that I cannot trust those who deal in these things," he replies. "In the past, I spent millions for things which I can never use. That will not happen again. I didn't like the way it was progressing, I didn't like the way others left things. So I did my job and took this over myself. When I first started my research, it was very basic. It started with learning the atomic numbers for uranium-92 and for plutonium-94, and from there I built a foundation of my own knowledge. What else do I have to do all day in this compound? I cannot be seen outside these walls.

"I learned that the gaseous diffusion method is only used to enrich uranium-92, but this is not applicable to plutonium-94, which needs to be placed in breeder reactors. Others combine uranium and plutonium fuels for the bombs. Basically they are what you would call a hybrid. This all sounds very basic and it is, but it was a starting point for me.

"The more I studied the problem, the more I realized we had to purchase the finished product. I was afraid that it would otherwise blow up in our own faces. I quickly realized that the nuclear suitcases were the answer."

I take a sip of my tea and look into the Sheik's eyes. They are like those of a wild animal, piercing and unblinking, without a hint of compassion. The image sends a sudden shiver down my spine, and leaves me feeling chilled to the bone. As bin Laden continues, it occurs to me that this must be how an animal feels when it is cornered by a predator.

"With the collapse of the Soviet Union, the Russian army units entrusted with nuclear material and weapons decided to indulge themselves in a new spirit of capitalism by clandestinely selling the material and weapons to the highest bidders. It did not stop there. You could purchase automatic weapons, rocket launchers, and even armored cars and tanks. Officers of the old Soviet military complex saw the opportunity to become incredibly rich, and took it. The former members of the KGB also took part in the negotiations and sale of the Soviet nuclear arsenal, and engaged in the acquisition and sale of all manner of war materials. It came down to a question of whom to trust. It was then that I realized that a complete, easily transportable weapon that could be activated at a future date, any place in the world, was the best choice. Once again, this reinforced my feeling that the suitcase nuclear bomb would be my best choice.

"The nuclear suitcases were terribly expensive, but people from a branch of the Russian mafia who traffic almost exclusively in the heroin that goes to Europe and the United States made it possible for us to purchase more and more of the bombs. We cultivated the poppy fields in Pakistan and Afghanistan and brought the flowers to our sophisticated modern laboratories where it was refined into high quality Number Four heroin, which the Russians wanted. It was a simple arrangement. The medical grade narcotic we produced was the preferred drug of choice for the European and American markets, and the shipments had been contributing hundreds of millions of dollars to our cause.

"Tons of the drugs were transported to Turkey and then on to Poland, where they left the harbor city of Gdañsk. My representatives would in turn purchase the nuclear suitcases from another branch of Chechen Mafia, using the drug money. I brokered the deal with thirty million U.S. dollars in cash that I had on hand, and traded them top grade heroin that had a street value in excess of eight hundred million U.S. dollars. In exchange, I obtained twenty-two functional nuclear suitcases. I'm not telling you anything that is a secret. The Russian security service reported the loss of the nuclear weapons to the United States, and it was later reported in an extensive story in newspapers around the world.

"Over the course of the next several years, Israeli intelligence reported that I had obtained more than forty nuclear suitcases and additional kilos of uranium-235, but their reports were wrong. As I said, we were not in the business of building bombs, and wanted to purchase only completed weapons, so we did not acquire the uranium-235. What would I do with it? Some of these twenty-two nuclear suitcases were smuggled into the United States and scattered to remote locations."

I think of my earlier discussions with my driver and bodyguard about the presence in the U.S. of nuclear suitcases. It is widely known that the Soviets produced more than seven hundred of these suitcases, which they had long kept secret, and which had never appeared in the U.S.S.R.'s official nuclear weapons inventory. Given the contacts and the money that Osama bin Laden has available, it is easy to imagine him coming to possess the weapons he claims to have purchased.

I further have no doubt that there are sleeper cells in Europe and the U.S. that have such weapons in their possession. It is rumored that these tactical nuclear devices are located in California, Texas, New York, Michigan, and elsewhere, locations that have been selected carefully and over a long period of time. It is wishful thinking to believe that their locations will be found or disclosed in the near future. No, I fear it is far more likely – even probable – that some or all of the nuclear suitcases will eventually be used as the Sheik intends them to be.

Osama interrupts my wandering thoughts, saying, "In addition to nuclear weapons, we have some chemical weapons as well. If America uses chemical or nuclear weapons against us, then I can and will respond with nuclear and chemical weapons of my own."

I take several deep breaths, then let out a long sigh. I wonder to myself, *Is this at all possible? The U.S., European, and Israeli governments are aware of this, yet the American public has been kept in the dark!* You would think these governments would have made the discovery and securing of these weapons their highest priority, but if such a massive undertaking has been ongoing, it is one of the world's best kept secrets.

Several decades have passed since the Russians produced these weapons, and at least a decade since bin Laden acquired them. I wonder whether they are still able to be activated, or whether the mechanisms have deteriorated. Are they still dangerous? I know that plutonium has a half-life greater than 20,000 years, but it comes down to the condition of the mechanisms that activate the bombs, and access to someone with sufficient background in physics and electronics to ensure that the mechanisms will work. These factors seem relatively minor when I see what bin Laden has been able to accomplish, but they might be the only reason we are all still here.

"May I ask how you got nuclear devices into Europe and the United States?"

At this point, Hamza joins the conversation. "You hide it in the middle of a large container of mechanical or industrial parts. They are almost never checked. Even in those that are checked, it's easy to miss such a small parcel amongst tons of large, heavy industrial products."

I have to admit that his explanation makes sense. "Sounds simple and straight forward."

"It is, it is. And, then there is your southern border with Mexico. You can bring anyone or anything across the Mexican border. It's very, very, easy."

I sit here looking at Hamza with mouth open but no words coming out. I keep thinking to myself that we have been talking ineptly about this back home. It's been in the newspapers and on television, but Congress has done nothing that serves to actually protect us. The U.S. government has spent three billion dollars on a virtual electronic fence that does not work. I find myself thinking that if we are really serious about securing the U.S.-Mexican border, we need to really do it. Perhaps we need to put up a concave twenty-two-foot-high concrete wall along the entire border. We need to install in-ground detection equipment to detect attempts to tunnel under it, or else establish a heavily mined no-man's land, fifty yards wide along its entire length.

This actually could have been constructed for less than half of the three billion dollars that has been spent on the non-functioning virtual electronic fence. I seriously doubt that the U.S. government has gotten a refund for that useless device, and I'm sure there are elected representatives and government officials who reaped their share of expensive kickbacks for supporting the project. Perhaps bin Laden should write them a nice thank-you note for the assistance they provide him. Meanwhile, the American public goes unprotected and worse yet, gets screwed again, while the members of Congress publicly congratulate and reward themselves for an illusion well done. I wonder, when – if ever – will Congress keep the oaths they took and do the right thing?

I realize that I'm still sitting here with my mouth half opened, staring into oblivion, when Hamza taps me on my arm and silently mouths, "Are you okay?"

Startled out of my ruminations, but not my anger, I snarl at him, "No! I'm not okay!" I immediately realize the inappropriateness of my response, and smile at him, saying, "I'm sorry. I was out of line snapping at you like that."

Breaking his own extended silence, bin Laden speaks up. "You are right to feel that way. You should expect more from your government and from the most powerful military force on earth. You have been quite placid during most of this conversation, but now I can see the indignation and outrage you must feel. I'm going to assume that you have learned more than you ever wanted to hear. These are not secrets that have been hidden from your government, and the world's leaders and journalists have tried to bring them to the forefront. You *should* be concerned, if not for yourself, for your family and loved ones. We have the same concerns for our families and loved ones."

I look sharply at bin Laden and almost shout, "So where will it end? Do you plan to use these weapons? Where will you use them? When?"

He responds, with an ominous calmness that brings to mind the predator I saw in his eyes before, "The plan is going ahead, and, God willing, it is being implemented. We are not in a hurry. It may not happen in my lifetime. It is a huge task.

It is beyond either of our will and comprehension. This is not a matter of weaponry. It is a matter of the extinction of the Infidels, and I know Allah is with me. We will win this struggle against the Zionist-Christian alliance. We will carry the jihad anywhere in the world until we achieve success. We practice the good terrorism – Allah is on our side."

He reaches out, gently picks up his cup and takes a sip of tea before continuing.

His mood has changed almost seamlessly from the cold predator of a moment ago to the gracious host. "It's cold, and the hour is late. I do not wish to be impolite, and I know I have not answered your last few questions. We will make contact, and you will return again. And at that time, I will do my best to reply to your questions: *What do I want? Will I use the nuclear suitcases, and under what circumstances?*"

I take this rather abrupt cue to thank my host and prepare to leave, "I thank you for the meal and the time you have spent to enlighten me. I have a lot to think about, and will probably have additional questions of you the next time we meet. I hope we can continue this exchange very soon."

I rise to my feet, and Hamza escorts me from the house to the courtyard. We maneuver our way around some of the animals as we stroll toward the gate on the outer wall. By the time we reach it, two armed guards have appeared, and slowly rotate and slide the heavy bolts back and pull the heavy iron door into the courtyard so that I can leave. The street is dark and deserted, and I am acutely aware of the fact that I'm walking alone and unarmed in the Northwest Frontier Province. This is the home to smugglers, gun runners, drug dealers, thieves, and cut-throats, all of whom have found refuge here.

On the other hand, it is the predominant tribal custom to subscribe to the Muslim code of hospitality, which calls for the protection and shelter of strangers, even if affording such hospitality means risking your own life. Paradoxically, everyone in the Northwest Frontier Province is heavily armed. Even the youngest male tribal members carry Kalashnikov automatic rifles. I know I have to walk at least a half mile or more on these unlit, pothole-ridden dirt roads, but at the moment, I am more concerned with not tripping and injuring myself than with evading armed attackers. Since I have no cell phone with me, and there are no emergency facilities readily available, being injured in a fall could be catastrophic, so I pick my way along the road slowly and carefully.

There is no rush. I know Mohammed and Sultan will be waiting in the van for my arrival. As a physician who lives in the U. S., I find it somewhat strange that I am more comfortable in my travels when I have my M-4 slung over my shoulder, especially when I am unaccompanied by my private armed guards. Few in this area can afford the luxury of such protectors, and I know how fortunate I am to be one of those few. But because my guards have not been allowed to accompany me on these interviews, I have to place my trust in my own caution, good luck, and the sense that those who might do me harm are somehow aware of my meetings with the Sheik, and that they leave me alone for that reason.

I have memorized the route by now, having seen it both at night and in the daytime, but I am still startled when I pass an adjacent walled compound and the dogs inside begin to bark. These homes all have armed guards, and I just pray that they aren't trigger-happy. I keep to the middle of the road to lessen the dogs' protective responses and continue briskly on my way. I glance at the luminescent dial of my watch and see that I have been walking for about fifteen minutes, and figure that I will soon see the van. As I turn another corner, I see that my calculations are correct. I see the van off to the side of the road, parked under some trees with the lights off. I can finally breathe a sigh of relief.

For now, anyway.

Be Careful What You Wish For...

*I*n 1998, Pakistan's esteemed nuclear scientist Dr. Abdul Qadeer Khan successfully tested five atomic bombs in the Balochistan desert, thus adding the Islamic Republic of Pakistan to the elite club of nuclear-armed nations. At the time, this group also included the United States, Great Britain, China, Russia, India, France, and Israel. Dr. Khan's demonstration shocked the world, since it came from a "Third World Country" that couldn't provide electricity reliably to its major cities, still employed centuries-old farming techniques, did not provide even rudimentary medical care for its population, and failed to develop an

479

adequate sanitation system. Many around the world were left wondering where the funds came from to support this type of program.

I am certain that a significant portion of the funds came in the form of financial aid money from the United Nations, the United States, and Europe – money that was intended to pay for humanitarian projects. That these funds could be diverted from their intended purpose, only to be used for the creation of a nuclear arsenal, doesn't say much for the Pakistani government, much less for our international intelligence gathering capabilities. But what if our intelligence service isn't as incompetent as such an oversight would indicate? What does that say about our own country's agenda and priorities?

Prime Minister Benazir Bhutto, our Pakistani "friend" during the first Reagan administration, as well as during the Carter, Bush (senior), and Clinton administrations, had assured the Americans that Pakistan's nuclear program had been halted – yet under her direction, Pakistan pursued the development even more aggressively, albeit discreetly. Once the Islamic Republic of Pakistan had successfully developed a workable nuclear weapon, it then was faced with the need for a means of delivery of their new toy.

At that time, Bhutto began discussions with the psychopathic North Korean officials for the purpose of obtaining long-range ballistic missiles. In exchange for the missiles that would be modified to carry the Pakistani atomic bomb, the Pakistanis provided the North Koreans with the technology for enriching uranium using gas centrifuges. What followed was an exchange of nuclear scientists and laboratory technicians between North Korea and Pakistan. Dr. Khan also offered this information to other Islamic countries – in particular, Iran – where he assisted them in implementing their uranium enrichment program.

On February 4, 2004, Dr. Khan publicly confessed on Pakistani state-run television to having been deeply involved in black-market trading of materials used in the manufacture of nuclear weapons. One would expect him to be tried for treason and imprisoned or even executed for such activities, but *on the very next day*, Federal President Pervez Musharraf granted the scientist a full pardon, praising him for his service to his country, and even referring to him as "my hero."

The response of the G. W. Bush Administration, according to a State Department spokesperson, was that Pakistan "was not involved in any of the proliferation activity," and that the decision as to how to deal with Khan was "a matter for Pakistan to decide." Such statements were likely borne of the administration's ill founded trust that the Musharraf regime would render assistance – or, at the very least, not resist – U.S. and NATO efforts to locate and kill Osama bin Laden.

The fact that bin Laden was ultimately located and killed within close proximity to a major Pakistani military installation demonstrates just how ill-founded that trust actually was. There is simply no way that the Pakistani Inter-Service Intelligence – the I.S.I. – was unaware of his presence.

American and European intelligence services had known for over twenty years that Khan and the I.S.I. had been complicit in the illegal sale of nuclear technology and materials, and Musharraf's claims of ignorance about these activities was ludicrous. Since the Pakistani government refused to acknowledge – much less act upon – this information, it has remained under tight sanctions. Despite the presence of the sanctions, however, there is every reason for the international community to be concerned about the security of Pakistan's nuclear weapons storage facilities. Adding to this concern is the fact that most of the technicians and even the highly educated nuclear scientists are strict Islamic fundamentalists, and hold with strong anti-American sentiments. Given these factors, it is not a question of *whether* radical Islamists will seize control of nuclear weapons, but of how long it will be before they do so.

Meanwhile, the world's attention is too narrowly focused, concerned only with the possibility of Iran's obtaining a nuclear weapon. The truth of the matter is that even if Iran already has such weapons, they are very crude, likely several generations behind those that Pakistan possesses. Furthermore, Iran lacks any delivery systems capable of striking a blow beyond the immediate region. However, Pakistan, which is far from being a friend of the United States, already has operable nuclear weapons, all of which are under the control of radical Islamic fundamentalists. While NATO and the United States focus on Iran, the explosive situation in Pakistan is overlooked and underestimated, and its ultimate detonation inevitable.

Why was the world surprised, and millions of people shocked by what happened on September 11, 2001? Did the world honestly believe that such a terrible event would never happen? What happened to America was an expected event – expected by those whose eyes were open, that is. It should have been anticipated and measures taken to prevent it. And now, after suffering subsequent attacks throughout the world, we need to come to grips with the fact that there are probably more than twenty-four one-kiloton nuclear suitcase bombs in the United States alone, and even more scattered throughout Europe – all held by sleeper cells who are impatiently awaiting orders to deploy the bombs in strategic locations throughout the country.

I imagine there are many people who would scoff at such an assertion. After all, we have this near-omnipotent Homeland Security network, adroitly rooting out potential terrorists and closely monitoring all suspicious shipments into the country, right? Think again. It is literally impossible to monitor everything that is transferred to the United States in shipping containers, especially when you consider that approximately ninety-seven percent of all containers are not inspected at all. The nuclear suitcases have been brought in at major U.S.

ports, across the unprotected, uncontrolled Mexican border, and across the even less tightly monitored Canadian border as well.

Is it even remotely reasonable to assume that in those ninety-seven percent of unmonitored and uninspected shipments, there have been no illegal materials – including easily-concealed nuclear suitcases? What will it take for America to learn that it needs to close its borders and regulate its border traffic? America always responds *after* a catastrophe. It would seem only prudent to close the borders and try to *prevent* a catastrophe. Unfortunately, it is already too late where the nuclear suitcases are concerned. They are already in the U.S.

As I had discussed in my conversations with bin Laden, I was an engineer and a scientist before I ever studied medicine. Living through an era that saw the development of the atomic and later hydrogen bombs, I was fascinated by the chemistry and mechanics that were involved in their development. The original weapons were large and bulky, but it was a new science, and people were feeling their way by trial and error. As techniques improved, the destructive potential went up exponentially. Gaseous effusion equipment became available, rendering possible the production of highly enriched uranium.

With this quantum leap in explosive energy provided by superior nuclear fuels, the design of the bomb itself became increasingly important. And with the advent of superior designs, either uranium or plutonium could be utilized as the active element, and conventional explosives could be used to squeeze the nuclear fuel into the critical mass that would result in the explosion. Eventually, the addition of a neutron reflector concentrated the neutrons in the center of the nuclear material, in what is referred to as the pit. By reflecting the neutrons back into the pit, the fissile material reaches an optimal state of supercritical mass. In other words, the longer the plutonium or uranium is allowed to react, the more atoms are split and the bigger the explosion.

With the improved designs, the explosive force achieved with a given amount of plutonium or uranium can be exponentially increased. One of the most effective designs uses a simple gold foil as the initiator component. And instead of using stainless steel for the reflector, tungsten carbides – with their higher density and strength – reflect more neutrons into the central area, further optimizing the supercritical mass and maximizing the result. With such technology, it is possible to create a small, portable bomb that would fit into a carry-on suitcase, yet be capable of taking out a major portion of New York City, Houston, or Los Angeles.

* * * * *

After my third meeting with bin Laden, I am facing another sleepless night. I am filled with uneasy feelings, the same feelings that have robbed me of sleep on previous occasions. I've come to interpret these feelings as an alarm triggered by instinct. In my gut, I know that something is not right.

After three meetings with Osama bin Laden, I've come to perceive him as an individual who harps incessantly about injustices, some quite real, but most existing only in his imagination. He seems to be reading messages hidden from the rational world, lingering between the lines of the Qur'an. He misinterprets these "messages" and passionately espouses them to his followers. The end result is that his misinterpretations, fueled by his psychopathic tendencies, have driven him to make the leap from verbalized fantasy to violent action. He no longer merely threatens. He destroys.

At no time during these interviews have I been convinced by bin Laden's protestations of innocence. He claims that he is God's messenger, following the demands of Allah. I've seen plenty of pathologically obsessed individuals out there whose outlook on life outside their own beliefs is reduced to violence through hatred, but I've yet to encounter one whose pathology finds as receptive an audience as does bin Laden's, or whose capabilities render widespread devastation as feasible – no, as probable – as do bin Laden's. And to make matters worse, his pathology is so infectious within his culture, and his machinations so well-established, that his delusions, not to mention the destruction that those delusions could manifest, have been given a life of their own, and will most certainly linger and continue to be manifested, long after bin Laden himself is gone.

I don't like the situation in which I've found myself, not for a moment. I've decided to play it safe at the next meeting with the Sheik, to ask my questions, but to listen more and add nothing of my own. There have already been times when bin Laden asked a question that I found particularly upsetting, and I would take the opportunity to voice my opinion, criticize his pattern of thinking and the references to the Qur'an that he would twist to support his statements.

I am very conscious of having been a guest in the house of bin Laden, and of the fact that our conversations have been very open. But I'm now having second thoughts about some of the comments I have made, and wondering about the wisdom of refuting the Sheik, especially his use of quotes from the Qur'an to support his actions. And for the first time, I find myself honestly wondering, *Am I in any danger?* Sure, the thought of physical danger has crossed my mind many times, but up to now, even after being shot in an ambush, those thoughts have been more hypothetical than gut-wrenchingly real.

At this point, there is nothing I can put my finger on that tells me I'm in real danger, but I've learned to listen to my instinct, and want to play it safe. On the other hand, I don't want to show any signs of weakness, and I feel pretty capable of reacting effectively to any situation that might occur. I just have to remind myself not to get too cocky, however, since that same sense of self-assurance has doubtless led many a soldier to his ultimate place in a body bag.

I know that my worry is contributing to the fact that the whole situation with bin Laden is not looking so good right now, but I still don't intend to back out of it. However, I find that my mind is working on a completely different level as I reconstruct the three visits I have had so far with bin Laden. I am naturally concerned about the implications of what I've already been told, and am thinking about where we will go from here in our next meeting. I prop up a couple of pillows and sit up in my bed, staring into the darkness of space within the room. I close my eyes again and think for a moment.

At my age, I do not have much to lose in the way of time. The direction our conversations have taken makes it very plain how dangerous this could get, and also makes it even clearer to me that I am no longer just on a medical mission. For more than three years, I have been spreading the word about my interest in interviewing Osama bin Laden in every city, town, village, *madrasa*, and hospital I have visited. I've spoken of my desires to every warlord, village chief, city mayor, and other political appointees I've met. Now that I have finally gotten my wish I am reminded of the old saying, "Be careful what you wish for, because it just might come true." Indeed, there are some things that perhaps you should not wish for.

Only Mohammed, Sultan, and Saleem know where I disappear to every few evenings. They know their lives, as well as my own, depend on secrecy. They have to remain composed and unflinching if we're going to continue with the interviews. I am all too aware that I, and my faithful gang of three, are in the battle of our lives. After all, we threaten to shine unwanted light, not only on bin Laden's terrorist operation, but upon his heroin trade and his attempts to acquire additional nuclear suitcases. Not to mention the complicity of the Pakistani government and the I.S.I., the bungling of the United States and its intelligence and diplomatic arms, and perhaps the international and Russian Mafia.... It's infinitely more far-reaching than I had ever imagined, and I know it's going to be tough – if not impossible – for anyone, myself included, to come out of it all unscathed.

At this point, Osama bin Laden's stature is so elevated that he is typically viewed in the region as being larger than life itself. Anything that is said or done against the Sheik is considered to be anti-Islam, and to many, anti-Pakistan, and therefore not to be tolerated. Not for the first time, I mull over the irony that he is so universally revered in Pakistan that he enjoys the protection of the Pakistani government, yet in the United States and Europe, he is viewed as a madman and the world's most dangerous individual. Across the international community, bin Laden is Number 1 on the Most Wanted list, with fellow Islamic extremist Dr. Abdul Qadeer Khan being a close tie for the dubious honor.

Over the years, numerous complaints have been voiced about Pakistan's nuclear weapons program, to which Dr. Abdul Khan has responded by saying, "All Western countries, including Israel, are not only the enemies of Pakistan, but, in fact, of all Islam. This [kind of complaint] is poisonous propaganda against the Muslim country."

I think we need to ask ourselves how Pakistan's official entry into the realm of nuclear-armed nations is any different from Osama bin Laden's acquisition of no telling how many nuclear suitcase bombs, or his using the funds that he acquires through the drug trade to obtain assistance from Russian and Chinese technicians and scientists in his pursuit of such weapons. In my mind, I see no difference at all. There is the common element of radical Islamic fundamentalism, which is fueled by and simultaneously fuels a widespread hatred of the West as a whole, and the United States in particular.

The United States has for many years been blind to (or unconcerned with) and taken no steps to thwart the clandestine development of the Islamic bomb, while at the same time ignoring the effects of our military adventures in the region that have served to reinforce the Muslim world's hatred of us. We are walking blindly and arrogantly into what will likely prove to be the most horrific confrontation in human history, and as has been said many times, but rarely listened to or considered, those who do not study history are doomed to repeat it.

I feel that the "relationship" between bin Laden and myself is becoming increasingly chaotic and ominous, and after the last interview, there is no doubt in my mind that I am now walking a very dangerous and narrow path, but I also feel that as long as the interviews continue in such an open and straightforward manner, I must not alienate the Sheik. The public verification of the existence of suitcase bombs in the hands of sleeper cells in the United States and Europe would generate mass chaos, and I honestly believe that bin Laden could unleash the use of the bombs without even a twinge of conscience. I will try to tone down the discussions, knowing I have to tread carefully, but my focus from this point forward must be to try and learn where these nuclear suitcases are being held.

Sitting here in the dark, stunned, I ask myself whether the whole thing has been an enormous mistake. I've always been an optimist, walking around feeling much younger than I am, and pretty much always thinking that if I put my mind to it, I can conquer anything. My wife Terry always says that throughout my whole life, I've gone into dangerous situations as if I were immortal. It's an attitude I've maintained, despite having been repeatedly proven wrong.

Suddenly, I feel as if there isn't much time left. I've come to the realization that this is more than a one-on-one experience, and that there are a great number of adversaries out there – thousands and thousands of them. They have formed their own little clubs that I couldn't join even if I wanted to. They will try to stretch the boundaries of their control in the name of Islam and Allah, and the rest of the world will have to fight hard to hold their own.

Above all, who makes these decisions? For years, it has been Osama bin Laden, and adding the Prophet's name to his own by taking the name Osama bin Mohammed bin Laden has only added to his mystique. By adding Mohammed to his own name, was he really sending the message that he saw himself as a godlike figure? Is he delusional, or just very clever? Is he trying to prove something with these interviews, and if so, what?

I feel that there is something that is eluding him. The feeling that something is not right just will not leave me. In our interviews, bin Laden harps on and on about imaginary injustices and messages hidden between the lines of the Qur'an that only he is capable of reading. In reality, I think, bin Laden is making the deadly leap from fantasy to action in the name of God – Allah – all the while protesting his own innocence.

I know, from more than forty years of medical experience, that there are many nut cases out there who are pathologically obsessed, and whose obsessions are frequently acted out in threatening, violent and even deadly ways. And the more I talk with bin Laden, the more convinced I am that he is both dangerously obsessed and equipped to wreak havoc on the world.

These interviews have opened some wide cracks in my perception of what is taking place in the world, making me realize how little of that is made public by my own government and the press. I've always had doubts about the I.S.I., but now those doubts carry over to the CIA and the rest of my country and the world's intelligence services. I know that I need to document what I've seen and heard, as well as my own instinctive feelings about the situation that faces all of us.

After taking several deep breaths and telling myself (not too convincingly) that everything is under control, I know that what is at risk is much more important than my own safety, and that I have to attempt to get some solid information, something that will convince my own government that it is on a path with no good end in sight. I quickly pull myself together, turn on the night table light, grab my notebook, and begin reviewing my notes from my latest interview.

It feels to me as if things are rapidly coming to a head, and that I'm rushing headlong into a situation where I might have only myself to rely on. I know that this is the very type of thing that worries Sultan, Saleem, and Mohammed the most. They are wonderfully devoted and loyal, and are determined not to leave me to face my fate alone. They have made a pact between themselves to watch me more closely, even to the point of hiding their presence from me as they watch over me. Even as my worry deepens, I am grateful for their presence, and realize that it just might save my life, yet again.

A Tense Meeting with Officials

n the evening, just as I am finishing my last surgery, one of the hospital orderlies appears at the operating room door, short of breath and panting from running up several flights of stairs to the operating room suites. Struggling to relay his message between breaths, he says that there is an urgent telephone call in the administrative office, and that I must come at once and personally take the call.

I've just completed the technical portion of the operation, and my two assistants can easily do the wound closure. I quickly review the wound closure technique with them and order the necessary suture material from the circulating nurse.

The local Pakistani surgeon and the resident have been working with me for more than a week now, and have completed this type of closure many times before, so I have complete confidence in their knowledge and abilities. I remove my gloves, mask, and gown and leave the operating room. As I push the doors open, I am surprised to see two orderlies waiting on the other side to escort me to the administrative office. As we briskly walk together, I can't help but wonder what could be so urgent.

I will know soon enough.

As we reach the administrative office, one of the orderlies steps forward and opens the door. The office is empty, and the orderly points to a telephone handset sitting in the middle of the desk. With some trepidation, I pick it up and speak into the mouthpiece, "Hello, this is the doctor."

The voice at the other end speaks in heavily accented English, slowly and clearly, with no pleasantries or introduction. "You're invited to a dinner meeting tonight at 10:00 PM."

Somewhat put off, I respond, "I'm still working in the operating room, and need to make evening rounds and check on my post-op patients."

"Sorry, you need to be at this meeting. This is not a request."

"What is the problem?"

"It will all be discussed at the meeting."

"Will you give me some idea? Give me some reason for the urgency of this meeting. I would like to prepare."

"National security – it's of national importance."

"Who will be there?"

"I am not at liberty to say. A car will pick you up at 10 PM. Please be prompt. I repeat, this is not a request. It is mandatory."

"I understand, I'll be at the main entrance at approximately 10 PM. That will give me just enough time to see my post-op patients and change into civilian clothing."

"We are not interested in how you are dressed. Just be there at 10 PM. A car will be waiting."

I don't like the tone of his voice, and feel compelled not to fully relinquish control to this faceless person. "I will do my best to be on time, but my patients come first. Just have the car and driver wait at the main entrance to the Medical College."

"You be there. Our driver will be there promptly at 10 PM. Thank you." The caller hangs up abruptly.

Reflexively, and with no small amount of irritation, I say "Goodbye" into the dead line, and stand there staring at the telephone receiver in my hand. I take several clearly audible deep breaths, and notice that the orderly is still standing at the door, looking at me with a quizzical expression. I then realize that I am still holding the telephone in my hand, but not talking. I reach across the desk and place the receiver into its carriage, then turn and walk quickly past the orderly without saying a word. I know my way back to the operating room, and it is probably obvious to him that I am irritated, though I am certain he has no idea as to the cause for my mood.

Upon arrival at the operating room, I see that they have just finished closing the wound, and have done a flawless job. It looks great. The anesthesiologist has stopped the intravenous medication, and the patient is already breathing on his own, his chest rising and falling in a smooth rhythm. He will open his eyes and be awake in a few minutes. All that is left to do is to apply the bandages. I praise my team members for their job well done, and tell them that I am going to the open ward to examine today's post-op patients, and those who stayed overnight from the day before. I request that they meet me there when they are finished with the patient.

No matter how urgent this mysterious meeting is, the patients always came first for me.

In fact, the more I think about that phone call, the more defiant I become. I decide that I am going to be appropriately late for this evening's unexpected meeting. I'm not going to let some faceless caller intimidate me. After all, I don't know the purpose for this sudden and unexpected gathering, and I don't have any idea who else will be in attendance.

I keep thinking about the telephone call. I didn't recognize the caller's heavily accented voice, but he had made it clear that my presence was required and that his call was a demand, rather than an invitation to dinner. As long as I can remember, I have not responded well to such attempts at intimidation. I know that there is no way to avoid this "invitation," but there is no way I'm going to be on time. Let them sit a while and wonder.

The student nurses, residents and local doctors join me on the patient ward, and we go from bed to bed, checking on each of the children and answering questions from their family members. We issue the evening's medical orders, first in the infant ward, and then in the female and male wards. As we finish up, I look at my watch and see that it is 9:50 PM. Everyone is obviously quite exhausted, having been working since 6:00 AM, almost sixteen hours, non-stop.

I thank everyone and leave the hospital, walking the rosebush-lined path to the main house, then descending the steps to the terrace garden along the flagstone path to my room. The glass door isn't locked, and I slide the door open slowly, suddenly realizing how profoundly tired I am. Glancing again at my watch as I remove it and set it on the nightstand, I see that it is ten o'clock, but I'm not going anyplace without a shower. Undressing quickly, I grab several aspirin from the bottle on the night table and wash them down with the ever-present bottle of water. I step into the shower, turning on the hot water and waiting for it to reach the desired temperature.

After sixteen hours on my feet, bent over the seemingly never-ending line of patients in the operating room, the hot water feels incredible, and I am more than a little irritated that I can't take the time to enjoy it to its fullest.

After washing and rinsing, I lather my face and wipe the steam from the mirror with the towel so I can see my reflection and quickly shave. I reach for the bottle of aftershave lotion next to the mirror and splash it generously on my face. It stings, but in a good way that I think most men understand. After toweling off, I put on a well-starched, hand-pressed, button-down collared dress shirt. I have a feeling the men I will be meeting tonight will either be in uniform or Western dress.

I quickly slip into a pair of gray slacks, black socks, and some comfortable shoes I had purchased in Karachi last year for only eight dollars. I retrieve my watch from the night table and place it on my wrist, then take my black double-breasted jacket with the gold colored buttons from the armoire and check to see that it is clean and well pressed. I slip a small recorder into the right jacket pocket, along with a pack of gum. I figure that if I'm careful enough, I can, under the pretense of reaching for the gum, discretely turn the recorder on and capture whatever is said. Finally, I grab my gold rimmed glasses from the top of the night table and walk out the door, a mere twelve minutes from the time I first walked into the room.

Exiting onto the terraced garden, I take the short stairway to the main path, two steps at a time. Even with the pressing concerns that fill my mind tonight, I still enjoy the smell of the roses that hangs sweetly in the night air. As I continue walking along, I briefly wonder whether I should have worn a tie, but set the question quickly aside. I figure I'm adequately impressive in my dark double-breasted jacket, which had been custom-made for me in Karachi, by a tailor who had been recommended to me by the then-chairman of the Pakistani senate.

It is very dark tonight, with only a quarter moon to light my way as I walk along the path toward the main entrance of the Medical College. As I near the entrance, I see it: a highly polished and spotless black SUV, with its driver standing alongside the automobile, smoking. No one else is in sight. The windows of the vehicle are blackened, and I can't see inside.

Upon seeing me, the driver quickly tosses the cigarette to the ground, stomps it out, comes to attention, and salutes me. He rushes to the rear of the car and opens the rear passenger door. Looking inside, I see that the SUV is empty and climb in. It smells of new leather, and looks as if it probably did on the day it was purchased.

Looking to the front, I watch the driver, already seated, start the car and release the brakes. We are instantly descending the mountain and barreling toward the main guard gate. As soon the guard sees the SUV approaching, he opens the gate, then whips to attention and salutes as we pass without stopping. As the driver approaches the main cross street, he leans on the horn and cuts into traffic, paying no heed to the pedestrians, three-wheeled motorized rickshaws, and a mini-bus, all of which swerve and slam on their brakes to avoid the SUV.

Turning left, we head into town, in the direction of the Pakistani Military College – Pakistan's West Point, you might say – and several other military bases that are located in the area. I start to introduce myself and ask the driver his name and where we are going, but notice that there is a glass divider separating us. So I just look out the window at the crowded streets and shops along the way, wondering the whole time what lies before me tonight.

I feel pretty certain that I can hold my own regardless of the circumstances I'll face. I won't allow them to put words into my mouth, and decide that the best approach is to say little, and let my "hosts" do the talking. Reaching into my jacket pocket and fumbling nervously with the recorder and the pack of gum, I notice that I have a packet of before and after Polaroid photos of some of my surgical procedures. I must have left them in the jacket pocket following a press conference that I gave a few days ago. I also find several of my business cards, and think to myself that they might come in handy.

My driver is a cowboy, with no regard for anyone or anything else on the road. He is driving at break-neck speed, using his horn constantly and his brakes very little, if at all – giving me a roller coaster of a ride. I realize that we are late, but I really want to get there in one piece, so I tap on the glass divider, and the driver pushes a button and lowers the divider. I tell him in Urdu to slow down, and that I don't care if we are late, I want to get there safely. I don't know how much English the driver understands, but I repeat it in English as well, this time, in the tone of a stern order, which seems to bring the driver to his senses, and he slows down considerably.

A few minutes pass, and the driver turns off the main street. After going several hundred yards, we are approaching a check-point. I suddenly realize that I'd rushed out without my passport or even my wallet. In fact, I have no identification with me at all, and being an American in Pakistan, this could have dire consequences for me. The driver slows, lowering his window and speaking to the guards. They respond by snapping to attention and saluting, and one of them scurries over to the steel barrier blocking the road and pulls on the rope, lowering the counter-weight and quickly raising the steel crossing bar, allowing us to pass. Beyond relieved, I make a mental note never to leave the hospital compound again without my identification papers.

Unlike most of the roads in the country, this portion of the street is smoothly paved and well illuminated by street-lights. All the homes appear to be relatively new, and much larger than what I've seen elsewhere in Pakistan. Some, I estimate to be in excess of fifteen thousand square feet, with two and three stories and ornately decorated balconies. Ten-foot-high walls surround every one of them, and guards holding automatic weapons are stationed at each gate. The driver moves slowly along the road, and as we approach two large, beautifully carved and highly polished wooden doors, set into a ten-foot-high wall, he honks the horn three times. The doors open, and he drives into a courtyard with a circular drive surrounding a large and well-lit fountain. In the drive are parked seven other black SUVs, and one white SUV is parked along the far wall. Some of the drivers busy themselves polishing their cars, while others are clustered together, talking and smoking. I count at least six armed guards circling the area, their AK-47s slung over their shoulders.

The car comes to a stop in front of an impressive main entrance, and the driver runs around to open my door. Before I even have time to step out of the car, a military type opens one of the front doors and salutes. I take my time exiting the SUV, and slowly and deliberately climb the four steps to the entrance. The guard stands frozen in his salute until I enter the house, where a houseboy in spotless tan and green traditional Pakistani garb greets me and motions for me to follow him.

The entryway is a strikingly large two-story affair, set off by a massive marble stairway with a polished brass handrail extending to the second floor. The houseboy guides me around it and down a wide hallway with closed double doors on either side. He opens one of the double doors on the right. It doesn't make a sound as it parts to allow me to step through. I stand there for a moment, taking in the massive room, decorated in a burnished gold and muted royal red trim. It is very impressive, even regal. Across the room, there are eight men seated together, engaged in a lively discussion. As I had expected, several are in military uniform, two more are dressed in Pakistani police outfits, albeit with no side arms visible, and the remainder are wearing Western style suits with white shirts and open collars. They are obviously the politicians.

The question is, who is here to represent the Pakistani secret police? I know they are here. As I stand here in the entryway to this room, the others are all so caught up in their conversation that none even looks up or takes any notice of me at all. I chuckle to myself and immediately formulate a plan to take them off guard and gain their respect. I stand quietly, looking from one to the other, first at the military men, and memorizing each of their features, their uniforms, and their ranks.

Then I turn my attention to the "suits." The men occasionally take a sip of their tea or fruit juice, or reach for a piece of fruit from a platter on the table, but continue talking to each other, totally unaware that I am standing in the room. Finally, one of the suits looks up and sees me standing here, watching. He jumps up and almost sprints to my side. Without introducing himself, he asks, "Have you been standing there long?"

"Yes, several minutes. Am I in the correct place?"

He says yes and apologizes profusely. "I am so sorry. Please come in and sit down." We walk slowly to where the others are sitting, and all of a sudden the room grows absolutely silent. Addressing the rest of the group, my greeter says, "The doctor has been standing there for several minutes, and we have been so engrossed in our conversation we were not being proper hosts." He turns back to me and says, "Please sit." With a subtle sweeping motion, he points to a large, very comfortable looking leather chair with pillows. "Can I get you something to drink?"

This is just the opening I am waiting for to bring my plan into action. In my best and most formal Urdu, I reply, "*Muja chi cha hay, Shakria.*" As I speak, my eyes remain riveted on my host's face, and I see the sudden change in his expression that I had hoped for: shock! Glancing around the silent room, I note that the expressions on the others' faces change as well as they focus on me. They are stunned, probably wondering just how long I've been standing there in the room, listening to their conversation, wondering what I had heard, and how much I had actually understood.

I keep a good poker face. Turning toward the houseboy, who stands with his hands clasped in front of him at the side door, I repeat my request – again in Urdu – for tea. The houseboy looks up at me, nods, and opens the door behind him to leave the room. The room remains deathly silent.

I have them right where I want them.

The Tension Builds

he room is silent for several seconds, but it feels like an eternity. The collected military men, secret police, and bureaucrats seem to be rather anxiously waiting for me to divulge how much of their conversation I had heard and understood, but I remain silent. Let them sweat a bit. Finally, the uneasy silence is broken. One by one, the men introduce themselves, using only their first names. None of them identifies his position, which doesn't particularly surprise me. After the introductions are over, one of the uniformed military men – a captain, judging by the insignia on his uniform – addresses me.

"Doctor, we understand that you came under attack recently. I am truly sorry you have had to endure such a trial, especially since your mission here in our country is one of mercy. My officers report that you saved a number of their men's lives, by means that are not entirely doctor-like, and that you were wounded in the process. I must admit that you look no worse for wear, so I assume your wounds were not too serious. I hope that our efforts on your behalf after the attack may in some small way repay your courage."

I can feel the tension behind his questions, and can almost hear the questions they would probably prefer to ask. I know that I have to be careful here, and not say anything that could put me at greater risk than I already am. Slowly I say, "As I'm sure you all know, there was a military patrol in the area that arrived a few minutes after we were attacked, and they began rescue operations immediately. They called for ambulances for myself and my driver, as well as their own injured. I told them that I would prefer to have my driver take me to our hospital because I felt it would be quicker than waiting for the ambulances to arrive.

"Besides, given the number of your own men who were wounded, I figured that you would need all the ambulances you could get, and didn't want to take one myself if it was not absolutely necessary. As it turned out, it wasn't. Your men righted our van and to our surprise, it started. They wrapped me in a blanket and placed me on the backseat, and my driver rushed us to the hospital."

"Doctor, we understand you actually operated upon yourself, and then helped take care of our soldiers who were being brought into the hospital as well."

I can sense that this officer is somewhat torn between his appreciation for my helping his men, and the doubts as to my objectives. I am sure those doubts had motivated them to "invite" me here to this meeting. "It was not that difficult. My adrenaline was pumping rather rapidly. I applied local anesthesia in my wound sites. With the resident doctor's help, we were able to remove the bullets and stop the bleeding. The local anesthesia kept me relatively comfortable, and I refused any narcotics. I knew there were casualties that needed to be taken care of, so we set about preparing the operating rooms and calling in additional personnel so we could take care of the wounded soldiers."

Our host speaks next, saying, "I understand you worked through the entire night and into the next day."

I respond, "You have to do what you have to do. And it wasn't the first time that I've stayed awake for a day and a half or more in an emergency situation. I always figure that there will be time to sleep later."

At this, the captain begins to clap his hands, and the others quickly stand up and clap along with him. At this point, I'm having trouble discerning what this has all been leading up to. I still have a feeling that they haven't even begun to broach the subject for which they have brought me to this meeting.

Our host must be quite intuitive, and seems to address the question without my having asked it. "Excuse us for summoning you to this meeting on such short notice. I assure you that this is a friendly invitation, and that you are not risking anything. What we are going to discuss stays within this room. As you know, it is imperative that we maintain an awareness of events that occur here in our country. This attack was unusual enough that we felt it necessary to look more deeply into it and weigh its implications. And now here we all are. You have just met some of us, and I can understand that you don't have any reason to trust us. Were I in your position, and especially so soon after experiencing an attempt on my life, I would be suspicious as well."

Despite their friendly overtures, I decide to reserve judgment until I know what direction this meeting is taking. I figure that I've already scored points. I feel that I am in a position of strength. They apparently need something from me, but what? I casually reach out and take some of the dried apricots I like so much, followed by a sip of tea. Now, I decide, is as good a time as any to go on the attack.

"Who here is from the I.S.I.?"

The room again becomes very quiet, and the smiles on the men's faces begin to fade somewhat. I make eye contact with each of the men, and the gentleman sitting to my host's left, who is also in military uniform, suddenly speaks up. "Not everyone who works for the I.S.I. is your enemy."

That answers my initial question without anything further needing to be said. However, I'm still not sure why - or how - this meeting has been set up with me on such short notice. I suspect that this gathering had been planned well before the attack had taken place. Otherwise, it would have been almost impossible to gather all of them in one place like this. Wanting, no, *needing* to maintain my position of strength, I speak with a confidence that I hope appears more genuine than it is at this point. "To be honest, being summoned like this makes me both uneasy and angry."

Our host, looking somewhat stunned by my statement, asks, "Why do you think I arranged this meeting and invited you to attend?"

In a strong voice, loud enough to be heard by all in the room, and in a tone that leaves no doubt as to my distrust for their assurances, I respond, "It wasn't exactly an invitation."

Growing impatient, the host blurts out, "That is not important, Doctor."

"Then please come to the point."

"This investigation...I am sorry. That is a poor choice of words. This *meeting* is being conducted in great secrecy, and concerns matters of great import to us. You are in Abbottabad teaching and operating at the Frontier Medical College, but you are also inquiring in many places about having a meeting with Osama bin Laden!"

I take another sip of tea, weighing the situation for a moment before responding. Shifting my position in the chair and sitting up straight, I maintain eye contact with my questioners as I begin to speak. "I am both fascinated and disturbed by Osama bin Laden. I am not interested in collecting a big reward for his capture. I will tell you exactly what I have told others over the past several years in my travels throughout Pakistan. I am writing a book. I would like to interview the Sheik, and the information I have gathered has led me to Abbottabad."

The gentleman from the I.S.I. looks particularly uneasy now. He says, "We need to find out what you know and what you intend to do with it. This is an exceptionally sensitive subject for the Pakistani government. The survival of Pakistan and my government, not to mention our relationship with the United States, are my only concerns. Which means that you are my problem, and my problem is definitely my government's problem. Let me say that my government has absolutely no hand in the matter regarding Osama bin Laden. No conspiracy exists. I can confirm that. We have never heard mention that Osama bin Laden has any connection with our wonderful city of Abbottabad. As I am sure you know, Abbottabad is the location of many of our military headquarters, and of course of the Pakistani Military College where we train our officer corps.

The others in this room have never heard a word about this matter, either."

As he speaks, I am thinking to himself that I don't believe his denials at all. I also know that the absolute worst thing I could do in this situation would be to disclose the meetings that I have had, much less the topics that have been discussed.

The I.S.I. representative is transparent in his clumsy attempt to adopt a more conciliatory tone. "Good doctor, we are all friends here. I understand you know more about Osama bin Laden than almost anyone else. We suggest that you share your knowledge with us tonight."

All eyes are on me, and the room is suddenly very quiet again. After a moment, I nod as if in agreement to sharing what I have learned, but I need to choose what I say very carefully, so I hesitate, taking a few sips of my tea. I know it will be almost impossible to satisfy them without divulging any real information, but know that it is exactly what I have to do. I've made some potentially damaging discoveries, the most significant of which is that Osama bin Laden is living in a compound in Abbottabad, only a few minutes' walk from their most prestigious military headquarters and school, and that he has been there for possibly up to five years.

If this information were to be made public, it would deal a serious blow to the credibility of the Pakistani government and the I.S.I. Not to mention the fact that the United States is spending tens of millions of dollars looking for bin Laden, but is looking in all the wrong places. While this wild goose chase reflects very poorly upon the Pakistani government's claim to be America's ally, it doesn't say much for the capabilities of our CIA and Secret Service, either. The really damaging thing is that I have written letters to President Obama and Secretary of State Hillary Clinton, stating what I've learned, but my letters were totally ignored. I even made a week-long trip to Washington, D.C. and spoke with Congressmen and Senators, but when I went to the Secretary of State's offices, I was turned away. Obviously, my trip to Washington hadn't set well, with me or with those in my government whom I tried to contact.

On the other hand, the men in this room know that I have returned to Pakistan again and again to renew my contacts. When my information is published, it will be impossible for the Pakistani government to claim ignorance. The inevitable media storm will lead to a public uproar and reprisals, both at home and in Pakistan. The resulting calamity is inevitable.

The I.S.I. agent is growing impatient with my silence, and it shows. "I need to ask, and I need an answer *now*. You know more than you ought to. How did you come by all this information?"

It is a bit of a challenge, but I manage to at least appear calm as I respond. "I have nothing to hide, I will tell you the truth as I see it. As you know, my team and I have taken care of more than 10,000 children and adults throughout Pakistan, including in the Northwest Territories. In my perhaps misguided attempt to meet and interview bin Laden, I have conferred with patients, shopkeepers, and *maulanas*. I have visited mosques and bazaars, asking the same questions, stating that I was writing a book and wanted to interview the Sheik. I was honest with those I spoke with, up-front and truthful. There was no hidden agenda.

"Most people are very open with their doctor and their religious leaders, especially if the doctor is one who has performed surgery on their child. Their candor is built upon a trust that you might have thought would never be extended to an outsider, especially an American. I have spoken to thousands of these parents throughout Pakistan, and the trail has led me to the Northwest Territories and Abbottabad. I must be getting close, or we wouldn't be sitting here in this room.

"You're asking for my cooperation, and I have given it to you. I don't know if I am any closer now than I was two years ago, or whether you would ever offer me the opportunity of interviewing Osama bin Laden. I can't know what is in his mind, and I certainly can't provide you with that insight. Even if I could, doing so would be placing myself and the Sheik in jeopardy."

The others in the room are growing impatient with me as well, judging by the dour expressions on their faces.

"We are asking you to cooperate in the interest of the country, Doctor."

"Gentlemen, the fact that I am in Abbottabad should be an answer in itself."

The I.S.I. agent is smiling at me now, but his eyes belie the animosity that he is trying to conceal. "You play your cards very close and very well."

"I have never had a confrontation with the I.S.I."

"Don't get us wrong. We are very appreciative of the work you've done for the children of Pakistan, and more recently of the care you have provided for the wounded soldiers following the attack near Mansehra, especially since you were wounded at that time. I understand that you would naturally claim that you did not know where Osama bin Laden is located, much less that you have met with him.

"I will accept what you have said. I request that you do not make any further inquiries regarding Osama bin Laden, for your own safety. Under normal circumstances, I would not have insisted that you attend such a gathering as this, but these are far from being normal. As I said before, we all have great respect for what you have done for Pakistan."

He pauses to let that sink in, and then continues, "Those are the rules, and I must insist that you abide by them. And, I know that you frequently walk through the bazaar and attend the mosque, but I suggest you keep a sharp eye on those around you. I hope you will trust in me, and that we can work together, rather than against each other."

His threat is clear. I turn to face him, offering him a cautious smile that I suspect looks no more genuine than his own, and ask him bluntly, "*Can* I trust you?"

"This country, its military, and the police officers who are here, are all at your disposal. Of course you can trust us. We are looking out for your safety and that of your team."

His threat widens, I think to myself, and I suppress an impulse to address the threat directly. They know more than they are willing to say, of course, and are most likely protecting Osama bin Laden. The knowledge makes me furious. These bastards who work for the government are probably being paid to keep bin Laden's whereabouts secret. But I have already met with him and I'll be damned if I will disclose any of my sources of information to them, because doing so would likely get people whose trust I cherish killed.

Besides, I would probably face retribution from my own government – that is, if I were allowed to leave Pakistan or even to continue living. I have received no replies from my own government to the letters I have written to them, and as I indicated earlier, I was treated as if I were some type of pariah when I went to Washington, D.C. So I know I can't depend on any kind of support back home if I happen to get myself into a bad situation in Pakistan. At this moment it hits me: I really have to be careful now.

I shrug and turn his question back on him, "Do you trust your own doctor? More than ten thousand of your country's children and their families have trusted me. The warlords have trusted me. The man in the street has trusted me, and those in your mosques have trusted me. I hope you gentlemen will trust what I have said here tonight. I believe in democracy for Pakistan, and realize that sometimes it has to be protected. Just as you have the I.S.I., we have the CIA and other intelligence gathering agencies to protect our democracy and freedoms. But by their very nature, institutions like the I.S.I. and CIA tend to function beyond the scope of governmental oversight and as such cannot always be trusted. So do I trust you? I don't really know."

"Are you married, doctor?"

"Yes. I am very committed and in love. She is my soul mate."

"You almost didn't make it back home to her."

Just as I am about to respond angrily to this reinforcement of his earlier threats, the door opens and the houseboy rings a small bell, firmly but softly. Our host stands and says, "We could continue questioning the doctor all evening, but I'm sure we are all hungry, and that we accept what he has told us."

I stand as well, biting my lip but keeping my face otherwise expressionless. Our host puts his arms around the two military men and approaches me, saying to them, obviously for my benefit, "The doctor is our guest, a true hero and treasure. I want you to promise to give him your fullest protection while he is in Abbottabad. Now, I am hungry. Let's eat."

The doors on the far side of the room are opened by two houseboys. The group crosses the hallway into a large dining room and gathers at a table that has been beautifully set. I've always liked to sit at the center of the table where I can converse with those next to me, as well as those on the opposite side. I start to pull out a chair, but the host stops me, insisting that I take a place at the head of the table, where the houseboy is already drawing the chair back for me. I never liked sitting at the head of any table, since it separates me from the others in the group. It is obvious that I have no choice but to take the seat being "offered" to me. As I settle into my chair, the others take their seats, and three of the houseboys begin serving the meal.

The officer to my left leans over and says to me, "This meeting never occurred, and we hope you shall honor your pledge never to discuss this matter with anyone."

I look at him, peering directly into his eyes. He is the shortest one in the group, bald, an older man with a round, clean-shaven face, wearing gold-rimmed half glasses.

"I pledge my secrecy, at the risk of ending up dead."

After that, and throughout the meal, nothing more is said about the subject, and the topics and tone of the conversations at the table remain light. They discuss business, travel, family, grandchildren, and any number of other benign topics. After about an hour, the men excuse themselves one by one, saying the hour is late and they need to return to their homes. I glance at my watch, and notice that it is almost 2:00 AM. I thank my host for the dinner and for the wonderful ice cream dessert.

He smiles broadly, saying, "We learned that ice cream was your favorite, and I wanted you to enjoy it with us at this dinner."

"Thank you for that consideration. It is a favorite. I see you know all about me, and that I truly have no secrets."

Still smiling, but with a slight return of the predatory look I had seen in his eyes before, he declares, "It's absurd that you should think otherwise, but I'm glad we could all meet and clear the air."

He walks me to the front entrance and down the steps. He waves his hand in the direction of the drivers standing beside the row of cars, and without saying a word, the man who had driven me here immediately brings the SUV to the front. He comes around and opens the door for me, and once more, I turn to thank my host.

Accepting my outstretched hand, he says, "We will see each other again before you leave. I would like to visit the hospital and see some of the children."

"It would be a pleasure to have you as a guest at the hospital and to give you a tour of the children's wards. Good night."

I turn away and step into the SUV, and the driver closes the door behind me. The drive back to the Frontier Medical College is uneventful, but I realize that my situation has become potentially explosive, and that I will be continually watched from this point on. I feel as though I'm holding a hand grenade from which the pin has been pulled. This is far from over, but all of a sudden, I realize that I am exhausted. I know that I will get less than four hours of sleep before I have to be up again and back in the operating room. I also know that I have no good reason to trust the police, the military, or the I.S.I. When I enter my room, I close, and for the first time lock, the door behind me. I draw the curtains closed over the glass entranceway, and then undress. I flip the switch to the small lamp on the night table, and the room falls instantly into absolute darkness. I crawl into bed, lay my head upon the pillow, and within thirty seconds I fall into yet another deep but uneasy sleep.

Fourth Meeting: The Stage is Set

In my previous meetings with the Sheik bin Laden, I have gotten a better picture of the man versus the myth, and have learned a lot about what drives him. That he is both highly revered and widely hated goes without question. And the more I speak with him, the more I am convinced that he represents a profound danger, both to his own homeland and to the rest of the world. If for no other reason than this, I continue to seek further meetings with him, not only to more clearly understand him and his mission, but also to learn how and when he hopes to bring his jihad to the rest of the world.

* * * * *

Tonight, I will be with Sultan and Mohammed. I leisurely stroll alone through the many small shops and alleyways of the Sarafa Bazaar, and visit the mosque located between Masjid Road and the main bazaar road. I linger for a bit at a couple of teahouses, but on this night my focus is upon matters more pressing than food or shopping. I have not been contacted by the Sheik for several days, and as I circle the mosque and walk through the streets of the Sarafa Bazaar, my mood is glum.

I finally come to the Iqbal Restaurant, just west of the mosque, where Mohammed and Sultan are waiting for me. This night, like most, is comfortably cool, and we each wear a traditional knit scarf wrapped around our shoulders to shield us from the chill.

I usually enjoy losing myself in the back streets of these bazaars and markets, the kind of places that never make it to the pages of the quick reference-style guide books. These are the back streets where real people get their hands dirty performing everyday tasks – emptying the trash bins into the donkey carts, making deliveries, stocking their shelves for customers, and busying themselves with ordinary everyday tasks. What we see here is very foreign to Americans or Europeans, who are more accustomed to lavish window displays, flickering neon signs, and well lit office facades. These are the places that people read about in those "off the beaten path" travel books, but never visit. I can't imagine any of my friends in this setting.

While I am as fascinated as always by the sights and smells of this area, I harbor no illusion that this is a tourist's journey, any more than these nightly wanderings have anything to do with my medical mission. And I find my gaze searching not for the manifestations of a centuries-old culture as much as for a look of cautious recognition in some stranger's eye. For it is that look that will tell me that the Sheik is ready to meet with me yet again.

As Mohammed guides us through the nearby maize of back streets and alleyways, Sultan watches my back. We cross Gumani Road, going north past a small café whose Urdu name roughly translates in English to the Rainbow Café. A few minutes later, we look in at the New Friends Café, but see no sign of anyone who might work for the Sheik.

As we continue away from the market, these cafés are the only two buildings that are lit, and the rest appear to be private homes or small businesses that don't cater to the evening crowds.

We continue walking for a while, until we come upon another restaurant. I don't know what has caught Sultan's attention, but he raises his hand and looks toward the restaurant. We can hear the murmur of voices from within and the clatter of kitchen utensils being struck against each other, but there seems to be something else that disturbs him. He is looking up at the balconies that extend from the second and third levels of the restaurant to our right. At first, I can't see anyone, but then the light breeze carries a wisp of smoke into the air from the second story balcony. From that vantage point, a person could not only observe the cobblestone courtyard in which we are standing, but also the streets north and west of the bazaar. Someone has obviously observed our movements, and is watching us now.

My adrenaline begins to rise very quickly as Sultan dashes toward the staircase that leads to the balconies. He moves quickly and silently upwards, his weapon at the ready. Mohammed quickly motions for us to move forward under the staircase and into the shadows. He too has his weapon ready. From our hiding place, we hear a door open and close, and assume it is at the top of the second story balcony. Looking back across the cobblestone courtyard, we see nothing out of place, nothing threatening.

Mohammed signals to me, and we cross behind the restaurant and start down the side alley, which leads us back out and onto the main street next to the restaurant's entrance. Just as we emerge from the alley and enter again upon the main road, we are startled by the loud crash of something substantially heavy slamming against the stonework in the courtyard. We turn to look down the narrow alleyway we have just exited and see that someone has thrown open the back door to the restaurant's kitchen, causing it to crash noisily into the stone wall. In the light emanating from the doorway, we see two men maneuvering an obviously heavy metal barrel from the kitchen and into the cobblestone courtyard. They move their load awkwardly across the cracks and irregular cobblestones to the far end of the alley. Having placed their load where they wanted it, the two men turn, paying no attention to us, and re-enter the kitchen, leaving the large door ajar.

Another man, this one with a scruffy beard and unkempt hair, and dressed in a chef's whites, steps out. Tied in the back of his head, and covering his forehead and all of his hair, is a white scarf. He takes out a cigarette and lights it, all the while looking down the alleyway in our direction. He holds our gaze for a few seconds, then turns and withdraws from our sight.

I'm getting worried about Sultan. Thirty seconds goes by. Then several minutes. Nothing happens, and everything remains quiet. Mohammed and I step out of the shadows and turn toward the restaurant.

Then we see Sultan, who reaches up and pulls his shawl down to conceal the weapon at his side. Lowering his arms, he descends the interior stairway, steps out the front entrance of the building, and walks briskly toward the front entrance of the New Jaghan Café, not knowing that Mohammed and I are headed in the same direction. We emerge from the alleyway to the main street, turn, and approach the several steps at the café's main entrance. The two large front doors are lashed open, held by loops of material draped over the door handles and attached to the building itself. We stand here in the doorway for several seconds, scanning the occupants of the crowded café.

Then, we see him. Seated at a table in the far corner near a stairway sits Sultan, accompanied by two young men. I recognize one of them, Abu Ahmed Al-Kuwaigi, whom I've met on previous occasions, and who goes by the name Ibrahim. Sultan sees us and waves for us to come join them, and as I draw near, I see a large vein throbbing above the other man's left temple. He looks up from the table and glares at us. His mouth opens as if he is going to say something, then snaps shut again. Looking more closely at his expression, I can see that his glare is probably borne of fear as much as anger.

The two men's hands rest flat on the table in front of them, fingers splayed in a position of submission. Glancing at Sultan, I begin to understand. His hands are at his side, below the table and out of view of the other patrons, clutching his pistol, which is pointed at the man seated across from him. Without allowing our demeanor to reflect the obvious tension at the table, we approach the three as if this is the casual meeting of friends. All three at the table are facing us now, their backs to the stone wall. A quick glance around the room is reassuring; nobody seems to notice us, and there is no apparent threat. The table is ten feet away from any other, and backed up against the wall.

I notice that Mohammed is also scanning the surroundings as I turn toward the young men and greet them. "*As-salam-alai-kum.*"

They both respond in kind, almost in unison.

I ask them, "*Aya ta pe po-he-gy Englesi?*" ("Do you speak English?")

"*Ho, leg leg.*" ("Yes, a little.")

I pull out a chair and sit down. Mohammed moves his chair to the far side of the table so he can observe the rest of the room, and he sits down too. A waiter arrives and Mohammed orders tea for all of us.

Ibrahim is the first to speak, introducing the other man, whom I've never met, as his brother Abrar. The brothers are ethnic Pashtun. Ibrahim tells us that they have been with Osama bin Laden for at least ten years. Ibrahim has long been bin Laden's front man, and has of late been known as his courier. I know that if there is going to be another meeting with the Sheik, Ibrahim is the one who is going to arrange it. The question is, will it be tonight?

The tension eases significantly, and Ibrahim smiles at me and greets me, "*As-salam-alaikum.*"

I return his smile and greeting, "*Wa Alaeikum Assalaam.*"

The conversation continues in a mixture of English, Urdu, and to a greater extent, Pashto. That may seem odd to many Americans, but mixed dialects and linked languages are common throughout the tribal area. After a few moments, our tea arrives. I take some tattered rupee notes from my pocket, but Ibrahim gently places his hand on my arm, saying "*Na. Na.*" ("No. No.") It appears that this is going to be Ibrahim's party. Not wanting to insult him, I slide the money back into my pocket. Ibrahim places some coins on the waiter's tray, and waves him away. I scan the restaurant again to reassure myself that nothing suspicious is going on, and I am relieved to note that nobody is paying particular attention to our little group.

Taking a sip of my tea, I turn toward Ibrahim, fixing on him a rather stern gaze. After a few seconds, Ibrahim begins to squirm a bit, and I ask him point blank, "Are there any others?"

My question elicits a nervous chuckle from Ibrahim, and a notable hesitation before he responds, "*Da. Da.*" I rotate in my chair and lean back, studying the two of them and thinking to myself that they are both mad as hatters. I can see it by looking behind their eyes. I consider Ibrahim's answer, still studying his expression for a few seconds before shaking my head and letting him know I don't believe him. I'm probably not quite as amenable as they might have expected. On the other hand, I think they also understand that as satisfying as I might find it, I know that it would not be a good thing to kill the Sheik's messenger.

Mohammed senses the tension and tries to ease it, addressing the two, "I'm sorry he said what he did. I have no idea where he comes up with such things."

Sultan, who has up to this point been sitting quietly taking all this in, pushes his empty teacup toward the center of the table. He looks up and studies the two men as if they are our enemies, knitting his brow and squinting as if taking aim.

I recognize his distrustful expression, as well as his own body language when he is trying to interpret the body language of an opponent. He often assumes that he is smarter than his opponents, and that might not be particularly fair or diplomatic, but he is usually correct, leaving him more often a step ahead of the game rather than a step behind. Though Sultan has always been one to quietly observe others, he is also strangely impatient with their failings.

That impatience shows itself now, as he raises himself up in his chair, again wrinkles his brow as only he can, and says, "We can all be friends and you can tell us what the plans are for this evening and who else will be taking part. Or you can continue with your little charade and risk making your boss angry. I am sure the Sheik has given you instructions. Will there or will there not be a meeting?"

Ibrahim responds, "Yes, we have instructions, but you may need to think about how you will respond to my answer."

Sultan looks up at him, and growls angrily, "What do we need to think about?"

"The Sheik very much enjoys the discussions with the doctor. He would like the doctor to stay with him for several days. For security reasons, we will not be going to the compound in Abbottabad. There are other safe houses that we use. One of them is about one and a half hours north of here. The Sheik is already there. We have been ordered to bring the doctor. Only the doctor."

"How will he get there?"

"We have a car available, and Al Sada will be driving the doctor."

I perk up at this, stating, "I know Al Sada. He was present at my recent dinner meeting with Osama bin Laden." Despite my reassurance, however, Sultan is still wary, and it shows clearly on his face.

Ibrahim sees this, and attempts to ease Sultan's concerns. "Al Sada is a thirty-year old Yemenite who has also been a close companion of bin Laden, and escaped with him from the Tora Bora cave fortress in 2001. Al Sada has been a close companion to the Sheik ever since."

My mind is racing; I know of at least three safe houses and assume that there are others. It wasn't that difficult to learn where they were, either, since there are no secrets among hospital personnel, and as I have noted, patients routinely say things to their caregivers that they might never divulge to anyone else. Anything unusual becomes quickly apparent, and is discussed by all the hospitals' staff. It was in the Civil Hospital at Haripur that bin Laden's youngest wife Fatah had given birth years ago to a baby girl, Aasia, and eighteen months later, to a son.

Fatah hadn't hesitated to discuss her home life with her doctors, or for that matter, where she and the Sheik took refuge from his enemies. From the staff, I have learned that there is a safe house located in Haripur, about an hour and a half south of Abbottabad, and I assume that this is the one to which I am to be taken. Mohammed and Sultan listen intently to Ibrahim's proposition, and while they are wary of me leaving with the two men, it sounds reasonable enough to me, at least while sitting here with my two friends at my side. I won't be travelling that far, but the road we will be taking is not a road most people would want to take at this time of night.

In an operation like this, everyone has a role to play, even if it isn't necessarily the one he is expecting or wanting to play. I have traveled often through this region, and know it very well, as do Mohammed and Sultan. I can well understand why bin Laden would choose this place for our meeting, because it is a place where no one can get to him, and where the physical environment itself helps to ensure his safety. It is as if the region had been specifically designed for the task. It is difficult enough to make the trip in daylight, and we will be doing it at night, when we will be less likely to attract unwanted attention. The location of our meeting, as well as the path we must take to get there, provide guaranteed access control, privacy, and the level of security the Sheik needs.

Judging by their expressions and body language, it is obvious to me, as well as to Sultan and Mohammed, that Ibrahim and Abrar are acting on orders from the Sheik. They are not trying to be aggressive, but they seem to be in a rush to get me out of here. This is a strange situation to observe, since I know that Sultan and Mohammed have spent a large portion of their lives on the outside looking in – yet now I find myself in the opposite situation. Here I am, an outsider, having been absorbed into bin Laden's very exclusive clique, and I am now on the inside, looking out. I've not known Osama bin Laden very long, but it is clear that he has put down roots in Abbotta-bad. He has been flourishing there for many years, so why this sudden transition to the safe house?

Mohammed gets up from the table and motions for Ibra-him to join him. They walk outside to the deck that extends to either side of the steps. I think to myself, *What is Mohammed up to?*

Just at this moment, more tea arrives, along with a plate of warm pita bread, and another with sliced cucumber, tomatoes, and other vegetables. The three of us sit in silence and eat, but my eyes follow Mohammed and Ibrahim as they descend the few steps from the porch, Ibrahim with his hands in his pock-ets, nervously kicking his toes into the dusty ground.

Then, almost as suddenly as they had exited, they return to the table. Mohammed seems tense and distant. Staring at the table, he picks up a piece of pita bread with his right hand and tears off a section, one-handed, in keeping with tradition-al Muslim etiquette. He seems more anxious by the moment. He doesn't break his silence until he finishes chewing, then says, "We have come to a compromise. The doctor will travel to Mansehra with us in the van. Al Sada and the brothers will lead the way in their car. At the junction of the Abbottabad road with Jaffar Road, just south of the Kashmir Bazaar, is a small hotel called the Zam Zam Hotel. We will transfer the doctor at that point. We will remain at the Zam Zam until the doctor returns to us in a few days or we receive a message there notifying us of any change in plans."

I am impressed with Mohammed's ability to find a unique means by which to achieve our seemingly divergent goals: mine, to meet with the Sheik; the Sheik's men, to minimize the risk to his security; and Mohammed's, to keep me safe at all costs. I have to confess that part of me is fascinated with the manner by which Mohammed has come to this compromise. I already know that he can get his hands dirty when he thinks he needs to, but he is working now in a different way than I've previously seen. Now that everyone involved knows what is going to happen, the tension and distrust that existed only moments ago seem to have lifted. Each of us knows what we were part of, and the enmity gives way to a bond that is developing amongst the players. This is a galaxy removed from the lies and deceit that seem to be the basic building blocks of the world I know, both here in Pakistan and back home in the U.S.

Abrar fills a round of the pita bread with vegetables, wraps it in a napkin, and starts walking toward the door, the rest of us following close behind. Once we arrive back at the van, Mohammed takes the driver's seat as usual, and I start to climb into the van next to him. But Sultan puts his hand on my shoulder and shakes his head sternly, saying, "No, no."

I can tell from the tone of his voice that he's not going to budge. He turns and slides the side door of the van open, then motions me in, and I climb in and stretch out on the bench seat in the back. The route Al Sada follows out of Abbottabad is crazy, dodging down an endless variety of back streets and alley ways, narrowly avoiding pedestrians, motorized three-wheeled rickshaws, and pushcarts. He is, I realize, making it difficult for any potential tails to catch up to and follow us. He is so adept at this dance of evasion that we hardly slow down until we come to the intersection with the KKH and turn north.

At this junction, Sultan asks me to remove his AK-47 from under the bench seat and hand it to him. Mohammed has already taken his Beretta from under the front seat and jammed it into the crack between the two front seats. I haven't seen anything that might have been a portent of danger, and ask him, "What are you doing?"

Sultan says, "Sorry. Old superstition. Always have to check my weapon one last time. Can't move, otherwise. This is not a friendly road at night, and you can never know what will happen next." The three of us sit in silence, each considering Sultan's words, and each gripping our own weapon a bit more tightly.

An Unsettling Journey

*D*espite the fact that we are under escort provided by the man who is probably the most revered individual in Pakistan, there is good reason for us to be on edge as we barrel down this isolated road, since there are a lot of people in this region who are even more wary than we are, and will shoot first and ask questions later. Scrubby, barren fields stretch out on both sides of the road. We pass the unmarked intersection of a narrow, winding country lane that leads from the KKH to a nearby village. The only lights we can see are from a single mud brick farmhouse that glows in the distance, and nowhere in sight is there anything resembling shelter.

Every one of us is scanning the fields, as well as the road in front of and behind us for anything unusual that might be a sign of threat. At this time of night, we don't have to worry about any traffic except for the occasional livestock that might inadvertently wander onto the road. We know, however, that if we encounter any motorized vehicles other than the large lorries that lumber along the highway, we have to be prepared for a danger that is always prevalent.

Of course, we travel with our lights out. This in itself is disturbing to me, since the road is not lit. It feels as if the world begins and ends right where we are, and that we are surrounded by nothingness. I check the florescent dial on my watch every few minutes, as if to make sure the hands are still moving. I see them creep around another five minutes, but begin to feel as if we are frozen in time. Suddenly, the car in front slows for a moment, and as we catch up, we see a three-wheeled bicycle rickshaw stacked high with firewood beginning to exit left from the KKH onto a side street.

Once we pass the rickshaw, the cars accelerate again, and are soon barreling along at a rapid clip. There is virtually no traffic, and the lead driver is relentless, weaving around pot-holes and trash that has blown onto the road. Before we even see it, the van bounces violently over a small ditch where water from melting glaciers has come down the mountainside and run across the road. We continue on, constantly scanning the area around us, straining our eyes across the unlit road into the adjacent small villages and fields.

The road suddenly drops down sharply and to the right. We navigate through a switchback, swing around, and double back to a place where the road suddenly levels off again. Here, we pass a half dozen burned-out military vehicles that had been left behind and pushed to the side of the road. Next, we pass several derelict buildings from which we surmise that the attack on the military convoy had taken place. It is easy, based upon the destruction, to imagine the carnage that must have occurred, but the spot seems altogether deserted now.

I find my mind wandering, perhaps as a means of diffusing the anxiety I feel here, quite literally in the middle of nowhere. In my world, I've gotten used to a degree of constant tension. Every time I walk into an operating room and pick up a scalpel, I am keenly aware of the risks involved, and that I literally hold another person's life in my hands. But it is the road I've chosen, and I have the experience and training to spot pitfalls along the way. Besides, in a modern, fully equipped hospital, there are people, albeit at arm's length, ready to help me at a moment's notice. It can be stressful enough, at times, but I can only imagine what life is like for the ordinary villagers living in their mud huts without electrical power, limited sanitation, and unpurified water.

With the hundreds of millions of dollars coming from the U.S., Europe, the United Nations, and others, why are these people still suffering so much? The money is literally gushing into this place, but none of that money is reaching them. The ruling elite – perhaps two or three hundred people – are siphoning it all off. None filters down to the bottom of the heap. And that's what I believe is fueling the discontent that makes this place so dangerous, leading more and more people to respond with their voices, but realizing they are not being heard. They have come to believe that the only alternative is to arm themselves, and when that happens, things begin to escalate out of control, as they have recently in Egypt, Syria, and other countries in the Arab and Persian World. And the writing is on the wall in Pakistan, as well.

It was bad enough when the only medium of exchange was power, but now it is a struggle for both power and money. Not just a few aid dollars from the U.S.A., but billions and billions of dollars. And such unimaginable riches can be a powerful motivator. There is so much at stake here, and bin Laden wields incredible influence. I have some pretty hard questions to ask him, and I need to determine whether his interest is truly in the protection of his faith and his people, or in the instigation of a global conflict that would result in the loss of millions of lives and the devastation of many millions more. And just as importantly, I must decide what I can do to avert the latter alternative, should that be his real objective.

I've been lost in my own thoughts for quite some time, emerging only now, as I notice that the van is beginning to slow down. Looking through the filthy windshield, I can see some lights, and am pretty certain that we are descending toward Mansehra. We pass the mosque to our right, then the bus stand on the left. A hundred yards away stands the Taj Mahal Hotel – a laughable misnomer, as the building is in an advanced state of decay, with a single bulb hanging from an exposed wire and swinging in the wind, welcoming guests at its front door.

We continue slowly now along Abbottabad Road to its junction with the Shinkiari Road, where we turn left and continue fifty meters past a bridge to the hidden alcove where the Zam Zam Hotel, which bears no resemblance whatsoever to its opulent namesake in Mecca, is located. The sign outside indicates that rooms cost one hundred fifty rupees – roughly two dollars – a night. The cars stop side by side on the gravel parking area in front of the hotel.

Al Sada remains behind the wheel, with the motor running. Ibrahim exits the car and walks toward the van. I tap Mohammed and Sultan on the shoulder, indicating that they should remain where they sit. I rummage through the back of the van, stuffing a black plastic sack with a change of clothing, as well as a second pair of sandals and a large gray woolen shawl, knowing it can get rather cold in the mountains. Sliding the side door of the van open, I hand the sack to Ibrahim, who nods as he takes it from my hand. I raise my arms, hands out and palms facing him, fully expecting to be subjected to a body search before I am allowed to enter the vehicle with the two men.

Ibrahim seems almost amused by my submissive gesture, and shaking his head, indicates that this is not necessary. We walk to the other car and get in. Almost before I am seated, Al Sada puts the car in gear and stomps the accelerator, spraying sand and small stones as he accelerates onto the main road, going north past the mosque and the bank in Old Town, and turning left to re-enter the KKH. He continues driving at a high speed with his lights off. We continue north through the mountains to the village of Shinkiari and onto the Siran River Valley. Where we will exit is anyone's guess.

I want to get a sense of the place before the car stops, but with the headlights off, and no streetlights or other structures of note, there is no way to do so. Al Sada abruptly exits the KKH onto a dirt road, immediately reducing his speed. I look down at my watch, trying to get some perspective as to how much distance we travel on this path. We bounce along for about six minutes, then turn right again. There are still no distinguishable features on the landscape for some time; then suddenly, out of the darkness, a two-story structure constructed of local handmade brick appears. It has large, evenly spaced windows, barred with a decorative iron façade, from which no lights shine.

As we draw closer, the building itself is completely obscured by a twenty-foot-high mud brick wall, topped with shards of broken glass to discourage those who might want to scale it. There is a pair of large double wooden doors centrally located and securely set into the wall, but no sign of guards at this entrance. The car continues slowly to the right, around the perimeter of the wall, until we come to a set of ornate iron gates large enough for a medium-sized truck to drive through, with steel sheeting on the back sides that completely blocks any view of the courtyard. To either side of the gate and along the wall are black metal boxes, which I suspect might contain surveillance cameras, motion detectors, and floodlights.

Al Sada stops and flashes his lights several times, but there is no response. There is no sign of inhabitants inside, and Al Sada waits a moment before flashing his lights again, whereupon the huge iron gates slowly open, and I see several men with automatic weapons laboring to open the gates so we can pass through. As soon as we enter, the gates are quickly closed. Still, no lights appear. Two of the men open the car doors, and using flashlights to light the way, they direct us to the house. Ibrahim carries my black plastic bag. The space surrounding the building is my first area of focus, and I don't see or feel anything out of the ordinary. The smell of livestock reaches my nostrils as I am guided across the courtyard to the main house.

Upon stepping across the threshold, I immediately enter a large central room with doors leading to hallways on either side of a central staircase. The floor is beautifully tiled, but otherwise the room lacks any decorations, and is minimally furnished. I am surprised – actually shaken – when in the far right doorway, the Sheik himself appears, smiling and greeting me, "Peace be with you."

Despite my surprise, I manage to respond in kind, "And to you too."

We exchange the usual pleasantries, and the Sheik asks me if I would like some tea. I politely decline and say, "*Paakaana*." ("Bathroom.")

At this, they all begin to laugh.

Ibrahim says, "Come with me, I will show you where the bathroom is, and to your room. It's been a long day and I know you must be tired."

I nod appreciatively, and when I turn back toward my host, Sheik bin Laden is gone. I turn again, and Ibrahim and Abrar escort me to my room, saying, "The Sheik will be up for Morning Prayer. We start our days early. I will come get you if you would like to join us."

"Yes, I would like that. Thank you, and good night."

They turn and leave, closing the door behind them. Glancing around, I see a small cabinet at the far end of the room, a table with one chair, and a typical Pakistani rope-style bed with a thin mattress, on top of which is a bright, multi-colored quilt with tassels and silver metal medallions sewn into it. The quilt, I note, is very similar to one given to me several years ago by the chairman of the Pakistani Senate. The room is sparse, but I can already tell that it will be comfortable and shield me from the chill night air.

I realize then that Ibrahim was right; I am extremely tired. After answering the most urgent of nature's calls, I remove my dusty sandals, lie down on the bed, and say a prayer... sort of. *Good Lord, what sort of a mess have I landed in? And how the hell am I going to get out of it?* The answer seems to come as a revelation: *Step back and allow common sense to guide you.* I don't even get under the quilt, and as soon as my head touches the pillow, I fall immediately into a sound sleep.

A Meeting on a Mountain

I awaken as the first hint of gray light begins to soften the blackness of the desert night. I find that I am thoroughly refreshed and relaxed. Then, as my head begins to clear and I orient myself, I remember with a start that I am in Osama bin Laden's safe house. And in spite of my disgust at my own country's "intelligence" failures at locating the Sheik, and despite the fact that this is not his compound in Abbottabad, I still feel a twinge of concern. *What if the CIA knows about this safe house as well, and has somehow found out that he will be here, and today is the day when they send a drone to take him out?*

Strangely enough, the possibility of my own impending demise seems almost inconsequential to me. I imagine what the Pakistani news would report about the attack, or for that matter, how the American media would interpret my presence here, lying dead among the members of bin Laden's household. My mind goes quickly to thoughts of my beloved Terry. She would know the truth, of course, but the public would be less understanding. They would concoct all kinds of stories to fill the void in their understanding, and Terry would be dogged and harassed unmercifully.

I have no choice but to put those "what if" scenarios out of my head. I am here to speak again with the Sheik, and hopefully to learn more about his mindset, not to mention his plans for the destruction of his despised infidels in Europe and the U. S. I cannot afford the distraction of worries that are unlikely to be realized.

I take my time washing up and dressing, still trying to calm myself, and reminding myself that I have to remain clear enough to ask the right questions, while managing to avoid giving the wrong answers to the questions I know the Sheik will have. I fear that this may be my last meeting with him, and I wonder what we will discuss. Will we cover any new ground, or will we just review what we've already talked about? Will anything happen that will change my mind and heart, or his? Will I come away from the meeting, or meetings, feeling as if I have accomplished anything?

Will I come away from the meeting at all?

I am startled from my reverie by a knock at my door, probably Ibrahim here to tell me that breakfast will be served soon. I open the door and to my surprise, there stands the Sheik himself, along with his son Khalid, both of them smiling as if they can read my shock. "Come, Doctor. After our brief talk last evening, I began thinking of your description of your travels, and find myself again chafing at my imprisonment behind these walls. Let us walk, as the free man I once was, and have our discussion in the sunlight, with the wind in our faces."

"But Sheik, surely you know that leaving your safe house is dangerous for you, and to be honest, I do not want to be caught in a barrage of bullets either."

At this, the Sheik lets loose a hearty laugh. "Even your words remind me of a freedom that is denied me. None of my household would dare speak that way to me, and yet, I know there is no disrespect in what you say. Come. We will wander to a place that is dear to me. There, we shall be safe, and we will be able to speak freely, as men and friends, with no other ears nearby to listen and misinterpret our words."

It is obvious to me that the Sheik has made up his mind, and as his "guest," I am bound by more than mere courtesy to accede to his wishes. I throw on a thick woolen shawl against the chill that still lingers in the pre-dawn air. Then the three of us walk across the courtyard toward the large gate, where we are immediately confronted by an armed guard.

The Sheik whispers to him, ordering him to keep silent and to open the gate.

As we slip through and into the empty street, the Sheik turns back to the man and tells him not to inform anyone that we have left, and that we shall return at midday. As the gate closes behind us, we walk for some time, with bin Laden putting his finger to his lips to silence me each time I begin to speak. I am feeling anxious again, and I want to ask him why he hasn't brought at least one of his bodyguards along. I also want to express concern about the fact that none of us is armed. But bin Laden will not allow me to speak, and I am not going to push the issue.

Khalid follows a few steps behind, also silent. I find myself looking around me, half expecting to see a troop of policemen or I.S.I. agents approaching, but we are altogether alone. The only sound is the occasional barking of dogs, each dutifully but unenthusiastically announcing our presence. Thankfully, their pronouncements are ignored by their owners, most of whom are probably still asleep.

After about fifteen minutes, we have gone beyond the neighborhood, and are at the edge of the grassy foothills that surround the city. We continue hiking until we begin a climb into the foothills, gentle at first, but growing increasingly steep and rugged as we proceed onward, I assume towards a spot that the Sheik has already chosen. As the path grows steeper, the Sheik no longer has to bid me to be silent, as I'm concentrating on both my footing and the thinness of the air.

We have walked for quite awhile now, and the sun has risen high above the peaks. The shadows have grown shorter, and the sky is clear as only a high-plains sky can be. Finally Osama indicates that we should sit and rest, and I am grateful. The only sounds are of the rushing water in the small stream just a few feet away from where we are sitting, and the pleasant sounds of birds.

After a while I break the silence with a question to Khalid, "Where is your brother Hamza? Did he come along to the safe house with you and your father and the rest of the household?"

There is silence, and I wonder if I have asked the wrong question. In truth I had been wondering about Hamza since I arrived here last night, hoping that if he is here, I can have some time to talk with him about his own experiences. There are many questions I have wanted to ask about the time he was placed under house arrest in Iran, and what happened immediately after he was released. There never seemed to be a good time to do that during my previous meetings with his father.

Yet Hamza has been a fascinating character in my eyes. I know he has been involved with various Al Qaeda activities in Pakistan's tribal regions. In particular, I had heard he was hiding out for a while in the increasingly dangerous territory of Waziristan, in the northwest part of Pakistan near the Afghanistan border. I imagine that if this were true, it had caused his father no small amount of concern. In fact, I had been very surprised to see Hamza at the compound in Abbottabad during our previous meetings, and now I find myself wishing I had made more of an effort to talk with him, one-on-one.

A sudden foreboding washes over me, along with a feeling of deep sadness. I cannot quite explain it.

"Hamza is not with us," Khalid finally answers, a little cryptically. I wait for him to say more but he only looks towards his father, who has been mostly silent up until now.

"Thank you for asking after his welfare," the Sheik says, after a few moments. "I will convey your good wishes to Hamza, who has remained behind at the compound in Abbottabad, against my wishes. I would rather he be close to me at all times."

"May I ask why you have come to this safe house?" I venture.

The Sheik says, "It is not a permanent situation. I just felt it would be best. That is all I want to say about this now, if you please."

And that's that. The subject of the safe house is closed.

The change in bin Laden's facial expression reflects his concern about Hamza. I get the feeling that he wants to talk some more about his absent son, however, so perhaps I can acquire some answers about Hamza from his father.

"Up until the time I met him at the compound in Abbottabad," I say, "I had assumed that Hamza, after his release from house arrest, was in hiding at one of Al Qaeda's supposedly secret camps in Waziristan, in the middle of Pakistan's tribal area. Of late, however, I would imagine that the CIA's stepped-up drone campaign and missile strikes have rendered those locations safe no longer."

The Sheik confirms that assessment, saying, "I am grateful that Hamza left, and I am working toward getting most of our lieutenants and other personnel away from the Waziristan area as well, because of the effectiveness of the American drone strikes there. I have prayed about all of these decisions. I recently sent a messenger back to the region, but it will take several weeks before he returns with an answer. The tribal areas are no longer safe. Hamza is back, but my lieutenants and other Al Qaeda members need to get out of Waziristan as well. But I do not know how long Hamza will be with me in Abbottabad. He is talking of going back to Waziristan, and that is the last thing I want him to do." He looks truly worried now.

"I will pray for your son's safety, no matter where he goes."

"I have asked that Hamza's fellows relocate to the Kunar Province in Afghanistan. And I would hope that this is where Hamza will go too. I think it will be much safer."

"Isn't that the area you were hiding in following the Battle of Tora Bora?"

"Yes, the high mountains and very dense tree cover of the Kunar area can easily hide my son and my lieutenants. It is a place where America's eyes in the sky will not be able to find them."

"As you know, I too have a son, and even though he is grown, with children of his own, I still worry about him. Also, I traveled through the tribal areas of Balochistan, Waziristan, and North to the Chinese border about a year ago. It is a difficult trip. It was unsafe then, but with the significant increase in drone attacks, remaining there can be suicide. I can see you are worried for your Hamza if he goes back there. But I pray it will all work out for the best."

The Sheik regards me for a moment without exactly smiling, but there is something approaching kindness in his eyes. Then he leans back against a large boulder, with his feet outstretched and his head down. I turn to study him, noticing that his freshly trimmed beard is even shorter than it had been at our previous meetings. I think again about how different he looks in person, compared to photos and videos that I had seen of him, with his beard extending over his simple tan *shalwar*. Looking at him now, in the natural sunlight, it appears that he must have recently dyed his beard, because it and his sideburns and temples no longer show the silver-gray that I had seen before.

It all makes sense to me, when I think about it. Bin Laden knows that a huge part of Al Qaeda's success is due to how it is presented in all forms of media. And since he is Al Qaeda's front man, public perception of him as a leader is particularly important. Hence he is always looking to improve his public image. Contrary to what I might have once assumed, trimming and dyeing his beard is not an attempt to disguise himself and evade capture; rather, it is an effective means to avoid projecting the image of himself as an aging leader of a terrorist group that is quickly being dispatched.

Raising his head and looking at me, he asks, "Doctor, I have knowledge of your efforts in Egypt, Syria, Jordan, Iraq, Pakistan, and many other countries worldwide. We have talked about some of these things before, but I never took the chance to ask you whether you contributed to efforts during the massive flooding that took place in Pakistan this past year."

Grateful to get away from more worrisome – for bin Laden – personal topics for a while, I respond, telling him that I, along with our medical team, traveled with considerable difficulty throughout the Indus Valley last year, following the flooding that had occurred there. More than twenty million Pakistani had been displaced. The Indus Valley had been decimated. Roads were washed away and transportation was very difficult. The roads that were passable were filled with caravans of lorries trying to bring in supplies, but their unbroken lines blocked the roads and made evacuation impossible.

The Sheik says, "Do you know that I released a tape that appeared on Al Jazzier and other websites criticizing the Pakistani government's slow response to this catastrophic event?" I nod, telling him I can understand the criticism.

"These people were farmers and small ranchers who lived off the land," bin Laden says angrily. "They were subsistence farmers, the poorest of the poor, and not only was the Pakistani government's response slow and inadequate, but the other countries throughout the world showed little or no interest in helping."

I know that he is right; there was minimal media coverage of the massive flooding that displaced so many millions of Pakistanis, and most people I spoke with knew nothing about it. There were a number of much smaller, though still catastrophic, events during the same year, and the world's response to those was overwhelming compared to the meager help that the Pakistani people received. I have to agree with bin Laden on this matter.

Now I am really warming up to the subject. "I visited the tent camps that lacked electricity and sanitation facilities. The only water these people had was brought by tanker trucks, and it was questionable whether it was even safe to drink. I have photographs showing how the money was spent for beautiful banners that were posted in the tent camps saying 'U.S.A. – Aid Center,' but when I visited there were no medications, no doctors, no nurses, and no real aid to speak of. Only an expensive, brightly colored banner in each of the camps. Propaganda? Yes. Aid? No. But since there was little or no television coverage of this catastrophic event, their banners went unseen and the propaganda effect was minimal."

Bin Laden seems somehow pleased that I agree with his assessment, but he still wants clearer validation of his complaints. "So, I was right in my statement about the Pakistani government's slow and inadequate response to this massive disaster?"

I feel the need to be careful in what I say now in response. "You know that I do not support the activities in which you and Al Qaeda have engaged, and those you have encouraged, over the past two decades. I never have supported those activities and I never will. I have to make that very clear. But I do commend you for speaking out in support of the flood victims."

I tell him how I spoke on American radio and tried to raise money to support the efforts of the doctors following this flood. "To my continual frustration, people told me that they were afraid to donate because the American government is monitoring all donations going to Pakistan. They were paranoid that the money would be passed through to you and Al Qaeda. And so there are millions of dollars in U.S. funds that have been placed on hold, left sitting in bank accounts in the U.S. and abroad, unavailable for use in legitimate humanitarian projects.

"I even spent six months working with several members of the Texas Congress to fly supplies in to the flood victims. It looked as if it was going to be possible, but then it ended suddenly, without any aid being transferred. Even so, working with my friend Hashmat Effendi and her charitable organization, five containers of supplies managed to arrive in Pakistan. Hashmat stayed almost six months to see that these supplies got to the people."

Bin Laden nods in approval as I continue, "That is another problem with American and U.N. sponsored programs. Without boots on the ground, supplies end up on the black market where they serve only to further enrich the corrupt, rather than getting to the needy victims of the catastrophe for whom they are intended. This is not limited to Pakistan. I have seen this worldwide. So much aid and so little help."

Khalid, who has been listening intensely to the conversation, gets up and walks over to the stream, splashing cold water on his face and wetting his scarf. He gently wrings it out over his head, then places the scarf back around his neck. As he sits down, he says, "Your response to all of this must have been discouragement and frustration."

"That's true," I respond. "But if you believe in what you are doing, you have to hold to the belief that there is always a way. The plain fact is that military assistance in a catastrophic event like this is a necessity. Everywhere I went in the region, I saw that anger toward the military was already high in Pakistan, and their failure to effectively participate in the aid efforts just made it worse. Criticism of the army, which is generally unthinkable in Pakistan, came from all quarters due to its lack of response. The anger – and the criticism – were ramped up in the days following the flood. The public directed their anger at General Ashfaq Parvez Kayani, and he was losing support both from the Pakistani citizenry and from those within the military. His reputation, and that of the military as the country's support structure, had been shattered. Even so, it seemed unlikely that Asif Ali Zardari's civilian government would remove General Kayani in response."

Bin Laden and Khalid both nod their heads in agreement. At this point, I feel it is an opportune time to press on some of the questions I have. "Help me understand more about Al Qaeda? Am I correct in my assumption that it is at least two decades old?"

Khalid is first to respond, saying, "My father conceived the idea of Al Qaeda while he was fighting the Soviets in Afghanistan. In 1988, when he was in Peshawar, Al Qaeda was conceived and became a reality."

Bin Laden, who has been listening intently to his son's reply, crosses his legs underneath him and strokes his beard in thought. And then with outstretched arms, hands open and palms pointing towards the heavens as if he is delivering a sermon, he says, "I created Al Qaeda in response to a conspiracy by the West, the Jews, and their allies, to destroy the Muslim world and Holy Islam. This conspiracy is led not by you and the people of the United States, Doctor, but by your political leaders. The leaders you have elected have declared war on Islam, and there is now a need for Islamic revenge on the West.

"Under the supervision of the United States, puppet governments that they work with collaborate and attack us on a daily basis. The West and the Jews prevent our people from establishing the Islamic Sharia, by using violence and lies.

The United States and these governments have surrendered to the Jews and handed them most of Palestine. They have acknowledged the existence of the Jewish State, while ignoring the dismembered limbs of my own people. Allah places an obligation upon us, on Al Qaeda, to take the necessary steps to free the *Ummah* and to make Sharia the supreme law of the land. Our fight against these governments and their leaders is separate from and not directed against you or the peoples of the West."

As he makes this statement, his eyes are closed and his head is turned toward the heavens. By now I have become accustomed to his histrionics, but once again I can't help thinking that his outlook is quite delusional, albeit somewhat inspirational, and unrealistically hopeful, considering Al Qaeda's current state of disarray.

Surprisingly (and probably foolishly), I am not intimidated by the intensity of bin Laden's statement, and I counter with a rather bold statement of my own. "Mustafa Abu Al-Yazid was recently killed by an American missile in a drone attack near the city of Miran Shah in Waziristan. If I'm not mistaken, he was Al Qaeda's main fundraiser and recruiter, and played a role in your internal security.

"You have also lost eight or more of your lieutenants to missile strikes, including your Chief of Operations in Pakistan, as well as several of your technical and weapons experts. I can truly understand why you have feared for your son Hamza and your men. Your leadership and infrastructure have been hammered by the drones. I too would be moving what was left of my followers from the Northern Waziristan tribal areas immediately."

With his arm outstretched, fists closed, and a long, thin finger pointing at me in a very un-Islamic gesture, the Sheik declares, "There are spies in the tribal areas who are working with the American CIA, providing them with the information they need for the drone-missile attack. They do this for money." This last statement, he spits out, sneering, as if the very words leave a bitter taste in his mouth.

I figure I've gotten this far without becoming the target of his rage, so I continue with a theme we have touched on before. "These are your people. Muslims, who as you say are doing this for money, but I also feel they are tired of the battles and the bloodshed, and want to return peace to their homeland."

"They are not true believers when they bring death to a brother Muslim. They have formed a counter-intelligence unit to locate the spies among us throughout the tribal area who are providing this information to the American CIA, if Allah wills it."

Once again it hits me that he doesn't see the incongruity in his own words and actions. And despite the very real chance that challenging him might incite his rage, I decide to press even harder, perhaps hoping to give him sufficient pause to reconsider his goals.

"I know we have discussed some of this before in our previous meetings. But I took an oath to cure my fellow man and to do no harm. For thirty-five years of my life, I have invested in mission trips worldwide to remove the barriers between people and to erase the obstacles of misunderstanding. And that is why I sit here with you, to put these words into action and try to make changes for everyone's good.

"I really would like to change things and make a real difference. You pinpoint flaws in my society and yours, yet you don't mind entering into battles, real and imaginary, that can tear both societies down, rather than improve them. To me, your real objective begins to appear very hazy. Forgive me, Sheik, and I mean no disrespect, but you have no loyalties to any values except your own, which you portray as being those of the Almighty Allah. Exactly what you wish to achieve remains unclear to me, even after all of our many hours of conversation."

As I speak, Khalid is looking out across the mountains, thinking he sees movement. He gets our attention by tossing a small pebble between us, then places his finger to his lips and points toward the movement with his other hand. He slowly rises to a standing position behind the boulder that he had been leaning against. He focuses his gaze, and though the sun is now directly in his eyes, he indicates to us that he sees someone.

And then we see them too: a couple of figures several hundred yards away, slowly moving towards us, along the narrow mountain path. The figures advance, occasionally taking brief pauses, and in the reflected sunlight, we can see that they are armed. For a minute, I can only stare, spellbound, at their steady approach. I feel my panic growing, and a cold sweat forms on my brow. Climbing up the sheer cliffs behind us would be impossible. At this moment, I regret the Sheik's insistence that we bring no weapons with us on this outing.

We are all looking over the edge of the boulder, searching along the long narrow path for more signs of the intruders, but they seem to have disappeared. This doesn't comfort me in the least. To make matters worse, even the cries of the occasional bird have been stilled, and we are surrounded by utter silence, increasing the foreboding I feel.

I hear Khalid whisper something, but cannot catch his words. He crawls to the other side of the clearing, stands up quickly, and peers out from between two large boulders. At this point, my body is shaking and my heart is pounding painfully in my chest. Khalid signals us to look down on the path. He holds up two fingers and gestures that he has seen the men again and they have weapons slung across their shoulders. We can now clearly see two armed men advancing along the path toward our position, and I find myself wondering again if I am in the wrong place at the wrong time. I close my eyes for a second, more an extended blink than anything else, and see the face of my wife.

When I open my eyes and look down the path, I notice something strange. The two men making their way up the narrow mountain path are making no attempt to hide their presence. They stay on the trail and are exposed along the approach to the clearing. As they come closer, it becomes obvious that they are armed, but their weapons are slung casually over their shoulders, rather than at the ready. Their faces are not discernible, but because they move so casually and openly, they do not appear to be a threatening force. Perhaps they do not know of our presence in the clearing. If they are hostile, we might be able to surprise and overpower them.

I peer out from behind the boulder to where Khalid is crouched, studying the movement of the two men ascending the trail. None of us dares to step out from our hiding place. However, the fact remains that the only way out of this clearing is down the path in front of us, from which two men, armed with automatic weapons, are steadily approaching. All this time, bin Laden sits quietly, saying nothing. I can only imagine what he is thinking. Suddenly, Khalid jumps to his feet, cups his hands and hollers down the path, "Ibrahim! We are up here. Abrar! We are sitting in the clearing next to the stream."

I recognize the names as soon as Khalid calls out to them, and the relief I feel is indescribable. The two men whom we had feared to be potential attackers are bin Laden's bodyguards, whom I'd been wishing had accompanied us in the first place.

"I've learned," I say, smiling as relief continues to flood my senses, "that you really can't shake your bodyguards, no matter how hard you try."

At this, bin Laden smiles, rises, and peers out over the trail, watching the two men carefully make the climb upward toward us. He waves to Ibrahim and Abrar, and they wave back. This seems to encourage them, and they begin to move more quickly at the sight of bin Laden and Khalid and me. In a few minutes, they reach the clearing and Ibrahim gives the Sheik a big hug and kiss on each cheek. He steps back a few feet, looks up at the Sheik, and says, "It was getting late in the day and we began to worry about you. We were already worried that you had left the house and refused to take any weapons with you."

Smiling at the two, the Sheik says, "We climbed the mountain to escape all the good and bad, and to come closer to our God. We are here to reaffirm our faith and honor Allah. Here on this mountain, we are closer to God and His Messenger, who have called out to all of us, that you should live a life of self-respect in this world and victory in the next. Our lives should be one of jihad for the sake of God Almighty.

"For the non-believers, God will punish them at your hands. He will disgrace them. He will help you conquer them. He will shield the believers and put love in their hearts. Those who obey Him will be proud and those who disobey Him will be humbled. You have climbed this mountain and followed the path to His guidance. Partake of the cool water that He has provided for us, rest a minute, then join us in prayer before we descend God's mountain."

Ibrahim and Abrar step to the edge of the stream of water, and Ibrahim kneels and plunges his face into the cool, fast-moving glacial stream, letting it run over his head and into his mouth and exclaiming joyfully, "It is so cold and refreshing!" Abrar is more conservative, kneeling along the edge of the stream and meticulously washing his hands, then cupping them to collect the water and bringing it to his lips. Ibrahim and Abrar then join us, leaning up against the same large boulders and crossing their legs underneath them.

After allowing his bodyguards a brief rest, bin Laden says it is time for us to return to the compound, as the day is ending, and it is best that he not be out and about during the evening when many people are about. We begin our descent from the clearing, returning along the same path we had taken this morning. Like this morning, we walk mostly in silence, but despite the relief I feel at the passing of what appeared to be imminent danger, I am filled with an even deeper worry.

I have seen the mind of a zealot who is bent upon destroying all those who do not share his beliefs or even his zeal, and I have learned that he does indeed have the capability of wreaking widespread destruction, all in the name of his God. I might not be able to stop the movement, or even the man himself, but I know now, without any doubt, that I have to try whatever I am capable of doing, even if my only means of doing so is sharing his story, his delusion, and his terrible plans.

Beginning of the End

ife goes on after my "meeting on the mountain" with Osama bin Laden. The overwhelming feeling of sadness that washed over me momentarily while I was up on the mountain has not returned to me with full force, yet there is an undercurrent of melancholy that wasn't there before, as well as a growing sense of anxiety. I try to push both aside and for the most part am successful – at least during the day – for as always, the workdays are long and my patients and colleagues take up most of my time and attention. But the late nights and early mornings, when I am finally alone with my thoughts and emotions, can sometimes be a challenge.

I have come to almost dread those fragile hours just before daybreak, when there are no work distractions to compete with the worries that swim below the surface.

It is not simply my unease about Osama bin Laden that disrupts my rest. I have become steadily more worried about Pakistan. After all, I have come to love this country and its people, having cared for so many Pakistani children and women – and men as well – for several years. And yet, having met twenty-four of the most powerful warlords, as well as political leaders and military police, and, of course, having spoken with bin Laden, I am rapidly reaching the conclusion that the Islamic Republic of Pakistan is presently at a tipping point. Will it emerge as a semi-peaceful nation or a conflagration of multiple, endless civil wars? I've kept coming here, thinking I could do some good in the region, and I know that I have in terms of medical care and the trust that has been established and the attitude changes I have seen towards myself and America in general. These changes have been clearly visible where the man in the street is concerned – and even in the tribal areas – but little has changed among the radical Muslims and the attitude of the central government in Islamabad. It's a bleak picture, and I wish I knew the answer, but another year or so should tell.

What seems clear to me is that Pakistan is as close to being a failed country as it has ever been. And what makes the situation really scary is that this country, teetering on a knife's edge of stability, is in possession of nuclear weapons.

These are the thoughts that continue to haunt me.

* * * * *

After four meetings with bin Laden, I continue to mull over the conversations in my head. It is impossible, really, to gauge either the short-term or long-term results of these interchanges. I can only go by the signs that Osama has been willing to give me. As far as I am concerned, the interviews have gone quite well for the most part. The schedule for our meetings has been very erratic, of course, but that's the way the Sheik has wanted it. I have known from the beginning that if I were going to even be granted the interviews – say nothing of obtain any useful information – I would have to follow his instructions to the letter.

Now it has been weeks since our last meeting. I've heard whispers that the Sheik is back in his compound in Abbottabad but have heard nothing directly from any of his people, and I wonder if – and when – we will ever get to meet again. Something about that meeting on the mountain had seemed so final, but perhaps it was just the extraordinary outdoor setting that made everything seem more dramatic. In any case, not hearing any word directly from the bin Laden camp for such an extended period has added to my general sense of anxiety.

Finally word does come, and I am given detailed instructions on how to proceed for the next meeting. I am instructed to arrive at the market in Abbottabad after sundown, where I will be taken to the meeting, without my bodyguards, of course. I am told I will be eating dinner with the Sheik and at least one of his sons. And so, per the Sheik's instructions, Mohammed takes me into the market and then makes his way through the roundabout that is north of the general bus stand. Saleem and Sultan are not with us tonight. From the bus stop, Mohammed proceeds along the west fork to Jinnah Road and into the bazaar. We make several stops in the bazaar, behaving as if we are casual shoppers, just like everyone else. We then continue past the military quarters and proceed to the mall. It is dinnertime, and the hectic evening traffic has dissipated. Some of the shops in the bazaar have already closed. From there, we drive on to an Internet café that is located in a relatively quiet area.

I tell Mohammed to return to the café around midnight, and to wait there for me. I have no idea what time I will actually be getting back, but I want to be sure that he will be waiting for me, regardless of the time. As he has been every time I have instructed him to leave me, Mohammed is extremely hesitant. But I assure him that I will be just fine, though inwardly I am far from certain about this.

I watch as his taillights disappear into the foggy dark evening, only to see a set of headlights reappear a minute later. It is Mohammed, making a circle and checking on me. This will not do! I wave him off, and once I'm certain that he has actually left, I walk to the door of the café and look inside. There is only one patron, who is intently working at a computer, and the proprietor, sitting behind the desk sipping tea. Neither raises his head nor pays much attention to my presence. That is good.

The sign on the door reads, "Twenty rupees per hour for Internet access." That's about twenty cents an hour U.S. What a bargain! Then again, my new handmade-to-order sandals cost only two dollars, and my very plain beige *shalwar kameez* was only two dollars. After a few minutes of trying to decide whether to go inside, I decide against it and begin pacing through shops up and back along Jinnah Road. The only lights are unshielded light bulbs dangling from the ceilings in the shops. An occasional Moped zooms past, and I can hear a dog barking in the distance. I know I am being watched, but from where? And what mode of transportation will be coming? Perhaps I'll just be walking to the house tonight, accompanied by one of the Sheik's bodyguards.

It still amazes me that I have managed to catch up with Osama bin Laden at all, much less meet with him not once but several times. After all, the whole world has been looking for him, and he is right under everyone's nose here in Abbottabad, the largest city in the Hazara Territory. Following the Pepsi Cola trail didn't require high-tech equipment or expensive surveillance, just plain old detective work and patience. I still smile to myself as I remember the day that my guys and I were out driving and came upon those pallets of Pepsi next to the shop. Ultimately, it was the Pepsi trail, along with the trust we had established with the religious leaders and many others that we met along the way, that took us to Osama bin Laden.

So much for the hundreds of millions spent on electronic eavesdropping. I suppose it has its place in today's world, but there is still nothing like just talking to the people. The longer we stay in Abbottabad, the more people I meet who are aware that the Sheik is here, living in a palatial home only a few hundred yards from the National Military Academy. It is hard to believe that the I.S.I., Pakistan's version of the CIA, is unaware of his presence. It is the proverbial fox-guarding-the-henhouse scenario. Funding, resources, and information seem to pass in both directions without ever revealing anything worthwhile. The I.S.I. is without a doubt the biggest dog on the block where receiving funds and arms from the U.S. is concerned. Any time one of these groups fails to cooperate with the I.S.I.'s agenda, the I.S.I. causes them to disappear, and unlike the local authorities, they stay gone. But not Osama bin Laden. Oh, he disappears all right, but he does so in plain sight, with everyone around him pretending not to see him.

I begin walking back toward the Internet café when I hear the sound of a motorcycle approaching. It stops in front of the café just as I reach the doorway, and the driver motions for me to get on behind him. He looks around for only a few seconds, then takes off so quickly that the front wheel leaves the ground for a few seconds, causing my adrenalin levels to nearly go through the roof. He continues down Jinnah Road, traveling at a speed that leaves me uncomfortable... no, terrified, as we fly past several cafés and The Pine View Hotel. He turns onto Pine View Road, then backtracks on the main Bazaar Road. An old man is trying to cross the street, and I think for sure that we're going to hit him, but my driver hits the brakes and jumps the curb onto the sidewalk, going behind the startled old man, then coming back down onto the road behind him.

I am accustomed by now to wildly varying modes of transportation, as well as to the backtracking and crisscrossing of routes on the way to the meetings with bin Laden. I've certainly had my share of uneasy experiences en route to these meetings. But tonight is the most nerve-wracking so far, for this young man on his motorcycle seems to have a death wish. He works his way through the Sarafa Bazaar and then backtracks through the Gurdwara Bazaar, again crossing the main Bazaar Road. Coming to Masjid Road, he hits the brakes, throwing me violently against his back and causing our heads to collide. He says nothing, and doesn't even turn around to see if I'm okay.

He looks up and down the streets, and I think he might be waiting for a change of vehicles (I can only hope), but there are no other vehicles in sight. He then proceeds at a much slower pace, to my great relief, down a street lined with cinderblock stores and multi-storied homes of hand-made baked brick with wooden roofs. They are all surrounded by high walls capped with broken shards of glass and barbed wire. The homes are larger and further apart now, with most being two or three stories tall, painted in pastel colors. The streets are not lit and only a few of the homes have any visible illumination. I recognize the area, and know that we are very close to our destination. There will be no further backtracking, and my wild ride is over. Most important – and surprisingly – I have survived it. As we pull up to the gates, I pat the young man on the shoulder, and for the first time, he turns and faces me and I say, "You're a good driver."

"That's my job, but thank you."

I am met at the entrance by a young man who introduces himself as Mahmood, a friend of Sheik bin Laden. Mahmood searches me, though he seems mildly apologetic, almost embarrassed, to be going through this now. Of course I've been through this on multiple occasions, and with each visit the routine becomes less intrusive, so I stand calmly with arms outstretched. Once Mahmood is finished, he pats me on the back of each hand and motions for me to follow him.

I follow Mahmood inside, and we walk down a hallway and turn right into the large room. As usual, there is no furniture, and the floor is covered with oriental rugs, with several ornate pillows stacked in the far corner. Mahmood and

I exchange pleasantries, and I learn that he has studied in England, which explains why his accent is tinged with the cadences of Northern London. He invites me to sit as he scurries across the room and brings one of the large embroidered pillows for my back.

Without my prompting him, Mahmood says he is very lucky to have someone like the Sheik as his friend and sponsor. He describes Osama as the most intelligent man he has ever met, and tells me how impressed he is that such a wealthy person gave up everything for his belief in Islamic causes, even risking his life to go fight in Afghanistan. His adulation of the Sheik is obvious as he explains much of what I already know about how Sheik bin Laden's role in the war against the Soviet occupation of Afghanistan has made him a hero throughout the Middle East.

He adds that bin Laden is violently opposed to the presence of U.S. troops in Saudi Arabia – troops that had arrived there in response to Saddam Hussein's 1990 invasion of Kuwait. "They should have left!" Mahmood says indignantly. "But I think it is important that people understand that the Sheik is not a revolutionary, but a reformer of all Islam and particularly the Saudi Rasheed."

I decide to push the issue, since he has brought it up. "Do you believe that the House of Saud, the family that has ruled Saudi Arabia for generations, are 'apostates' from Islam?" I have been aware of reports that the members of Al Saud have been struggling to "reclaim" Islam from what they see as abuses by radical Muslim groups such as Al Qaeda. Of course the extremists have a different perspective.

Mahmood has gotten himself a pillow, and seats himself across from me. He sits silent for a moment, contemplating what I've said.

"Apostasy is a grave charge to level against the Saudi royal family. The Saudi King and his family are the protectors of the two holiest places in Islam, Mecca and Medina. They are true traditional Sunni Islamists." He seems unwilling to say anything more.

Then I decide to shock him and say, "Abdullah Bin Aziz Al-sar, the King of Saudi Arabia, has been my patient. I operated on His Highness at the Methodist Hospital in the Texas Medical Center in Houston, Texas. I attended to him for six weeks after his surgery. I visited him every day in his hospital room, and we had long discussions regarding the political situation in the Middle East, as well as oil, religion, and the attitudes of East versus West."

Mahmood sits with his mouth open, his eyes wide, but says nothing. Then suddenly he jumps up and with an elaborate courtesy I've come to recognize as a defining characteristic of Middle Easterners, says, "Forgive me. You must be thirsty. Can I get you something?"

I respond that I would appreciate some tea.

No sooner have I spoken the words than Osama bin Laden

enters from the far side of the room. I rise from my seat and greet him, "*Asallam Aleikum*." As Mahmood rushes past him to get the tea, the Sheik places a hand on his shoulder and tells him to bring some dates and nuts as well when he returns.

Osama takes his time crossing the large room and sits directly across from me, propping up the pillows Mahmood just vacated. He must have been standing in the shadows of the doorway when I was talking to Mahmood, because the first thing he says to me once the tea and dates have arrived is, "You were surgeon to His Highness?"

"Yes, several years ago, he was my patient in Houston, Texas."

"Tell me what you thought about His Royal Majesty – the inner man."

"Just like the conversations you and I have shared, there are things that we have discussed that I consider a sacred part of the doctor-patient relationship, and will not discuss. There were other aspects of our conversation that were less personal, however, and did not fall within the realm of physician-patient privilege. Those, I am free to discuss."

"First, how did he select you as his physician, and Houston, Texas as his destination?"

"The House of Saud and its family members have been coming to the Methodist Hospital and the Texas Medical Center for their medical care for many years. I have written several medical books and many articles, and have operated and lectured in Egypt, Syria, Jordan, Turkey, and throughout the Muslim world. I actually asked His Highness the same question. He told me that several of my books had reached the medical libraries in Saudi Arabia, and been reviewed by his personal physician, who suggested to His Highness that he should come to Houston and consult with me."

"He came with his physician and others?"

"The King came in his private jet with his personal physician, his spiritual advisor, his personal secretary, several gentlemen who were in the oil and gas business and were planning on making contacts in Houston and in Dallas – and of course his personal bodyguards. There were some other family members as well, but I had little contact with them."

"Where did he stay?"

"We have special secure facilities within the hospital for our VIP patients. This includes a secure area and additional personnel for security when necessary. The Marriott Hotel, where the other members of his delegation stayed, is connected to the hospital by crosswalks."

"Everything went well?"

"Everything went extremely well, and we were both pleased with the outcome, but as I said, I will not discuss his medical care or treatment any further. I trust that you understand."

"I completely understand and respect your integrity and honesty. Now, I suspect you have some more questions for me?"

"Thank you, Sheik. I know we have discussed this before – at our first meeting – but since we have been talking about health, I continue to be amused by rumors in the American media regarding your own health."

Osama smiles as he responds, "Well, as you can see, I'm still in good physical condition, as I was when you first met me and inquired about my health, with no limitations of body or mind."

I muse, "Some of the information that we were receiving I found difficult to believe as a physician. For example, the rumors of dialysis equipment in the caves of Tora Bora in the mountains of Pakistan and Afghanistan. Even with the amount of money you have available, providing this type of medical care under those conditions would be impossible, and if the diagnosis that was rumored were true, you would have to be assumed to be dead some three years ago."

At this point, bin Laden's smile broadens and grows into laughter, just as Mahmood returns with a woven basket that contains fresh dried apricots, and another filled with pistachios and figs. Another young man comes out bearing tea. He places the service on the floor between us, and Mahmood does the same with the baskets of dried fruits. At that, bin Laden reaches out with his long arms and pushes the baskets closer to me, saying, "I know you like these." Then he smiles and adds, "But don't eat too many, because they are preparing a wonderful dinner for us, as usual."

"Sheik, when I mentioned the rumors in the media about your ill health and your supposed death, it is one of the few times I've seen you actually laughing."

Nodding, he responds, "After my not having made a public appearance or statement for many months, there were those who believed that they were not just rumors, but actual fact."

I reach down, place a date in my mouth, take a sip of the tea, and look directly at Sheik bin Laden, who is sitting there with a broad smile but not saying anything. And then I have an epiphany of sorts, and blurt out, "You fooled the world by leaking this information. It gave you time to make your plans and to travel from Afghanistan to Pakistan and establish a residence in Abbottabad, right under everyone's nose!"

He continues smiling. We make eye contact for a few seconds, then he picks up his cup and takes a sip of tea. He then reaches out, and I push the woven basket closer to him as he takes some of the apricots. Finally, he looks up at me and winks. About that moment several young men begin bringing in dishes of the hot food, placing them on the floor around us. There is a vegetable and yogurt salad, lentil stew (one of my favorites), and a dish of chicken and rice with red sauce that I know from previous experience will be very hot.

I wonder why I haven't seen any signs of Osama's sons, as I was promised that at least one of them would be joining us for dinner. And then as if on cue, his son Khalid, who had accompanied us on our mountain trek, comes in with a large bowl of rice pudding. This is a dish to which I have taken a ravenous liking, and which, to everyone's surprise (and on a few past occasions, to my hosts' chagrin), I sometimes eat with the main meal.

The others leave, including Mahmood, and the Sheik gestures for Khalid to sit down and join us. As I eat, I find that I am savoring every moment, all of my senses alert, as if this were a completely new experience for me. And once again, I find myself thinking, *Here I am, sitting with Osama bin Laden, and the entire world is looking for him.*

I was never really worried about my safety in the hospital or in the market. The attack on the Karakoram Highway left me shaken, of course, but both the emotional and physical scars from that experience are healing. But it suddenly occurs to me that I am truly in the hot seat right now. The uneasy feelings I have been fighting since the last meeting now threaten to come to the surface. *Should Osama be discovered here in Abbottabad, and I be found interviewing him, I am probably as good as dead.* If one of those stealth bombs is flown across the Afghan border into Pakistan to take out high-ranking terrorists, as the U.S. had been doing for the past year, it will be all over in seconds. Then again, they might prefer to keep bin Laden alive, but a long drawn-out trial in an international court of justice could take years, and would provide him with continued ongoing publicity for many years to come. I know my country well enough to know that this is the last thing they would want.

On the other hand, I muse, killing Osama bin Laden would require documenting his death for the world to see, but not allowing his body to fall into the hands of the Islamic extremists, who would entomb him as a martyr. This would be a monument to him and to his cause. I wonder if these circumstances have been considered carefully by those in Washington, D.C. who think they have all the answers although, interestingly enough, some of them have never visited this part of the world.

Well, I can't allow myself to think about these things now. I willfully return my focus to the meal that is set before me. I try some of the lentil stew, and it is absolutely delicious, easily my favorite so far. I decide to show proper manners and behave myself by not indulging in the rice pudding too quickly this time.

But even as I savor the meal, my thoughts return to matters at hand, most particularly the fact that I am here with the Sheik in Abbottabad. Truly, he could have been anywhere he chose. Had he shaved off his beard, had some plastic surgery, dressed in Western clothes like a businessman, and obtained the appropriate papers and passports, he could just as easily be in San Francisco, Houston, or even Washington, D.C., and no one would be the wiser.

What is stopping him from moving to Europe or the U.S.? As I see it, not a damned thing but his own choices. Departments of the U.S. government such as the CIA, and every other intelligence and military branch, have all been looking for him, and all of them have mistakenly assumed that he is somewhere in the mountains along the Afghan/Pakistani border, or in the northern tribal areas of Pakistan itself. Do they make these assumptions because those were his last reported whereabouts? It surely couldn't be that they have any actual evidence that places him there.

I know that my government has a standing offer of a twenty-five million-dollar reward for information as to Osama's location. When I first started on my quest, I did the same thing, albeit on a much smaller scale, and with a nonviolent end in mind. I remember how I tossed money around, looking for that individual who might know his whereabouts or be willing to provide me with information. At the same time, there have been many U.S. and Pakistani government agents doing the same thing, with a lot more cash than I ever had. The only difference between the governments' efforts and my own is that I am seen as a benefactor, someone who builds trust rather than fear.

Meanwhile the Pakistan Special Forces, with the aid of the United States government's military advisors, have been combing the mountains along the Pakistani/Afghan borders and looking into every cave, visiting villages and asking innumerable questions. They are handing out money and, in some cases, small arms or ammunition, in hopes of finding that one person who will lead them to Osama bin Laden. Yet nothing has turned up, as far as I know. In addition, every form of communication in and out of Afghanistan and Pakistan is being monitored by mega computer programs, in hopes of intercepting information that will ultimately lead to Osama. And all those billions of dollars spent have ultimately been wasted.

Osama, of course, is keenly aware of the scale of the efforts to locate and kill him. That is why he has restricted the number of people around him to several members of his family and some close lieutenants, all of whom have come with him to this location. These were people who have been with him for many years, and whose loyalty he could absolutely trust. In return, he has the funds to take special care of them. He reinforces their loyalty and desire to maintain his trust by providing them not only with necessities, but also in some cases, as the situation has permitted, with whatever luxuries his wealth could afford. The more I observe him, the more I realize how cleverly and completely he has utilized the people's loyalty and adoration to reinforce their faith in Allah – and by extension, in himself. He truly has set himself up in the people's eyes as a source of divine authority.

And yet, despite these precautions, Osama can never feel secure. There are only a few bodyguards at the home, and when I've visited, I've occasionally spotted one or two of them on the upper balconies, but never within the family quarters. In addition, all the photos I have seen of Osama bin Laden on American television and in the newspapers show him with an automatic weapon across his lap or at his side. When we've met, he has never been armed, nor have I ever seen any weapons in the room. Perhaps he has been trying to show me his best hospitality and make me feel at ease. It is working.

Not only is every intelligence agency worldwide hunting him, there are also many private bounty hunters doing the same, eager to earn that multimillion dollar reward, and dreaming of an instant, comfortable retirement, with all the luxuries that would come with it. Several of these bounty hunters have lost their lives in the attempt to collect the bounty. I, however, have been meeting with him for one reason and one reason only: to better understand this man and his goals.

Yet after many hours of conversation with him, I've discovered an even more important objective. As a physician, I have spent my years saving lives, essentially using a more conservative approach toward roughly the same goal he claims to want to achieve for his own people. Not the goal of annihilating perceived enemies, of course, but of providing a safe place where the people of the Muslim world can live happy lives, according to their own culture and beliefs. And in that sense the Sheik and I are at cross-purposes. I am not saying that the people of the region should turn the other cheek and continue to allow themselves to be dominated by outside forces with their own agendas. However, the approach that bin Laden has taken has united the world against him and his supporters, dooming the very people he would defend to inevitable defeat. And I find this enormously frustrating and heartbreaking.

The silence is broken when Osama's son Khalid says to me, "I know you and my father have probably spoken at length about this, but I would like to learn more about your work, if you don't mind answering some of the same questions again."

"Of course I don't mind," I reply. "I am always happy to talk about my work."

Khalid, encouraged, says, "What type of surgery do you do for our people?"

"I am a plastic and reconstructive surgeon. When I come to the Middle East, I operate mostly on children and young people like you. We have many patients with burns and burn contracture. There are also some with war injuries. This is an agricultural community, as you know, and there are many injuries that occur on the farm as well. There are many children that have birth defects such as cleft lip and cleft palate."

"I like medicine and it interests me. Tell me why they have cleft lips and palates."

"In the poor countries around the world, the women do not receive adequate prenatal care. Their diet is limited and prenatal multi-vitamins are not available to them. Also in many of these countries there is a lot of inter-marriage, and that increases the possibility of cleft lip and palate, among other birth defects. But it's not just the surgical procedures that make a difference. The lectures and teaching are even more important."

"No, doctor! It is what you do for the children that changes their lives!"

I shake my head. "Well, that's debatable. You're looking only at the short term. My team and I cannot all be here full time, and I am getting older. So it's very important that we educate the youngest surgeons and the interns and residents who will carry on this work. The only way they can continue is if I bring them to the operating room and teach them these procedures. In addition, I leave them with the equipment they will need to continue the work. By establishing clinics and teaching the local surgeons and the next generation of residents and interns, thousands more children will be treated, and the process will continue, when I am gone."

Osama nods appreciatively, then says, "But we can't underestimate what you are doing medically as well as emotionally for these children. You are returning their lives to them, and bringing their families back together. What I am doing is changing the spiritual attitude of the Muslim world. We are both doing the work of Allah."

In the interests of politeness and preserving the sanctity of the guest-host relationship, I don't want to come right out and contradict his statement. But it still makes me uncomfortable to be placed in the same category as one of the world's most wanted men. It is an "honor" I have never sought.

However, I recognize a good conversational window when it opens – and indeed, this is an opening for which I've been waiting. We have covered some of this ground before in previous conversations, but somehow I have never been completely satisfied with the results. Maybe this time I can reach Osama in a way I hadn't previously been able to do, or perhaps I can at least come away with a feeling that we have approached some new level of mutual understanding. I do not harbor any delusions that I can change his mind or his heart... but you never know until you try. I take the leap.

"Forgive me, Sheik, for bringing up some subjects we have touched on before, but I am still puzzled about some things. I've read the English version of the Qur'an several times, and it professes tolerance of other religions. The only exception to that tolerance is in how you interpret what is said to be the Prophet's last words, when he proclaimed that there should be only 'one religion on the Arabian Peninsula.' But even this is still open for interpretation. It does not mean that non-Muslims cannot walk the sand of Saudi Arabia. Nowhere in the text is it said that non-Muslims cannot enter the cities of Mecca and Medina. In fact, seeing the greatness of the mosques in Mecca and Medina is more likely to produce a convert than is threatening them. In other verses, the Qur'an states that other religions are to be understood, accepted, and tolerated. Lest we forget, both Christ and the prophet Mohammad originated as Jews."

At that, Khalid suddenly stops eating and looks from me to his father, and then back to me. His expression makes it clear that he has a bad feeling about the direction the discussion is taking.

Bin Laden looks up from his meal, contemplating his response. After spending some time with him, I've learned that he does not answer abruptly, and thinks through his statements before making them. I remain quiet, turning my head gently in his direction. As nonchalantly as possible, I partake of some of the delicious milk and rice pudding dessert.

After a moment, he speaks. "When things go wrong in this society, in ways and to degrees that can no longer be hidden, then there are those who must step forward and ask why and what needs to be done. What did we as Muslims do wrong? This has been debated with ever-increasing passion for the past several decades, culminating in the Russian invasion of Afghanistan. And you are right, in a sense it is still going on today.

"Is it an external problem foisted upon us by foreigners from abroad, or is it a domestic problem caused by minorities from within? Debates about what is wrong with society are nothing new, as you know. There are always those suggesting causes and others proposing remedies. Many have written on the subject, each offering – if I may be allowed to use a physician's frame of reference – a diagnosis of the flaws, and a prescription for the remedies, that they think should be adopted. Weaknesses have occurred in Islamic society in both the civilian sector and the state. Proposed reforms to deal with them have all failed. The basic fault was in straying from the old ways and losing sight of the original Islamic intent as put forth in the Qur'an. The remedy, of course, is to return to those ways. This diagnosis, and its prescription, are what I adhere to."

He again grows silent and contemplative, and with a smile, he pushes the plate of rice pudding closer to me, at which point we both partake of it. I glance towards Khalid, who seems, of course, young and inexperienced, and does not know what to make of this conversation. What I don't think he realizes, but that I see quite clearly, is that he is being given a lesson in leadership, religious fundamentals, and statesmanship.

Bin Laden continues, "In modern society, including most Muslim ones, the people are in a *Jahiliyyah*, a state of individual ignorance that existed in pre-Islamic Middle East societies. Then the Prophet Mohammed, blessed be He, provided us with the perfect revelation of the Qur'an."

"I cannot argue against the written word of the Qur'an," I respond. "Like other religious texts, it has produced significant changes on a local and worldwide level."

"No, Doctor. It is more than that. True Muslims must free themselves from *Jahil* (ignorant) society."

"But Sheik, you are professing that the only way to do that is by eliminating the non-believers?"

"I am saying the only way to achieve this is thru jihad."

"Yet in numerous places, the Qur'an states that jihad is to be used only in the defense against aggression." I try not to let my growing frustration get the better of me. We certainly have covered this ground before, and I think it is finally hitting me that I am no more likely to change his mind than he is to change mine. But I listen intently as he forms his next words.

"The only way to establish a worldwide Islamic order is through an offensive jihad aimed at the enemies of Islam," he says, his tone growing slightly more emphatic, and I detect a bit of impatience in his voice. "This would include Muslim societies such as the apostates in Saudi Arabia, who do not follow the Qur'an precepts, as well as the non-Islamic societies of the world. To question this argument is to refute the greatness of the Islamic way of life. It is a time for change in the Muslim world. We have discussed this before, you know."

"Yes, I know, but as I said, I am still trying to understand. What I see is a man who has embarked on a life devoted to a Holy War."

Then I decide to approach it from an angle we haven't covered before. "This vision you now project didn't just appear before you. Who do you see as the real inspiration for jihad?"

"My father. He was very insistent that one of his sons should fight against the enemies of Islam, so I am the one son who is acting according to the wishes of my father."

"Other than the wishes of your father, who do you feel had the greatest impact on your life?"

His son interrupts, saying, "We are followers of the writing of Sayyid Qutb."

Osama looks at him with a harsh expression upon his face, but I want to hear what the young man has to say, so I intercede on his behalf, saying, "Your father and I have discussed some of this, and I have read some of the writings of Sayyid Qutb and of Mohammed Azzam, but I'm not familiar with their life's history. Perhaps you can tell me something about each of these men's lives."

I turn and smile at bin Laden, and with a nod I turn my attention back toward his son. Osama's harsh expression is gone, and like any proud father, he smiles broadly and says to the young man, "Tell us what you have learned of Abdullah Yusuf Azzam and Sayyid Qutb."

The momentary tension borne of an elder's frustration with youthful impetuousness passes quickly, overwhelmed by a father's pride in his son's intelligence. I return to the task of devouring my dessert as the young man begins his dissertation.

"I know that Abdullah Azzam was born in a small village in the land that is referred to as Palestine in 1941. Assam was a theologian who studied at Damascus University. As a Palestinian, he had a passionate dislike for Israel and for the Jews, whom he blamed for usurping Palestinian territory to create their own county in 1948. Like my father, Azzam was a soldier .He fought Israel in the 1967 war and became a firm believer in the jihad. After the war, I believe he went to the University in Cairo and studied Sharia law, receiving a degree in Islamic jurisprudence. He was a well-educated man. I believe he had an opportunity to travel abroad and study under infidel teachers, but doing so was inconceivable to him, as he despised the Infidels who lived beyond the frontiers of Islamic civilization."

"Isn't that very narrow minded?" I asked. "I am one of those infidels. And in order to understand the world, you need to read and to travel if that's available to you, and as I have told your father, I have read the Qur'an several times, as well as the writings of the man we are now discussing."

Here, bin Laden speaks, saying, "The question you have voiced is centuries old. You are asking if it is permissible to imitate the infidels. The answer – according to Azzam, Qutb, and the high religious authorities – is that it is permissible to imitate the infidels in order more effectively fight against them.

"The *ulama* – the religious establishment – has been consulted on this question throughout the centuries, particularly about the lawfulness of copying Westernized reforms in the military, and more especially about studying in foreign schools under non-Muslim teachers and utilizing unapproved textbooks. The question came down to adopting or copying infidel devices. While this involved learning from infidel teachers, it has nonetheless become necessary. The question to be answered is why it is that in the past, the Muslim world was always able to catch up with the New World ideas and devices, and yet we are now no longer able to do so."

"But Sheik bin Laden, this extends beyond scientific advances and military tactics," I reply. "It extends to woman's rights and general reform on their behalf. In the Qur'an and the Book there is nothing that says a woman must be covered. There is also nothing that I am aware of that says women cannot go to school and become educated. In fact, only a few years ago there was a decree from the high counsel that women were entitled to a full education, with the only limitation being that classes for boys and girls should be kept separate. And, I know nothing in Sharia law that supports any man's right to throw acid upon the woman or carve up her face."

Once again I am going over topics that the Sheik and I have previously discussed, but I am doing this as much for the benefit of his son as to emphasize some points that I feel need more attention.

Osama's son quickly interjects, "Girls go to school."

"But in many areas, Khalid, once they reach the twelfth grade, their education ceases."

Here, the dutiful son obviously rushes to defend the practice. "That is because it is time for them to consider family and learn the ways of their mothers and grandmothers."

As has happened on other occasions, I sense my blood pressure rising, and my agitation shows in my response. "You are saying that a woman doesn't have the right to be a doctor, scientist, or lawyer, or to participate in the military, but she is allowed to strap a bomb on her body, walk into a crowded market, and blow herself up."

Oddly enough, Osama finds himself in the position of peacemaker, saying, "These are things beyond what we can correct here. We have gotten away from the subject we were pursuing: the lives of Mohammed Azzam and Sayyid Qutb."

His son resumes his commentary. "I know Abdullah Azzam participated, as did my father, in the jihad in Afghanistan. My father told me that Azzam later moved to Islamabad, where he taught at the University and preached that the jihad was absolutely necessary to restore the *Khalifa*. My father told me his motto was *'Jihad and the rifle alone; no negotiations, no conferences, and no dialog.'*

"It was in Afghanistan that he put this belief into practice, joining the Mujahadeen with my father in battles against the Soviets. The fight against the Soviets was an obligation for every Muslim male, and I wish I were old enough to have participated.

"Azzam believed that the jihad should continue until all Muslim countries were restored as a single Islamic Nation. Toward this goal, Azzam worked with my father and traveled the world to recruit men and money. In his preaching, my father would always say, 'Standing one hour in the battle line in the cause of Allah is better than sixty years of daily prayer.' My father told me Azzam even went to the United States to preach recruitment, and to raise millions of dollars for the jihad. He gave me a videotape of one of Azzam's speeches, and he was such a powerful speaker that I too could feel the need to become a holy warrior in the jihad."

I look at Osama, then turn toward his son and say, "You have taught him well. But from what you have said, if Islam is to reign supreme again, the countries of Spain, Burma, Yemen, Uzbekistan, the Philippines, Palestine, Somalia, Lebanon, Chad, and many others throughout the world need to be re-conquered. Not to mention that there are countries you do not consider to be Muslim enough, such as Egypt, Jordan, Turkey, and even Saudi Arabia, which will need to be converted. There is also Malaysia, with the world's largest Muslim population, but whose people are moderate in their attitudes and beliefs. I just don't see this happening."

"You will not see it. I will not see it, and most likely my son and his sons will not see it, but even if it takes a hundred years or two hundred years, the International Jihad Network that Azzam created will avail itself. Praise be to Allah."

Then he adds, "But again we are deviating from tonight's topics."

I know it is useless to press the point, so I turn back to his son. "Educate me. Tell me more about Sayyid Qutb and his philosophy as you have learned it, or as your father has passed it on to you."

Khalid says, "Sayyid's brother Mohammed was also a well-known Islamic scholar, but it was Sayyid who wrote the most important text for the jihadist movement. Sayyid Qutb was an Egyptian, influential with the jihadists' groups throughout Egypt. My father told me that Qutb also visited the United

States, and was so appalled by the permissiveness of its population that he returned to Egypt with an uncompromising hatred for the West. I am told that he did most of his writing while he spent some ten to twelve years in Gamal Abdel Nasser's prisons. Part of the reason for his imprisonment was because his writings deemed the Egyptian regime un-Islamic. To Qutb, the Egyptian hierarchy was *jahiliyya*. He felt that they created a society in which Islam was not being applied, and would therefore be considered *kufr* (infidel).

"Qutb believed that he was trying to establish the reign of God on Earth, and in so doing, he would eliminate the reign of man. My father told me that Qutd was executed for his beliefs, and that his writings became the basis for the militant Islamic movement. The Egyptian government thought that Qutb's execution would bring to an end to this struggle, but it only resulted in his being elevated to a martyr's status; and his writings became the Islamic movement's Bible."

I turn again to bin Laden, saying, "This is the same logic that you now apply to the Saudi regime. You are reading the Islamic book and selectively taking sections out of context to support your reasoning. Is it not true that the Prophet Mohammed himself said *"To insult a brother Muslim is sinful, to kill him is unbelief?"*"

Osama responds more quickly to this challenge, saying, "The Egyptian officials were infidels. And yes, I have applied this to the Saudi regime and others as well. The purpose of the jihad is to remove them with actions, not words. Qutb's blueprint for jihadist action is complicated. I have simplified it. Action rather than words is what speaks for us, and it seems to be working."

I repeat myself, trying again to drive home what I feel to be a critical point. "The Prophet Mohammed said it is sinful to attack or involve the innocents, that it is sinful to utilize women and children in the manner which you have, and rather than kill another Muslim, followers would do better by killing themselves. I am not a theologian, but this seems to be very straightforward. There doesn't seem to be any insistence upon being Muslim *enough*. Muslim equals Muslim. Whether you are ultra orthodox, orthodox, or conservative in your beliefs, you are still Muslim.

"Like you, I believe in the Ten Commandments, and one of the commandments is *Thou Shalt Not Kill*. On the other hand, I am also a believer in the justice of *An Eye for An Eye*. If you help me, then I will be more than happy to help you. If you profess harm to me or my family, I will kill you. I realize that this is a dichotomy of beliefs versus actions, but I have to profess that they both exist in my mind as well."

The dinner meal and main dessert had been removed some time ago, and tea and sweets are now being served. This is the time when a gracious guest says thank you and gets up and take his leave. I glance at my watch and realize that it is quite late. Before leaving, I express my thanks to the Sheik for the evening meal and the opportunity to meet again with Khalid and have him participate in our discussion. I tell the Sheik, "You have taught him well and he is very knowledgeable. I hope that he is given the opportunity to see both sides of the equation."

Bin Laden smiles, though not quite as warmly as before. "That he will learn for himself as he grows older. And I would like for us to meet again tomorrow night."

"My instructions for tomorrow night's meeting?"

"A courier will find you tomorrow and provide you with the information in the late afternoon. Perhaps you will need to purchase some fruit and vegetables at the market."

"I will be there."

The Sheik nods to Khalid, who also stands up and escorts me past the guest quarters, from which an armed guard suddenly appears and joins us as we continue across the open area from the main house to the portal in the outer wall. The bodyguard unlocks the gate, slides back two large steel bolts that run the length of the door, and then slowly peers through, into the darkness. He turns and nods towards us, indicating he is satisfied that it is all clear.

Khalid wishes me a safe journey to my destination, expressing his wishes that Allah should look over me. I push the heavy iron gate open so I can exit, and in the silence of the night the hinges seem to scream aloud as they creak under the weight. As soon as I step through the gates, I hear the metal bolts being drawn into place. A dog begins to bark, but is quickly quieted.

I begin to walk slowly away from the home in the direction of the National Military Academy, as planned, but my mind is elsewhere, thinking back on the conversation with the Sheik's son and the young man's indoctrination of radical Islamic idealism, as professed by Azzam's and Qutb's writings. I wish I had my penlight with me, but my agreement, as usual, was that I bring only my notebook and pen. The Sheik has always been very insistent about this, and I have abided by the rules as much for my safety as for that of the women and children that would also be in the household. As is my habit, I will stay up all night if necessary to transcribe my notes while the conversations are fresh in my memory.

As I walk, the only sound I hear is that of my sandals on the gravel. I am tired, and not in any hurry, when suddenly everything changes. There are helicopters flying very low overhead, and they are coming in directly over the house that I have just left. All of a sudden, I find myself drenched in a cold sweat, and I begin to shake. I freeze in my tracks, my eyes scanning the sky. I spot two helicopters.

There are countless unspoken questions fighting for attention in my mind, but I have only one simple but ominous answer: I know that this is not going to end well.

Takedown

There is a vendor's cart chained to the tree near where I am standing. I attempt to climb onto the cart so I can see better, but the full-length *shalwar kameez* that I am wearing hinders my climbing ability. I quickly roll up the bottom part and tuck it into the trousers, which allows me to sit sideways on the cart, swing my feet over and come to a standing position. I reach a lower limb of the tree and hoist myself up, moving from branch to branch until I climb onto a fork near the top of the tree, from which I can see into the courtyard of the bin Laden compound. One of the helicopters strikes the high outer wall of the compound, breaking off the tail rotor section, which crumples as it drops eight or ten feet to the ground. I can see men exiting the crashed Black Hawk and spreading out over the compound.

The second Black Hawk successfully lands in a field just off the road outside and behind the compound, and its occupants spill out to join the others. I hear the barking of dogs, but cannot determine whether the animals are with the troops that have just landed or are the same ones from neighboring homes that had barked at me earlier in the evening when I approached the compound. All of a sudden, I see, then hear, the flash of automatic weapons fire coming from the guesthouse that I had walked past just minutes ago. I assume it is coming from bin Laden's bodyguards. The gunfire is sporadic and short, and I don't hear any return fire, only a *pfft-pfft* sound like a motorbike engine that refuses to start. Then it occurs to me that the invaders' weapons must be fitted with flash suppressors and silencers.

Next I hear the muffled sound of an explosive device, and assume that the attackers have either blown the reinforced main house entrance door or blasted a hole in the wall. Lights suddenly go on in the second floor of the residences across from the bin Laden compound. Everything seems to be happening very quickly, and I find myself transfixed by what is happening. I keep thinking that only a few minutes ago, I too was in the compound. What if I had still been inside? On my trips to Pakistan, I figure that I have already used up my nine lives.

After a few surreal moments, I realize that I am gripping the branch of the tree so hard that my fingers have begun to cramp. I slowly straighten up, then lower myself into the crotch of the two main branches as if sitting in a saddle, and I lean forward, resting my chest against the limb in front of me. Finally, I can relax my grip and let the circulation return to my fingers. I am unhurt and – I hope – not visible to anyone. I feel reasonably safe, but I am visibly shaken.

About thirty minutes pass, and I am finally beginning to relax and catch my breath when an explosion occurs within the compound, followed by a ball of flame. I can see that the damaged helicopter has been detonated, but don't know whether it is a delayed response to its crashing or if it has been purposely detonated by the military team to prevent it falling into the hands of the Pakistanis or others. One thing I do know is that the commotion will certainly bring the local police and the local militia. For all I know, they may have already been summoned by the residents of the neighboring homes, all of which are now well lit. I have to get out of here now, to get as far away from this place as quickly as possible. As I begin descending the trunk of the tree to the wagon below, I see several helicopters lifting off. All I can think of is that it is a long walk back to where I am staying, if I can even find my way in the dark.

I am hoping and praying that Mohammed was not scared off by the commotion, and is still waiting for me in the vicinity of the military college. While I know that I need to be well away from the area before the local police or military arrive, I don't dare risk running. That would only attract unwanted attention to me, not to mention putting me at risk of tripping over one of the many potholes or falling into a roadside ditch. Instead, I walk at a pace that is brisk enough to cover some ground, but not so fast that I appear to be fleeing whatever happened back at the compound.

I wonder what did happen. Whatever it was, I know it can't be good, but I guess that depends on which side you're viewing it from. I suddenly realize that my *shalwar kameez* is still rolled up and tucked into my bloomer-like bottoms, and that if anyone sees me like this, it will be difficult to explain. I stop for a few seconds, catch my breath, and pulled the *shalwar kameez* out and roll it down to its normal position around my ankles.

Once I'm far enough away from the compound to not appear connected to it, I begin moving faster. In the distance, I can see what looks like the glow of a cigarette about 100 yards down the road, and I am desperately hoping that it is Mohammed. If so, he will flash the van's headlights, our usual signal. I wait a minute, but the signal doesn't come. I finally decide that I really have no choice but to continue moving in the same direction, hoping all the while that there isn't a policeman or militiaman or worse on the other end of that cigarette. As I continue walking, I finally spot the van at the side of the road, partially hidden by some trees. The driver's window is halfway down, and someone is smoking, causing the faint glow that I had seen from over 100 yards away. As I draw closer, I call out to Mohammed in a low voice, almost a whisper, and see the cigarette get flipped out the window onto the road. A hand appears in the window, emphatically beckoning me to come forward. I can't even begin to express the relief I feel when I see that it is indeed Mohammed.

His words come out in rapid staccato. "Helicopters. I saw them. I was very worried for you. I was afraid to turn the lights on in the van to signal you. I didn't know what was happening. I'm sorry. I know you don't like me to smoke in the van. But I was very nervous."

"Mohammed, I don't like you to smoke in the van or anywhere else, but I'm very happy that you did. When you drew on the cigarette, I could see the tip glow and that's how I knew how to find you. Let's get out of here. There are going to be a lot of police and local militia showing up pretty soon, and we don't want to be around when they do."

"You are right, doctor. I'm going to drive slowly because I don't want to turn the headlights on just yet. What happened?"

"We had just finished the interview, which was very productive. The Sheik's son Khalid joined us for dinner and the evening's discussions. I had just left the compound and heard the bodyguard slide the bolts across the entrance as I began walking to find you. I was tired and not in a great hurry, dragging my feet and thinking about the interview... when I saw the helicopters suddenly appear. I was scared and my adrenaline was pumping like crazy, but I had to know what was going on. I climbed into a wooden cart that was chained to a tree across from the compound, and from there, grabbed a low branch and climbed up into the tree. It was dark, but I had a good view into the compound.

"One of the helicopters crashed when the tail fin struck the outer wall. I don't think anyone was significantly hurt, because I could see men scrambling from the helicopter into the courtyard. Then another helicopter managed to land safely. There was some automatic weapons fire from the guesthouse, and I could see the flashes, but that was over almost as soon as it had started. I did not see or hear any gunfire from the ground, but I did hear some sounds that led me to believe they had silencers and flash suppressors on their weapons. About the time the gunfire in the guesthouse and second floor porch area ceased, there was a small, muffled explosion coming from the direction of the main house, and I assume that they blew the door or punched a hole in the wall. There was a lot of activity, but no further gunfire that I could detect. Then there was a large explosion near the compound wall."

Mohammed interrupts. "They probably blew the fallen helicopter so no one could utilize the electronic gear that it carried or retrieve any codes or secret information that was in it."

"That was exactly my feeling. It all happened so quickly, and when I looked up, the helicopters were already lifting off. I was afraid the local police and military would be cordoning off the area very soon, I just wanted out. You cannot imagine how happy I was when I saw you."

Even as I say this, my relief falls prey to my fear that Mohammed is about to get us both killed. "I don't know how you are driving on this miserable road without your headlights, Mohammed. You are making me nervous."

"Doctor, I'm driving very carefully, but I think we are far enough away that I can turn the headlights on." I feel a renewed sense of relief as he turns the headlights on and slows down. After a short distance, he turns off the main boulevard and continues slowly along side roads until we reach our destination.

Once we stop, Mohammed looks at me with a worried expression and says, "If they captured Osama bin Laden, it is not going to be safe around here for anyone, especially an American. There will be a lot of confusion for the next several hours, and I think that will give us the opportunity to leave. We will go north to Mansehra; that's about thirty kilometers away. The road to Mansehra is satisfactory. I slept earlier today, so I am not tired. I know you do not like the idea of driving at night, but I promise you I am very familiar with these roads, and we can connect with the Karakoram Highway before we reach Mansehra, and we will then cross the Pakhli plains. It is a farming district of rice and cornfields. There are no checkpoints along that section to worry about.

"We will pass thru the Saran River valley, continuing to climb through the pine belt near Badar. There we can find a secluded area in the pine forest where we can safely park and sleep in the van. As soon as the sun comes up, we will begin to move north again. We will be in the tribal area of the Northwest Frontier Province. We will be taking some of the same trails along the original Silk Route that Marco Polo traveled. It is beautiful country and we will be much safer traveling this route than taking the Karakoram Highway in daylight.

"Beyond Naran we will pass through the Kaghan Valley and then we will be crossing Babusar Pass. There will probably be field officers and checkpoints before entering the Pass, and again when we come to the city of Chilas.

"At Chilas will be turning east and then north along the curve of the Indus River. Chilas is located on a high plateau. There is a fort there, in which the police are stationed. You will show your papers and sign the book, and we may be able to find out some information about what took place tonight. There are also some teahouses in Chilas where we can get some breakfast, and one place that I know of that has satellite television. If it's working, that might be our best source of information. Right now, I'm going to ask that you pack and meet me at the van in ten minutes. I will awaken Sultan and Saleem and we will all be ready to leave. Remember: ten minutes."

I have a fleeting thought that I still have patients and commitments back at the medical center, but I know Mohammed is right. I cannot do any good for my patients or my colleagues if I am killed or captured. I must leave, and the sooner, the better. So I rush to my room and hastily throw my things into the pack, then gather up my camera equipment and carefully place it into its padded carrier. I am moving so quickly that I almost collide with Saleem as I pass through the doorway into the hall. The house is dark, and we move very quietly so as to not disturb any of the occupants, who are still asleep. I ask Saleem to write out a note, thanking our hosts for the hospitality. When he is finished, I attach it to it a small bundle of gifts for the children. I add a little note at the bottom, "You will understand after you see the news in the morning. We are returning to Islamabad. I will call you from there in a few days." I feel bad enough for leaving in the dead of night, and even worse about the misdirection in the note, but I know that for our own safety, I cannot let them know which direction we are actually taking.

Mohammed is already behind the wheel as we throw our clothing and equipment packs into the back of the van. He turns to us and says, "I am not putting on my headlights. Also I'm not starting the engine near the house, because if the noise awakens anyone, they will have questions that we cannot answer. The three of you can push me through the gates and onto the road."

I nod and respond, "That should be no problem for the three of us." Then, the physician part of me decides to add an altogether unnecessary warning. "Slowly. I don't want anyone to slip or get hurt."

Sultan, Saleem, and I return to the van, and with our backs up against the rear bumper, we began pushing with our feet. The van moves very easily on the flat surface of the courtyard, and it is only a few minutes until we have exited the gate and are on the road. We slide open the side door and jump in. Before we even have the door closed, Mohammed starts the engine and we are on our way north to Mansehra, about 30 kilometers away. Saleem is the first to speak "Tell us what you saw. Tell us what you think happened. What took place at the bin Laden compound tonight?"

Mohammed, of course, already knows the story but is eager to hear it again. And I am glad to tell it again, knowing that it is a story I will not be able to share with many other people any time soon.

"I had dinner with the Sheik, and his son Khalid joined us. Then we sat and sipped tea for several hours, discussing social and political philosophies, the Qur'an and jihad. His son participated in the discussion. It quickly became very apparent what the basis was for Khalid's philosophical and religious beliefs. The Sheik taught him well, as he taught his son Hamza."

"It was sometime after midnight; I think we had all lost track of the time. We were all tired when I stood up and thanked my host for the dinner and the discussion. I told Osama that I was particularly appreciative of having his son sit with us and discuss these topics, and that he was welcome to join us any time.

"Then I asked about our next meeting and the Sheik said he wanted to meet again tomorrow night. He said there would be a messenger who would locate me in the market and inform me of the details. I was then escorted by his son out of the main house, and past the guest quarters where the bodyguards were staying. A bodyguard opened the gate just enough for me to pass through, and I shook hands with Osama's son, thanked him, and slipped through the gate and proceeded to walk down the road.

"I was only a couple of minutes away when the dogs in the neighborhood started barking, and I looked up and saw the helicopters. One of the helicopters crash-landed when it struck the high outer wall of bin Laden's compound, but it did not explode. Only the tail section struck the wall and folded in on itself.

"I was stunned. I wasn't sure how to react. My curiosity got the best of me, and I wanted to see what was going on, but I didn't want to get too close to the action. I was afraid I could end up being a target."

Saleem interjects, "If it had been me, I would have run and run very fast."

"Actually, Saleem, that was the first thing that came to mind. But you know me better than that. I just had to know what was going on. Lights had already come on in several of the adjacent homes as a result of the noise when the helicopter crashed. That is when I saw the donkey cart chained to a tree and I thought I could climb up and have a better view. It was easy enough. Once I got on top of the donkey cart, I could reach the larger lower limbs and pull myself up in the tree, where I was hidden from sight but had a good view into the courtyard of bin Laden's compound.

"From my perch in the tree, I could easily see the helicopter that had just crashed. Shortly thereafter, it exploded. I felt it was purposely destroyed by the troops themselves, since it could not fly and they would not want to leave any high-tech gear and other information for others to find. There was gunfire from the bodyguards on the balcony and in the area of the guesthouse, but it only lasted a few seconds. I'm sure the bodyguards were no match for whoever was in those helicopters, whom I assume were Special Forces such as the Navy SEALs or Delta Force troops, equipped with night scopes and sniper rifles. It seemed like only minutes passed, and then the helicopters lifted off.

"It was only then that I realized that I better get the hell out of there as fast as I could, and that we needed to be gone from this area before the police and local military arrived. That's pretty much it. I'm sure when we arrive in Chilas in the morning we will be able to get more news."

We leave the main road at Mansehra City and continue north, albeit at a slower pace, toward the town of Balakot. We don't see or pass any other vehicles on this rough secondary road, and we are all happy about that. There are no other lights except our headlights, and I find myself thinking – as I often do in this part of the world – that driving this road at night is suicidal. About every fifteen or twenty kilometers we pass a small village of mud brick houses along curving alleyways. The alleyways open into courtyards planted with neat rows of trees, which I assume to be either the apricot or apple trees common to this area.

Between these small villages, the headlights play on great fields of wheat, sorghum, and of course poppy. We continue along this narrow section of road, kicking up dust as we go, which casts weird shadows in our headlights. We are still on the plateau within the tree line, but gradually climbing higher as we go. Still no oncoming traffic. Near Balakot, the road curves to run parallel to the Kunhar River. We pass a small building marked "Telephone Exchange," and then the police station, which is the only building with a light on inside. We continue north, passing a mosque, then cross over the Kunhar River Bridge from west to east. There are still no other vehicles on the road.

Our goal is to reach Naran Village in the upper Kaghan Valley regions, where we can rest. That is a good hour and a half or two hours away. We are passing through the Danna Meadows, where the road is hilly and twisting, adding to our discomfort about making this drive at night. There are no other vehicles on the road, and no challenges from police or military patrols. We pass through Balakot, where the road is more or less paved, but it becomes steeper as we climb into the mountains. There are areas where the road is not much more than a gravel jeep track, and Mohammed has to gear down along this stretch. I think he might be getting sleepy, and that worries me. He puts a disc into the player on the dash and begins singing along with it. I keep telling myself that it is not too much longer now, and we will pull off the road and get a few hours of sleep before continuing.

We have climbed more than a mile in altitude over these roads, and it has become a little chilly. Unfortunately, the van has no heater or air conditioning, so I wrap myself in one of the multi-colored quilts piled on the bench in the back of the van. It is early May, about a month before the beginning of the tourist season in this area, which is something of a summer resort for people who wish to escape the heat of Islamabad, Abbottabad, and Muzaffarabad. This lovely area also attracts hikers, trekkers, and photographers from all parts of the world. The tourist season is relatively short, and by late September or early October, most of the accommodations have closed for the very cold winter, and are boarded up against the heavy snows that invariably come through the area. By November, the roads are often impassable, and the village completely shuts down.

No matter what time of the year it is, there is always a chance of encountering snow as the road climbs higher and higher through the Himalayas. If a road is blocked by snow, there is no other way in or out except on a helicopter. Hopefully there will be no snow to block our passing.

It isn't long before we enter the southern end of the village of Naran. We pass several hotels, whose signs I can just barely read in the glare of our headlights: "Naran Hotel" and "New Park Hotel." A few hundred meters up the road is a mud brick building marked "Post Office," and we then come to a cross street on our left with a small mosque. There are very few lights on in any of the buildings. Many look as if they are still closed for the winter.

The last building in this cluster has a sign that says "Paradise Inn," but there are no lights on. We then come to a crossroad on our right that parallels a small stream. Mohammed says, "This takes us to Lake Saiful Muluk. It's only about a kilometer away. We should be able to find a place off the road where we can stop and sleep for several hours before returning to the main road in the morning. I'd like to get started as soon as the sun is up."

Saleem is wrapped in his blanket with his head resting against the side of the van, fast asleep, and hears none of this.

Sultan, barely more awake than Saleem, responds groggily, "I agree. We can get to Chilas in the early morning and find a place where we can wash and have something to eat."

I tell him, "You are familiar with this territory, and I'll go along with what you think is best. We all need some sleep."

It is only a few moments before we reach Lake Saiful Muluk, which sits amongst snow-capped mountains at about 3,200 meters (approximately 9,000 feet). Legend has it that in ancient times, Prince Saiful Muluk – a mortal – fell in love with a fairy who lived in the lake. The Prince married her, and now, according to legend, the lake is inhabited by a mirage of fairies. There is a forestry rest house adjacent to the lake, part of a national forest conservancy program, where we will be able to rest. Mohammed says there will probably be no one else around and we will have the place all to ourselves. He adds, "I am too big a man to sleep comfortably in this seat. I have been driving for a long time. I'm going to sleep on the porch."

When we reach the forestry house and park, Mohammed grabs his blanket from the shotgun seat, and I reach over and give him another from the back seat of the van. As he is leaving I say, "There are no lights."

Mohammed starts to laugh. "There is no electricity. But don't worry. In the morning, you will see that you are at the top of the world." He goes on to describe the snow-capped mountains, open fields, and flocks of birds that I will be able to see and enjoy – and photograph.

"When it is light," he continues, "we can take a walk across the Kunhar River from Naran. There is a small bridge, and if you are not in a hurry, it is only a short walk to Darseri Village on the shore opposite from Naran. Bring your cameras. There are some excellent views, and if you are awake when the sun comes up, your photos will capture some splendid scenery. Good night."

I slide the window back several inches, drinking in the fresh, cool air. I wrap myself in a blanket and stretch out across the bench in the rear of the mini-van, altogether exhausted, and fall immediately into a deep and surprisingly untroubled sleep. The next thing I know, the sun is coming through the window, announcing the arrival of morning. I glance through the window and see that Mohammed is already up, and is standing on the porch of the cabin, folding blankets. I don't see Sultan, and assume that he must be up as well, and is stretching his legs.

On the seat in front of me, Saleem is still asleep. I nudge him several times. I hate waking him, but we will need to be on our way soon. We are at least 160 to 180 kilometers from Abbottabad, but since we had gone all night without encountering other vehicles, and there were no police or military checkpoints along this section of the Karakoram Highway, I feel we are good to go. I'm anxious to get to the boarding house in Chilas, in hopes that their satellite television is working. Mohammed had said they can get programs from all over the world, including the U.S., when the TV is functioning.

We relocate the small armory of weapons, hand grenades, and flash bangs into a compartment in the floor of the van, and place the larger weapons under the seats. Then we place our bedrolls and personal items in front of the weapons, leaving them well concealed but still readily accessible should we need them. The pistols and extra ammunition we stick into the side pockets across from each of us.

The van packed, Sultan says, "Doctor, get your cameras and let's take a walk. It is a beautiful clear day. You will probably see women and children coming down to fetch water, and others starting to wash clothes along the rocks that border the river."

Despite the fact that I've only slept a few hours, I feel great, and welcome the idea of taking a leisurely – if necessarily brief – stroll amid this incredible scenery. The adrenaline and anxieties of last night's surprise have significantly subsided. And despite the fact that I might actually be fleeing for my life, at this moment I feel that life is good.

It occurs to me that almost no one comes here, particularly Americans. I'm getting to experience and photograph what few people, other than locals, have ever seen. Our walk takes us along the Kunhar River and across the bridge from Naran. We turn left and walk to the village of Darseri. As we approach, the smell of cooking fires reaches our nostrils, and as Sultan predicted, there are half a dozen children filling water jugs along the stream and carrying them back up the mountain, balanced on their heads. They are friendly and stop to look at the strangers, which gives me a few seconds to get a photo of them in their colorful tribal outfits. They are adorned with a myriad assortment of earrings and pierced nosepieces, and are quite a striking sight.

It is cool and there is a light breeze, which feels very good. I feel almost at home. My companions and I are dressed in fashion typical of the region, and other than my very obviously non-native language abilities, I blend in quite well. I have not shaved for several weeks now, which makes me look even more the native, rather than the Western outsider I am.

The events of last evening are at the far back corners of my mind as we walk along. There is simply too much beauty everywhere I look to even consider the events in Abbottabad or the greater world. Today, at this moment, I stand at the top of that world, drinking in sights that few people will ever get to see, except perhaps in photographs. My only real regret at this moment is that I cannot share this experience with Terry. I know that she would be as enthralled as I am. If only...

After the Takedown: Onward to Chilas

*T*he interlude at the glorious mountain resort provides only a brief respite. For a time I am spellbound, feeling as if I truly am perched at the top of the world, utterly removed from the mayhem at the compound in Abbottabad. I am able to get some amazing shots of the mountains and the "enchanted" lake. But the magic does not last. My looming anxiety, fueled by the need to know exactly what happened at bin Laden's compound, breaks the spell all too soon, and I know it is time to go. Mohammed, Sultan, Saleem, and I pile into the van and continue on our way to the boarding house in Chilas.

Mohammed drives slowly along the rock-strewn, pothole riddled road, which is easily the most dangerous road I have ever been on in all my world travels. He downshifts, and the van begrudgingly climbs upward, traversing the switchbacks. I look over my shoulder toward the far wall of the canyon and see a cluster of eight or nine ramshackle huts and barns, made of freely-available local stone which is cut and shaped at the lower elevations and carried up the steep trails by donkeys. Billows of white-gray smoke waft from several of the chimneys. When I open the side window of the van to photograph the scene, we can smell the faint aroma of cooking meat.

The canyon at this point is not particularly deep, opening into a broad valley with several armed tribal guards at the entrance. They are dressed in black from head to foot, their heads wrapped with black turbans, and their deep-set eyes are focused on our van and its occupants. Despite their threatening appearance, however, they remain at ease, with their Russian-made AK-47s slung leisurely on their shoulders. As usual, I am dressed in a *shalwar kameez*, with a locally made wool scarf resting on my shoulders. As we approach, I pull one end of the scarf up over my head and across my face, leaving only my eyes exposed. Mohammed rolls down his window and addresses the guards, "*Ashalaam Aleikum.*"

One of the guards answers, "*Wa Aleikum Asalaam,*" and nothing further is said. No questions asked. But their gaze remains fixed upon the van as it moves forward, and we pass the checkpoint and proceed into the valley below.

The valley floor is covered in wild grasses, with goats and sheep grazing contentedly. I peer through my telephoto lens at a villa complex in the distance. No one is outside. *Nothing of interest here*, I think. As I continue watching, a cool breeze suddenly gusts through the narrow canyon, blowing sand and dust in my face. You can actually hear the sand particles as they strike the windshield. We slowly plod along the valley floor, which is not much more than a trail created over untold centuries by the passage of donkeys and sheepherders. There are still large rocks present in the path, and Mohammed periodically has to zigzag around them.

In the distance, I spot a secondary trail that extends further into the mountains, winding along the high rocky rim, roughly a thousand feet to our right. Above this trail, the snow-covered peaks of the Himalayan Mountains rise majestically in a scene rarely viewed by Westerners, but well worthy of a postcard. Through my telescopic lens, I can see a group of men partially hidden along the far side of the canyon wall. There are no clouds in the sky, and the sun reflects off the peaks and glaciers that extend like long fingers into the valleys below. But there are other more ominous reflections as well – those of the gun barrels in the hands of the distant tribesmen.

There is another group of low-roofed huts, and I see a woman and two small children dressed in beautifully colorful tribal outfits. As the van approaches, they quickly move behind a high stone wall. There is also a man on the ridge behind us, but we can see no path or road that leads to his location, and we all find ourselves wondering how he got there. The one thing we are certain of is that he is closely observing the van's movements. He has a very long rifle slung over his shoulder, and even at this distance, looking through my telephoto lens, I can identify it as an old British Enfield, which is in itself worrisome. While the AK-47s that are so common here are deadly up close, the old British rifles are capable of reaching out and touching someone at far greater ranges. The man has his back to the village, and he continues to track our progress with binoculars. Each of us is thinking the same thing: *Should we be expecting something?*

I peer again through the telephoto lens at the far side of the ridge. With the blanket of white snow in the background, it is easy to spot another observer along the skyline who is also following our progress through binoculars. He is obviously not hiding. We figure that these men are only spotters, and since they are on the far side of the canyon, they don't present any threat to us... at least for the time being.

We haven't seen another vehicle on the road all day, but suddenly, as if out of nowhere, we see a cloud of dust that tells us a vehicle is coming toward us along the canyon trail, moving at a much faster clip than we are. A scan with my telephoto lens reveals it to be an old pickup truck, with several men standing in the rear hanging onto a rail behind the truck's cab. This might be trouble. The truck is coming up fast, and the men on the ridge above us continue to watch the movement of the van through their binoculars. I'm starting to get a little anxious, but everyone else seems calm and unconcerned. I instinctively reach down and run my hand over the M-4 rifle that is wedged between the driver's seat and my own. I again turn my tele-photo lens toward the oncoming truck, but it is gone. It has either stopped or turned onto a mountain road leading away from the canyon proper. The apparent threat removed, I begin to relax. Looking out the window over this desert wasteland I can't imagine how people could manage to live here.

"No wonder they are willing to die and go to Paradise," I say. "The next life has to be better than this one."

This being said, the conversation turns once again to a discussion of religion – actually, it's more of a friendly religious debate – when Mohammed blurts out, "All religion is bunk... mine, yours – everyone's. The whole religious house of cards is built on the supposition that man is a special animal. There is nothing special about man. We are cousins of the monkey, and I don't know any monkeys that worry about getting into Heaven or ending up in Hell."

Then, after a brief pause, he continues, "As you well know, I am a Muslim, but not a religious extremist or a terrorist in any sense of the word. The real problem as I see it is that we are all being placed into a mold and expected to look, speak, and act like everyone else. There are terrorist killers who plot murder

of the innocent, people like Osama bin Laden and his followers. They have perverted Islam and insulted the Prophet, as
well as everyone who believes. Even worse, they have betrayed
Allah."

Sultan jumps into the conversation. "To pervert the Holiest
of the Holy is a great crime."

Not wishing to be outdone, Mohammed responds, "These
terrorists are beyond paranoid. They are criminals. They are
psychopaths who kill thousands of innocent people, hoping
that one of them is guilty. They have killed thousands of people for publicity. They will kill you, believing that if you are
innocent, you'll end up in Paradise anyway, so murdering you
is not really a sin."

We've been over this conversational terrain before, of course,
but it helps to pass the time. And since it's a topic of endless
interest to me – because it is something that ultimately affects
all of us – I never have an objection to revisiting the issues.

Saleem comes up with an interesting comparison. "The
Islamic terrorists are the new Nazis." I think about this for a
while and acknowledge that even though the Nazi comparison
has been overused – and misused – countless times over the
years, this is one of those cases where it may be appropriate.

The conversation continues in the same vein as countless
other discussions we've had, eventually trailing off as we drift
off into our respective reveries. The ride is far from smooth,
and I once again find myself grumbling inwardly about the

rutty camel path that has been so egregiously misnamed the Karakoram "Highway." Some highway, I think to myself for the millionth time.

But this is not a matter worth fretting about for very long. It's a beautiful day, and there is wonder all around me. I've seen many amazing things in my travels, but have never beheld scenery or mountains quite like this. Despite my earlier grousing about the bleak desert wastelands, the mountains are stunningly beautiful. It is a land of contrasts, no doubt about it. I have three cameras with me in the front of the van, each with a different lens. I switch among the cameras, taking one picture after another in the lovely morning light. We are climbing again. The road twists ever higher until we are above the timberline; the trees are all gone, replaced by scrub bushes and scattered areas of grass and wildflowers. We are now traveling between a couple of foothills – well, they are considered foothills in this part of the world. However, with elevations ranging from 11,000 to 12,000 feet, they would be considered mountains by the people back home. From this vantage point we can see another open valley below.

We pass a scattering of several mud brick homes, and past these dwellings is a small white mosque standing alone. Then we see a barn and what appears to be an exercise yard for livestock, its grayish-brown dirt pounded down from the trampling of countless hooves. All of the buildings are constructed with wood beam roofs, covered with tin sheeting that reflects the sunlight.

Shortly thereafter, the mountains again begin their steep inclination to the sky, and the road becomes rougher. I have one camera hanging from a strap around my neck, and another sits on my lap. I really want to continue taking pictures, but I need to keep one hand on the front dash of the van as we bounce along from pothole to pothole.

We are the only vehicle in sight as we approach a desolate mountain village. Rough road or not, I still manage to take some photos as the village slides by. Who knows when, or if, I will ever pass this way again? I want to capture everything I possibly can. We make our way past the last roadside abutment and continue to climb. The van rocks back and forth over the winding and rutted gravel road, and the sharp wind smacks against the window as if trying to force its way inside. If the weather only stays like this through the next several weeks, I think, we will be just fine.

There are no living things at this altitude; it is a total dead zone. Our path is littered with gray and brown rocks, making driving a challenge. Fortunately Mohammed is up to the challenge, as always. To make things even more interesting, fast-moving small streams race down the side of the mountain from the melting glaciers, cutting across the road. These are dangerous areas, I realize, and a washout is always possible.

With the window open it is chilly, so I turn and ask Saleem to hand me my favorite, decades-old faded sweater. I button my shirt collar all the way to my neck and then pull the sweater over the shirt. It isn't long before I become lulled again by the almost hypnotic rocking of the van, and I settle far back into my seat, content to let my mind run where it may as I gaze upon the most fascinating landscape in the entire world. I don't know what the outcome of this trip will be, but I hope we are lucky enough to live through this. For now I am just going to concentrate on burning these striking visuals into my memory.

I slip off my sandals and enjoy the coolness of the metal floorboard against the soles of my feet. This portion of the trip, I think to myself, is obviously going to challenge me at every level – physically, mentally, emotionally... even spiritually. My thoughts drift towards the philosophical, and I find myself reviewing my life and everything that has brought me to this moment, and to this place.

Why live if one cannot fulfill one's desires? For me life is precious, and I want to enjoy every moment of it. I go, go, go because I know that one day it will all be over, and no matter how much money I have, or how fine is my home or anything else I own, it will all be gone for me when I breathe my last breath.

In truth, I realize, I have reached the point where I care little for the routine of my current life, apart from being with my wife, and experiencing the pleasure of working in the operating room, where I can still achieve results that will change people's lives. All things beyond that are just superficial trappings.

I think about wealth and what it means to me, as opposed to the meaning it has been given by the culture in which I grew up. I myself am not rich, but I am very comfortable. But money has never been my primary goal, and over the last thirty-five years I've given much more away than I have saved.

I was born into a comfortable home in Brooklyn, New York, the oldest of three brothers. Our home was not far from the old Ebbets Field, where the Brooklyn Dodgers used to play baseball. My father was a dentist and my mother a housewife who worked part time as a dental assistant in Dad's office. Unfortunately, when I was ten years old my father died. My mother was still very young and had no formal education. But she knew right from wrong, and even though dealing with three young boys was a handful, she managed.

After my father's death, Mom felt New York was not where she wanted to raise her three boys, and we really didn't have the income necessary to live within the city anyway. So we relocated to Asbury Park, a small seaside town on the Jersey Shore. We moved into a first-floor rental that consisted of nothing more than two small bedrooms, a kitchen, and a sitting area. Our only luxury was that the apartment did have its own bathroom and shower. The telephone was a party line, and if it rang once it was for us. If it rang twice it was for our neighbor on the second floor, and three rings meant the call was for those living in the attic apartment.

Life changed quickly for my brothers and me, and it took us at least a year to acclimate. I can only imagine how difficult it must have been for Mom, but she was wonderful, and seemed to understand our emotions perfectly. We lived a short distance from Sunset Lake and the much larger Deal Lake, where we could fish from the shore or the bridge on a sunny weekend afternoon. Sunset Park had a rambling path where we rode our bikes and met other children our age.

There was only one grammar school at the time, Bond Street School. Though it was co-ed, the genders were segregated to a great extent. The word "Boys" was chiseled into the stone above the north side entrance, and above the south side entrance was the word "Girls." The schoolyard itself was divided down the middle with a ten-foot-high chain-link fence, and during recess the boys and girls were separated. That didn't bother me a bit. Who was interested in girls at that age anyway? They weren't good for much of anything, and they talked too much. At recess we boys played stickball using an old broom handle, while the girls did whatever girls do on their side of the schoolyard. In the fall, however, everyone's attention in this small town turned to the high school football team.

By the age of eleven I was working; I suppose I was a natural-born capitalist. In the summer I cut lawns, painted houses and did odd jobs. I became the richest kid in school and the envy of many of my peers. I got good grades and had money in my pocket. A couple of years later, I was able to get my local working papers. The minimum age to acquire these papers legally was fourteen, but I was muscular and tall for my age, and I made a little "adjustment" on my birth certificate so I could get a regular job at a seaside resort along the Asbury Park ocean front. I worked a ten-hour day for 15 cents an hour. I knew I could make a lot more cutting grass, but this was a "real" job.

I wasn't satisfied with the limited duties of my job. I learned the mechanics of running the Boardwalk's Ferris wheel, and this increased my job responsibilities. With those increased responsibilities came a significant jump in pay: I was now making 55 cents an hour. I was very proud of myself, and particularly proud that I made enough money that summer to purchase a bicycle. This was important, because it was my only means of transportation. It was nothing to me to ride ten to fifteen miles in one direction to a concert, or to go to Shark River on a Sunday with my fishing rod. I would chain my bike to a lamppost and walk across the sand to a rock jetty, where I would claim my several feet of territory and fish for striped bass or blues.

I had my share of friends, but I was never a joiner. Most of my activities were more or less solitary and self-challenging. I enjoyed fishing, for instance, because it allowed me to enjoy the spray of the ocean and the warmth of the sun. And best of all, while holding the rod between my legs I could read a book. I loved reading. Nobody used the term multi-tasking at that time, but I was already doing it.

Winter brought opportunities as well. I made money shoveling sidewalks and digging out automobiles that were buried under the snow by the city's snowplows. In addition, I trapped Deal Lake for muskrats, which at the time were still popular for men's winter coats and hats, as well as for muskrat collars to adorn women's winter wear. I learned how to stretch and salt the skins and take them to the fur market, where haggling for the best price was an everyday occurrence. That was definitely an art, and I became good at it – a skill that would serve me well in later years.

My family didn't have much in the way of material wealth, but we were happy, and school and work kept me busy and out of trouble. However, I have to admit that when I got to high school I was occasionally envious of the kids who lived in the large beautiful homes in Deal Township, and drove to school in expensive cars that their parents had given them. But eventually I learned that there was a price they paid for having everything given to them. Because they didn't have to work for anything, many of them had no goals or ambitions. They came from very nice families, but some of them drank, some got involved with drugs, and some drove too fast in their fancy cars. Some lost their lives, and others eventually ended up in prison. Most of them are not alive today. At any rate, apart from my envy of my richer classmates, my years at Asbury Park High School were busy and fulfilling. I worked on the yearbook and was on the track team. And I graduated at the top of my class.

With some help from the family I was able to go to Rutgers, the State University of New Jersey. After that I left for the dental school at Temple University in Philadelphia, where I graduated at the top of my class with honors and then went on to get a medical degree. I was accepted into a residency in general surgery at the University of Pennsylvania for six years. This was followed by a plastic surgery residency in Ann Arbor, Michigan, with additional training in hand surgery in Detroit.

After I graduated, I was headhunted by several universities for a faculty position. The truth is that I like warmer weather and was looking to make my home in a Southern state. When I received the letter from Baylor College of Medicine in Houston, Texas, inviting me to "look them over," I had a feeling that I would accept the offer even before I got there. I joined the Plastic Surgery Department at the Baylor College of Medicine in Houston's world-famous Texas Medical Center, and have been there ever since. I spent most of my time working at the Methodist Hospital, the adjacent St. Luke's Hospital, and the Texas Children's Hospital.

It wasn't long before I wanted to give back. I met Marvin Zindler, a consumer advocate and firebrand investigative reporter who worked for the local ABC-TV station; I mentioned him a few times earlier in this narrative. We became good friends and eventually established the Agris-Zindler Children's Foundation. The Foundation provided medical care for people who "fell between the cracks" in Houston and the surrounding counties. Later we extended the Foundation to the Children's Fund International, undertaking three to four overseas trips a year to teach surgical procedures, perform operations, and provide medical supplies in Third World Countries.

Marvin and I had plenty of hair-raising adventures in our travels, and we always joked that we were protected by the "angel on his shoulder" – his guardian angel. Well, Marvin is gone, but his legacy lives on through our Foundation. And I can't help sometimes believing that I must have inherited his angel. I sure hope that angel is looking out for me on this trip...

Saleem taps me on the shoulder, startling me out of my trance, and asks that I bring the window up. It is getting colder, and the wind has become brisk as we move up the mountain, even though the sun seems to continue the upward march right along with us, burning fire in the sky. The ridge of the mountains and the plain of the valley make me feel suddenly very alive, as if I have received a transfusion of fresh blood. Breathing the clear mountain air, and looking out over a world so barren and yet so beautiful, fills me with new strength and even optimism. As I look up at the next set of switchbacks, I can see – and hear – one of those colorfully painted fourteen-wheel jingle trucks coming towards us, its metal discs sounding like wind chimes as it approaches.

Mohammed tells me again about the scary adventures he had driving a jingle truck when he was younger. Of course I have heard the story before, but I happily listen. "Allah definitely looked after me and I am still here today," he declares as he concludes his tale. "I was young, foolish, and enticed by the amount of money a driver was paid to make this dangerous trip. Something I would not do today in one of those trucks."

"There are a lot of things we did when we were younger, that we'd never dare try today," I reply, laughing. "I think Allah has looked out for all of us." (Not to give short shrift to my friend Marvin's guardian angel, of course.)

We are now slowly and carefully approaching the base of the next set of switchbacks. Here the road flattens out and is wide enough to allow the jingle truck to pass us – just barely. Our mirrors touch as the driver slowly slides by. I can hear the gravel from the tires cascading down several thousand feet to the floor of the gully below, and am once again unwillingly reminded of just how far it is to the bottom. We then begin our climb up the switchback and into the Babusar Pass. We are only going five miles an hour, ten at most, so I lower the window on my side and begin taking photos again.

The road is certainly not improving as we climb. It is nothing more than a gravel track, one that continues to get steeper as we progress. We are now entering the Indus Kohistan tribal area. We're at the western end of the Himalayas, and the Indus River has cut a gorge so deep that I can neither see nor hear the river below. It is such a desolate, inhospitable area that even the ancient caravan routes bypassed it. I am awestruck at the crumbling terrain all around us, with the steep rock wall on one side and the deep gorges and crags dropping away on the other. The mountain is a stone wall rising more than 20,000 feet, and looking down is not recommended.

Stone watchtowers and fortified houses can still be seen along the mountainside. Outsiders are emphatically not welcome, and historically, outlaws camped out in these mountains without fear of capture. Today, the Taliban and Al Qaeda do the same. Tribal warfare and blood feuds are common in this area, as you can imagine. Another name for the Indus Kohistan was Yaghistan, "The Land of the Ungoverned." A most appropriate name that was; it should have told us something.

Big forts are scattered throughout the valley below. This is part of the N.W.F.P. Frontier Constabulary, which tries to control this area. Since this is deep in the tribal region, the only purpose for the Constabulary and the forts is to protect this section of the Karakoram Highway.

This is probably the most dramatic of all of Pakistan's mountainous roads, especially traveling it on a clear day like today. Viewing the side canyons and the corduroy hillside takes my breath away. To our west the Lesser Himalayas stretch more than eight kilometers toward the Punjab, and to the north is the Hindu Raj.

We are now coming to the outskirts of Chilas. The British built the large forts in Chilas to protect their supply lines that ran through the Babusar Pass. It is now a police post that attempts to maintain some control over the town. However, I have been told that they are not as successful as they would like to have people think. And that is hardly surprising. Chilas and the surrounding valleys of Darel and Panjgur are a beehive of tiny tribal republics, each controlled by a tribal lord and a counsel of elders. They have been at war with each other for centuries, feuding internally. It is a hostile environment, inhabited by orthodox Sunni Muslims, and foreigners – particularly women – will feel unwelcome.

Given all of this, I admit that I am a little nervous when we stop at the police checkpoint, where we all get out of the van and go into the station. I show my passport and sign the registry book. I get the usual question: "American?" This is accompanied by the standard wide-eyed expression of surprise.

"Yes, American doctor," I respond.

Saleem elaborates. "He is the Doctor Angel of Quat Valley."

That seems to break the ice. The police officer smiles and replies, "We have heard many good things about him. Our district hospital is located on Ranoi Road, just past the bazaar. I would be pleased to show you."

Saleem responds, "We have been driving most of the morning and would like to wash and get something to eat first."

The policeman says, "Then let me suggest the restaurant at the Panorama Hotel. It has a very wide veranda and a beautiful view of the valley. May I suggest the korma? It is a tasty rice and chicken dish with a thick brown curry sauce."

I smile and say that sounds good. I am beginning to get a little hungry. But Mohammed has his mind on something else besides food. "Do they have satellite TV? We have heard some disturbing rumors along the road and would like to see the news."

"Not rumors!" the policeman responds. "Terrible news. Our Sheik, the new leader of the Muslim world... we fear he is dead."

"That's what we have heard," says Mohammed. "We want to find out more."

"There are many men having tea and watching the international news program, waiting for confirmation from America of what happened," says our new friend. "Be careful, many people are angered at this news. It is best that I and two of my men accompany you there."

Saleem asks him, "Have you eaten your mid-day meal yet?" The policeman shakes his head, and Saleem says, "Then join us as our guest, and we will view the American news program together."

The policeman agrees, saying, "I will bring several of my officers and meet you in front."

As we walk back to our van, I tell Saleem that this was a good move. Just as I'm saying this, three police officers and the captain come out, each with an AK-47 over his shoulder, as well as a sidearm. I glance over toward Saleem and Sultan. They make eye contact and nod their heads. We climb into our van and follow the policemen's Jeep as it leaves the station for the restaurant.

As we approach, there are all sorts of wagons and animals hitched along the roadside. We follow the Jeep as it is waved through the gate, and we park behind it. I reach down to pick up my camera, and Saleem emphatically shakes his head and whispers, "No!"

I reach over the seat and point to the photo albums of my young patients. Saleem thinks that is a good idea, so I gather up several of them and we open the doors to get out of the van.

I have never been able to get over the fact that Mohammed almost never locks our van. All of our valuables are in that van: cameras, a small stash of weapons and ammunition, our clothes, money – everything. Given the volatile events that have just occurred, I wonder if perhaps he will become a little more security conscious. As I get out, Mohammed slides the van's side door closed. I stand there for a few seconds, but Mohammed shakes his head and waves me on. "It's all right!" he assures me.

And I suppose it is. People in this region just don't mess

with what isn't theirs, for the penalty is swift and severe. There are no lawyers in the tribal area; it is pure Sharia law, and the tribal or clan leaders have the final say. Sometimes I think that maybe we could learn something from this back home, but such thoughts are quickly dispelled when I consider the other, less desirable ramifications inherent in such a system...

When we walk into the restaurant with our police escort, all eyes turn in our direction. The owner – or perhaps he is just the manager – scurries over to us, and I can see from his expression that he is quite upset and wants to know what is wrong. The police captain reassures him, saying, "I have some guests and would like a nice table facing the satellite TV area."

Several tables are hurriedly placed together, and wooden benches are brought out. Once we all take our places, those in the room turn their attention back to the international news program on TV.

Saleem orders tea for everyone, as well as the chicken korma that our policeman friend had recommended. Everyone nods in approval. I whisper to Sultan that I will pay for all of it, including for the police officers who have accompanied us. Since dinner only costs 100 rupees – about eighty cents – per person, I think I can handle it.

One by one we each get up to use the bathroom and wash up, and then return to the table. When it is my turn I walk out onto the semi-circular porch to view the mountains and valley below before returning to the table. Once again I am struck with the thought that there is nothing in the world that compares with the Himalayas.

I return to the table and the tea is already there; Saleem has a cup waiting for me. I realize how thirsty I am, and how ravenous.

Saleem whispers in my ear that the broadcast has been picked up from the United States and transmitted via satellite, with subtitles in Urdu and Pashto. The announcer says that several Black Hawk and Chinook helicopters, with a strike force of Navy Seals and Delta commandos, traveled 160 miles from Afghanistan to Abbottabad. They flew very low, and these new top-secret stealth Black Hawks avoided detection by the Pakistani radar along the border.

The plan had been for the helicopters to hover over the Osama bin Laden compound, and the Special Forces would deploy by rappelling. I was there, though, and I know that is not what happened. One of the helicopters landed, and the attack force proceeded on the ground. No one rappelled down.

The commentator goes on to say that the tail section of one of the helicopters struck the high wall surrounding the compound, causing the tail rotor to dislodge and the tail section to crumple upon itself. When this happened, the helicopter was only a few feet off the ground, and the pilot brought the damaged helicopter in, safely embarking the Special Forces without any injuries. This is exactly what I had seen from my perch in the tree overlooking the compound. So far, it seems to me that the commentator is reporting the events accurately.

The commentator informs us that there was a live satellite feed directly to the U.S. war room, where President Obama and others were watching what was taking place in real time. It appears that we are being shown video taken from the live feed, because we hear an explosion at the door to bin Laden's house. We're told that twenty-four commandos then stormed into the house, wearing body armor and night vision goggles. I could see the explosion from my vantage point in the tree, but it was too far away and too dark for me to see the individuals. However, I do not doubt what the commentator is now telling us. He adds that dogs were also used in this assault, which would explain the racket from the neighbors' dogs in the adjoining houses.

The announcer tells us that each room was cleared and women and children were bound together in order to prevent them from either interfering with the operation or getting injured themselves. He describes the home as having an elaborate series of hallways, almost like a maze, and even some false doors to add to the confusion. But the Special Forces plunged ahead. They went up the stairs, having found the iron gate at the base of the stairs unlocked. One of Osama bin Laden's sons was shot.

We're told that bin Laden left his third-floor bedroom and looked down over the railing, at which time the Special Forces opened fire, but missed him as he ducked back into his bedroom. As they rushed up towards him, two young girls ran from the room and the Special Forces entered. According to the announcer, bin Laden was shot twice and pronounced dead. We're told that one of the wives was present when this took place, and she confirmed that the man who had been shot was Osama bin Laden. He was placed into a body bag and quickly removed.

Once the all-clear was given, a security team entered the house and cleaned out books, papers, computers, and everything they could find that looked as if it might be of strategic value.

As the commentator is relaying this part of the story, we hear a second, louder explosion, and he explains that the downed helicopter was purposely destroyed. This also coincides with what I saw and heard from my perch up in the tree. The program ends with the announcement that four of the dead were left behind, but the women and children were all okay. The entire action lasted about thirty minutes.

The whole narrative has coincided pretty closely with what I was able to see and hear. Saleem and Sultan, wanting to know what I think, look at me from across the table, and I answer by raising my eyebrows. That tells them all they need to know.

About this time the waiter arrives with fresh hot flatbread and plates of steaming hot curry. I sip my tea and eat the delicious curry. The commentary on the satellite TV continues, explaining that facial recognition photos were sent to CIA headquarters, where it was confirmed that the man who had been killed was indeed Osama bin Laden. We're then shown footage of President Obama announcing, "We got him." We're told that the body was then immediately flown to the USS Carl Vinson, a ship that was in the North Arabian Sea. It was planned that Osama bin Laden would receive a Muslim shipboard ceremony and would be buried at sea. The commentator states, "There will be no martyr's burial site to visit."

The announcer wraps up the program by informing us that significant information about Al Qaeda had been obtained in the form of notebooks, journals, computer programs, and videos. This information included the organization's internal structure, its finances, and its plans for future targets. The announcer states that President Obama will visit Ground Zero in New York City this week. We are told that the surprise attack on bin Laden's compound has been declared a monumentally successful military strike, and that the members of the SEAL team and Special Forces who participated will remain anonymous. I think to myself, *I wonder how long that anonymity will last.*

After a few minutes, the entire news segment begins to play again. I have heard all I need to hear for now; I won't learn anything more here. It is time now to continue on our journey north, while we still have some daylight. We have decided not to spend the night in Chilas; with any luck we will reach Gilgit – where we have been told there is very comfortable lodging and good restaurants – just as the sun is setting. And I will have more opportunities to take photographs along the way, so I am eager to leave. We thank our hosts and make our departure.

For the most part I am satisfied that my observations from the other night have been confirmed. I know that the rumors will be flying, and that in the months to come it may be difficult to separate truth from speculation. I have no doubt that over the next few weeks, President Obama's supporters will laud him as a hero (and, of course, will praise the teams who actually carried out the orders), while the president's detractors will be busy with their own spin. Already some people are questioning the veracity of the reports, wondering if the Sheik really was taken out, despite the news reports that his identity had been confirmed. The conspiracy theorists will be kept busy fueling people's mistrust of the media. For now, though, the consensus seems to be that Osama bin Laden – the world's most wanted man – is dead. And for me, the adrenalin that had subsided for a while has returned full force, along with a rush of conflicting emotions.

Jacobabad –
After the Takedown

One thing seems clear to me: I know that at some point, I will have to leave Pakistan, but it cannot be now. It is almost certainly unsafe for me to be near Abbottabad right now, but I also have commitments at the Civil Hospital down in Jacobabad, and I know I must get there as soon as possible. So after a few hours of rest – if you can call it that – at the hotel in Gilgit, we are on our way down to Jacobabad. It's a long drive, more than 900 miles, but the plan is to go straight through without stopping anywhere to spend the night, and Sultan will take over the driving when Mohammed gets tired.

During that long drive I have a lot of time to think – and fret. I have a heavy surgical schedule waiting for me in Jacobabad, and am looking forward to having something else besides the Abbottabad raid to occupy my mind.

It is impossible to overstate how relieved I am when we finally reach Jacobabad. Although outwardly I am calm, inside I am a wreck. When I am finally alone in my room at the Civil House where I will be staying for the duration of this mission, I push my door shut and drop the steel bolt.

The adrenaline rush has subsided again. The attack on the compound itself – and the realization of how close I came to being caught up in the attackers' net – seem almost surreal to me. For obvious reasons, primarily my own safety as well as that of my associates here in Jacobabad, I know that I must try to appear as normal as possible, so as to avoid having to answer questions that are best left unasked. Especially since the I.S.I. is aware of my efforts to meet with the Sheik, I fully expect my staff and I will be questioned at some point about my whereabouts on the night of the attack on the compound, and whether I might have had any part in that attack. So I take a few deep breaths, thankful again to still be alive, and I lie down on my bed for a few hours of restless sleep.

All too soon it is time to get up again, and I stumble to the bathroom, hoping that the cantankerous light bulb over the mirror will work this time. I'd had trouble with it the night before. I flick the light switch and this time the bulb actually lights up, which I take as a good omen. I am beginning to feel much better. I turn the handles to start the shower, but all I get is a measly trickle. I let it run, hoping the pressure will increase, but of course, it doesn't. Meanwhile, I grab the ladle from the large blue plastic tub and pour the water over myself and begin my daily routine. The shower is still not much more than a drip, but at least it is marginally enough to rinse off. I towel off, then walk over to the mirror and shave. I put on clean scrubs and my white lab coat and head out the door, hungry for the breakfast that awaits me.

As I retrace my steps back down the staircase to the first floor, I pass several doors to my left. One is a pantry with large shelves, containing what appear to be several months worth of food supplies, including bags of rice and other grains, and hundreds of cans of other foods. Further down the hallway is a linen closet, stocked with clean sheets, towels, and cleaning supplies. The third door leads into the dining area, dimly lit in these early morning hours, in the center of which is a large table with sixteen chairs. The cook, who has already placed a tray with English tea and hot milk at one end of the table, appears from a side door, startling me. Apparently, my adrenaline is still looking for reason to begin pumping again. The cook asks if I would like eggs, and I gratefully say yes, and thank him.

I hear voices in the hallway, and other members of the surgical team begin to file in. Having gotten only three hours of sleep, I'm hoping that my adrenaline surge will continue and will get me through the day. Like most people, I have done my share of foolish things, and will likely do more in the future. Hopefully, I can put the last couple of nights behind me and keep my imagination from getting the best of me, so I can focus on the patients who rely on me. After our breakfast, I return to my room, get my medical equipment and camera bag together, and return to the main entrance to await Mohammed.

The sun is just now rising, an asymmetrical reddish-orange ball glowing in the sky and patiently brushing the heavy mist from the hollows. As we traverse the narrow unpaved streets on our way to the hospital, the dust and sand is kicked up by the van and swirls about us. Though the shops are still closed, there are still a few people about, and Mohammed is moving along faster than I like. There is always that goat or water buffalo wandering these narrow roads, and a collision is the last thing I need, especially this morning. But despite my concerns, we arrive at the hospital unscathed, with nary a victim – four-legged or two – left in our wake.

The team operates all morning, and everything is going smoothly. By mid-afternoon, I have been in the operating room for more than ten hours. The temperature in here is over a hundred degrees, and I've sweated so much that I have completely soaked through my operating scrubs. My eyes burn from the sweat that drips constantly from my brow, and I must look pretty bad, because the rest of the O.R. staff take pity on me and tell me to take a break. I realize that they are probably right, so I grab my camera and leave the operating room, just as my last little patient is extubated and begins breathing on his own.

I walk to the small doctors' lounge and pick up a bottle of water, which I drink down in about thirty seconds. I sit back on an old chair whose stuffing is popping out in several places, but I am comfortable and couldn't care less. I lay my head back, just for a second, and promptly fall asleep. When I awaken, my head is turned to the side up against my shoulder, leaving me with a painfully stiff neck. I gently rub my shoulder, then my watery eyes. I glance up at my watch and see that I've gotten a thirty-minute power nap, and notice that Dr. Nur is looking down at me with an expression of either bemused sympathy or gentle disgust. He smiles at me and says, "Get a shower and change your clothes. We will be having something to eat shortly."

His statement does nothing to clarify the meaning of his facial expression, but I realize that I have gotten pretty ripe, and must assume he has noticed it as well. I take his advice, and head back to my quarters, where to my surprise, the water pressure in the shower has improved markedly. The shower feels exquisite, and in no time, I feel refreshed and ready to take on another round of patients... after I eat, of course. Dr. Nur's mention of food reminded me that I am famished. Adrenalin eprocessing, you see, is very hard work, especially when added to what would be a couple of days' worth of surgeries in places with more civilized conditions. I hurriedly put on a fresh set of scrubs and stroll down to the dining room, led by the delicious smells of the meal that I know is waiting for me there.

As I mentioned earlier, there is no food in the hospital. Given the quality of food served at many hospital cafeterias in the States, is probably a blessing. Each day at between four and five in the afternoon, one of the doctors' wives or some of the nurses cook at home and bring the food to the hospital for the doctors, operating room staff, and other hospital personnel. And each day, I am always asked something like, "Did you like the meal? Isn't this the best meal you ever had at this hospital?" I always compliment them on the meals, which is not just a matter of being polite, because the meals are always excellent.

I have learned that these late lunches have become a cooking contest between the wives, and that I have unknowingly been appointed the judge. They want me to say that so-and-so's wife makes the best chicken and rice curry, or that Dr. Nur's wife makes the best fried fish and vegetables, or that the head nurse's lamb stew and yogurt dessert are exceptionally good. Each hopes to earn bragging rights, so that she can gloat over the others with claims that her cooking is the finest. I know that I'll really be in trouble if I single out a specific dish, but my inherently diplomatic approach saves me, and I say, "I've enjoyed each and every meal. They are all different, and I can't honestly say that I like one better than the other."

At today's mealtime we experience yet another of the frequent electrical brown-outs, and the large generators, located at the junction of the main hallways with the operating rooms, are started. I always dislike it when they come on because they produce a loud, constant hum, and the smell of diesel exhaust, made worse by temperatures of over a hundred degrees, circulates throughout the hallways and even into the operating rooms.

We finish lunch, and the nurses busy themselves restocking and cleaning the operating rooms and preparing for the evening's group of young surgical patients. I decide to take a walk, accompanied by two bodyguards who have temporarily been assigned to me, since I have given Sultan and Saleem a well-earned day off. I put on my white lab coat and fill a black plastic sack with some candies and small stuffed toys. In my other hand I carry my camera. As I approach the main entrance to the hospital on my way out, two of the four guards with their AK-47s over their shoulders step in behind me and offer me a quick salute. I pass through the front doors and go outside, under the porte-cochère, and turn right down the dusty gravel road toward the front gate. I wave to six military men standing around a jeep with its mounted .50-caliber machine gun, and they wave me over and point to my camera. They want me to take some photos of them, and I happily oblige them, then I pass the camera to one of my bodyguards so that he can take a picture of me with the group. As it turns out, that is what they really want.

Joseph Agris, M.D.

I pass through the gate onto the main street with its shoulder-to-shoulder people doing their day's-end shopping. All the shops are open. As is the case with so many places I've been in Pakistan, most homes here don't have electricity, and by extension they also lack refrigerators. Purchases of meat and other products that would spoil in this heat are made every evening in preparation for the late meal.

Having been to Jacobabad on several occasions, I recognize several of the merchants along the main street, and I stop to say hello and make some small purchases. Curious onlookers always gather when I enter a shop, but my bodyguards always have my back. I walk along the main road, dodging donkey carts and rickshaw drivers. I notice a man sitting in a barber chair that has been placed on the sidewalk, with the barber standing over him, deftly trimming around the man's beard with a long, thin straight razor. I watch the process – a scene out of an old Western movie depicting life 150 years ago – for several minutes. I point to my camera, and they laugh and nod in agreement. After I take a series of photos, I thank them and continue on my way.

After walking several blocks, I enter a particularly dilapidated section of town, and one of my bodyguards comes up to me and tells me, "These are the poorest of the poor." I can believe it. This is a scene unlike anything we typically see back home, crowded with people living in mud brick houses with tin roofs or in tents patched together with cloth and plastic or whatever materials they are able to scavenge. There is no running water or sewer system, and as I mentioned, no electric service at all. Adults and children are sitting cross-legged in front of the mud brick structures, weaving baskets from reeds that they harvest at no cost along the streams and canals that flow around and through the city of Jacobabad. The baskets are beautifully done, with designs that are quite intricate, reminding me of the baskets woven by the American Indians. Seeing my interest, one of the bodyguards explains, "It will take them about a day to weave a basket." I inquire as to the price and I am dumbfounded when he tells me that it is equal to about twenty-five cents U.S.

As I walk along, I give the candy and small stuffed animals I've brought with me to the children who seem so fascinated with the stranger in their neighborhood. The smiles on their faces are delightful, and the sparkle in their eyes is unbelievable, and brings me pleasure far greater than anything else I might get for the money I have spent. Some of the older children hold up baby lambs and baby goats for me to see, and they all giggle when I reach out to pet the animals. It occurs to me that their purpose for showing the animals is not to allow me to pet the little creatures; they are offering them up for sale.

Glancing beyond the open doorways into the mud huts and tents, I can see a few pots and pans, some blankets, and not much else. Since they have so little in the way of possessions, I assume that the small gifts I've given them are quite likely the only toys these children have ever had. Some of the mothers and older children come forward to show me their woven baskets, offering them in exchange for the gifts. I am touched by their offers, but of course, I refuse, instead telling them that I really like their work and would be happy to purchase the baskets. As this is taking place, a crowd of thirty to forty onlookers has gathered, and my security personnel are getting upset. They turn to face the crowd and attempt to keep them back, away from where I am negotiating the price of the baskets.

Someone in the crowd asks, "Who is he?"

The guard answers, "He is the Crazy Texas doctor who is helping the children here in the Jacobabad Civil Hospital."

I will never forget his answer. My bodyguard did not say, "*He is a doctor.*" My bodyguard did not say, "*He is the American doctor.*" My bodyguard did not say, "*This is the doctor from Texas who is helping the children.*" He said, "*This is the Crazy Texas Doctor.*" And I think that is great.

I purchase several of the woven baskets and happily overpay for them. Then I continue walking and, with the onlookers' approval, I distribute the remainder of the toys to the children, who begin clapping. An older man with a long silver-gray beard, high cheekbones, and large, tired-looking eyes steps forward. He shouts out, "The doctor is doing Allah's work. Bless those who give to the poor."

He continues, quoting several passages from the Qur'an. The onlookers and even my bodyguards now begin to clap and nod their heads in approval. I shouldn't be embarrassed but I am, and I turn and start walking back toward the Civil Hospital.

Upon reaching the hospital, I thank the two bodyguards for escorting me. Then I continue into the building and through the double doors to the surgical suites. I hang up my white lab coat, push open the door to the operating room, and ask the staff if they are ready. Their reply is instantaneous: "*Da, da.*" I slip into the doctors' lounge, change out of my sweat-soaked scrubs into a dry pair, put on my operating room sandals, and walk over to the scrub sink to wash.

Dr. Nur has already started his case, and I am at the adjacent operating room table. Having had my power nap, something to eat, and a nice walk to clear my mind and stretch my legs, I am refreshed and moving quickly again. I am in the flow, completing procedure after procedure... when at some point I realize that I am all alone in the operating room except for my anesthesiologist and one scrub nurse. I glance at the clock on the wall and see that it is almost two in the morning. It occurs to me that the old saying really needs to be revised to read, "*Time flies when you're doing what you love.*"

For a few hours, I have been able to push aside my anxiety about possible repercussions for the events in Abbottabad. But I know that sooner or later I may have to face some uncomfortable consequences.

Joseph Agris, M.D.

Aftermath: Reflections

I have been so engrossed in what I have been doing that I didn't realize that the other members of the team had retired to the doctor's lounge. I finish the operation, apply the bandages, and look at my anesthesiologist and nurse. I put on a big smile and say, "We should stop." They smile, their own weariness obvious in their agreement. I leave the operating room for the doctors' lounge, where I expect to find the team members asleep. When I get there, I am told that they were exhausted, and that the driver has already taken them and the other technicians back to the Civil Hospital House. I tell the driver I will get my camera equipment and be ready to leave

661

in a few minutes. I return to the operating room, and as I open the door I overhear the anesthesiologist say to the nurse, "Did you ever meet someone with such a volcanic personality?"

The scrub nurse, who is busy cleaning the instruments, looks over her shoulder and says, "Dr. Agris has an inner fire. It can be difficult to understand at times, but the children all get good care because of it, and that is what matters."

We've nicknamed the anesthesiologist "Mr. One Hundred Percent" because he always keeps the oxygen monitor for the infants and children not at 98% or 99%, but always 100%. I even had a T-shirt with the nickname printed in bold letters made for him as a gift, which he seemed quite proud of. Mr. One Hundred Percent responds to the nurse, "I have met only a few doctors with a personality like our Dr. Agris. He seems sometimes like a lion, and we are his cubs, to be taught, scolded, or praised by him, depending upon the situation. And we never know what he will be like when he has been let out of the cage."

I continue to slowly push open one of the big swinging doors, whereupon Mr. One Hundred Percent's voice suddenly drops as I enter, and his face betrays his shock at having been overheard.

I flash a big smile at them to put them at their ease, saying, "The Lion just wants to know if his cubs are okay, and whether they are ready to transfer our little patient to his bed on the open ward so we can all go home?"

The anesthesiologist turns to face me full-on, and haltingly half-asks and half-proclaims, "You heard what we just said."

I roll my eyes, laugh, and tell him, "I take it as a great compliment. But now, it's time for us to return to the Civil House and get some sleep. We have a long day again tomorrow." Both of them still have the classic "deer in the headlights" expression on their faces, and say nothing more as I exit the room.

The driver is obviously anxious to get home, too, but his driving is pretty tame compared to what I've experienced before. I see no need to chide him for being in a hurry, and the ride to the Civil House where our medical team is staying goes quickly. The lights are on when we arrive, which makes me feel a lot better than I did the night before. I head directly up to my room, thoroughly exhausted. I spend a few moments contemplating what the team has accomplished today as I look out my window into the black Pakistani night. In the utter silence of the evening, it is difficult to even imagine the conflict that so colors this region. It is easier – and more pleasant – to simply put the thoughts of that conflict aside and relish the stillness.

The Civil House, built by the British a hundred years ago, is just outside of town. From my vantage point here, there are no lights visible anywhere, either in the nearby homes or in the streets themselves. As I stand here, lost in thought, I find myself wondering what it is that I am searching for as I gaze out the window into the blackness. Obviously punchy from fatigue, all I can think of is that it is probably blacker here than at the entrance to hell. I stare off into this emptiness for a moment, take a deep breath, exhale slowly, and then begin preparing for bed. Tomorrow morning (what tomorrow? It is 3:00 A.M, and in four hours the sun will rise again), we will start the same routine all over again, and I need to get a few hours sleep. I keep thinking about all the preparation I need to do before tomorrow's surgeries, but decide it can wait until I get some sleep.

I virtually fall into the bed, adjust my pillow, and as I close my eyes, I think to myself how much I appreciate the work the team is doing: the pre-op assessments by Hashmat, the way Hajji Sob is looking after me and the team, and even the way Jacob Ababa had arranged for our Civil House accommodations. The area around the Civil House is nicer than most. The streets are not as riddled with garbage as most, and our team is safely ensconced behind the high walls, with armed guards at the gate and doors. Lying here with my eyes closed, safe in the serenity of the night, I am reminded again of how I have fallen love with Pakistan and its people, and how fascinated I am at how they can be so caught up in the turbulence of current tides, yet still very much enmeshed in a lifestyle and culture that goes back so many centuries.

Ultimately, my exhaustion wins out, and I drift into sleep. Tomorrow will be yet another day of surgeries, of crises, of triumphs, and at its end, a re-emergence of exhaustion – just like pretty much any other day in Pakistan. These last weeks have held many surprises for me, from the joys in the newly-repaired children's smiles to the terror of having barely escaped the bloodshed at the Sheik's compound. From being shot to being befriended by some of the most feared individuals in the world. From the deep compassion and devotion of my driver, interpreter, and bodyguard, and my fellow doctors, nurses, and other medical staff, to the cynical opportunism exhibited by some of the lower-level officials I've encountered. From the anguish at seeing young women and girls horribly disfigured or murdered for actions and words that wouldn't even raise an eyebrow back home, to my joy at being able to help at least some of them have a better life. From the searing heat of the desert valleys to the bone-chilling cold of the high Himalayas, Pakistan has, for me, been a land of profound contrasts that alternately fill me with exhilaration and sorrow.

I do not know if I will ever again be allowed to journey here, as even the minor role I have played may well come to be seen as a threat to those who would keep the country mired in the challenges of its past, rather than guide it to the promise of its future. I hold in my heart the hope that the violence and suffering will one day pass, so that the people I've grown to love and respect will have a chance at living joyous lives, freed from fears and petty conflicts. Not mirror images of life back in the United States, certainly, but lives that are filled with hope, with joy, and with the very real promise of happiness that they so greatly deserve, yet have been denied for so long.

The Faces of Pakistan

Most Photos by Dr. Agris - The "Crazy Texan"

In this section is an assortment of photographs, most of which I have taken. They offer a peek into a world that is completely foreign to most Westerners, but to say that they fall far short of giving anyone who has not been there a taste of what life is like in the cities, towns, villages, and tribal regions of Pakistan is a gross understatement. I might as well try to describe the delicious smells that emanate from the tribal kitchens.

I realize that the pictures of the burn victims might be quite upsetting to some, but to be honest, that is my intent; to hopefully spur readers to add their voices to the demand for such atrocities to stop.

667

It is just as much an understatement to describe the countryside in Pakistan as breathtaking. From the withering desert floor to the "top of the world" Himalayan peaks, there are panoramas that aren't matched anywhere else on earth. Unfortunately, between the condition of what pass for "highways" and the ever-looming threat of attack by Taliban, Al Qaeda, or tribal warriors, a journey through the country is likely to be a heart-stopping adventure.

The Karakoram Highway (KKH) is, in most stretches, little more than a dirt track, winding through Northern Pakistan. It is part of the ancient Silk Road to China.

Caravan traveling South from China
along the Karakoram Highway. This was the most
dangerous of all the the routes I travelled. Below, a
tanker truck follows this perilous path.

Posing with a couple of my young patients, with the majestic Himalayas in the background.

A typical "neighborhood" in the tribal areas. Homes have no electricity or running water. Virtually no Americans are ever seen in these warlord-controlled areas due to the extreme danger.

Everyday life in Pakistan

These men are dressed in the traditional attire typical in the northern tribal areas of Pakistan.

671

These are typical scenes from marketplaces in Pakistani cities.
The woman at the lower right, however, is anything but typical, as most
women cover their faces to avoid severe punishment by the Taliban for
not adhering to strict Sharia law. One of my bodyguards is to her right.

These photos are of a typical marketplace
in the tribal area of the Northern Territories. You will note
that there are no women to be seen, as virtually all
business transactions are handled by men.

Two men selling their loads of hay in the market in Jacobabad City.

These women are representative of "proper" dress according to Sharia.

This is what commuting looks like in most areas
of Pakistan. The fare from their village
to work in the city is five cents.

Our travels were in a van very similar to this one.

In Jacobabad City, donkey carts are the most common form of transportation.

Yes, we do make house calls! I even drove.

Traveling in the Northern Territories with my small private army. My bodyguards, armed with machine guns, clear the way in their Jeep.

Virtually every male child over the age of ten is armed with an automatic weapon. This boy's machine gun has two high-capacity magazines taped together, enough firepower to wage a significant attack, Is this how he should be spending his childhood?

**With my faithful driver, interpreter,
and bodyguard: The Four Musketeers!**

**It is sometimes necessary to "go native" for one's own safety.
(And to maintain my "Doctor Angel / Crazy Texan" image!)**

**With Muhammad Mian Soomro, President of Pakistan
in 2008, and Chairman of the Senate.**

**At dinner with
Mr. Soomro**

**As a guest of the
Pakistani Air Force**

**The Frontier Medical College in Abbottabad,
where I taught and operated,
only blocks from bin Laden's home**

**Burn Center in Karachi –
the only burn center
in Pakistan.**

**Typical dress in the
tribal areas. I must blend
in to remain safe.**

Human beings in all cultures have built
beautiful temples to glorify God.
I can't help but wonder
how they can also subjugate, torture,
and even murder innocents,
all for the same purpose.

The archaeological site of the ancient
city of Mohenjo-daro, located in Sindh
Province, in the Northern Indus Valley
of Pakistan. This is the site of one of the
oldest cities in the world, built around
2,600 BCE, located in an area
too dangerous for most people –
especially Americans – to visit.

Joseph Agris, M.D.

The Children
Why we're here in the first place

"This is what I write on in school and practice on at home." I am humbled by the joy in the faces of children who, despite living in abject poverty, take such pride in what they do have. For most of the children in the tribal areas, there are no school supplies – no paper, no pens, and often no books beyond a single copy that is held by the teacher.

682

Before and after surgery...

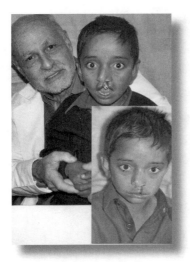

Left-sided cleft lip
(before & after surgery)

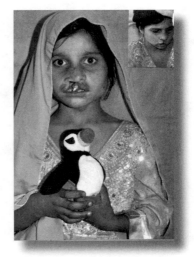

Severe wide right cleft

Double cleft
(before & after surgery)

We give stuffed toys
and school supplies

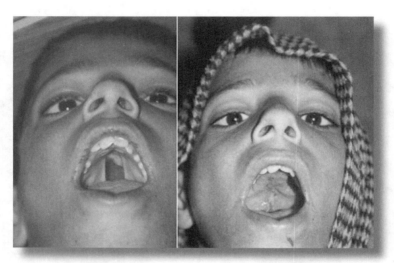

Before Surgery   **After Surgery**
Cleft palate defect

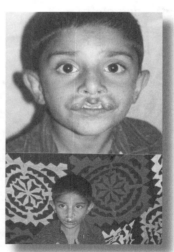

Burns and other war-related injuries do not
discriminate by age. The very young are
not immune, and are the most tragic of the
thousands of innocent victims
caught up in the ravages of war.

Double wide cleft
Below: after repair

**Henna painted on hands
to ward off evil spirits**

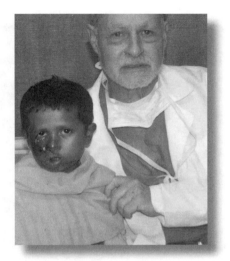

Recent burn

**With my patient & new-
found friend, I *feel* like
Dr. Angel**

**Burned hand
after surgical correction**

**Post-op of one of 500 cleft lip repairs
I made him an honorary Texan**

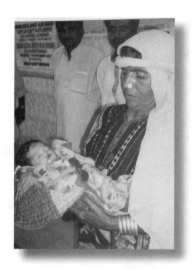

**These women's colorful apparel is typical of that worn in the tribal area
of Northern Pakistan. The woman on the right is one of our nurses.**

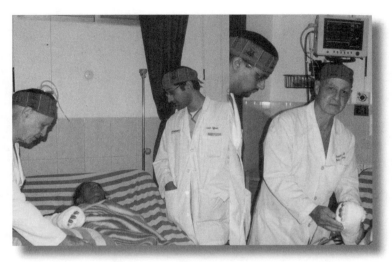

Here, I'm making post-op rounds on the hospital ward, teaching young doctors

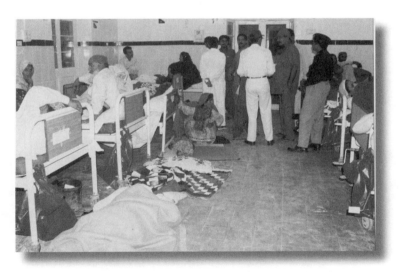

When we run out of beds (which happens often), our young patients have to sleep on blankets spread out on the floor. And none of them complain.

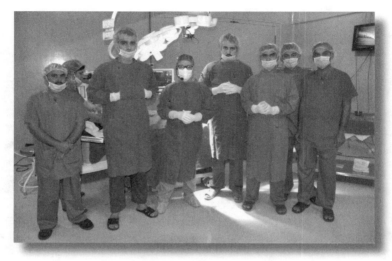

With my Pakistani students and local doctors.

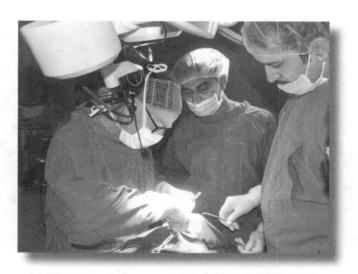

**In the operating room at the Frontier Medical
College in Abbottabad, only blocks away from
Osama bin Laden's home and compound**

With Arsala, Senior Nurse, student doctors, and a mother and her post-op cleft-lip child.

Stopping for an evening meal at the hospital in Jacobabad. All meals are prepared and brought in by the local doctors' wives, as there is no food in the hospital.

Burn Victims

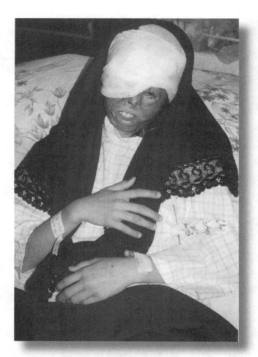

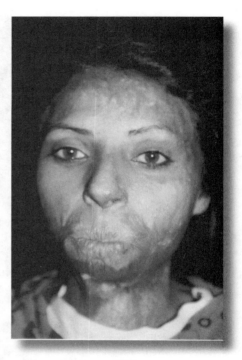

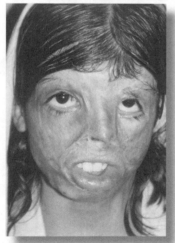

Caustic acid, intentionally thrown in these young girls' faces, often resulting in blindness, as well as severe facial destruction, distortion, and scarring. They are treated as burn patients, requiring multiple surgical procedures and skin grafts.

The perpetrators of these violent attacks are rarely even questioned, much less prosecuted, and go about their lives as if nothing had happened, while their victims' lives are often ruined.

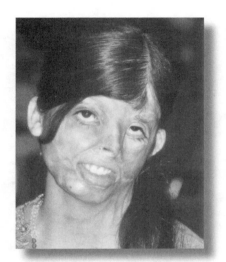

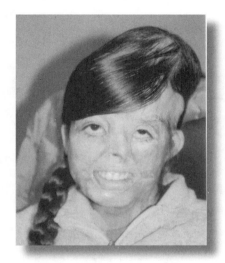

**Before surgery and after
Giving them their lives back**

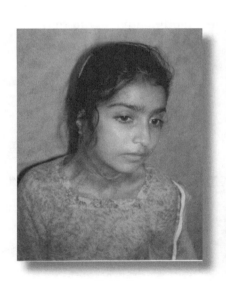

Fatima

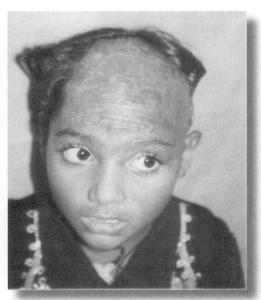

Komal

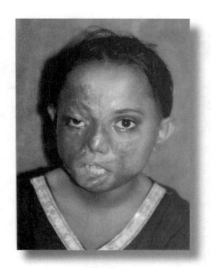

Mafia

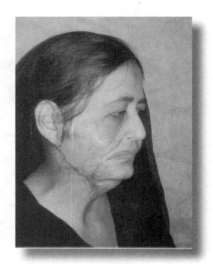

Noureen Reza

The burns such as these women and children suffer are among the most painful and difficult to treat of all injuries, requiring twenty to thirty surgical procedures as the children grow up

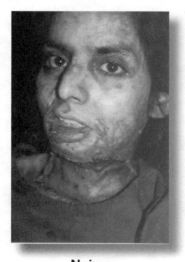

Najma

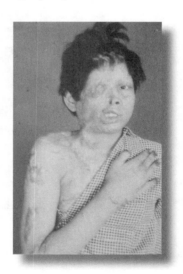

This woman suffered a burn contracture, adhering her chin to her neck. After surgery, she was able, for the first time in years, to lift her head enough to look directly at someone and smile.

Shakira, The thankful one

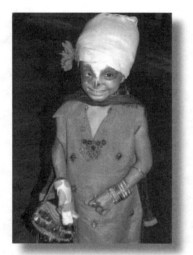 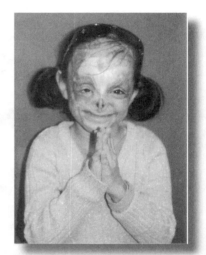

She is the only survivor of a U.S. unmanned drone rocket attack on her village. Her parents, grandparents, brothers, sisters, and friends were all annihilated in the misplaced attack, which did not yield any "high-value" targets.

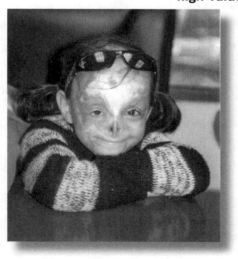 

Shakira, along with two other Pakistani children
posing with Dr. Agris, are very privileged to have been
selected and sponsored to be brought to Houston
for their medical care. The treatments they receive here
are not available to them in Pakistan.
Without these treatments and surgeries, the children
would be doomed to a life of further abuse and rejection,
even by their own families and friends.
Now, however, they can once again smile.
Sadly, there are scores of innocents with similar – and
worse – injuries and birth defects
who aren't as fortunate, and remain in Pakistan
with little hope of a happy life.

Joseph Agris, M.D.

Takedown
Osama bin Laden's compound

**The bin Laden compound in Abbottabad.
It has since been bulldozed, leaving no sign it ever existed.**

In the days following the attack, hundreds of people would come to look, and many came to pay homage to the Sheik Osama bin Laden.

This is a rare night shot of the actual raid on bin Laden's compound, taken by a curious (and very brave) neighbor. The white specks are actually muzzle flashes from the Sheik's bodyguards' rifles as they tried to defend the compound from attack.

Major Roads of Pakistan

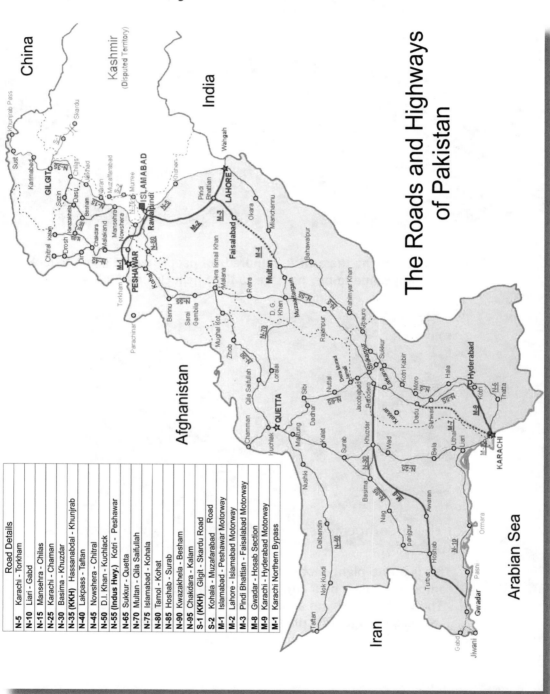

Road Details
N-5 Karachi - Torkham
N-10 Liari - Gabd
N-15 Mansehra - Chilas
N-25 Karachi - Chaman
N-30 Basima - Khuzdar
N-35 (KKH) Hassanabdal - Khunjrab
N-40 Lakpass - Taftan
N-45 Nowshera - Chitral
N-50 D.I. Khan - Kuchlack
N-55 (Indus Hwy.) Kotri - Peshawar
N-65 Sukkur - Quetta
N-70 Multan - Qila Saifullah
N-75 Islamabad - Kohala
N-80 Tarnol - Kohat
N-85 Hoshab - Surab
N-90 Kwazakhela - Besham
N-95 Chakdara - Kalam
S-1 (KKH) Gilgit - Skardu Road
S-2 Kohala - Muzafarabad Road
M-1 Islamabad - Peshawar Motorway
M-2 Lahore - Islamabad Motorway
M-3 Pindi Bhattian - Faisalabad Motorway
M-8 Gwadar - Hosab Section
M-9 Karachi - Hyderabad Motorway
M-1 Karachi Northern Bypass

Afterword

As I look back upon the things I learned, both in my travels and during the interviews with Osama bin Laden, I've come to recognize that what faces us as a species is much more than just a clash of asynchronous cultures, of people from two different worlds, or even of the incompetence and misdeeds of a given regime, administration, or party. For even the most committed enemies can at some point reach a place of peaceful, if not friendly, coexistence. But such a state can only exist when both parties are upfront in their agendas, and remain committed to the prospect of coexistence.

Unfortunately, we are, at present, far from finding such a place. We in the West might scoff at the barbarism of tribal wars, yet we engage in our own form of tribal warfare right here in the U.S., with opposing political parties so entrenched in their own narrow visions that they refuse to even consider the possibility of working together. And behind the scenes – in political parties, in the myriad bureaucracies within our respective governments, and in the grand vision of nations, there are forces at work that literally feed off the discord and relish the confrontation, all in the service of their own cynical agendas.

My own country pursues objectives that cannot and never will be realized, since the very core of those objectives eliminates the ability to realize a positive outcome. In my own travels throughout the Middle East, I have been able to establish relationships built upon a trust that cannot be achieved, and indeed is destroyed, through strength of arms.

From a purely pragmatic standpoint, I have come to understand that we will never win a war against the radical Islamic fundamentalist mindset, but we could certainly win the hearts of the Islamic world. Not with weapons, but with acts of genuine altruism. Having established myself as Doctor Angel and the Crazy Texan, I have been able to walk unmolested in places where an armed battalion would be slaughtered on sight. Not because I'm some kind of super human, but because the people of the Middle East have come to know and trust that I come to them with only one purpose: to help them.

The plain truth is that the United States could minimize or even eliminate the threats to our security and safety at much lower cost, in both lives and treasure. A clinic in a tribal village could be built and equipped for about the same cost as one of the rockets we presently fire from our drones. And where the drone attacks might eliminate a specific "high-value" target, they also take a great toll in innocent human lives, thereby creating a fertile soil in which the seeds of hatred can continue to flourish.

Were the killing to stop, and our only actions in the region be humanitarian in nature, with no ulterior motive, we would win the hearts of the people, and leave no place for the hatred to take root. The radicals would ultimately be marginalized to the point where they posed little threat to us, and their continued efforts would come to be seen as desperate attempts to sustain the hatred and continue the deaths of innocents.

Beyond helping the Pakistani people to develop their own medical care system, we could provide them with assistance and advice as to the best ways to improve the infrastructure that will make their lives less difficult. We could even help them to develop an agricultural economy that produces food to feed themselves and the world, rather than the poppies that only serve to enslave and ruin lives.

And while this would require a financial commitment for years to come, that commitment would be infinitely less costly than is the military commitment required just to douse the fires of hatred that will continue to spring up as long as we pursue our present path.

In short, we must ask ourselves – and answer honestly – what it is we truly want, and what we can honestly expect in return for our efforts. It boils down to a clear decision, between a quest for peaceful progress or a never-ending legacy of death, both in the Middle East and right here in our hometowns. The decision will be made, whether by choice or by inaction. But it must be made now, before it is too late.

About the Author

Besides being one of Houston's premier cosmetic, plastic, and reconstructive surgeons, with a bustling practice in the world-famous Texas Medical Center, Dr. Joe Agris is an activist and philanthropist, especially when it comes to children's health problems and education issues. More recently he has also become more involved with fighting the effects of the horrible abuses to which women in the Muslim world are subjected, and the devastating effects of drone attacks in Pakistan and Afghanistan.

Years ago, Doc Joe and the late Marvin Zindler formed The Agris-Zindler Children's Foundation to deliver needed medical care to kids all over the world. A true Renaissance man, well-read in the arts and sciences, Doc Joe is a world traveler and a photographer (he took the vast majority of the photographs that appear in this book).

When he's not off on a medical mission to some remote corner of the world, Doc Joe is in Houston, Texas, tending to his practice, enjoying time with his lovely wife Terry, and planning the next project or mission. The photo on this page was taken on his most recent mission to Pakistan, where he treated hundreds of men, women, and children who had suffered everything from crippling birth defects to burns from acid attacks, attempted "honor killings," and on rare occasions, wounds resulting from drone rocket attacks, which most people in the immediate vicinity – including scores of innocent women and children – do not survive.

About the
U.S.A. International Children's Foundation
and
Smiles Gone Wild

The way a society treats children is a measure not only of its social responsibility and qualities of compassion but also of its commitment to enhancing the human condition for future generations. If today we can guarantee the dignity, equality and basic human rights of children, as the Convention on the Rights of the Child seeks to ensure, the men and women of tomorrow will be able to bring this planet closer to the goal of peace, progress and justice for which we are all striving.

- Javier Perez de Cuellar
Secretary-General of the United Nations

Every two minutes a child is born with a birth defect. Cleft palates, disfiguring birthmarks and other defects are "silent catastrophes" that can ravage any child. Even if the condition does not threaten a child's health and is "merely" cosmetic, it can be psychologically and emotionally devastating. These children need special attention, yet a heartbreaking number of them fall between the cracks of the system.

The Children's Foundation, a non-profit 501(c)(3) organization founded in 1981 by Joseph Agris, M.D., and the late Marvin Zindler, exists to help these forgotten children. With your help, we have been able to deliver badly needed care to children in some of the poorest areas on the planet, including Central America, the Middle East, the former Soviet bloc, China and many other places. We have also helped many children and their families in the United States.

The Children's Foundation & Smiles Forever are dedicated to identifying the problems, bringing about solutions, and mobilizing resources for the implementation of needed care and support services. This encompasses medical care, surgery, medications, and prostheses, as well as family support. And, while these clinical applications are certainly needed, research leading to cure or prevention is also paramount.

We owe to children the best that we can give. Every child has a right to necessary medical care. But not all children are born equal. The world is full of desperately poor children whose families can scarcely afford food and shelter, say nothing of medical care. However, though medical care is often costly, it is an affordable cost... if we all give something.

Give a child a chance, by giving your tax-deductible gift to the Children's Foundation & Smiles Forever today. Send your check or money order, made payable to
THE CHILDREN'S FUND,
to:
The Children's Foundation
6560 Fannin Street, Suite 1730, Scurlock Tower
Houston, Texas 77030

Please include your name, address and daytime phone number. We also accept Visa, MasterCard or American Express. Please call (713) 797-1700 to give credit card information, to obtain information about matching funds for employers, or to find out how you can volunteer of your time and services to help "Doc Joe and his kids."

And remember... a portion of the profits from the sale of *Tears On The Sand* will be donated to the Children's Foundation and Smiles Forever.

"The kids" thank you!

A message from "Doc Joe"…
Your support is urgently needed.

"Smiles Gone Wild": the new site for The Children's Fund
http://www.smilesgonewild.org

Click. Donate. Smile.

To my readers:

Thank you for purchasing and reading *Tears on the Sand*. This big book has been a labor of love for me, but there is something even dearer to my heart than writing: my nonprofit charity, The Children's Fund (aka the Agris-Zindler Children's Foundation). The Children's Fund has become my passion and my obsession.

But I urgently need your help to carry it on.

Your support of The Children's Fund allows my team and me to help patients such as those you've read about in *Tears on the Sand*. There are so many in need: the children born with devastating congenital abnormalities…the women whose faces and bodies have been nearly destroyed by acid attacks or deliberately-inflicted kerosene burns…the men and boys who have suffered gruesome injuries from farming accidents… the innocents who, against all odds, survived unmanned drone attacks but are left horribly burned. Your generosity also makes it possible for us to provide medical equipment and supplies for the clinics and hospitals, and hands-on training for the doctors and nurses, in the areas we visit.

Every dollar you give to The Children's Fund is needed and deeply appreciated. You can read more about The Children's Fund in these back pages. Or you can visit the link I listed above, and I hope you will! Here's that link again: http://www.smilesgonewild.org

You can also find information here:
http://www.agriscosmeticcenter.com/childrens-fund-childcare
Or you can call the phone number or write to the address below my name.

Giving feels good, and by giving to The Children's Fund, you'll not only help put a smile on the face of a child, but a big smile on your own face as well. Thank you in advance for helping make life better for so many people in need.

Sincerely yours,
"Doc Joe" Agris

PS ~ If you are considering plastic, cosmetic, or reconstructive surgery, please know that by choosing our services you are doing more than helping yourself: you are also helping "the cause." While donations to The Children's Fund are certainly important, the continued success of our practice has also helped make it possible for my team and me to carry on our medical missions. For more information about our practice, qualifications, and the many different procedures available, I urge you to visit the Agris Cosmetic Center Web site:
http://www.agriscosmeticcenter.com/index.html

Dr. Joseph Agris, M.D., D.D.S., F.A.C.S.
Member of the American Board of Plastic Surgery
6560 Fannin St.
Suite 1730
Houston, TX 77030
713-797-1700

Help yourself, and help the children too!

To order additional copies of

Tears On The Sand

Name _____
(as it appears on card)

Address _____

City, State, Zip _____
Please send me:

[ ] copy / copies of the hardcover Collector's Edition at US $34.95*
per copy. TOTAL: $ _____

[ ] copy / copies of the quality softcover edition at US $24.950* per
copy. TOTAL: $ _____
* Add US $4.00 per copy for shipping & handling ($8.50 outside
Continental US)

Enclosed is my check [ ] money order [ ]

in the amount of $ _____
(Please make payable to The Children's Fund)

Please charge the above amount to my Visa [ ] MasterCard [ ]
American Express [ ]

Account number _____

Expiration date _____ Security code _____

Signature _____

A portion of the proceeds from the sale of this book will be donated to
THE CHILDREN'S FOUNDATION and SMILES GONE WILD